The Internet For Dummies, 10th Edition

Cheat Sheet

Firefox, the World's Best Web Browser

- ✔ The latest browser from the open-source Mozilla project. Download it for free from `www.mozilla.org`.
- ✔ **Go directly to a Web site:** Type its address into the Address box and press Enter. (You can leave the `http://` off.)
- ✔ **Reload the current page:** Press Ctrl+R or click Reload.
- ✔ **Open a new tab in your Firefox window:** Press Ctrl+T.
- ✔ **Add the current page to your bookmarks:** Press Ctrl+D.
- ✔ **Edit your bookmarks:** Press Ctrl+B.
- ✔ **Set your browsing preferences:** Choose Tools⇨Options.
- ✔ **Set the current page to be your start page:** Choose Tools⇨Options, click General, and click Use Current Page in the Home Page section.
- ✔ **Exit Full Screen mode:** If the whole top of the window is gone, press F11 to return to normal.
- ✔ **Erase the history of what Web sites you've viewed:** Choose Tool⇨Options, click Privacy and click History.
- ✔ **Control cookies on your computer:** Choose Tools⇨Options, click the Privacy category, and click Cookies.
- ✔ **Block popup windows:** Choose Tools⇨Options, click the Web Features category, and make sure that Block Popup Windows is checked. Click Allowed Sites to specify sites that can or can't open popups.

Internet Explorer (IE), Microsoft's Web Browser

- ✔ Comes with Windows. Download and install new versions from `www.microsoft.com/windows/ie`. Beware of Internet Explorer's many security holes, which Microsoft issues frequent updates to patch. Check for updates at `windowsupdate.com`.
- ✔ **Go directly to a Web site:** Type its address into the Address box and press Enter. (You can leave the `http://` off.)
- ✔ **Refresh the current page:** Press Ctrl+R or click Refresh.
- ✔ **Add the current page to your favorites:** Choose Favorites⇨Add To Favorites.
- ✔ **Edit your favorites:** Choose Favorites⇨Organize Favorites.
- ✔ **Set your browsing preferences:** Choose Tools (or View)⇨Internet Options.
- ✔ **Set the current page to be your start page:** Choose Tools (or View)⇨Internet Options, click the General tab, and click Use Current in the Home Page section.
- ✔ **Exit Full Screen mode:** If the whole top of the window is gone, press F11 to return to normal.
- ✔ **Erase the history of what Web sites you've viewed:** Choose Tools (or View)⇨Internet Options, click the General tab, and click Clear History.
- ✔ **Control cookies on your computer (IE 6 only):** Choose Tools (or View)⇨Internet Options, click the Privacy tab, and click Advanced. Set First-party Cookies to Accept and Third-party Cookies to Block.
- ✔ **Block popup windows (IE 6 only):** Choose Tools⇨Options, click the Privacy tab, and look at the Pop-Up Blocker section.

For Dummies: Bestselling Book Series for Beginners

The Internet For Dummies, 10th Edition

Cheat Sheet

Thunderbird, an Excellent E-mail Program

- The latest e-mail program from the open-source Mozilla project. Download it for free from www.mozilla.org.
- **Connect to an e-mail account:** Choose Tools⇨Account Settings.
- **Set your e-mail preferences:** Choose Tools⇨Options.
- **Compose a new message:** Press Ctrl+M or click the Write button.
- **Attach a file:** Click the Attach button or choose File⇨Attach.
- **Send and receive messages:** Press Ctrl+Shift+T or choose File⇨Get New Messages For⇨Get All New Messages.
- **Block JavaScript and images:** Choose Tools⇨Options, click the Advanced category, deselect Enable JavaScript In Mail Messages and select Block Loading Of Remote Images In Mail Messages.
- **Delete the current message:** Press Delete or click the Delete button.
- **Reply to the current message:** Press Ctrl+R or click the Reply button.
- **Forward the current message:** Press Ctrl+L or click the Forward button.
- **Display your Address Book:** Press Ctrl+2 or click the Address Book button.
- **Create a new mail folder:** Choose File⇨New⇨New Folder, type a name, and set the Create As A Subfolder Of box to the folder name in which you want the new folder to live.
- **Configure junk mail filtering:** Choose Tools⇨Junk Mail Controls.
- **Create mail filters:** Choose Tools⇨Message Filters to display the Message Filters window, where you can create, edit, and delete filters.

Outlook Express, the E-mail Program that Comes with Windows

- Beware of security holes, for which Microsoft issues frequent security updates. Download new versions from www.microsoft.com/windows/ie. Check for updates at windowsupdate.com.
- **Connect to an e-mail account:** Choose Tools⇨Accounts, click the Mail tab, and click Add.
- **Set your e-mail preferences:** Choose Tools⇨Options.
- **Compose a new message:** Press Ctrl+N or click the Create button.
- **Send and receive messages:** Press Ctrl+M or click Send/Recv button.
- **Block images (OE 6):** Choose Tools⇨Options, click the Security tab, and select Block Images And Other External Content In HTML E-mail.
- **Delete the current message:** Press Ctrl+D or click the Delete button.
- **Reply to the current message:** Press Ctrl+R or click the Reply button.
- **Forward the current message:** Press Ctrl+F or click the Forward button.
- **Display your Address Book:** Click the Addresses button.
- **Create a new mail folder:** Choose File⇨Folder⇨New or File⇨New⇨Folder from the menu, type in a folder name, and choose which folder to put this new folder into.
- **Attach a file:** Click the Insert⇨File Attachment from the menu or by clicking the Attach button.
- **Create mail filters:** Choose Tools⇨Message Rules⇨Mail.

For Dummies: Bestselling Book Series for Beginners

The Internet

FOR

DUMMIES®

10TH EDITION

The Internet
FOR
DUMMIES®
10TH EDITION

by John Levine
Margaret Levine Young
Carol Baroudi

WILEY

Wiley Publishing, Inc.

The Internet For Dummies®, 10th Edition

Published by
Wiley Publishing, Inc.
111 River Street
Hoboken, NJ 07030-5774
www.wiley.com

Copyright © 2005 by Wiley Publishing, Inc., Indianapolis, Indiana

Published by Wiley Publishing, Inc., Indianapolis, Indiana

Published simultaneously in Canada

For general information on our other products and services, please contact our Customer Care Department within the U.S. at 800-762-2974, outside the U.S. at 317-572-3993, or fax 317-572-4002.

For technical support, please visit www.wiley.com/techsupport.

Wiley also publishes its books in a variety of electronic formats. Some content that appears in print may not be available in electronic books.

Library of Congress Control Number: 2005924599

ISBN-13: 978-0-7645-8996-6

ISBN-10: 0-7645-8996-2

Manufactured in the United States of America

10 9 8 7 6 5 4 3 2 1

10B/RV/QZ/QV/IN

WILEY

About the Authors

Please visit all three authors online at net.gurus.com.

John Levine was a member of a computer club in high school — before high school students, or even high schools, had computers — where he met Theodor H. Nelson, the author of *Computer Lib/Dream Machines* and the inventor of hypertext, who reminded us that computers should not be taken seriously and that everyone can and should understand and use computers.

John wrote his first program in 1967 on an IBM 1130 (a computer somewhat less powerful than your typical modern digital wristwatch, only more difficult to use). He became an official system administrator of a networked computer at Yale in 1975. He began working part-time — for a computer company, of course — in 1977 and has been in and out of the computer and network biz ever since. He got his company on Usenet (the Internet's worldwide bulletin-board system) early enough that it appears in a 1982 *Byte* magazine article on a map of Usenet, which then was so small that the map fit on half a page.

Although John used to spend most of his time writing software, he now mostly writes books (including *UNIX For Dummies* and *Internet Secrets,* both published by Wiley Publishing, Inc.) because it's more fun and he can do so at home in the tiny village of Trumansburg, New York, where in his spare time he is the mayor (yes, really, see www.Trumansburg.ny.us) and can play with his small daughter when he's supposed to be writing. John also does a fair amount of public speaking. (Go to www.johnlevine.com, to see where he'll be.) He holds a B.A. and a Ph.D. in computer science from Yale University, but please don't hold that against him.

Carol Baroudi first began playing with computers in 1971 at Colgate University, where two things were new: the PDP-10 and women. She was lucky to have unlimited access to the state-of-the-art PDP-10, on which she learned to program, operate the machine, and talk to Eliza (a computer-based shrink). She taught ALGOL and helped to design the curricula for computer science and women's studies. She majored in Spanish and studied French, which, thanks to the Internet, she can now use every day.

Carol's been working in the computer industry since 1975. Today she's an industry analyst, consulting to emerging technology companies. (Check out what she's doing at www.baroudi.com.)

Carol loves Europe and is always looking for reasons to go. She believes that we are living in a very interesting time when technology is changing faster than people can imagine. Carol hopes that as we learn to use the new technologies, we don't lose sight of our humanity. She feels that computers can be useful and fun, but are no substitute for real life.

In high school, **Margaret Levine Young** was in the same computer club as her big brother John. She stayed in the field throughout college against her better judgment and despite John's presence as a graduate student in the computer science department. Margy graduated from Yale and went on to become one of the first PC managers in the early 1980s at Columbia Pictures, where she rode the elevator with big stars whose names she wouldn't dream of dropping here.

Since then, Margy has co-authored more than 25 computer books about topics that include the Internet, UNIX, WordPerfect, Microsoft Access, and (stab from the past) PC-File and Javelin; including *The Internet For Dummies Quick Reference, Dummies 101: The Internet For Windows 98*, and *UNIX For Dummies* (all published by Wiley Publishing, Inc.), *Poor Richard's Building Online Communities* (published by Top Floor Publishing), and *Windows XP Home Edition: The Complete Reference* and *Internet: The Complete Reference* (published by Osborne/McGraw-Hill). She met her future husband, Jordan, in the R.E.S.I.S.T.O.R.S. (that computer club we mentioned). Her other passion is her children, along with music, Unitarian Universalism (www.uua.org), reading, and anything to do with eating. She lives in Vermont (see www.gurus.com/margy for some scenery) and works as a software engineer for the Unitarian Universalist Association (www.uua.org).

Dedications

John dedicates his part of the book (the particularly lame jokes) to Sarah Willow, who surprises and delights him every day, and to Tonia, now and always.

Carol dedicates her part of the book to Joshua, with all her love, and to her friends, who remind her that there's more to life than writing books — or business, for that matter.

Margy dedicates this book to Jordan, Meg, and Zac, who make life worth living, and to Susan, the world's best cousin.

Author's Acknowledgments

Mark Enochs hustled us through the editorial process despite our attempts to drag it out while (no doubt at great personal cost) making us look like better writers than we are. Thanks also to the rest of the gang at Wiley Publishing, Inc. especially those listed on the Publisher's Acknowledgment page.

For childcare, Margy thanks Jordan (actually, she thanks him for everything else, too). John likewise thanks Tonia and the Trumansburg Elementary School, where the kids hug the principal and the superintendent when they walk down the hall, whose faculty and staff provided vital and high-quality education and care to the aforementioned surprising person. Carol thanks Patrick, Arnold, Suzanne, and Laura, the wonderful folks at Kesher, and her family and friends for their unending help and support. We all thank Matt Wagner and Bill Gladstone at Waterside Productions for encouragement. The entire contents of this book were edited and submitted to the publisher using the Web — practicing what we preach. We thank our Internet providers: Finger Lakes Technologies Group (Trumansburg, N.Y. Hi, Paul!), Lightlink (Ithaca, N.Y. Hi, Homer!), and Shoreham.net (Shoreham, Vermont. Hi, Don and Jim!).

Finally, thanks to all the smarties (we wouldn't say wiseacres) who sent us comments on the previous editions and helped make this one better. If you have ideas, comments, or complaints, about the book, whisk them to us at internet10@gurus.com.

Visit our Web site at net.gurus.com for updates and more information about the topics in this book.

Publisher's Acknowledgments

We're proud of this book; please send us your comments through our online registration form located at www.dummies.com/register/.

Some of the people who helped bring this book to market include the following:

Acquisitions, Editorial, and Media Development

Project Editor: Mark Enochs
   (Previous Editions: Linda Morris, Rebecca Whitney)

Senior Acquisitions Editor: Steven Hayes

Copy Editors: Barry Childs-Helton, Andy Hollandbeck, Virginia Sanders, Heidi Unger

Technical Editor: Tom Riegsecker

Editorial Manager: Leah Cameron

Editorial Assistant: Amanda Foxworth

Cartoons: Rich Tennant (www.the5thwave.com)

Composition Services

Project Coordinators: Adrienne Martinez Nancee Reeves,

Layout and Graphics: Lauren Goddard, Joyce Haughey, Melanee Prendergast, Heather Ryan

Proofreaders: Leeann Harney, Joe Niesen, Carl William Pierce, TECHBOOKS Production Services

Indexer: TECHBOOKS Production Services

Publishing and Editorial for Technology Dummies

   Richard Swadley, Vice President and Executive Group Publisher

   Andy Cummings, Vice President and Publisher

   Mary Bednarek, Executive Acquisitions Director

   Mary C. Corder, Editorial Director

Publishing for Consumer Dummies

   Diane Graves Steele, Vice President and Publisher

   Joyce Pepple, Acquisitions Director

Composition Services

   Gerry Fahey, Vice President of Production Services

   Debbie Stailey, Director of Composition Services

Contents at a Glance

Table of Contents

Introduction

Welcome to *The Internet For Dummies,* 10th Edition. Although lots of books about the Internet are available, traditionally most of them have assumed that you have a degree in computer science, would love to know about every strange and useless wart of the Internet, and enjoy memorizing unpronounceable commands and options. We want this book to be different.

Instead, this book describes what you actually do to become an *Internaut* (someone who navigates the Internet with skill) — how to get started, what you really need to know, and where to go for help. And we describe it in plain old English.

For this tenth edition, we've extensively revised and updated the entire book. When we first wrote *The Internet For Dummies* twelve years ago (yikes!), a typical Internet user was a student who connected from college or a technical worker who had access through work. The World Wide Web was so new that it had only a few hundred pages. Now, over a decade later, the Net has grown like crazy to include half a billion (dare we say it?) normal people, connecting from computers at home or work, along with students ranging from elementary school to adult education. We now focus on the parts of the Net that are of the most interest to typical users — how to find things on the World Wide Web, how to use Firefox and Internet Explorer (the most popular and/or useful Web programs), how to send and receive electronic mail (e-mail), and how to shop online, invest online, chat online, and download interesting things from the Net.

About This Book

We don't flatter ourselves to think you're interested enough in the Internet to sit down and read the entire book (although it should be a fine book for the bathroom). When you run into a problem using the Internet ("Hmm, I *thought* that I knew how to find somebody on the Net, but I don't seem to remember . . ."), just dip into the book long enough to solve your problem.

Pertinent sections include

- Understanding what the Internet is
- Knowing how to get connected to the Net
- Climbing around the World Wide Web
- Finding people, places, and things
- Communicating by e-mail
- Hanging out with friends using instant messaging and chat
- Getting stuff from the Net

How to Use This Book

To begin, please read the first three chapters. They give you an overview of the Internet and some important tips and terminology. (Besides, we think they're interesting.) When you're ready to get yourself on the Internet, turn to Part II and pick the option that best suits you and your circumstances. Parts III through VI egg you on and provide extra support — they describe the Web, e-mail, and other stuff you can do on the Internet.

Although we try hard not to introduce a technical term without defining it, sometimes we slip. Sometimes, too, you may read a section out of order and find a term we defined a few chapters before that. To fill in the gaps, we include a glossary at the end of the book.

Because the Internet is ever-changing, we have expanded our book to include an online area to help keep you up to date. Whenever you see our special Whoosh icon, it means we have more up-to-the-minute information available on our Web site, at

```
net.gurus.com
```

When you have to follow a complicated procedure, we spell it out step by step wherever possible. We then tell you what happens in response and what your options are. When you have to type something, it appears in the book in **boldface**. Type it just as it appears. Use the same capitalization we do — a few systems care deeply about CAPITAL and small letters. Then press the Enter key. The book tells you what should happen when you give each command and what your options are.

When you have to choose commands from menus, we write File⇨Exit when we want you to choose the File command from the menu bar and then choose the Exit command from the menu that appears.

Who Are You?

In writing the book, we made a few assumptions about you:

- ✔ You have or would like to have access to the Internet.
- ✔ You want to get some work done with it. (We consider the term "work" to include the concept "play.")
- ✔ You are not interested in becoming the world's next great Internet expert, at least not this week.

How This Book Is Organized

This book has six parts. The parts stand on their own — although you can begin reading wherever you like, you should at least skim Parts I and II first to get acquainted with some unavoidable Internet jargon and find out how to get your computer on the Net.

Here are the parts of the book and what they contain:

In Part I, "Welcome to the Internet," you find out what the Internet is and why it's interesting (at least why we think it's interesting). Also, this part has stuff about vital Internet terminology and concepts that help you as you read through the later parts of the book. Part I discusses security and privacy issues and gives some thoughts about children's use of the Net.

For the nuts and bolts of getting on the Net, read Part II, "Internet, Here I Come!" For most users, by far the most difficult part of using the Net is getting to that first connection, with software loaded, configuration configured, and modem modeming or broadband banding broadly. After that, it's (relatively) smooth sailing.

Part III, "Web Mania," dives into the World Wide Web, the part of the Internet that has powered the Net's leap from obscurity to fame. We discuss how to get around on the Web, how to find stuff (which is not as easy as it should be), and how to shop online on the Web.

Part IV, "E-Mail, Chat, and Other Ways to Hang Out Online," looks at the important Net communication services: sending and receiving e-mail, instant messages, and chatting. You find out how to exchange e-mail with people down the hall or on other continents, how to use e-mail mailing lists to keep in touch with people of similar interests, and how to use instant messaging programs to chat with your online pals. You also get a briefing on avoiding and blocking online hazards like viruses and spam.

Part V, "Advanced Internet Activities," covers two important topics that don't fit in Parts I through IV: making your own Web page, and using weblogs, which let anyone be an online journalist.

Part VI, "The Part of Tens," comprises a compendium of ready references and useful facts (which, we suppose, suggests that the rest of the book is full of useless facts).

Icons Used in This Book

Lets you know that some particularly nerdy, technoid information is coming up so you can skip it if you want. (On the other hand, you may want to read it.)

Indicates that a nifty little shortcut or timesaver is explained.

Gaack! We found out about this the hard way! Don't let it happen to you!

Indicates something to file away in your memory archives.

Points out a resource on the World Wide Web that you can use with Netscape, Internet Explorer, or other Web software.

Points you to more up-to-the-minute information on our very own Web site. Hey, this book is *alive*.

What Now?

That's all you need to know to get started. Whenever you hit a snag using the Internet, just look up the problem in the table of contents or index in this book. Either you'll have the problem solved in a flash or know where you need to go to find some expert help.

Because the Internet has been evolving for over 30 years, largely under the influence of some extremely nerdy people, it was not designed to be particularly easy for normal people to use. Don't feel bad if you have to look up a number of topics before you feel comfortable using the Internet. Until recently, most computer users never had to face anything as complex as the Internet.

Feedback, Please

We love to hear from our readers. If you want to contact us, please feel free to do so, in care of

Dummies Press
10475 Crosspoint Blvd.
Indianapolis, IN 46256

Better yet, send us Internet e-mail at `internet10@gurus.com` (our friendly robot will answer immediately; the human authors read all the e-mail and answer as much as we can), or visit this book's Web home page, at `net.gurus.com`. These e-mail addresses put you in contact with the authors of this book; to contact the publisher or authors of other *For Dummies* books, visit the publisher's Web site, at `www.dummies.com`, or send paper mail to the address just listed.

Part I

Welcome to the Internet

The 5th Wave   By Rich Tennant

INTERNET ACCESS
.50¢ - Min.

In this part . . .

The Internet is an amazing place. But, because it's full of computers, everything's more complicated than it should be. We start with a look at what the Internet is and how it got that way. We tell you what's happening, what people are doing, and why you should care. We give special attention to security problems, privacy issues, and family concerns — particularly the knotty question of what's the best way for kids to work with the Internet.

Chapter 1

What Is the Internet, and Why Do You Care?

In This Chapter

▶ What, really, is the Internet?

▶ For that matter, what is a network?

▶ What is the Internet good for?

▶ Is the Internet a safe place?

*I*t's huge, it's sprawling, it's globe spanning, it's become part of our lives, it must be . . . the Internet. We all know something about it, and most of us have tried to use it, with more or less success. (If you've had less, you've come to the right place.) In this chapter, we look at what the Internet is and what it can do before we dive into details in the rest of book.

If you're new to the Internet, and especially if you don't have much computer experience, *be patient with yourself.* Many of the ideas here are completely new. Allow yourself some time to read and reread. The Internet is a different world with its own language, and it takes some getting used to.

Even experienced computer users can find the Internet more complex than other things they've tackled before. The Internet is not a single software package, and it doesn't easily lend itself to the kind of step-by-step instructions we would provide for a single, fixed program. This book is as step-by-step as we can make it, but the Internet resembles a living organism mutating at an astonishing rate more than it resembles Microsoft Word or Excel, which sit quietly on your computer. After you get set up and get a little practice, using the Internet seems like second nature; in the beginning, however, it can be daunting.

Okay, So What Is the Internet?

The Internet — also known as the *Net* — is the world's largest computer network. "What is a network?" you may ask. Even if you already know, you may want to read the next couple of paragraphs to make sure that we're speaking the same language.

A computer *network* is a bunch of computers hooked together to communicate somehow. In concept, it's sort of like a radio or TV network that connects a bunch of radio or TV stations so that they can share the latest episode of *American Idol*.

But don't take the analogy too far. TV networks send the same information to all the stations at the same time (it's called *broadcast* networking); usually, in computer networks, each particular message is routed to a particular computer, so different computers can display different things. Unlike TV networks, computer networks are invariably two-way: When computer A sends a message to computer B, B can send a reply back to A.

Some computer networks consist of a central computer and a bunch of remote stations that report to it (for example, a central airline-reservation computer with thousands of screens and keyboards in airports and travel agencies). Other networks, including the Internet, are more egalitarian and permit any computer on the network to communicate with any other computer. Many new wireless devices — mobile phones, Palm Pilots, Blackberries, and their ilk — are linked to the Net, expanding the reach of the Internet to our very persons.

The Internet isn't really one network — it's a network of networks, all freely exchanging information. The networks range from the big and formal (such as the corporate networks at AT&T, General Motors, and Hewlett-Packard) to the small and informal (such as the one in John's back bedroom, made from a couple of old PCs bought at an electronics parts store) and everything in between. College and university networks have long been part of the Internet, and now high schools and elementary schools are joining in. Lately, computers and the Internet have become so popular that more and more households have more than one computer and are creating their own networks at home from which they connect to the Internet.

So What's All the Hoopla?

Everywhere you turn, you can find traces of the Internet. Household products, business cards, radio shows, and movie credits list their Web site addresses (usually starting with "www" and ending with "dot com") and their e-mail addresses. New people you meet would rather give you an e-mail address than a phone number. Everyone seems to be "going online" and "Googling it." Are they really talking about this same "network of networks"? Yes, *and* there's more.

The Internet affects our lives on a scale as significant as the telephone and television. When it comes to disseminating information, the Internet is the most significant invention since the printing press. If you use a telephone, write letters, read a newspaper or magazine, or do business or any kind of research, the Internet can radically alter your worldview.

With networks, size counts a great deal: The larger a network is, the more stuff it has to offer. Because the Internet is the world's largest interconnected group of computer networks, it has an amazing array of information to offer.

When people talk about the Internet, they usually talk about what they can do, what they have found, and whom they have met. Millions of computers connected to the Internet exchange information in a bunch of different ways. The number and type of available services are so expansive that we don't have room to give a complete list in this chapter, but here's a quick summary:

- **Electronic mail (e-mail):** This service is certainly the most widely used — you can exchange e-mail with millions of people all over the world. People use e-mail for anything that they might use paper (mail, faxes, special delivery of documents) or the telephone (gossip, recipes, love letters) to communicate — you name it. (We hear that some people even use it for stuff related to work.) Electronic *mailing lists* enable you to join group discussions with people who have similar interests and to meet people over the Net. Chapters 13 through 16 have all the details.

- **The World Wide Web:** When people talk these days about surfing the Net, they often mean checking out sites on this (buzzword alert) multimedia hyperlinked database that spans the globe. In fact, people are talking more about the Web and less about the Net. Are they the same thing? Technically, the answer is "no." But practically speaking, the answer for many people is "pretty close." We tell you the truth, the whole truth, and nothing but the truth in Chapter 6.

The Web, unlike earlier Internet services, combines text, pictures, sound, video clips, animation, and even live broadcasts of news, concerts, and wildlife. You can move around with a click of your mouse. New Web sites (sets of Web pages) are growing faster than you can say "Big Mac with cheese," with new sites appearing every minute. In 1993, when we wrote the first edition of this book, the Internet contained 130 Web sites. Today, it has many millions, and statistics indicate that the number is doubling every few months.

The software used to navigate the Web is known as a *browser*. The most popular browsers today are Firefox and Internet Explorer. We tell you all about them in Chapter 6.

✔ **Chat services:** People are talking to people all over the globe about everything under the sun. They enter chat rooms with several other people or with one special someone. They're using the chat facilities of America Online, Microsoft, Yahoo, Internet Relay Chat (IRC), or Web-based chat rooms. We tell you how to get chatting in Chapter 16.

✔ **Instant Messaging (IMing):** With the help of special programs on your computer and your friend's computer, you can start up a conversation in a heartbeat. Paging programs like Windows Messenger, Yahoo Messenger, ICQ, and AOL Instant Messenger let you send messages that "pop up" on the recipient's screen. We hear tales of nimble-fingered youth carrying on upwards of 13 IM sessions simultaneously. We tell you about IM programs in Chapter 16.

A Few Real-Life Stories

Seventh-grade students in San Diego use the Internet to exchange letters and stories with kids in Israel. Although it's partly just for fun and to make friends in a foreign country, a sober academic study reported that when kids have a real audience for their stuff, they write better. (Big surprise.)

For many purposes, the Internet is the fastest and most reliable way to move information. In September 1998, when special prosecutor Kenneth Starr delivered his report on the scandal involving President Clinton and Monica Lewinsky to the U.S. House of Representatives, the House quickly put the report online, thus allowing millions of people to read it the day it came out. (We can still debate whether it was a good idea to do that, but the Internet is what made it possible.) And Matt Drudge's *Drudge Report* online gossip sheet broke much of the scandal first.

In the hours and days following the terrorist attacks of September 11, 2001, people gave up on the overloaded phone system (cell phones were particularly useless) and turned to e-mail to find out whether their loved ones and coworkers had survived. The Web provided folks in the United States with news coverage from all over the world, thus allowing Americans a glimpse at how the rest of the world saw the situation.

During the Iraq war, soldiers and civilians have kept in touch with friends and relatives by e-mail. One young man in Baghdad kept a widely read weblog (or *blog* — see Chapter 18) that gave people all over the world a view of the lead up to the war.

Medical researchers around the world use the Internet to maintain databases of rapidly changing data. People with medical conditions use the Internet to communicate with each other in support groups and to compare experiences.

Forward-thinking physicians make themselves available to their patients via e-mail and encourage their patients to use e-mail instead of the phone for non-emergency questions.

The Internet has more prosaic uses, too. Here are some from our personal experiences:

- ✔ When we began writing our megabook, *Internet Secrets,* we posted notices on the Internet asking for contributions. We got responses from all over the world. Many of these contributors became our friends. Now we have people to visit all over the world. It could happen to *you.*

- ✔ We get mail every day from all over the world from readers of our *For Dummies* books and are often the happy recipients of readers' first-ever e-mail messages.

- ✔ The Internet is its own best source of software. Whenever we hear about a new service, it usually takes only a few minutes to find software for our computers (various computers running various versions of Windows, as well as a Macintosh), download it, and start it up. Much of the software available on the Internet is free or inexpensive shareware.

- ✔ When Margy wanted to buy a used Subaru, she and her husband found listings of the models they wanted at dealers all over their state. They could even get insurance and registration information about the cars before they went to the dealer, so they knew where and when the cars had been driven, and whether they'd been in major accidents.

The Internet has local and regional parts, too. When John wanted to sell a trusty but tired pickup truck, a note on the Internet in a local for-sale area found a buyer within two days. Margy's husband sold his used computer within a half-hour of posting a message in the relevant Usenet newsgroup. Carol checks local movie listings and cultural events faster and more comprehensively than looking in the paper.

Why Is This Medium Different from Any Other Medium?

The Internet is unlike all the other communications media we've ever encountered. People of all ages, colors, creeds, and countries freely share ideas, stories, data, opinions, and products.

Anybody can access it

One great thing about the Internet is that it's probably the most open network in the world. Thousands of computers provide facilities that are available to anyone who has Internet access. Older networks limited what users could do and required specific arrangements for each service, but the Internet connects everyone to everything. Although pay services exist (and more are added every day), most Internet services are free for the taking after you're online. If you don't already have access to the Internet through your company, your school, your library, or a friend's attic, you probably have to pay for access by using an Internet service provider (ISP). We talk about some ISPs in Chapter 4.

It's politically, socially, and religiously correct

Another great thing about the Internet is that it is what one may call "socially unstratified." That is, one computer is no better than any other, and no person is any better than any other. Who you are on the Internet depends solely on how you present yourself through your keyboard. If what you say makes you sound like an intelligent, interesting person, that's who you are. It doesn't matter how old you are or what you look like or whether you're a student, a business executive, or a construction worker. Physical disabilities don't matter — we correspond with deaf and blind people. If they hadn't felt like telling us, we never would have known. People become famous (and infamous) in the Internet community through their own efforts.

Does the Internet really reach every continent?

Some skeptical readers, after reading the claim that the Internet spans every continent, may point out that Antarctica is a continent, even though its population consists largely of penguins, who (as far as we know) are not interested in computer networks. Does the Internet go there? It does. A few machines at the Scott Base on McMurdo Sound in Antarctica are on the Internet, connected by radio link to New Zealand. The base at the South Pole is reported to have a link to the United States, but it doesn't publish its electronic address.

At the time of this writing, the largest Internet-free land mass in the world is probably one of the uninhabited islands in the Canadian arctic — Melville Island — perhaps (you can look it up on the Internet). We used to say New Guinea, a large jungle island north of Australia, until a reader there sent us e-mail in 1997 telling us about his new Internet provider. *Note:* If you live on Melville Island and you're online there, please e-mail us right away!

The Net advantage

The Internet has become totally mainstream, and you're falling further behind the curve — and at a faster rate — if you haven't yet gotten started. Increasingly, news gets out on the Internet before it's available any other way, and the cyber-deprived are losing ground.

Here are some of the ways people use the Internet:

- **Getting information:** Many Web sites have information free for the taking. Information ranges from IRS tax forms that you can print out and use to help-wanted ads, real estate listings, and recipes. From U.S. Supreme Court decisions and library card catalogs to the text of old books, digitized pictures (many suitable for family audiences), and an enormous variety of software — from games to operating systems — you can find virtually anything on the Net. You can find out the weather, view movie listings, and even see school closings for anywhere in the world, from anywhere in the world.

  Special tools known as *search engines, directories,* and *indices* help you find information on the Web. Lots of people are trying to create the fastest, smartest search engine and the most complete Web index. We tell you about Google, the most complete one at this point, so you at least get the picture. As mentioned in the Introduction to this book, when you see a Web icon in the margin of this book, we describe resources that you can retrieve from the Internet (usually the Web), as described in Chapters 8 and 12.

- **Finding people:** If you've lost track of your childhood sweetheart, now's your chance to find him or her anywhere in the country. You can use one of the directory services to search the phone books of the entire United States. We tell you more about this subject in Chapter 8.

- **Finding businesses, products, and services:** New yellow pages directory services enable you to search by the type of company you're looking for. You can indicate the area code or zip code to help specify the location. Also, many people are shopping for that hard-to-find, special gift item. A friend told us of her search for a bear pendant that led her to a company in Alaska that had just what she was looking for. John and Margy's dad found exactly the crystal he wanted — in Australia.

- **Research:** Law firms find that information they formerly paid $600 an hour to get from commercial services can be found for free when they go directly to the Internet. Real estate appraisers use demographic data available on the Net, including unemployment statistics, to help assess property values. Genetics researchers and other scientists download up-to-date research results from around the world. Businesses and potential businesses research their competition over the Net.

✔ **Education:** Schoolteachers coordinate projects with classrooms all over the globe. College students and their families exchange e-mail to facilitate letter writing and keep down the cost of phone calls. Students do research from their home computers. The latest encyclopedias are online.

✔ **Buying and selling stuff:** On the Internet, you can buy anything from books about beer making to stock in microbreweries. And we hear you can make a mint by cleaning out your closets and selling your old junk on eBay. We talk about the relevant issues later in this chapter and in Chapter 10.

✔ **Travel:** Cities, towns, states, and countries are using the Web to put up (or *post*) tourist and event information. Travelers find weather information; maps; plane, train, and bus schedules and tickets; and museum hours online.

✔ **Intranets:** Wouldn't ya know? Businesses have figured out that this Internet stuff is really useful and have created their own, private networks — like mini-Internets. On these *intranets*, companies use e-mail to communicate with employees, customers, and vendors. Many companies use Web pages for company information like corporate benefits, for filing expense reports and time sheets, and for ordering supplies. An intranet provides a way for an organization to provide stuff you can see from inside a company that folks on the outside can't see, including manuals, forms, videos of boring meetings, and, of course, endless memos. In some organizations, e-mail and intranets reduce the amount of paper wasted on this stuff.

✔ **Marketing and sales:** Software companies sell software and provide updates via the Net. (Aside from the large pile of AOL CDs that we now use as coasters, most software distribution is migrating to the Internet, where customers can download and install programs without waiting for a CD to arrive.) Companies are selling products over the Net. Online bookstores and music stores enable people to browse online, choose titles, and pay for stuff over the Internet.

✔ **Games:** Internet-based multi-user games can easily absorb all your waking hours and an alarming number of what would otherwise be your sleeping hours. You can challenge other players who can be anywhere in the world. Many kinds of games are available on the Web, including such traditionally addictive games as bridge, hearts, chess, checkers, and go. In Chapter 21, we tell where to find these games.

✔ **Love:** People are finding romance on the Net. Singles ads and matchmaking sites vie for users. The Internet long ago stopped being a magnet for a bunch of socially challenged 22-year-old nerdy guys and now has turned into the world's biggest matchmaker for people of all ages, genders, preferences, and life situations.

- ✔ **Healing:** Patients and doctors keep up-to-date with the latest medical findings, share treatment experience, and give one another support around medical problems. We even know of some practitioners who exchange e-mail directly with their patients.

- ✔ **Investing:** People do financial research, buy stock, and invest money online. Some online companies trade their own shares. Investors are finding new ventures, and new ventures are finding capital.

- ✔ **Organizing events:** Conference and trade-show organizers are finding that the best way to disseminate information, call for papers, and register participants is to do it on the Web. Information can be updated regularly, and paper and shipping costs are dramatically reduced. Registering online saves the cost of on-site registration staff and the hassle of on-site registration lines.

- ✔ **Nonprofits:** Churches, synagogues, mosques, and other community organizations put up pages telling Web users about themselves and inviting new people. The online church newsletter *always* comes before Sunday.

Where did the Internet come from?

The ancestor of the Internet was the *ARPANET,* a project funded by the Department of Defense (DOD) in 1969, both as an experiment in reliable networking and to link DOD and military research contractors, including the large number of universities doing military-funded research. (*ARPA* stands for Advanced Research Projects Administration, the branch of the DOD in charge of handing out grant money. For enhanced confusion, the agency is now known as *DARPA* — the added *D* is for *Defense,* in case anyone had doubts about where the money was coming from.) Although the ARPANET started small — connecting three computers in California with one in Utah — it quickly grew to span the continent.

In the early 1980s, the ARPANET grew into the early Internet, a group of interlinked networks connecting many educational and research sites funded by the National Science Foundation (NSF), along with the original military sites. By 1990, it was clear that the Internet was here to stay, and DARPA and the NSF bowed out in favor of the commercially run networks that make up today's Internet. (And, yes, although Al Gore didn't invent the Internet, he was instrumental in keeping it funded so that it could turn into the Internet we know today.) Familiar companies such as AT&T, Sprint, Verizon, and Quest run some of the networks; others belong to specialty companies such as Level3 and Verio. No matter which one you're attached to, they all interconnect, so it's all one giant Internet. For more information, read our Web page located at

    net.gurus.com/history

Some Thoughts about Safety and Privacy

The Internet is a funny place. Although it seems completely anonymous, it's not. People used to have Internet usernames that bore some resemblance to their true identities — their names or initials or some such combination in conjunction with their university or corporation names gave a fairly traceable route to an actual person. Today, with the phenomenon of screen names (courtesy of America Online) and multiple e-mail addresses (courtesy of many Internet providers), revealing your identity is definitely optional.

Depending on who you are and what you want to do on the Net, you may, in fact, want different names and different accounts. Here are some legitimate reasons for wanting them:

- ✔ You're a professional — a physician, for example — and you want to participate in a mailing list or newsgroup without being asked for your professional opinion.
- ✔ You want help with an area of concern that you feel is private and you don't want your problem known to people close to you who may find out if your name were associated with it.
- ✔ You do business on the Internet, and you socialize on the Net. You may want to keep those activities separate.

And a warning to those who may consider abusing the anonymous nature of the Internet: Most Net activities can be traced. If you start to abuse the Net, you'll find you're not so anonymous after all.

Safety first

The anonymous, faceless nature of the Internet has its downside, too. To protect you and your family, take the following simple precautions:

- ✔ In chat rooms and other getting-to-know-you situations, don't use your full name.
- ✔ Never provide your name, address, or phone number to someone you don't know.
- ✔ Never believe anyone who says that he is from "AOL Tech Support," "eBay Fraud Prevention," or some such authority and asks you for your password. No legitimate entity will ever ask you for your password.
- ✔ Be especially careful about disclosing information about kids. Don't fill out profiles in chat rooms that ask for a kid's name, hometown, school, age, address, or phone number, because they are invariably used for "targeted marketing" (also known as junk mail).

Although relatively rare, horrible things have happened to a few people who have taken their Internet encounters into real life. Many wonderful things have happened, too. We've met some of our best friends over the Net, and some people have met and subsequently married. We just want to encourage you to use common sense when you set up a meeting with a Net friend. A person you've e-mailed or swapped instant messages with is still largely a stranger, and if you want to meet in person, take the same precautions you would on a first date with someone you don't know: Meet in a public place, perhaps with a friend along, and be sure your family knows where you are and when you're planning to be back.

The Net is a wonderful place, and meeting new people and making new friends is one of the big attractions. We just want to make sure that you're as careful as you would be in the rest of your life.

Protect your privacy

Here in the United States, we've grown up with certain attitudes about freedom and privacy, many of which we take for granted. We tend to feel that who we are, where we go, and what we do is our own business as long as we don't bother anyone else. However, bunches of people are extremely interested in who we are, where we go (on the Net, at least), and, most especially, what we buy.

Some people worry that snoops on the Net will intercept their private e-mail or Web pages. That's fairly unlikely, although if you're worried about it, you can lock them with a secret password. The more serious problem is advertisers who build profiles of the sites you visit and the stuff you buy. Most Web ads are provided through a handful of companies like DoubleClick.com and Advertising.com, who can use their ads to tell that the same person (you) is visiting a lot of different Web sites and create a profile. They say they don't, but they don't say they won't.

Throughout this book, we point out when your privacy or security may be in danger and suggest ways to protect yourself. Be sure to read the next chapter for our overview of safety concerns and tips.

Chapter 2

Is the Internet Safe? Viruses, Spyware, Spam, and Other Yucky Stuff

We like the Internet. It's been part of our lives — and livelihoods — for years. We'd love to tell you that all the stuff you may have read about the dangers of connecting a computer to the Internet is hype. We can't. The success of the Internet has attracted unsavory people who view you as a money tree ready to be plucked. (Nothing personal. They see everybody that way.) In a few countries, perpetrating Internet fraud is now a major part of the national economy.

Even if no one steals your money, information about your online activities can be gathered and result in a real loss of privacy. And there are people who are trying to take over your computer so they can use it for nefarious purposes. When a new computer is hooked up to the Internet it's not a question of whether it will come under cyberattack, but when. And the answer is not measured in months or days — but in hours or minutes.

Relax — the Internet doesn't have to be a dangerous place. Using the Internet is like walking around a big city. Yes, you need to be careful, use some protection, and stay out of dangerous areas, but you can safely take advantage of the wonders that the Net has to offer.

This chapter describes the types of privacy, security, and annoyance issues that abound on the Internet:

- ✓ **Privacy issues** involve how much people can find out about you over the Internet.

- ✓ **Security issues** have to do with keeping control over what programs are running on your computer.

- ✓ Just plain **annoyance issues** include ending up with a mailbox full of spam (junk e-mail) or Web browser windows popping up with advertisements.

Through the rest of this book, we include instructions for staying safe by using a firewall, a virus checker, a spyware scanner, and some common sense. Chapter 3 talks about rules for letting kids use the Internet, and most of the suggestions make sense for grown-ups, too.

What People Can Learn about You

Advances in technology are eroding the privacy that most of us take for granted. Innovations we use every day — credit cards, cellphones, electronic key cards, and automobile tollway transponders — allow our every purchase and movement to be tracked. The Internet is an extension of this trend. Much of what you do online may be watched and recorded — sometimes for innocent reasons and sometimes not.

All this is further compounded by the amount of publicly available information that is now conveniently available to a far *greater* public over the Internet. When paper records were kept by government officials and people had to visit the office and dig through the files for the specific information they wanted, a lot less information abuse was possible. Now the potential exists for anyone, anywhere to access information about people heretofore unknown, and gather information from various sources, including online directories. No longer are geography or time deterrents enough.

Several techniques for gathering information about you as you use the Internet, or tricking you into providing information, are described in the next few sections.

Phishing for inphormation

Phishing is the hot new Internet crime and you're the target. The good news is that protecting yourself is easy when you and your family know how to spot the phish-hook.

What does phish look like?

Once you start using the Internet and receiving e-mail (as described in Chapter 13), there's an excellent chance that you'll get a message like this:

Subject: Ebay Important Warning

From: eBay Billing Department! <Service@eBay.com>

eBay Fraud Mediation Request

You have recieved this email because you or someone had used your account to make fake bids at eBay. For security purposes, we are required to open an investigation into this matter.

THE FRAUD ALERT ID CODE CONTAINED IN THIS MESSAGE WILL BE ATTACHED IN OUR FRAUD MEDIATION REQUEST FORM, IN ORDER TO VERIFY YOUR EBAY ACCOUNT REGISTRATION INFORMATIONS.

Fraud Alert ID CODE: 00937614

(Please save this Fraud Alert ID Code for your reference.)

To help speed up this process, please access the following form to complete the verification of your eBay account registration informations:

http://www.eBay.com/cgi_bin/secure/Fraud Alert ID CODE: 00937614

Please Note:

If we do not receive the appropriate eBay account verification within 48 hours, then we will assume this eBay account is fraudulent and will be suspended.

Regards, Safeharbor Department (Trust and Safety Department), eBay Inc.

Copyright © 2004 eBay Inc. All Rights Reserved. Designated trademarks and brands are the property of their respective owners.

Sounds authentic and scary. Think you'd better deal with this right away? Better think again. You are the phish and this message is the bait. That underlined text in the middle is the hook. Click it and soon an official-looking page appears that looks just like an eBay sign-in page. After you enter your username and password, another official-looking page asks for your credit card number, PIN, billing address, checking account details (complete with a helpful graphic so you can find the right numbers on your personal checks), social security number, date of birth, mother's maiden name, and drivers' license number. The page is smart enough to reject an invalid credit card number. If you fill in all the information and press continue, you see a valid eBay page that says you've logged out. Then, who knows? You are wide open for anything from a small purchase paid for by your credit card to full scale identity theft that can take months or years to straighten out.

This message did not come from eBay. Millions of these messages are sent over the Internet every day.

Some clues might alert you. The misspellings of "recieved" and "informations" suggest the author is someone whose English skills are limited. And if you take the trouble to save the email to a file and then print it out, the underlined link in the middle of the messages looks like this:

```
<http://192.168.45.67/cgi_bin>http://www.eBay.com/cgi_bin/
            secure/Fraud Alert ID CODE: 00937614
```

The text between the angle brackets ("<" and ">") is where the link really goes, to a Web site with a numeric address. (When we tried clicking the link two days after we got the mail, the Web site had already been shut down. Those eBay security folks are on the ball.)

Don't take the bait

Sooner or later the phishers will find good editors or learn how to use a spell checker, so you can't rely on spelling and grammar mistakes, though they are a dead giveaway when you spot one. Here are a few additional tips:

- ✔ Assume that every e-mail that leads you to a page seeking passwords or credit card numbers or other personal information is a phishing expedition.

- ✔ If the e-mail purports to be from a company you've never heard of, ignore it.

- ✔ If it says it's from a company with whom you have an account, go to the company's Web site by typing in the company's URL into your browser (see Chapter 6), *not* by clicking a link in the e-mail. When you get to the company's Web site, look for a "My account" link. When you log in there, if there is a problem you should see a notice. If there is no way to log in and you are still concerned, forward a copy of the e-mail to the customer service department.

One trick phishers use to fool Internet users is *Web site spoofing* — tricking your browser into displaying one address when you are actually at another site. Some browsers allow Web sites to only show their main address, so they don't look so geeky. Phishers take advantage of this ability. Better browsers like Firefox (see Chapter 6) offer protection against Web site spoofing — they always show the actual Web address of the page you are on.

If you want to know for sure where a link is taking you, you can download SpoofStick — free software available from `www.spoofstick.com` for example — that shows you the top level name of the Web site you are actually visiting. (See Chapter 12 for how to download and install programs.)

To summarize: Make sure your family knows this rule well: Never, *never*, **never** enter passwords, credit card numbers, or other personal information at a Web page you got to by clicking a link in an e-mail.

Web beacons and bugs that track where you browse

Ever since the World Wide Web became a household word (okay, three words), companies have increasingly viewed their Internet presence as a vital way to advertise their goods and services and conduct their business. They spend millions of dollars on their Web sites — and would very much like to know just how people use them. Small wonder that when you visit a site, companies can keep track of your actions as you go from link to link within the site. But they *really* want to know what you were doing before you entered their site — and what you do after you leave. To gather this intelligence, they insert special pieces of code they call *Web beacons* and everyone else calls *Web bugs* — these report your actions to a central site, often run by a separate company that places ads on Web sites. By piecing together the information from many Web sites, these tracking companies get a pretty clear picture of where you go online — and what you look at when you get there. Many are careful to provide only statistical information to their clients, but the potential for abuse is there. And it's worth noting that U. S. courts set a lower standard of protection for "business records" gathered in this way than they do for personal papers stored in our homes.

Cookies aren't so bad

When you browse the Web (as described in Chapter 6), the Web server needs to know who you are if you want to do things that require logging in, or putting items in a virtual shopping cart, or any other process that requires that the Web site remember information about you as you move from page to page. The most commonly-used trick that allows Web sites to keep track of what you are doing is called *setting cookies*. A *cookie* is a tiny little file that is stored on your computer. It contains the address of the Web site and ID codes of some kind that identify you. Cookies don't usually contain personal information or anything dangerous at all; they are usually innocuous and useful.

Google yourself

One of the big attractions of the Internet is *all that data out there* that is now so easy to access. Some of that data is about you. If you have a personal Web site, have participated in newsgroups or mailing lists or have your own blog (see Chapters 17, 16, and 18 respectively), then you expect that all the information you put up there is available for everyone to see, usually forever. (We still find stuff about ourselves from over 20 years ago.) But other people put up information as well — newsletters, event listings, pictures from events, other pictures, and so on. Your electronic data trail on the Internet may be longer than you think. If you haven't done it before, try Googling yourself. Enter your name in quotes in the Google search box and click Go. If you have a common name you may need to throw in your middle initial or add the name of your town or school. (If you do this all the time it's called *ego surfing*.)

If you plan to shop on the Web, use Web-based message boards (explained in Chapter 16), or many other Web services, cookies make it all possible. When you're using an airline reservation site, for example, the site uses cookies to keep the flights you're reserving separate from the ones other users are reserving at the same time. On the other hand, suppose that you use your credit card to purchase something on a Web site and the site uses a cookie to remember the account with your credit card number. Suppose that you provide this information from a computer at work and the next person to visit that site uses the same computer. That person could, possibly, make purchases on your credit card. Oops.

Internet users have various feelings about cookies. Some of us don't care about them, and some of us view them as an unconscionable invasion of privacy. You get to decide for yourself. Contrary to rumor, cookie files cannot get other information from your hard disk, give you a bad haircut, or otherwise mess up your life. They collect only information that the browser tells them about. Internet Explorer and Firefox let you control whether and when cookies are stored on your computer. See Chapter 7 for how to tell your Web browser whether and when to allow a Web site to set a cookie.

How People Can Take Over Your PC

You can download and install software right over the Internet, which is a wonderful feature. It's wonderful when you need a viewer program to display and print a tax form, or when you want to install a free upgrade to a program that you purchased earlier. How convenient! We tell you all about it in Chapter 12.

However, it's also possible for other people to install programs on your computer without your permission. Hey, wait a minute — whose computer is it, anyway? These programs can arrive in a number of ways, mainly by e-mail and via your Web browser.

Viruses arrive via e-mail

Computer viruses are programs that jump from computer to computer, just as real viruses jump from person to person. Computer viruses can spread using any mechanism that computers use to talk to each other, like networks, floppy disks, even infrared beaming. Viruses have been around the Internet for a long time. Originally, they lived in program files that people downloaded using a file transfer program or their Web browser. Now, most viruses are spread through files that are sent via e-mail, as attachments to mail messages, though instant messaging (IM, see Chapter 16) is a fast-growing alternative.

There was a time when people in the know (like we thought we were) laughed at newcomers to the Internet who worried about getting viruses by e-mail. E-mail messages back then were just text files and could not contain programs. Then e-mail attachments were introduced. People could now send computer software — including those sneaky viruses — via e-mail. Isn't progress wonderful?

What do viruses do?

When a virus lands on your computer it has to somehow manage to get executed. *Getting executed* in computer jargon means being brought to life; a virus is a program and programs have to be run — they have to be "turned on," "launched," or "started." Once it's running, the virus does two things. First, it looks around and tries to find your address book, which it uses to courteously send copies of itself to all your friends and acquaintances, often wrapped up in very convincing sounding messages ("Hey, enjoyed the other night, thought this file would amuse you!"). Second, it executes its *payload*, the reason the virus writer went through all that trouble and risk (they do occasionally end up in jail).

The payload is the illegal activity that the virus is running from your machine. It could be recording your every keystroke (include your passwords). It could be launching an attack at specific or random targets over the Internet. It could be sending spam from your computer. Whatever it's doing, you don't want it to do. Trust us. If your computer starts to act quirky or really sluggish, chances are, you've contracted a virus or twenty.

In the good old days, virus writers were content just to see their viruses spread, but like everything else about the Internet, virus writing is now a big business, in many cases controlled by organized crime syndicates.

What can you do about viruses?

Don't worry *too* much about viruses — excellent virus-checking programs are available that check all incoming mail before the viruses can attack. In Chapter 4, which describes getting connected to the Internet, we recommend installing a virus checker.

Worms come right over the Net

A *worm* is like a virus, except it doesn't need a vector like e-mail. It just jumps directly from one computer to another over the Net, entering your computer via security flaws in its network software. Unfortunately, the most popular kind of network software on the Net, the kind in Microsoft Windows, is riddled with security holes, so many that if you attach a nice fresh Windows machine to a broadband Net connection, it'll be overrun with worms in less than a minute.

If you rigorously apply all of the security updates from Microsoft, they'll fix most of the known security flaws, but it takes a lot longer than a minute to apply them all. Hence we strongly encourage anyone using a broadband connection to use a hardware *firewall*, a box that sits between the net and your computer and keeps the worms out. If you have a broadband connection, you'll probably want to use an inexpensive device called a *router* to hook up your computers anyway, and routers all include a firewall as a standard feature. See Chapter 4 for more information.

Spyware arrives via Web sites

Spyware is like a virus, except that your computer catches it in a different way. Instead of arriving by e-mail, spyware gets downloaded by your browser. Generally, you need to click something on a Web page to download and install spyware, but many people have been easily mislead into installing spyware that purports to be a graphics viewer or some other program you think you might want.

What does spyware do?

Spyware is called that because it is frequently used for nefarious purposes like spying on what you are typing. Some spyware gathers information about you, and sends it off to some other site without your knowledge or consent. A common kind of spyware called adware finds out what sites you visit so advertisers can display popup ads (described in the section "Popup browser windows" later in this chapter) that are targeted to your interests.

Note: Targeted advertising is not evil in itself. Google's Adsense program places ads on participating Web pages based on the contents of those pages. Targeted ads are worth more to advertisers because you are more likely to respond to an ad about something you are already seeking.

Spyware can also send spam from your computer, capture every keystroke you type and send it to a malefactor over the Net, and other Bad Things.

Don't voluntarily install spyware

Lots of cute little free programs are available for download, but don't install them unless you are convinced that they are both safe and useful. Many toolbars, screensavers, news tickers, and other utilities are spyware in disguise. Besides, the more programs you run on your computer, the slower all your other programs run. Check with friends before downloading the latest program. Or search the Web for the program's name (see Chapter 8 for how) to find positive or negative reviews.

Protecting your computer from spyware

Spyware programs are often designed to be hard to remove — which can mess up your operating system. Rather than waiting until you contract a bad case of spyware and then trying to uninstalling it, a better idea is to inoculate your computer against spyware. To block spyware, be careful about what you click. And install a spyware checking program that can scan your system periodically. See Chapter 4 for details.

Adware — just another name for spyware

Adware is a controversial type of software that many people consider to be spyware. Adware is installed as part of some programs that are distributed for free. It watches what you do on your computer and displays targeted ads — even when you run other programs. Adware opponents say that no users in their right minds would knowingly install a program that peppers them with ads — and they want laws to ban the practice, pointing out that adware often behaves like a parasite, obscuring or replacing ads from competing Web sites. Adware supporters claim it's a way for new software from small companies to gain wide acceptance quickly, and they don't want the government eliminating these marketing choices.

Before downloading a free program, make sure you understand what the deal is. If you aren't sure, don't download it. Make sure your kids know not to download free games, song lyrics, and the like — most are infested with adware — and before you know it, you'll have so many popup ads that you'll have to unplug your computer to shut it up.

Popup browser windows

One of the worst innovations in recent decades is *popup* windows that appear on your screen unbidden (by you), when you visit some Web sites. Some popups appear immediately, while others are *pop-unders* that are hidden under your main window until you close the main window. The pop-ups you're most likely to see are ads for mortgages and airline tickets. (No, we're not going to give their names here; they have plenty of publicity already.)

Several mechanisms can make popups appear on your computer:

✔ A Web site can open a new browser window. Sometimes this new window displays an ad or some other annoying information. But sometimes the new window has useful information — some Web sites use popup windows as a sort of help system for using the site.

✔ Spyware or other programs can display popup windows.

Luckily, Web browsers now include features to prevent Web sites from opening browser windows. See Chapter 7 for how to tell your browser not to pop anything up.

Spam, Bacon, Spam, Eggs, and Spam

Pink tender morsel,
Glistening with salty gel.
What the hell is it?

— SPAM haiku, found on the Internet

More and more often, we get unsolicited e-mail (*spam*) from some organization or person we don't know. Spam is the online equivalent to junk mail. Off line, junk mailers have to pay postage. Unfortunately, online, the cost of sending out a bizzillion pieces of junk mail is virtually zilch.

E-mail spam (not to be confused with SPAM, a meat-related product from Minnesota) means that thousands of copies of the same unwanted message are sent to individual e-mail accounts, newsgroups in Usenet, the net's shared bulletin board, and even instant message programs. It's also known as *junk e-mail* or unsolicited bulk e-mail (UBE). The message usually consists of unsavory advertising for get-rich-quick schemes or pornographic offers — something you may not want to see and something you definitely don't want your children to see. The message is *spam,* the practice is *spamming,* and the person sending the spam is a *spammer.*

Spam, unfortunately, is a major problem on the Internet because sleazy business entrepreneurs have decided that it's the ideal way to advertise. We get hundreds of pieces of spam a day (yes, really) and the number continues to increase. Spam doesn't have to be commercial (we've gotten religious and political spam) but it has to be unsolicited; if you asked for it, it's not spam.

Why call it spam?

The meat? Nobody knows. Oh, you mean the unwanted e-mail? It came from the Monty Python skit in which a group of Vikings sing the word *spam* repeatedly in a march tempo, drowning out all other discourse. (Google for "Monty Python spam" and you'll find plenty of sites where you can listen to it.) Spam can drown out all other mail, because some people get so much spam that they stop using e-mail entirely. Another problem is that spam filters, which are supposed to catch and throw away spam, can throw away good messages by mistake.

Why is it so bad?

You may think that spam, like postal junk mail, is just a nuisance we have to live with. But it's worse than junk mail, in several ways. Spam costs you money. E-mail recipients pay much more than the sender does to deliver a message. Sending e-mail is cheap: A spammer can send thousands of messages an hour from a PC and a dialup connection. After that, it costs you time to download, read (at least the subject line), and dispose of the mail. The amount of spam has surpassed the amount of real e-mail, and if spam volume continues to grow at its alarming pace, pretty soon e-mail will prove to be useless because the real e-mail is buried under the junk.

Not only do spam recipients have to bear a cost, but all this volume of e-mail also strains the resources of the e-mail servers and the entire Internet. ISPs have to pass along the added costs to its users. America Online has been reported to estimate that more than half of its incoming e-mail is spam, and many ISPs have told us that as much as $2 of the $20 monthly fee goes to handling and cleaning up after spam. And as ISPs and companies try harder to filter out spam, more and more legitimate mail is being mistaken for spam and bounced.

Many spams include a line that instructs you how to get off their lists, something like "Send us a message with the word REMOVE in it." Why should you have to waste your time to get off the list? But don't bother, spammers' remove lists rarely work. In fact, they can be a method for verifying that your address is real, and you will likely receive *more* spam.

What can you do about it?

You don't have to put up with spam. Spam filters can weed out most of the spam that you receive. See Chapter 14 for how to use the spam filter that may already be built into your e-mail program, or how to install a separate spam filtering program.

What's the Secret Word, Mr. Potter?

Everywhere you go these days, someone wants you to enter a password or passcode. Even Harry Potter has to tell his password to a magic portrait just to enter the Gryffindor dormitory (though there is apparently no security between the boys' and girls' wings). Security experts are pretty unanimous in telling us how we should protect all our passwords:

✔ Pick passwords that are long and complex enough that no on can guess them. Never use a word that occurs in the dictionary as a password. Consider sticking a number or two into your password.

✔ Never use the same password for different accounts.

✔ Memorize your passwords and never write them down.

✔ Change your passwords frequently.

Be careful with password hints

Web sites are tired of dealing with customers who forget their password, so a new computer tool has emerged in the last few years — the password hint. When you create a new account, the friendly identity manager software asks for your username and new password. It then makes you select and answer a couple of security questions, like "What's your favorite color?" or "What's your pet's name?"

Some time in the future, you try to log in to that account — and find you forgot that pesky password. No problemo! You'll be asked the security questions you picked; if you type in the right answer, you're in. The problem is, a thief pretending to be you will get the same challenge.

Instead of guessing your password, all he has to guess is your favorite color (blue, maybe?) and figure out your pet's name (and did your kid post captioned photos of Rover on the school Web site as part of his third-grade computer-literacy project?).

If you encounter one of these password hints when you sign up for an important account, pick questions whose answers an attacker can't glean by researching you. And there's no rule that says you have to answer the security questions truthfully. You could pick a friend's pet, for example, or a color you detest, or you could say that your favorite color is Rover and your pet's name is Purple.

This is very sound advice for everyone — except ordinary human beings. Most of us have far too many passwords to keep track of, and too little brain to keep them in.

One common-sense approach is to use a single password for accounts where there is little risk of loss, such as the one you need to read an online newspaper. Use separate, stronger passwords for the accounts that really matter (such as your online banking). If you feel you can't remember them all, write them down, but keep them in a safe place, not on a PostIt note stuck to your monitor.

Keeping Yourself and Your Family Safe

Viruses, spyware, phishing, popups, spam . . . is the Internet worth all this trouble? No, you don't have to give up on the Internet in despair or disgust. You just have to put in a little extra effort to use it safely. In addition to the technological fixes that we suggest (virus-checkers, spyware scanners, and popup blockers), you need to develop some smarts about online security. Here's a quick checklist:

- ✔ **Develop healthy skepticism.** If it sounds too good to be true, it probably isn't true. No one in Africa has $25 million they will share with you if you help them get it out of the country. P.T. Barnum said there is a sucker born every minute. Today's sucker doesn't have to be you.

- ✔ **Keep your computer's software up to date.** Both Microsoft and Apple have features that do this more or less painlessly. Use them. The latest versions of software often fix security flaws that could otherwise be exploited.

- ✔ **Use a firewall and keep it updated.** Your computer probably has firewall software built in. Make sure your firewall is turned on. Some malware knows how to turn protective software off so check it every week or so. We recommend using a router — a device that lets you share Internet connections among several computers (whether wired or wireless) — because routers include built-in firewall programs that are much harder for a malware program to disable or bypass. These units are so cheap that you should get one even if you only have one computer. (See Chapter 5 for details.)

- ✔ **Install virus-protection and spyware-protection software and keep it current.** It will cost $25 per year or so. Pay it. Chapter 4 tells you how to install virus- and spyware-checkers.

It's absolutely essential to keep the virus-description files in your antivirus software updated — automatically if possible, and every week for sure. (New viruses are launched every week.) The maker of your antivirus software should have a Web site from which you can download the updates; check your documentation.

- ✔ **Don't open an e-mail attachment unless it's from someone you know** *and* **you are expecting it.** Contact the sender if you aren't sure.

- ✔ **Don't click any links in e-mail messages unless you're sure you know where they lead.** And if you do — and the site you end up at wants your password, or credit card number, or dog's name — close your browser window. Don't even think about giving out any information.

- ✔ **Pick passwords that are hard to guess and never give them to anyone else.** Not to the nice lady who says she is from the help desk, not to the bogus FBI special agent who claims to need it for tracking down a kidnapped child. No one.

- ✔ **Be consistent.** If you share your computer with several family members or housemates, make sure that each understands these rules and agrees to follow them.

Are Macs the solution?

We hear you Apple Macintosh users gloating as they read this chapter: "We don't have these problems. Why don't people just use Macs?" Mac users still have to put up with phishing and other forms of junk e-mail. But to date, almost none of the viruses, worms, or spyware affect Macs. While this could change, we think Mac users will always have an easier time on the Net. First, Macs are so scarce (compared to Windows machines) that it's not worth the virus writer's time to attack them — partly because this scarcity also makes it hard to spread Mac viruses. Most e-mail addresses in a Mac user's address book belong to Windows users anyway, so if a Mac virus copies of itself, the copies it mails out won't find nice vulnerable homes. (Designing a virus that will run on *both* Windows and Macs is hard, even today.) Finally,

Apple's Mac OS X is designed to be more secure than Windows, and is harder to infect.

The new, lower-cost Mac Mini can use your existing keyboard, mouse, speakers and monitor, and can even share them with your PC if you buy a gadget called a KVM switch. If you still need to use programs that run only under Windows, adding a Mac as your e-mail and Internet-surfing machine may be a reasonable compromise. Or you can buy Microsoft's Virtual PC package, which lets you run Windows programs on a Mac.

We know companies whose support staff runs *everything* on a Mac — because it doesn't get infected. When they need to run something on a PC, they do it in a window on the Mac screen. Cool.

Chapter 3

Kids and the Net

· ·

In This Chapter

▶ Finding the good stuff for kids on the Internet

▶ Getting wise to some concerns about the Internet

▶ Working up parental guidelines for using the Internet

▶ Finding mailing lists and Web sites for kids

▶ Finding online help for kids (and parents) with problems

▶ Looking at the Internet in schools, and school on the Net

· ·

*W*ith millions of kids online, a discussion about family Internet use is critical. (Obviously, if you don't have any kids, and you aren't one yourself, just skip this chapter and go to the next.)

Can We Talk?

In earlier editions of this book, we called this chapter "The Internet, Your Kids, and You," but we've wised up and now realize who is really in charge of the family Internet connection: kids. Face it, most kids are way more comfortable on the Internet than their parents are. Schools assign kids to do research on the Web and e-mail information to other students or the teachers. Online games are designed for kids of all ages. Forbidding your kids from using the Net altogether is hopeless (unless they are younger than about 8), but you want to keep your kids safe (and reading this chapter together is going to help you do that). This chapter talks about what's great — and what's scary — about children and youth using the Internet. We still feel it would be better if you parents had some say about what your kids do online, but let's face it — many parents don't have a clue. So in this chapter, we'll talk to you, the kids and throw in some comments for your parents, in case they happen to read this. We'll try not to say anything too embarrassing.

High on the list of parents' concerns about the Internet is the question of children's access to inappropriate material, including businesses that try to market and sell directly to children. This concern is legitimate: As time has gone by, both the good stuff and the grody stuff on the Net have increased dramatically. We have no simple answers, but one thing is crystal clear to us: Parents *have* to be involved. Considering the direction of education and edicts from on high, *kids will be involved* with the Internet, as schools hook up at a rapid clip.

What's in it for you?

Kids are often the first to discover the myriad ways in which the Internet can be exciting. Here are some ways we think the Internet rocks:

- It provides information about every topic imaginable.
- It's a great way to hang out with your friends and be at home at the same time.
- It's a great source of new music and videos.
- It provides personal contact with new people and cultures.
- It helps develop and improve reading, writing, research, and language skills.
- It provides support for kids with special needs and for their parents.
- It is an exciting outlet for artistic expression.

But not everything new is wonderful, and not everything wonderful is new. Many of you will spend more of your working life than you'd like in front of a computer. There *are* other things to do — without a computer (what a concept) — such as playing sports, reading a printed book, playing music, cooking, painting, hiking, skating, swimming, biking, skiing, or sculpting, just to name a few.

Okay, if you're still stuck to that screen, here are some things you can do online, broken down into four sections: Really cool, so-so, not such a good idea, and truly brain-dead. We aren't the only people who think this way. For extra credit, see what the folks in the United Kingdom are saying at www.kidsmart.org.uk/.

Really cool ways to use the Net

The capabilities of the Net are impressive; they can help you with what you have to do as well as what you want to do. For instance, you can impress your parents by using the Internet in these ways:

✔ **Research homework assignments:** The Internet is an incredible way to expand the walls of a school. The Net can connect you to other schools, libraries, research resources, museums, and other people. You can visit the American Museum of Natural History (at `www.amnh.org`) for information about dinosaurs (as shown in Figure 3-1), the Louvre (at `www.louvre.fr`) and the Sistine Chapel (`www.vatican.va` — select your language, click Vatican Museums, and then click Online Tours); you can watch spotted newts in their native habitat; you can hear new music; and make new friends.

Figure 3-1:
Many museums have great information online.

✔ **Find out how to evaluate the stuff you read:** When you search for a topic, you may get pages written by the world's greatest authority on that topic, some crackpot pushing a hare-brained theory, some college kid's term paper, or some guy on a bulletin board who thinks he's an expert. Some Web sites are maintained by hate groups and push really nasty venom. Becoming able to tell all those types of information apart is one of the most valuable skills you can acquire.

✔ **Make e-friends in other countries:** School projects such as the Global Schoolhouse connect kids around the world by working collaboratively on all types of projects. The first annual global learning project drew more than 10,000 students from 360 schools in 30 different countries. Since then, annual cyberfairs have brought together over 500,000 students from hundreds of schools in at least 37 countries! You can find out more at the Global Schoolhouse Web site, `www.globalschoolhouse.org`, where you can also subscribe to lots of mailing lists. (We explain how to actually get to these locations in Chapter 6, so you can come back here later and follow up on them.)

✔ **Practice foreign languages:** You can visit online chat rooms, where you can try out your French or Spanish or Portuguese or Russian or Japanese or even Esperanto.

✔ **Pay for music you download:** You can now buy music over the Internet in several ways. Apple's iTunes music store, `www.apple.com/itunes/`, sells songs for 99¢. Other sites, like `www.napster.com`, let you download as may songs as you like for a monthly fee (but beware, all the songs evaporate if you stop paying the fee). See Chapter 9 for details.

✔ **Write an encyclopedia article:** Wikipedia, `wikipedia.org`, is a free online encyclopedia that anyone can contribute to. It's a great research tool, but, even better, you can add the material you found while you were researching that term paper to make Wikipedia even better. A worldwide team of writers and editors updates the material constantly, and you can be one of them.

✔ **Discover how to make your own Web page:** A Web page can be as clever or as stupid as you like. Put your stories or artwork up for family and friends to admire. You even can start an online business. You can make a home page for a local cause you support. We tell you how to do these things in Chapter 17.

So-so ways to use the Net

Here are some ideas that your parents may consider a waste of time, but hey, we can't be serious all the time. If they give you a hard time, ask if you can inspect their Web time log. (There is no such thing, but they don't know that.)

✔ **Play games:** Many popular games (both traditional — like chess, bridge, hearts, and go — and video) have options that let you compete against other players on the Internet.

✔ **IM your friends:** Instant messaging (IM) has become the cool way to get in touch — *instantly.* Wireless options are already happening in many parts of the world. We reveal all in Chapter 16.

✔ **Talk on a videophone:** Thanks to software such as Yahoo Messenger, you can see your friends while you talk to them (not recommended on bad hair days). Chapter 16 talks about free video programs, which you may need after you get your parents to spring for that webcam.

✔ **Shop:** What can we say? Internet shopping is like the mall, but it's always open and you don't have to hunt for a parking spot. You can sell stuff too. Chapter 10 gets you started.

✔ **Role-play:** Any number of Internet sites let you pretend to be a character in your favorite science-fiction or fantasy book.

Not-so-good ways to use the Net

Stay away from the following ideas, which will just get you into trouble, some of it pretty serious:

- ✔ **Plagiarism:** That's the fancy word for passing off other people's work as your own. Plagiarizing from the Internet is just as wrong as plagiarizing from a book — and (for that matter) a lot easier for teachers to catch because your teachers can Google for stuff just like you can.

- ✔ **Cheating:** Using translating software to do your language homework is also no good. (You're gonna get caught, so save yourself the embarrassment.)

- ✔ **Revealing too much about yourself:** When chatting on the Net with people you don't know, it's tempting to give out identifying information about yourself or your family, but this is dangerous — it can get you stalked, ripped off, or worse. Even revealing your e-mail address can get you unwanted junk mail. Some seemingly innocent questions that strangers ask online aren't so innocent, so we go into more detail later in this chapter about what to watch for.

- ✔ **Sharing copyrighted music and videos:** Now that it's easy to buy music online, there isn't much excuse for using file-sharing software to trade copyrighted music or videos without permission. The music and movie industries are getting better at finding people who do that — and are taking legal action against them. It could cost your parents a lot of money. If you do take advantage of free downloads, consider sending money to the recording artists. One Web site, www.musiclink.com, has been set up especially for that purpose.

- ✔ **Visiting porn and hate sites:** This is between you and your parents, but find out what rules your parents have made for your online behavior and stick to them.

- ✔ **Pretending you are someone else online:** Go ahead and make up a pseudonym so you don't have to use your real name (that can be one way to limit how much any stranger knows about you). But, *don't* pretend you're a talent agent for *American Idol* or the latest reality show looking for a date.

- ✔ **Hanging out in adult chat rooms:** This can get both you and the chat room hosts into big trouble, so don't do it.

- ✔ **Let the Internet take over your life:** If the only thing you want to do after school is get online, maybe you should talk to someone about it.

Truly brain-dead ideas

Here are some ideas that you should *never* consider because they can lead right into major trouble:

- ✔ **Meeting online friends in person without telling a parent:** If you meet someone great online and you want to meet him or her in person, fine — maybe. But take precautions! First, tell your parents about it and decide with them how to proceed. Second, never meet someone you met online in a private place: Always meet in a public place, such as a restaurant. Finally, bring someone (preferably your parents) with you. (Even if some adults are stupid enough to meet a stranger without letting someone else know about it, you've already got a clue — right?)

- ✔ **Doing anything illegal — online or off:** The Internet feels totally anonymous, but it's not. If you commit a crime, the police can get the Internet connection records from your Internet service provider (ISP) and find out who was connected via which modem on what day at what time with what numeric Internet (IP) address, and they'll find you.

- ✔ **Breaking into other computers or creating viruses:** This little escapade might have been considered a prank back in the 1980s, but the authorities have long since lost their sense of humor about it. Kids *are* going to jail for it these days.

The Internet and little kids

We are strong advocates of allowing kids to be kids, and we believe that humans are better teachers than computers are. (None of our kids watches commercial TV.) Now that you know our predisposition, maybe you can guess what we're going to say next: We are not in favor of sticking a young child in front of a screen. How young is too young? We believe that younger than age seven is too young. We recommend that your younger siblings get as much human attention as possible. At young ages, kids benefit more from playing with trees, balls, clay, crayons, paint, mud, monkey bars, bicycles, other kids, and especially older sibs. Yeah, that means you. We know little kids can be a pain in the neck, but computers make lousy babysitters.

We think that Internet access is more appropriate for somewhat older kids (fourth or fifth grade and older), but your mileage may vary. Even so, we think it's a good idea to limit the amount of time that anyone, especially kids, spends online. We (despite our good looks) have been playing with computers for 35 years (holy cow!), and we know what happens to kids who are allowed to stay glued to their computers for unlimited time — trust us, *it is not good.* Remember those old sayings, "You are what you eat?" and "Garbage in, garbage out?" What your brain devours all the time makes a difference.

As human beings (what a concept), kids need to be able to communicate with other human beings. Too often, kids who have difficulty doing that prefer to get absorbed in computers, which doesn't help develop their social skills. Existing problems in that department get worse, leading to more isolation. If you're starting to feel out of touch and you want to put the machine in its place (maybe even get your life back), here are some quick self-defense tips:

- Keep a private log of all time you spend in front of the screen during one week. Then ask yourself if this is really how you want to spend your life.

- Find a hobby that doesn't involve a screen. Join a team. Form a band. Create art.

- Set aside one computer-free day each week.

- Try to have meals and conversations with actual human beings, face to face, in real time.

Your grandparents and the Net

More and more senior citizens have Internet access. Letting your grandparents and other older relatives know what you're up to via e-mail or instant message takes very little effort and can mean a lot to them. Sending them pictures of you and your siblings is even better. Next time you visit, set up their computer screen saver to display the family photo album.

Surf safe

Make sure you know the safety rules for using the Net. Rule numero uno is to never reveal exactly who you are. Use only your first name (or not even that) and don't provide your last name, your address, your phone number, or the name of your school. And never, ever, tell anyone your password. No honest person will ever ask you for it.

Many kids don't have a clue about this. They reveal who they are without even meaning to do so. They may mention the name of their hometown ball team. They may talk about a teacher who they hate at school. They may say what their parents do for a living. They may say which church or synagogue they attend. Such information may be revealed over the course of many messages spread over weeks or months. These seemingly harmless bits of information can help a determined person "triangulate" to home in on a kid. So be very careful about what you say online — in a chat room or instant message or e-mail. Be suspicious of strangers who seem to know a lot about you. Maybe they say they're a friend of your parents who is supposed to pick you up after school or to pick up a package from your house. Never go with a stranger or let him or her into the house without asking a trusted (offline) adult first.

Here are a few more guidelines for sidestepping online trouble:

- ✔ **Think before you give your e-mail address to anybody.** Many Web sites ask you to register, and many require you to provide a working e-mail address that they verify by sending you a message. Before registering with a Web site, make sure that it's run by a reputable company from which you won't mind getting junk mail.

- ✔ **Never agree to talk to someone on the phone or meet someone in person without checking it out with your parents.** Most people you meet online are okay, but a few creepy types out there have made the Internet their hunting ground.

- ✔ **Don't assume that people are telling you the truth.** That "kid" who's your age and gender and who shares your interests and hobbies may actually be a lonely, creepy, 40-year-old. And watch out for the safety of your younger sibs. They may not understand what a stranger is and believe that everything people tell them online is always true.

- ✔ **If someone is scaring you or making you uncomfortable — especially if the person says not to tell your parents — *tell* your parents.** Ask your parents to talk to your Internet service provider. And remember that you can always turn off the computer.

College and the Net

Although the Internet has had a home in universities for a long time, the Web has made online resources — and skills — a basic part of higher education. Much of the inspiration and perspiration of the volunteers who are making information available to everyone comes from universities, both students and faculty, who see in the Web incredible potential for

- ✔ Preparing for entrance exams
- ✔ Finding a school and applying
- ✔ Learning and doing research
- ✔ Keeping faculty and students in touch
- ✔ Networking with potential employers and professional organizations

Most campuses provide free or low-cost access to the Internet for their students and staff. Schools that enable you to register early sometimes give you Internet access when you register, even months in advance. If you're going to go anyway, you can get a jump on your Internet education before you even get to campus.

Checking out colleges on the Net

Most colleges and universities have sites on the Web. You can find a directory of online campus tours at www.campustours.com, with links to lots more info about the colleges and universities.

After you're a little more adept at using the Net, you can use it to take a closer look at classes and professors to get a better idea of what appeals to you.

Colleges have found dozens of ways to make the Net useful inside school as well as out. We like what the folks at Thunderbird, The American Graduate School of International Business (www.thunderbird.edu), did when they created My Thunderbird, a password-protected site that enables both students and professors to share and update profiles. Professors love the opportunity to get to know their students with the pictures and profiles that My Thunderbird provides. Class rosters stay current and the campus stays connected.

Internet technologies such as e-mail, chat, and instant messages are great ways for parents and college kids to stay in touch. They're much cheaper than phoning home and easier than coordinating schedules. Forwarding mail to other family members allows for broader communication. We noticed another surprising benefit: In our experience, families tend to fight less when they're communicating by e-mail. Somehow, when folks have time to think about what they're going to say before they say it, it comes out better.

Going back to school

Your education isn't over when you finish high school or college or (for those of us seriously dedicated to avoiding real life) graduate school. There's always more to learn. Nothing's quite like learning directly from a first-rate teacher in a classroom, but learning over the Net can be the next best thing to being there — particularly for students who live far from school or have irregular schedules. You can now take everything online from high-school-equivalency exams to professional continuing education to college and graduate courses leading to degrees. Some courses are strictly online; others use a combination of classroom, lab, and online instruction.

A few schools, like the University of Phoenix (www.phoenix.edu), specialize in online education, but schools all over the world now offer online instruction, and some (such as MIT at web.mit.edu) make all their course material available online for free. If the course is on the Net, it doesn't matter whether the school is across the street or across the ocean. You can find thousands of schools and courses in directories such as www.petersons.com/distance learning and www.online-colleges-courses-degrees-classes.org.

Sell, sell, sell!

If you spend a lot of time online, you will soon notice that everyone seems to be trying to sell you something. Kids, particularly those from middle- and upper-income families, are a lucrative target market, and the Net is being viewed as another way to capture this market.

Targeting kids for selling isn't new. Maybe you are old enough to remember Joe Camel of the Camel cigarette campaign that many people claimed was aimed at kids. Your school may make you may watch Channel One at school, a system that brings advertising directly to the classroom. If you watch TV, you know how TV programs for kids push their own lines of toys and action figures.

You should know that big-company marketing departments have designed kid-friendly, fascinating, captivating software to help them better market to you. Delightful, familiar cartoon characters deftly elicit strategic marketing information directly from the keyboard in your home. You should be aware of this situation and know what to do when someone on the Web asks for information. Parents, keep in mind that if your kids have access to your credit cards, they can spend big bucks over the Internet. Beware of online stores for which you have configured your Web browser to remember your passwords because your kids will be able to waltz right in and start buying. Kids, if you spend your parents' money online without permission, we have trouble believing that you aren't going to get into big trouble for it.

The Federal Trade Commission has also weighed in on this topic. They are on the Web at www.ftc.gov; when you visit this site, click Privacy Initiatives➪ Children's Privacy.

The Children's Online Privacy Protection Act (COPPA) limits the information that companies can collect from children under 13 (or, at least, children who *admit* they're under 13) without explicit parental consent — which, by the way, we think parents should rarely give. We heard of one marketer who said he wanted to use the Net to create a personal relationship with all the kids who use his product. Ugh. We have names for guys who want relationships that get things from kids, and they're not very nice names.

The FTC's Kidz Privacy site (www.ftc.gov/bcp/conline/edcams/ kidzprivacy) has more useful information for both kids and parents about COPPA and online privacy.

Who's online?

Lots of kids — and grown-ups — are putting up Web sites about themselves and their families. We think that this is really cool, but we strongly encourage families who use the Net for personal reasons (distinct from businesspeople who use the Net for business purposes) *not* to use their full or real names. We also advise you never to disclose your address, phone number, Social Security number, or account passwords in online social situations to anyone who asks for this kind of information — online or off. This advice applies especially when you receive information requests from people who claim to be in positions of authority — for example, instant messages from people claiming that they're from America Online (AOL) tech support. They're not legit.

To parents: All hands on Net

Parents, educators, and free-speech advocates alike agree that there's no substitute for parental guidance when it comes to the subject of Internet access. Just as you want your children to read good books and see quality films, you also want them to find the good stuff on the Net. (After all, someday they'll have to if they want to get ahead.) If you take the time to discover the good stuff with your children, you have the opportunity to share the experience and to impart critical values and a sense of discrimination that your children need in all areas of their lives.

The good stuff on the Net vastly outweighs the bad. Plenty of software is available to help parents and educators tap the invaluable resources of the Net without opening Pandora's box. Remember that every child is different — and that what may be appropriate for *your* children may not be appropriate for other kids. You have to find what's right for you.

Establish rules for your family's use of the Net; spell out (and consistently enforce) specific consequences for breaking those rules. Outline areas that are off limits. Limit the time spent online and be explicit about what information kids can give out over the Net. Margy made a poster with her family's online rules and hung it next to the computer that the kids use.

It takes extra effort from you to establish limits and at the same time give your children the freedom they need to explore. Some families prefer to keep their computers in a family space, as opposed to in kids' bedrooms. Wherever they are, check them often; don't let the screen be your babysitter. Don't buy into the hype that just because it's on a computer, it's educational. We're reminded of a cartoon featuring wishful parents reading the newspaper's Help Wanted section and finding that Nintendo players are making $70,000 a year testing games. Bottom line: That isn't the vast majority of us. Everyone knows kids whose lives seem to be lost in front of a screen. Don't let that be your kid. Some Internet routers have a feature that lets you set time limits on Internet access. Consider paying someone to set one of these up for you and use a password your kids can't guess.

Kids also (and especially) need explicit rules about talking with and meeting with people they meet on the Net. Even if you have reason to believe that someone your kids have met online is legit, never let your kids go to meet that person by themselves. Keep an eye on your phone bill (including cell phones) for unusual calls.

People with real authority *never* ask those types of questions. For one thing, AOL doesn't handle member accounts via instant messages, and never asks for credit card info via e-mail. It all makes a great case for knowing exactly how your Internet service provider works.

More than ever, children need to develop critical thinking skills. They have to be able to evaluate what they read and see — especially on the Web.

Regrettably, the amount of trash e-mail (*spam*) keeps going up. This situation is likely to get worse until we have effective laws — as well as technology — against unsolicited e-mail. In the meantime, one important rule to remember is this: If what an e-mail offers sounds too good to be true, assume it isn't true — and if an ad for it showed up from someone you don't know, that's also pretty good evidence that it's not true. See Chapter 14 for weapons on the war against spam.

Consumer's choice

Parents pay for online services, so services that want to remain competitive vie for parental dollars by providing features that help families control Internet access. America Online, for example, enables parents to block access to chat rooms that may not be appropriate for kids and to restrict access to discussion groups and newsgroups based on keywords you choose. Parental blocking is available at no extra cost. AOL and MSN TV (formerly WebTV) enable the master account holder to restrict the material that subaccount holders can view. Even your kids' iPods and cell phones can play or display material from the Internet.

Software sentries

Protecting kids online is a serious matter — and becomes more serious (and difficult) every day as we contend not only with inappropriate sites and spam, but also with spyware and adware that targets our kids and IMing and chatting with total strangers. Figuring out what makes sense in your house has to take into account your Internet service provider (ISP) and the services it does and doesn't offer, as well as your own hardware and software. The Google search engine has broken up the topic into these categories:

- ✔ Filtering Software
- ✔ Internet Safety for Kids
- ✔ Monitoring Software
- ✔ Windows Key Logger Shareware
- ✔ Parental Control Shareware

We encourage you to find out about these programs, but more importantly, we encourage you to *be involved* with what your kids are doing online. Software can help but it's no substitute for your direct involvement. Filtering software uses keywords and fixed lists of systems that the programs' authors believe to have objectionable material. None of them tells you exactly what they block, and your idea of what's appropriate and inappropriate may well not be the same as theirs. Many software sentries seem to have political agendas, blocking sites whose political content doesn't conform to that of the programs' authors. Kids have the best chance to learn to decide for themselves when their parents model that behavior.

If you leave monitoring software or key-logger software unchecked, you'll likely wake up one morning and find your disk clogged with screenshots or unending logs of keystrokes. Bogging down all computer use is *one* way to curtail it, but that might not be ideal.

You can try before you buy by downloading evaluation copies of software-blocking packages. (We cover how to do that when we discuss navigating the Web in Chapters 6 and 7.)

Internet Resources for Kids

As you may have guessed, the Internet is replete with resources for kids — and for parents, by the way. As we have learned from writing this book ten times in twelve years, nothing is as ephemeral as a Net address. To help keep this information as accurate as possible, we're putting our lists of resources on our Web site, both to keep them up to date and because they're too long to list here completely. From there, you can get right to the source — and we do our best to keep the sources current.

Visit `net.gurus.com/kids`, which puts you one mouse click away from the pages described in this section.

Mailing lists for parents and kids

Chapter 16 tells you how to subscribe to mailing lists. Lots of mailing lists for and about kids are listed on our Web page at `net.gurus.com/kids`. Because mailing lists enable you to swap questions and advice with other parents, they can be a great source of information, especially if your child has a specific challenge.

Web sites for kids

Okay, we admit it. Web sites can be the coolest thing since sliced bread. Our Web site has links to sites from around the world, especially for kids. To get to these sites, you have to know how to use a browser, such as Firefox or Internet Explorer. We tell you how in Chapter 6. (But watch out — when your 9-year-old sib finds a Web site that lists 1,000 knock-knock jokes, you'll be hearing them for weeks!)

Help for parents of kids with problems

Your child may have a physical challenge or learning disability that you want to know more about, and the Net is a great source. One of the most heartening experiences available on the Net — when it works right and everybody knows what to expect — is the help that total strangers freely offer to one another. The bonds that form from people sharing their experiences, struggles, strengths, and hopes redefine what it means to reach out and touch someone. We encourage everyone who has a concern to look for people who share that concern. Our experience of participating in mailing lists and newsgroups related to our own problems compels us to enthusiastically encourage you to check things out online. You can do so with complete anonymity, if you want. You can watch and learn for a long time, or you can jump into the fray and ask for help.

Not everyone who gives advice is an expert. You have to involve your own practitioners in whatever process you're seeking help with. Also, don't reveal too much about yourself (specifics of your children's names or exactly where you live), in case unscrupulous folks are around. Many people have found enormous help, however, from people who have gone down similar paths before them. For many of us, it has made all the difference in the world.

Our Web site at net.gurus.com/lists lists a few of the available online mailing lists and discussion groups. A mailing list or group that's specific to your needs almost certainly exists regardless of whether we list it, and new groups are created every day. Commercial online services such as America Online have special forums that may interest you as well. Or, visit Google Groups on the Web at groups.google.com to read and participate in Usenet newsgroups, an ancient (well, 20-year-old) system of discussion groups.

Notice that some lists are talk lists, which feature free-flowing discussions; some lists have focused discussions; some lists are almost purely academic. The type of discussion is not always obvious from the name. If it looks interesting, subscribe and see what sort of discussion is going on there. It's easy enough to unsubscribe if you don't like it or it's not appropriate.

The Internet in Schools

As schools hook up to the Net, they are actively debating Internet access for their students. Find out as much as you can and get involved. The more you know, the more you can advocate for appropriate access.

Contractually speaking

Some schools and libraries use software to filter Internet access for kids. A variety of filtering systems are available, at a range of costs and installation hassles, that promise to filter out inappropriate and harmful Web sites. Sounds good, but many kids are smart enough to find ways around rules, and *really* smart kids can find ways around software systems designed to "protect" them.

For more information on the Children's Internet Protection Act (CIPA), a law upheld by the Supreme Court that mandates filtering software in U.S. schools and libraries, see the America Library Association's page about it at www.ala.org/cipa.

We believe that Internet filtering in schools is not a good approach. Kids are quicker, more highly motivated, and have more time to spend breaking into and out of systems than most adults we know, and this method doesn't encourage them to do something more productive than electronic lock-picking.

Many institutions rely successfully on students' signed contracts that detail explicitly what is appropriate and what is inappropriate to use. Students who violate these contracts lose their Internet or computer privileges. We recommend the approach of contracts and consequences, from which kids can really learn.

Real education

Used effectively, the Internet is a terrific educational resource. Used ineffectively, it's a terrific waste of time and money. The difference is research and planning. Just recently, we were chatting with our local elementary school principal who'd just spent four hours of one weekend afternoon searching the Net to help her son (who teaches third grade in a nearby district) develop a unit on Canada — that sounds like a great use of the Internet to us. Lots of educational material is out there. After you get a little familiarity with the Web and the ways to find things online, offer to help your local teachers look for material to bolster their teaching. For teachers, we particularly recommend the Gateway to Educational Materials (www.thegateway.org) and the ERIC Clearinghouse on Information & Technology (www.ericit.org), both funded by the U.S. Department of Education.

Part II
Internet, Here I Come!

The 5th Wave   By Rich Tennant

"Since we got it, he hasn't moved from that spot for eleven straight days. Oddly enough they call this 'getting up and running' on the Internet."

In this part . . .

After you're ready to get started, where do you start? Probably the hardest part of using the Internet is getting connected. We help you figure out which kind of Internet service is right for you and help you get connected, with plenty of advice for broadband (fast) and WiFi (wireless) users.

Chapter 4

Climbing onto the Net: What Do You Need to Go Online?

In This Chapter

▶ Choosing a computer for Internet access

▶ Dialing into slow, old-fashioned Internet accounts

▶ Hooking up to new, faster broadband accounts

▶ Staying safe with firewalls, virus checkers, and spyware checkers

▶ Our favorite Internet setup: broadband with a router

▶ What you can do after you're connected

*G*reat, you say, *How do I get connected to the Internet?* The answer is *It depends.* (You'll be hearing that answer perhaps more often than you'd like.) The Internet isn't one network — it's 100,000 separate networks hooked together, each with its own rules and procedures, and you can get to the Net from any one of them. Readers of previous editions of this book pleaded (they said other things too, but this is a family-oriented book) for step-by-step directions on how to get on, so we made ours as one-size-fits-all as possible.

Here (drum roll, please) are those basic steps:

1. **Figure out what type of computer you have or can use.**

2. **Figure out which types of Internet connections are available where you are.**

3. **Sign up for your connection.**

4. **Set up your computer to use your new connection and decide whether you like it.**

5. **Install the software you need to protect your computer from viruses and spyware. (See Chapter 2 for scary descriptions of the types of Internet dangers that you need to protect yourself from.)**

You need four things in order to connect to the Internet:

- ✔ A computer, even a little tiny computer like a Palm or other handheld
- ✔ A modem (a piece of computer equipment) to hook your computer to the phone line or cable system
- ✔ An account with an Internet service provider (ISP) or online service, to give your modem somewhere to call
- ✔ Software to run on your computer

We look at each of these items in turn.

If you've got more than one computer to connect to the Internet, or if your computer is a laptop, see Chapter 5.

Internet accounts are easy to use, but they can be tricky to set up. In fact, connecting for the first time can be the most difficult part of your Internet experience. Installing and setting up Internet connection software used to require you to type lots of scary-looking numerical Internet addresses, host names, communications-port numbers — you name it. These days, making the connection is much easier, partly because Internet software can now figure out most of the numbers itself, but mostly because Windows XP comes with the New Connection Wizard, which can step you through the process.

What Kind of Computer Do You Need?

Because the Internet is a computer network, the only way to hook up to it is by using a computer. But computers are starting to appear in all sorts of disguises, and they may well already be in your home, whether you know it or not.

Hey, I don't even have a computer!

If you don't have a computer and aren't ready or able to buy one, you still have some options.

A likely place to find Internet access is in your public library. Most libraries have added Internet access centers, with clusters of Internet-connected computers among the bookshelves. These computers tend to be popular, so call ahead to reserve time or find out which hours are less crowded.

Another option is your local cybercafé. You can surf the Net while sipping your favorite beverage and sharing your cyber-experience. If you want to check out the Internet, cybercafés are a great place to try before you buy.

WiFi plus Starbucks and other hotspots

If you have a laptop computer, you can use public wireless (WiFi) Internet connections, which are available at many cafés, libraries, airports, and hotels. Your laptop needs a WiFi adapter to connect. Some of these connections cost anywhere from $6/hour to $10/day; others are free (if you don't include the cost of the latté). Some handheld devices have WiFi, too. See Chapter 5 for details.

Some have computers ready for you to use, while others require you to bring your own laptop (see the sidebar, "WiFi plus Starbucks and other hotspots").

If you want to use the Internet from your very own home, you're stuck getting some kind of computer. Luckily, almost any new-ish computers can connect to the Internet, and you can get quite decent ones for under $500.

Yup, I got this old beige box in the closet

Almost any personal computer made since 1980 is adequate for *some* type of connection to the Internet. But unless you have a really good friend who is a computer geek and wants to spend a lot of time at your house helping you get online, it isn't worth fooling with that old clunker — unless, of course, you're looking for a reason for the geek to spend a lot of time at your house, but that's your business.

If you can possibly afford it, we strongly encourage you to buy a new computer or at least one that's not more than two years old. New computers come with Internet software already installed and are configured for the latest in Web technology. If you already own an older computer, you will spend more time and energy, and ultimately just as much money, just trying to get the thing to work the way you want. We think that you're best off buying a brand-new computer.

One problem with old computers is that they tend to run old versions of Windows. The oldest version we'd suggest using is Windows 98; anything older will be hard to set up and hard to find software for. Macintoshes have the basic TCP/IP stuff, called MacTCP, built in as of System 7, but the improvements in System 10 (the latest) are particularly helpful for Net access. Your online life will be easier if you upgrade to System 10 — and it's a pretty good bet that all your Mac-using friends already have.

Yup, I got a brand new Thunderstick 2006

Ah, you *do* have a computer. (Or maybe you're thinking about buying one.) Most Internet users connect by having their computer dial in to an Internet service provider, or ISP. When you first turn on your new computer, or when you run one of the Internet programs that come installed, your computer will offer to call an ISP and set up an account right then and there. Don't dial (or let your computer dial) until you've read the rest of this chapter. We have some warnings and some options we think you ought to consider first.

Yup, I got this little Blackberry, Palm, or phone

Modern mobile phones have little bitty screens and little bitty keypads, so an industry group called WAP (Wireless Access Protocol) devised a way to show little bitty Web pages on those screens and navigate around them. WAP is quite popular in Japan (where teenage girls use it to get updates on Hello Kitty), but it's not catching on very fast in the United States.

At this point, we'd advise against paying extra for a WAP-ish phone unless you have a specific use in mind and you've tried it out on someone else's phone to see if you can stand using its teeny screen.

On the other hand, there are lots of other WAP-compatible devices that work okay with the Internet. Palm Pilots, Blackberries, and many other handhelds are designed to display text messages, e-mail, and very simple Web pages on their small screens. Go to a store that sells phones or electronics and ask to see a demonstration.

Internet appliances

If you're not ready to buy a computer, you might consider an *Internet appliance,* a box that just connects to the Internet and does Internet-ish things such as Web browsing and e-mail. In reality, these are small computers with the software already built in. They're usually quite cheap, $100 or so, but you have to use an ISP that supports your particular appliance.

Note: We don't think that Internet appliances are a good investment. For one thing, if the service that supports your appliance goes away, you're left with an expensive paperweight. For another, if you spend a little (well, a few hundred dollars) more to get a real computer, you can do all the Internet stuff an appliance can do, but you can also install new Internet applications from the Net. You can also use computer programs to write letters, balance your checkbook, figure your taxes, and all the other things that people do with computers. The oldest and best-known Internet appliance is WebTV, now called MSN TV. You can find out more on the Web at www.webtv.com.

Types of Internet Connections

If you're using a computer at a library, at work, at a cybercafé, or at someone else's house, you don't need to worry about how it connects to the Internet because someone else has already done the work. But if you have your own computer, you have several options:

- Dial into the Internet using a regular phone line and an Internet account.
- Connect via a faster phone line (DSL line) and Internet account.
- Connect via your cable TV company, which provides an Internet account.
- Connect via AOL (American Online): AOL isn't the Internet, but it connects to the Internet.

Here are the details about each method.

Dialing — the old-fashioned way

The Internet really started to take off when *Internet service providers* (*ISPs*) started offering Internet accounts that you could dial in to. Back in about 1992, dialup accounts allowed anyone with a computer to become part of the Internet by using a *modem* — a box that enables a computer to connect to a phone line or other communications line. A *dialup modem* connects to a normal, everyday phone line — using the same little plug (a RJ-11 jack) and phone wire. You can unplug a phone and plug a dialup modem in its place.

Dialup modems come in all shapes and sizes. Some are separate boxes, known as *external modems,* with cables that plug into the computer, the phone jack, and a power outlet. Others are inside the computer, with just a cable for the phone; some are tiny, credit-card-sized things you slide into the side of your laptop computer. (They still have a cable for the phone — some things never change.)

Matching the variety of physical sizes of dialup modems is an equally wide variety of internal features. The speed at which a dialup modem operates (or the rate at which it can stuff computer data into a phone line) is 56,000 bits per second (*bps,* commonly but erroneously called *baud*), usually abbreviated 56K. Most dialup modems can act as fax machines, and some even have more exotic features, such as built-in answering machines.

Most computers sold in recent years come with built-in dialup modems. If you already have a modem, use it — just examine your computer carefully for a phone jack, and if you find one, plug a phone cord into it. For external modems, be sure to get a cable to connect the modem to your computer, and also be sure that its connectors match the ones on your computer — either serial or Universal Serial Bus (USB).

Note to laptop computer owners: If your computer has credit-card-size PC Card slots but no built-in modem, get a PC Card modem that fits in a slot so that you don't have to carry around a separate modem when you take your computer on the road. See Chapter 5 for more information.

Phone charges

If you're not careful, you can end up paying more for the phone call than you do for your Internet account. One of the things you do when you sign up for an ISP is determine the phone number to call. *If at all possible, use an ISP whose number is a free or untimed local call* (that is, you're not paying by the minute). If you use a local or regional ISP, the service has a short list of phone numbers you can use. Some national ISPs (including AT&T) have their own national networks of dial-in numbers; the rest piggyback on other networks. If one national ISP has a local number in your area, they probably all do.

If you can't find an ISP that's a local call for you, your options are limited. If you shop around, you'll probably be able to find long-distance service for 4 cents per minute or less. (Of course, that's still $2.40 per hour.) Be sure to compare rates for in-state and out-of-state calls because an out-of-state call is usually cheaper even though it's farther away. Beware of toll-free numbers, which almost always levy a stiff hourly surcharge.

Some ISPs give you software that automatically selects a local phone number to dial. Usually it chooses correctly, but we've heard enough horror stories to warn you that you should always verify that the number your computer is calling is, in fact, a local call. Check the front of your phone book or call your phone company's local business office.

Names, passwords, and prices

The next step is for you to sign up with an ISP for an Internet account. You need an Internet account because when your computer's modem dials into the ISP, they are going to ask you for a username and password. No account, no username and no password.

The features and services that one ISP offers are much like those of another, with important differences such as price, service, and reliability. Think of it as the difference between a Ford and a Buick, with the differences between your local dealers being at least as important in the purchase decision as the differences between the cars. Most ISP accounts come with

✔ That all-important username and password, so you can connect.

✔ One or more e-mail addresses, each with its own mailbox. Most accounts come with from one to five e-mail addresses. If you have a family, each family member can have a separate address.

✔ Web mail — that is, a Web site where you can read your mail. Web mail is great when you want to check your mail and you're not at your own computer with your own e-mail program. You can use a Web browser to display your messages from any computer.

Pricing schemes vary all over the lot. Most ISPs charge about $20 per month and give you either unlimited hours or a large monthly allotment of 80 to 100 hours. Often, you can get a cheaper $5 rate that only includes three or four hours, with time beyond the included amount charged at $2 per hour or so. Most people prefer a flat rate — or at least a large enough allotment that they're unlikely to use it up. Studies have shown that the average Internet use is from 47 to 54 hours per month. More specifically, the Pew Internet & American Life Project Report, at www.pewinternet.org, reported in 2004 that experienced dial-up users average 94 minutes online per day, or 47 hours a month. Folks with faster broadband connections average 107 minutes a day, or 54 hours a month. (We *Internet For Dummies* authors average approximately one zillion minutes online a month, although we try not to exceed 24 hours a day.)

Here are the best ways we know to find an ISP close to home:

✔ Check the business pages of your local newspaper for advertisements from local ISPs.

✔ Ask your public library's research librarian or online services staff.

✔ Look in your local Yellow Pages under Internet Services.

✔ Ask anyone you know in your area who already has access what she's using and whether she likes it.

If you or your kids become regular online users, you will find that time stands still while you're online and that you use much more online time than you think you do. Even if you think that you will be online for only a few minutes a day, if you don't have a flat-rate plan, you may be surprised when your bill arrives at the end of the month.

Signing up

ISPs list two numbers: a voice number and a modem number. We think that it's useful, if you're new at this stuff (some of us have been "new at it" for *years* — don't take it personally) to call and talk to the human beings on the other end of the voice line to get their helpful guidance. If you don't get understandable answers (or if the person you're talking to sounds like he has better things to do than answer customer questions), look for a different ISP.

A word about usernames and passwords

Hundreds of millions of people are on the Internet. Because only one of them is you, it would be nice if the rest of them couldn't go snooping through your files and e-mail messages. For that reason — no matter which type of Internet account you have — your account has a username and a secret password associated with it.

Your *username* (or *user ID, login name, logon name,* or *screen name*) is unique among all the names assigned to your provider's users. It's usually also your e-mail address, so don't pick a name like *snickerdoodle* unless that's what you want to tell your friends and put on your business cards.

Your password is secret and is the main thing that keeps bad guys from borrowing an account. Don't use a real word or a name. A good way to make up a password is to invent a somewhat memorable phrase and turn each word in the phrase into a single letter or digit. "Computers cost too much money for me" turns into Cc2m$4m, for example. *Never tell anyone else your password.* Particularly, don't tell people who contact you and claim to be from your ISP — they're not.

Most ISPs now have sign-up programs that come on a CD-ROM or preinstalled on your computer. Windows XP comes with a New Connection Wizard that can show you a list of ISPs. Windows 98 and Me came with sign-up software for AOL and a few national ISPs (choose Start⇨Programs⇨Online Services from the taskbar). Some local ISPs provide a CD full of sign-up software, but if you have Windows XP, even without a CD, the Network Connection Wizard makes setup relatively painless.

Signing up for an account with an ISP generally involves providing your name, address, and telephone number along with billing information, which almost invariably includes a credit card number. Access is often granted immediately, or the service may call you on the phone to verify that you are who you said you were. If you don't use credit cards, call the ISP and find out whether you can pay your account by check.

 If you can bribe or coerce a friend or relative into helping you set up your account, do so. (**Hint:** Look for someone roughly between the ages of 12 and 16 who can be very knowledgeable, after you get past your humiliation. Chocolate-chip cookies always help.)

Because each ISP is just a tad different from the next, we can't go into exact step-by-step directions for everyone. We figure if we give the usual steps, help you understand the terms, and coax you through the whole process of setting up your Internet account and connection program, you're on your way.

Make sure that your phone line doesn't have call waiting. If it does, you (or your Internet connection program) have to type ***70** or **1170** at the beginning of your provider's phone number to tell your phone company to turn off call waiting for this phone call; otherwise, an incoming phone call will disturb your Internet connection. Most connection software has this ability built in. Just look for a Call Waiting option or one that uses the deactivation number for your phone system.

Connecting to dialup accounts for Windows XP users

Windows XP is the latest, greatest version of Windows and replaces all previous versions. It comes with an Internet dialup connection program, along with a New Connection Wizard for setting up your computer to use your Internet account. It also comes with Outlook Express for e-mail and Internet Explorer for Web browsing.

Telling Windows XP about your account

To set up Windows XP to access an Internet account, follow these steps:

1. **Double-click the Connect to the Internet icon on your desktop.**

   If you don't see it, click the Start button and choose All Programs⇔ Accessories⇔Communications⇔New Connection Wizard.

2. **Click Next on the New Connection Wizard's opening screen.**

   You see a window that looks like Figure 4-1.

3. **Click Connect to the Internet and then click Next.**

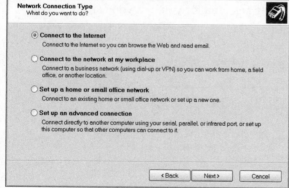

Figure 4-1:
The New Connection Wizard helps you get connected.

4. **If you don't have an Internet account yet, click the top button on the screen that appears (Choose from a List of Internet Service Providers) and click Next.**

The wizard leaves you with two options: sign up with MSN, Microsoft's own ISP, or dial the Microsoft Internet Referral Service (a toll-free call in the U.S.) to display a list of ISPs near you. The list is usually pretty short because it includes only big ISPs that have paid Microsoft enough to be included in the service. There may be terrific local ISPs (not on the list) that you can use instead.

Another problem is that the ISPs listed may not be a local call for you (especially if you live in the boondocks), so you may be in for some big phone bills. If you do choose an ISP from Microsoft's list, you can sign up on the spot — just check with your phone company to make sure that the phone number they give you is really a local call.

Skip Microsoft's referral service and do your own shopping.

5. **If you already have an Internet account, click the middle button (Set Up My Connection Manually) and then click Next.**

Setting up your account manually isn't as scary as it sounds; it mostly means that you have to type in the ISP's name and phone number and your username and password yourself. (Wow, makes our fingers hurt just to think about it! Not.)

The wizard asks how you connect to the Internet (over a regular, dialup phone line? a broadband DSL or cable Internet connection that requires a password? broadband DSL or cable Internet connection that doesn't require a password?), your ISP's name, the phone number to dial, your username, and your password. See the section "Getting faster connections: DSL and cable Internet" later in this chapter for information about broadband connections.

The wizard also offers two or three check boxes that you can select, depending on which version of Windows XP you have (see Figure 4-2). (They are usually selected for you, but you can click them to remove the check mark.)

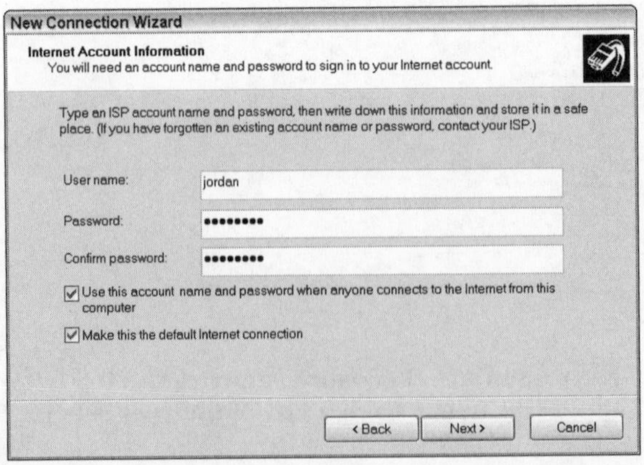

Figure 4-2:
Telling
Windows
XP's New
Connection
Wizard
about your
Internet
account.

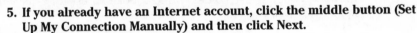

- **Use This Account Name and Password When Anyone Connects to the Internet from This Computer:** If your Windows computer is set up for multiple users, choosing this option enables all users to connect with this account. Unless you have some users on your computer whom you severely distrust, leave this option selected.

- **Make This the Default Internet Connection:** If you have several Internet accounts, one is the *default* (that is, the connection that Windows uses unless you specify otherwise). If you have only one Internet account (like most normal non-geeks), leave this selected, too.

6. **When you click Next and then Finish, the New Connection Wizard creates a dialup connection for your account.**

   The wizard also configures Windows to dial that number automagically whenever you try to browse the Web or send or receive e-mail.

Tweaking your account information with Windows XP

To take a look at your settings, choose Start⇨Control Panel⇨Network and Internet Settings and then click Set Up or Change Your Internet Connection. You see the Connections tab of the Internet Properties dialog box (shown in Figure 4-3) with your Internet account and other settings. To see the properties of this account, click Settings.

Figure 4-3:
You can use the Internet Properties dialog box to create or change dialup connections.

You can see all your network connections (Internet as well as local area network) by choosing Start➪Control Panel➪Network and Internet Connections➪Network Connections. (If you use the "Classic" Control Panel, choose Start➪Control Panel➪Network Connections.) The dialup connection that the New Connection Wizard created for you appears in the dialup section. If you need to change your account settings (for example, if your ISP tells you that the access phone number has changed), right-click the icon for your Internet account, choose Properties from the menu that appears, and make your changes.

Signing on and off with Windows XP

To connect to the Internet, run your browser and request a Web page, or run your e-mail program and tell it to check your mail. When Windows sees you requesting information from the Internet, it dials the phone for you. If you see a dialog box that asks for your username and password, type them in and then click Connect.

You can tell when you are connected because a two-computer-screen icon appears in the lower-right corner of the screen (just to the left of the digital clock). Double-click this icon to check the speed of your Internet connection — or, if you want to hang up, click the Disconnect button on the dialog box that appears.

Connecting to dialup accounts for Windows Me, 2000, and 98 users

Windows 98 came in two flavors: Original and Second Edition. Windows Me should have been called Windows 98 Third Edition because it's not that different. Windows 2000 is the business-oriented version of Windows (based on Windows NT). These versions of Windows came with an Internet connection program called Dial-Up Networking. They also came with automated signup programs for several ISPs (usually AT&T WorldNet and Microsoft Network in the United States — in other countries, other services appeared) and AOL.

Microsoft barely supports Windows 98 and Me anymore, so if you want a version of Windows that is supported and updated, consider upgrading to Windows XP. We tend to complain about Windows, we know, but Windows XP really is better.

Telling older versions of Windows about your account

To sign up for an account or to use an existing account with one of these services, click the Start button on the taskbar, choose Programs➪Online Services, and then choose the service. An MSN signup icon may also appear on your desktop.

If you want to use an account other than the ones with automated signup programs (and the service didn't send you an automated signup CD), you can run the Internet Connection Wizard to configure Dial-Up Networking to work with your account. Run the wizard by clicking the Connect to the Internet button on your Windows desktop, if there is one, or by choosing Start➪Programs➪Accessories➪Communications➪Internet Connection Wizard or Start➪

Programs➪Internet Explorer➪Connection Wizard, which is similar to the version that comes with Windows XP but with only three buttons.

If you have no account set up and want Windows to look for an ISP in your area, click the top "new account" button. If you've already arranged for an account, click the middle Transfer My Existing Internet Account button — even if you haven't set it up on another computer before. If you tried the middle "transfer" button and your ISP is not in the list that Microsoft suggests (which is quite likely if you're using a local ISP), click the bottom Set Up Manually or Do Nothing button.

We recommend using the Set Up Manually button at the bottom and then typing your ISP information in yourself — it's not hard. All you usually have to know is your ISP's access number (the phone number your computer calls to connect, which should be provided by your ISP), your username, and your password. We think you're better off choosing your ISP yourself than turning over the choice to Microsoft.

When you're done, you have an icon for your ISP in your Dial-Up Networking folder. To see it in Windows 98, open the My Computer folder on the desktop and open the Dial-Up Networking folder. In Windows Me, choose Start➪Settings➪Dial-Up Networking. In Windows 2000, choose Start➪Settings➪Network➪Dial-Up Connections.

Tweaking your account information in older versions of Windows

To change the settings for your ISP, right-click its icon in the Dial-Up Networking window and choose Properties from the menu that appears.

You can tell Windows to dial your Internet account automatically when your Web browser or e-mail program needs to connect to the Internet. This setting is in the Internet Properties dialog box (which may appear as the Internet Options dialog box — don't ask us why!). Follow these steps:

1. **Choose Start➪Settings➪Control Panel.**

2. **Double-click the Internet Options icon.**

3. **Click the Connections tab along the top.**

4. **Choose the Internet account to use (if you have more than one listed).**

5. **Click Always Dial My Default Connection (as shown in Figure 4-4).**

If you dial your ISP yourself (rather than letting Windows dial it when you run your browser or e-mail program), you may want to make the connection icon more convenient. If you drag the ISP's icon from the Dial-Up Networking folder to the desktop, Windows creates a shortcut on your Windows desktop. You can also add your Internet-connection program to your Start menu: Right-click the Start button and choose Open to display the Start Menu items in a window. Drag your ISP's icon from the Dial-Up Connection window to the Start Menu window. Way cool!

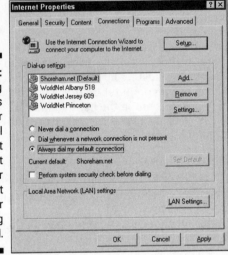

Figure 4-4:
Telling
Windows
2000, Me, or
98 to dial
your Internet
account
whenever
you start
browsing or
fetching
e-mail.

Signing on to and off of your ISP in older Windows versions

To call your account, double-click the icon for your ISP, type your username
and password if they don't already appear, and click the Connect button.
When you're connected, the Dial-Up Networking two-flickering-boxes icon
appears on the taskbar to the left of the digital clock. To hang up, double-
click the icon and then click Disconnect.

Connecting to dialup accounts for Mac users

Newer Macs already have all the software you need to connect to the
Internet. (Very old Macs — pre-System 8 — need a Mac TCP/IP modem program, such as FreePPP, which your ISP should be able to give you.) The only
things you usually need to set are the ISP's phone number, your account
name, and your password.

Getting faster connections: DSL and cable Internet

A snazzier way to connect, available not quite everywhere, is a *broadband*
(high-speed) connection. Broadband connections can provide greater *band-
width* — that is, more data transferred per second — than a connection over
a regular phone line. Such connections can be really fast, nominally up to
20 million bits per second, with downloads (in practice) often exceeding
140,000 bytes per second.

The good news is that high-speed connections are now available and afford-able by mere mortals in all but the most rural locations in the United States and Canada.

After you get used to having a high-speed connection, you will never be able to tolerate an ordinary dialup connection again. It's that good.

What is broadband, anyway?

There are two types of broadband Internet connections — DSL and cable, as follows:

✔ A *Digital Subscriber Line (DSL)* is a special kind of phone line that you or your ISP orders from your local telephone company.

✔ A cable Internet account is provided by your local cable TV company, using the same cable connection that brings you 250 brain-numbing TV channels.

DSL and cable Internet accounts have a lot in common: They're fast, they don't use a regular phone line, they don't use a dialup modem, and they don't use the Dial-Up Networking program that dialup accounts use. Some broad-band accounts have a permanent connection that works a lot like a connec-tion to a local network in an office. Others require you to log on, just as you would with a dialup connection. The good news about both DSL and cable accounts is that the ISP usually provides most of the equipment — for exam-ple, the modem — and can send an installer to set it up with your computer. With broadband, your local cable or telephone company can bring nifty equipment to your house and connect your computer to a high-speed con-nection while you sit back and watch. Ask your cable company whether it offers cable-modem Internet access or ask your phone company whether it offers DSL. If you get a yes to either question, consider getting broadband.

High-speed cable and DSL connections appear to cost more, usually $30 to $50 per month, plus installation and the cost of the special modem you need, minus whatever discount they give you for buying a package of broadband and the other services you get from them. However, neither cable nor DSL ties up your phone while you're online. Many people who use ordinary modems end up paying for the installation and use of a second phone line. When you add the cost of a second phone line to the cost of your ISP, you may find that DSL or cable is no more expensive. Cable and DSL connections are always available — there's no calling-in process, and they are significantly faster (and, we think, more fun).

A hidden cost in getting either cable or DSL Internet access is having to take a day off from work to wait for the installers, unless you feel brave enough to install them yourself. Sometimes it takes them two trips to get things work-ing. Try to get the first appointment in the morning. Also, the cable company or phone company is usually also your ISP unless you pay extra, so you don't have a choice of ISPs. In theory, the phone company provides DSL access on equal terms to all ISPs — but in practice, its own ISP somehow always seems to be more equal than the others.

Cable and DSL modems

To connect to a DSL or cable account, you use a DSL or a cable modem, so keep the following in mind:

- **If you have a cable Internet account, you need a cable modem.** Your cable company generally provides the modem as part of the service.

- **DSL modems are for connecting to high-speed DSL phone lines.** Don't buy one yourself — you need to make sure that the modem you use is compatible with your DSL line, so smart Internauts get their DSL modems from the ISP that provides their DSL service.

The moral of the story is: Don't buy a DSL or cable modem yourself. Get your cable or phone company to provide and install it.

You may need a network adapter

DSL and cable modems connect to your computer in one of two ways:

- **Network adapter:** A *network adapter* (also called a *LAN adapter, Ethernet adapter,* or *network interface card [NIC]*) was originally designed for connecting computers together into networks. If you have more than one computer in your home or office, you can use network adapters to connect the computers together into a *local area network* (*LAN*), as described in Chapter 5. Network adapters use an *RJ-45* plug, which looks like a regular phone jack but is a little bigger, into which you plug your modem or network cable. Check the back and sides of your computer for holes that look like overgrown phone plugs. Most computers (and all Macs) have a network adapter built in.

- **USB:** Newer computers come with one or more *USB* (Universal Serial Bus, if you care) connectors, which are used for connecting all kinds of stuff to your computer, from mice to cameras to printers. A USB port looks like a small, narrow, rectangular hole. Older (pre-1998) computers don't have USB connectors.

Most DSL and cable modems connect to a network adapter with a cable that plugs into an RJ-45 jack. You can get a DSL or cable modem with a USB connector.

If your cable or DSL modem installer reports that your computer doesn't have the network adapter or USB port that's needed to connect your high-speed modem, don't panic. If the installer can't provide the needed adapter, contact a local computer store about adding a network card or USB adapter — neither one should cost more than $20. Desktop computers need PCI card network adapters, which you install by turning off the computer, opening the case, finding an empty slot, sliding the card in, screwing it down, and closing up the computer. Laptops use PC Card network adapters, which look like fat credit cards and just slide into a slot on the side of the laptop.

Getting your DSL hooked up

DSL service is supposed to use your existing phone line and in-house wiring. But DSL often works better if the phone company runs a new wire from outside your building to where you use your computer. (Phone companies call this a *home run.*) For most kinds of DSL to work, you have to live within a couple of miles of your telephone central office, so DSL is unavailable in many rural areas.

DSL is available at different speeds. The higher speeds cost more (surprise, surprise!). The lowest speed (usually 640 Kbps) is fast enough for most users. (Compare 640 Kbps to the fastest dial-up line, which is 56 Kbps.)

If DSL service is available in your area, you call either your phone company or an ISP that will arrange for DSL service. Either they ship you the equipment to install yourself, or a phone installer comes with a network connection box (a glorified modem) that you or the installer hook up to your computer. DSL modems connect to a network card (which you may need to add to your computer) or to a USB port (which most new computers already have).

Getting your cable Internet hooked up

To sign up for a cable account, call your local cable company to open an account. Unless you decide to install it yourself (which isn't all that hard), a technician comes and installs a network-connection doozus (technical term) where your TV cable comes into your house, installs a network card in your computer if it doesn't already have one, brings a special modem (which can look like a laptop computer with a spike hairdo), and hooks them all together. Magic.

If you have cable television, the cable is split, and one segment goes to your computer. If you don't have cable television, the cable company may have to install the actual cable before it can wire up your computer. When the technician goes away, however, you have a permanent, high-speed connection to the Internet (as long as you pay your bill, about $40 to $50 a month). It may be cheaper if you also get their TV channels as well. In addition to the high speed and constant access at a fixed price, you aren't tying up a phone line.

Cable access comes in two forms: the older one-way and the newer two-way. With one-way cable, incoming data comes from the Net to your PC at high speed via the cable, but outgoing data still uses a modem and a phone line. With two-way cable, everything goes over the cable. One-way has nearly disappeared, but check with your cable company to find out for sure which kind it offers.

Do-it-yourself DSL

Hooking up your DSL modem shouldn't be so tough. One side plugs into the phone line, the other side into your computer. How hard can that be? Well, there are a few little details.

We'll assume you have a DSL modem that connects to a LAN or USB connector. If you have a LAN connector, you need a *crossover LAN cable* that should have come with the DSL modem. (Regular, noncrossover cables plug into a router or network hub, not directly from a modem to a computer.) If you're using USB, you should have a USB cable with a flat connector on one end and a squarish connector on the other. Turn off and unplug both your computer and the modem from the wall socket, plug in the LAN or USB cable, and then plug everything back in. The modem also connects to the phone line with a regular phone cord. The phone and LAN jacks on the modem are similar, but the LAN connector is the bigger one.

Now skip ahead to the section "After the DSL or cable Internet installer." And be sure to read the sidebar "Avoiding the DSL buzz."

Do-it-yourself cable modems

Connecting a cable modem is not unlike connecting a DSL modem, except that you connect it to your TV cable rather than to your phone line. If a TV is already attached to the cable, unscrew the cable from the TV and throw the TV away because you'll be having much too much fun with your Internet

---

Avoiding the DSL buzz

One of the clever things about DSL is that the DSL connection shares the same phone wires with your phone. You can tell that this is so because on all the phones on the line with DSL, you will hear a loud buzz of Data Hornets swarming up and down your phone line. (Well, not really, but it sounds like it.)

To get rid of the buzz, you need to install a *DSL filter* (which filters out the buzz) between the phone line and all your phones, but of course not between the phone line and your DSL modem. Filters are available from your DSL ISP, but you can probably find them cheaper at stores like RadioShack. The ideal way to install a filter is to run a separate wire from the box where the phone line enters your house to the DSL modem, and to install one DSL filter in that box into which you plug the wire leading to all the phones. But life is rarely ideal, so most of us install a filter for each phone.

For the phone plug where your DSL modem is connected, you'll want a *splitter* filter with a filtered jack into which you plug a phone (the one you use to call tech support when your computer doesn't work) and an unfiltered jack for the DSL modem. For all the other phones, the filter just plugs into the phone jack, and the phone code plugs into the filter. For that tidy look, you can also get wall-phone filters (which fit between the phone and the wall plate that the phone's mounted on) and baseboard phone jacks with filters built in.

connection to waste time watching TV. (If you're not yet ready to throw away your TV, move it to another cable outlet or get a cable splitter available at any store that sells cable accessories.) Screw the cable into the cable modem and plug the LAN or USB cable from the modem to the computer, just as we describe for a DSL modem in the previous section.

After the DSL or cable Internet installer

The installer (which is you, if you installed the modem yourself) configures your computer to communicate with the Internet. Most DSL and cable modems come with a software CD. If you're using a Mac or a version of Windows older than XP, run the software on the CD to install the necessary stuff to set up your connection.

If you're running Windows XP, you can either use the CD or set up the connection using Windows XP's built-in New Connection Wizard. We recommend the wizard because the CD usually has a pile of software that isn't of much use to you. To set up your connection using the wizard, follow these steps:

1. **Choose Start⇨All Programs⇨Accessories⇨Communications⇨ New Connection Wizard.**

   (They sure don't make it easy to find.)

2. **In the Network Connection Type, choose Connect to the Internet and click Next.**

3. **Select Set Up My Connection Manually.**

   Here you can choose either Connect Using a Broadband Connection That Requires a User Name and Password (if your ISP gave you a username and password), or Connect Using a Broadband Connection That Is Always On. A connection that is always on means that your computer is more vulnerable to hackers because it's never disconnected, but it's nice to be able to saunter up to your computer any time and not have to wait for it to connect. If you are worried about your computer being connected to the Internet all the time, you can shut down your computer — when it's turned off, it's definitely hacker-proof! See the section "Essential Software to Keep Your System Safe" later in this chapter.

4. **Choose a connection type, enter the required information in the boxes, and accept the suggested check boxes, particularly the Internet firewall.**

After your connection is installed, you should be able to start up a Web browser like Internet Explorer and type the name of a Web site into the address box at the top (try ours: net.gurus.com). The Web page should appear momentarily. If you have a connection with a username, it may ask you whether to connect. (Well, yeah, that's the idea.)

After you're connected, you can check the status of your connection:

- ✔ **Windows XP:** Display the Network Connections box by choosing Start➪Control Panel➪Network and Internet Connections➪Network Connections — broadband connections appear in the LAN or High-Speed Internet section.

- ✔ **Windows 98/Me/2000:** Display the dialog box by choosing Start➪ Settings➪Control Panel and double-clicking the Network icon. To change the connection's configuration, right-click it and choose Properties from the menu that appears.

- ✔ **Macs:** Use the TCP/IP Control Panel in OS 8 and 9. For OS X, choose System Preferences under the Apple menu and click the Network icon. Then select the TCP/IP tab.

On the other side of the pond

The ISP situation in the United Kingdom is a little different from the one in the North America. Traditionally, all phone calls in the U.K. have been charged by the minute, including even local calls, which can make long online sessions mighty pricey. As a result, there are now four different kinds of ISPs in the U.K.:

- ✔ **Traditional:** These ISPs charge a modest monthly fee and provide access via either local numbers or national rate numbers. Unless you are sure you won't spend much time online, or your ISP provides another service you're using such as Web hosting, these are probably not what you want.

- ✔ **Free:** These ISPs charge no monthly fee; they support themselves by splitting the per-minute charges with BT (British Telecom). (BT would rather not, but OFTEL, the telecom industry regulator, insists.) If you just want to try out the Net, free ISPs are a good way to start. We don't recommend them for long-term use because the per-minute split is less lucrative than the ISPs hoped, and free ISPs have a disconcerting habit of going out of business on short notice. The tech support

also tends to be pretty weak. (It's free — what do you want, your money back?)

- ✔ **Flat-rate:** These ISPs charge a monthly fee of about £20 but provide an 0800 or other number you can call without per-minute fees. Most users find this the best choice because it makes the bill predictable. The largest flat-rate ISPs are AOL (yes, *that* AOL) and BT. Be warned that even though access is nominally unlimited, if you "camp" on the phone 20 hours a day, your ISP will invoke small print you never noticed and cancel your account.

- ✔ **Broadband:** BT offer quite decent DSL service in most places in the U.K. at lower prices than American DSL so long as you agree to keep your service for at least a year. (Amazing but true.) If you use the Net enough to consider a flat-rate ISP, you might as well skip directly to DSL.

Depending on where you are and where your ISP is, your dialup phone connection may be anywhere from wonderful to dreadful. If you try one ISP and keep getting slow or unreliable connections, try another.

Your PC communicates with the Internet using the TCP/IP protocol, and you should see it listed on the Properties dialog box for the connection (in Windows XP) or in the Network dialog box (in earlier versions of Windows). Don't fool with these settings unless you are sure you know what you are doing!

AOL isn't exactly the Internet, but close enough

America Online (AOL), the world's largest online service, provides access to both the Internet and its own proprietary services. AOL has more than 20 million subscribers worldwide. To use AOL, you use software it provides. (Windows and Mac versions are available.) You can also use other software with your AOL account, such as Firefox and Microsoft Internet Explorer. Like most ISPs, AOL started as a dialup service and has since added DSL and cable connections — or you can use their "bring your own access" version with any other dialup or broadband Internet account.

Note: America Online, despite its name, is available outside America. AOL has access numbers in Canada and throughout the United Kingdom, at no extra charge, as well as versions for several other countries. If you travel internationally with your computer, AOL has more international phone numbers than anyone else, although some involve a high per-minute surcharge.

If you want to sign up for an AOL account, go to any post office and pick up one of the zillion AOL signup CDs lying around. (In fact, check around your house or apartment first. You are likely to find a few under the furniture.) Or call 1-800-827-3338 and ask for a trial membership. The introductory package has instructions and (surprise!) a disc containing the AOL access program. Follow the instructions on its cover to install the program and sign up for an account. You need a credit card to sign up.

For more information about how to use AOL, get *AOL For Dummies*, 2nd Edition, by John Kaufeld and Ted Leonsis (from Wiley Publishing, Inc.).

Essential Software to Keep Your System Safe

Okay, you're connected. But before you start surfing the Web, e-mailing, and instant messaging, you need to protect your computer from the Terrors of the Internet: viruses and spyware. Chapter 2 describes them in gory detail, and now is the time to use protection.

Fire at the wall!

A *firewall* is a barrier between your computer (or computers) and the Internet. In big companies, the firewall may consist of a computer that does nothing but monitor the incoming and outgoing traffic, checking for bad stuff. At your home or office, you have two good options:

- ✔ You can use firewall software built into Windows XP. To check your firewall settings in Windows XP SP2, choose Start➪Control Panel➪Security Center. In original Windows XP, choose Start➪Control Panel➪Network and Internet Connections➪Network Connections. (If you use the "Classic" Control Panel, choose Start➪Control Panel➪Network Connections.) Right-click the icon for your Internet account, choose Properties from the menu that appears, click the Advanced tab, and look for the Internet Connection Firewall or Windows Firewall section. If it's not already selected, mark the check box to turn on Internet Connection Firewall. When that's done, your computers have basic protection from hackers.

- ✔ You can use a *router*, a small box that sits between your computer(s) and your broadband modem. A router has one plug for a cable to your DSL or cable modem, and several plugs (usually four) to which you can connect computers. The router has firewall software running all the time. See Chapter 5 for how to use a router to connect more than one computer to one Internet account.

We recommend using a router because they cost only about $40 and we're sure that you'll want to hook up a second computer to the Internet before long. But the firewall program included in Windows XP works fine, too.

A router is a particularly good idea if you have a broadband connection that is always on (that is, always connected). The router is always on, too.

No viruses need apply

Viruses are sneaky programs that arrive via e-mail or in downloaded programs and immediately get up to no good. (See Chapter 2 for details.) You need to run a virus-checker program all the time, and you need to update its list of viruses regularly so that the program can detect the latest viruses.

Many commercial virus-checkers are available. The two most widely used programs are McAfee VirusScan, which you can download from the McAfee Web site at www.mcafee.com and Norton AntiVirus, at www.symantec.com. If you have more than one computer on the Internet, consider F-Prot, at www.f-prot.com, because you only have to pay for one license to run the program on all the computers in your house.

You'll need to pay for these programs (we don't know of a good, free virus-checker). Most require that you pay annually for a subscription to updates. Do it — without updates to the list of viruses that it's looking for, your program won't spot and block the latest viruses. Some bundle the virus-checker with other security packages, so you can get all the protection you need with one purchase.

Don't think that you are saving money if you don't subscribe to a virus-checking service. New viruses come out every day (well, every week, anyway). Your virus-checker can check only for the viruses that it knows about. You need a service that updates your list of viruses to check for. It's like the FBI sending out new "Wanted" posters to the local police.

A good virus-checker automatically connects to its home base over the Internet about once a week and downloads updates to its virus lists. You may see a dialog box on your screen when this is happening. Your subscription usually lasts a year, and you should see warnings to update your subscription (that is, pay again) when you year is almost up.

For help downloading and installing a virus program, see Chapter 12.

Detecting spyware

Spyware is a class of programs that sneak onto your computer, usually when you are browsing the Web, and run unbeknownst to you, doing God knows what. (See Chapter 2 for details.) A number of anti-spyware programs are available for free, although no single program seems to spot all types of spyware. We recommend that you run several anti-spyware programs from time to time, sweeping your hard disk and looking for bad stuff.

The programs we use are

✔ **Spybot Search & Destroy,** at www.spybot.info (shareware; donations appreciated)

Note that several unscrupulous programs have started using the word "spybot" in their names, so don't just Google to find the program. Go to the official Web site at www.spybot.info to download the program.

✔ **Ad-aware Personal Edition,** at www.lavasoftusa.com (free)

These programs (and many others) are also available for free download from www.download.com. For help downloading and installing a spyware-checking program, see Chapter 12.

Get rid of your Dell or Gateway software

Some computers come with Internet software created by the hardware manufacturers, designed to give you an easier Internet experience. Unfortunately, we find that these programs just give you a more *confusing* Internet experience, because each program is renamed to add the name of the hardware manufacturer. (AOL used to do this, too.) If your Dell, Gateway, or other new computer comes with Dell, Gateway, or other Internet programs, we recommend that you ignore them and use the Windows standard stuff described in this chapter.

In addition, follow a few basic rules, which will make more sense once you've read the later chapters of this book (don't worry, we'll mention them again in those later chapters, too). Here they are:

✔ **Don't use Internet Explorer as your browser.** Most spyware is designed to use features of Internet Explorer to worm its way onto your computer. Instead, use Firefox, as described in Chapter 6.

✔ **Don't use Internet Explorer within other applications.** For example, some e-mail programs have an option to use Internet Explorer to display messages that contain HTML (Web formatting). Turn off these options.

✔ **If you use Windows, turn on Automatic Updates, and download and install the updates that it suggests.** Microsoft issues security fixes to Windows at least once a month. To turn on Automatic Updates in Windows XP SP2, choose Start ⇨Control Panel⇨Security Center. In original Windows XP, choose Start⇨Control Panel⇨Performance and Maintenance⇨System. In the System Properties dialog box that appears, click the Automatic Updates tab. Choose the first or second option so that Windows lets you know when updates are available.

Our Favorite Internet Setup

You're probably wondering, "The authors of this book have used the Internet forever. What do they recommend as the very best way to connect to the Internet?" Okay, you're probably not wondering that, but we wish you were. And we've got the answer.

The best Internet setup (in our humble opinions) is this:

✔ A computer (Windows, Mac, or Linux — they are all good)

✔ A DSL or cable Internet account — broadband rocks!

✔ A *router*, providing a firewall between your computer(s) and the Internet

You're Connected — Now What?

When you connect to your ISP (whether by dialup, DSL line, or cable Internet account), your computer becomes part of the Internet. You type stuff or click in programs running on your computer, and those programs communicate over the Net to do whatever it is they do for you.

Running lots of Internet programs

You can run several Internet applications at a time, which can be quite handy. You may be reading your electronic mail, for example, and receive a message describing a cool, new site on the World Wide Web. You can switch immediately to your Web browser program (usually Internet Explorer or — as we recommend — Firefox), look at the Web page, and then return to the mail program and pick up where you left off. Most e-mail programs highlight *URLs* (Web addresses) and enable you to go straight to your browser by clicking the URL in your e-mail message.

You're not limited to running programs that your Internet provider gives you. You can download a new Internet application from the Net and begin using it immediately — your ISP just acts as a data conduit between your computer and the rest of the Net.

To find out more about using the Web, see Chapter 6. If you want to start off with e-mail, read Chapter 13. Or just flip through the rest of the book to see what looks interesting!

Getting off the Internet

If you dial in to the Internet (or AOL), you'll eventually want to disconnect (hang up). You don't have to log off, in most cases, but you do need to hang up the phone.

If you use a broadband account, you never need to disconnect. We love being able to saunter up to our computers any time to check the weather, our e-mail, or what movies Joe E. Brown was in, without having to wait for our computer to reconnect.

You may have a bunch of programs running while you use the Internet, including your Web browser and your e-mail program. Only one of these programs, however, is the program that connects you to the Internet. That's the one you talk to when you're disconnecting from the Internet. In Windows, you disconnect from a dialup account using the Dial-Up Networking or Dial-Up Connection program, which is usually a little icon on the Windows taskbar at the bottom of the screen, showing two flickering boxes. You can leave the rest of your programs (such as your Web browser and e-mail program) running even when you're not connected to the Net.

Chapter 5

Sharing Your Internet Connection

. . . .

. . . .

These days lots of families have more than one computer — perhaps one in the office, one in the family room, and one in your teenager's bedroom. Hey, one of us has one in the kitchen for our family's calendar and address book. (And that's not to mention the road-warrior laptop.)

Luckily, you don't need a separate Internet connection for each computer. Instead, you can connect the computers into a network — either with cables or through thin air with wireless connections — and then set them up to share one Internet connection. This chapter shows you how to set up both types of networks.

And for those of you who already have a laptop or just got one, this chapter talks about ways you can connect your laptop at home or on the road.

Don't Limit Your Internet Access to One Computer

Many years ago, back when computers were large hulking things found only in glass-walled computer rooms, a wild-eyed visionary friend of ours claimed (to great skepticism) that computers would be everywhere, and so small and cheap that they'd show up as prizes in cereal boxes. We're not sure about the cereal boxes, but it's certainly true that the last time we went to put an old computer in the closet, there wasn't room because of all the other old computers in there. Rather than let them rust in the closet, you may as well get some use out of them by connecting them all to the Internet.

With a broadband connection, that turns out to be pretty easy. No more arguing about who's going to use the phone line next! No more pouting from the computer users who didn't get the cable or DSL hookup! Everyone can send e-mail, receive e-mail, chat, and browse the Web — all at the same time.

To share an Internet connection, you connect your computers together into a type of network called a *local-area network (LAN)*, and then you connect the LAN (rather than an individual computer) to the Internet. A local area network is (drum roll, please!) a network that's entirely contained in one local area, like one building, and is connected via wires or wireless connections, with no phone lines within the LAN. Once the exclusive tool of businesses, LANs have become affordable enough that they're showing up in homes. As long as your home is in one building, if you've got some computers connected together, it's a LAN.

Figure 5-1 shows a typical home network: A cable or DSL modem connects to a *hardware router,* a device that connects your LAN to your Internet connection. Normally, you'd connect your PC to a network hub (for a wired network) or an access point (for wireless) — but a hardware router has a hub or access point built in. Then you connect the LAN to the rest of the computers around the house.

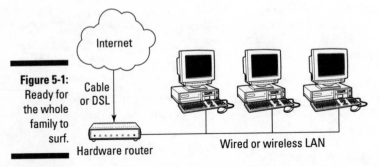

Figure 5-1:
Ready for
the whole
family to
surf.

Internet

Cable
or DSL

Hardware router

Wired or wireless LAN

The computers on your LAN don't all have to be running the same version of Windows — or running Windows at all. You can connect Windows computers, Macs, and Linux computers on the same LAN; they all speak the same networking protocol, the same protocol that the Internet itself uses.

First, Make a LAN

LANs come in two basic varieties: wired and wireless. In a wired network, a cable runs from each computer to a central box, whereas a wireless network uses radio signals instead of wires. If all your computers are in one room (or you're good at playing home electrician), a wired network's for you; otherwise, wireless is far easier to set up, although the pieces can be more expensive and the resulting network runs slower. Combos are also possible; most wireless equipment has a few jacks for wires to connect to the computers that are close enough to run cables.

The box in the middle — a hub or router

For any variety of current LAN, you need a special box that connects everything together. Here are the main kinds of boxes you have to choose from:

✔ A *hub* is a phone-book-sized box with a bunch of jacks for network cables and serves as a wired connection point that links all your computers into a LAN.

✔ A *switch* is the same thing as a hub, but it's got a little extra circuitry to speed things up.

✔ An *access point* is the wireless equivalent of a hub, with a radio antenna or two rather than jacks.

✔ A *router* is like a hub with the addition of Internet connection smarts, like a firewall (described in Chapter 4).

Our advice is to go for a router; they're cheap and they'll save you days of hair-tearing grief because they keep most Windows worms out of your network. Routers come in both wired and wireless versions. The wired versions have varying numbers of jacks, depending on how many computers you plan to have in your wired LAN; the wireless ones have one jack for the cable to the modem, an antenna for the wireless network, and usually a few jacks for wires running to computers in the same room.

Setting up a router

Routers invariably come with a short Ethernet cable to connect the router to the cable or DSL modem, so connect your router to your modem, plug them in, and turn them on. An Ethernet cable (also known as *Category-5* or *Cat-5*) looks like a fat phone cable, with little plastic connectors that look just like phone plugs, but a little larger. (Even their technical names are a little larger; a phone connector is called an RJ-11 jack, while an Ethernet connector is an RJ-45 jack.)

Configuring routers for DSL connections that require a username and password

For the most part, routers take care of themselves, but if you have the kind of DSL connection that requires a username and password, you need to put those into the router. If your DSL connection doesn't require a username and password, you can probably just skip this section, although you can come back later if a program you are installing requires you to change the router's configuration. Setup instructions for routers are all the same in concept but they differ in detail from one router to another — so you may have to (gack!) glance at the instructions that came with the router.

To set up the router, you use the Web browser on your computer, so first you have to get the browser in touch with the router. Since the router doesn't have a screen or keyboard that would enable you to configure it, you use a computer connected to the router instead. Even if you plan to have an entirely wireless LAN, the initial setup is a lot easier if you connect a PC (or Mac) to the router via an Ethernet cable (at least for now) so the router can figure out which computer it's supposed to be talking to ("Hey, there it is at the other end of that wire.") Follow these steps:

 1. **Turn off the router and the PC (or Mac).**

    Computers are usually happier if you plug and unplug stuff while the computer is turned off.

 2. **Plug an Ethernet cable into the network adapter on your computer and plug the other end into one of the jacks on the router.**

 3. **Turn on the router and then turn on the computer.**

 4. **Fire up your Web browser and type the address of the router's control page — its home page, with configuration settings.**

    Usually this page is at 192.168.0.1 (a special address reserved by the Internet powers-that-be for private networks like yours). If that Web address doesn't work, check the router's instructions.

 5. **If your router's configuration page requires a password, check your router's manual to find out what it is and then type it in.**

    You see the configuration page for your router.

 6. **If you have a broadband connection that uses a login and password, find the text box or field to enter your login name and password for your broadband connection.**

    Either follow the instructions in your router manual, or try clicking the tabs or links on the page until you find boxes with names like "Username" and "Password." Type them in. (With the D-Link router configuration page shown in Figure 5-2, clicking Tools displays the right page.)

 7. **If there's a Save, Done, or OK button or link, click it to make sure that the router saves your changes.**

    If there ain't no such button or link, don't worry.

Now your router knows how to log in to your DSL account.

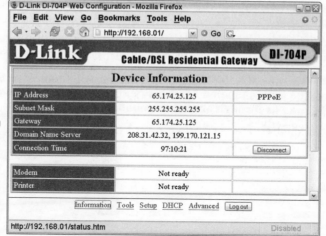

Figure 5-2:
You talk with
your router
via your
Web
browser.

Connecting your LAN to the modem

Plug the router into your DSL or cable modem, turn the modem on (if it's not on yet), restart the router, and check that you can connect to the outside Internet. (Try a visit to our home page at net.gurus.com.) If that doesn't work, check the modem cable and check that the username and password setup is correct if your Internet connection needs them.

Wiring up your computers into a LAN

After you have the router set up, if you want to create a wired LAN, you need wires. (Duh!) Specifically, LANs use Ethernet cable called *Category-5* (or *Cat-5*) cable, which is available at any office supply store, electrical supply store, computer store, and even the occasional supermarket. At each end of a Cat-5 cable is an RJ-45 connector, which looks like a larger version of a phone connector. You need one cable for each computer, plus one extra for the modem (if the modem didn't come with its own cable).

For each computer — PCs, Macs, or whatever — plug one end of a Cat-5 cable into the computer's network adapter, the same jack into which the DSL and cable Internet modems plug. (See Chapter 4 for information about network adapters and whether you need one.) Plug the other end of the cable into the router.

When you've got your computers connected together, tell each computer about the LAN. On each Windows computer on the network, follow this drill:

1. **Choose Start➪All Programs➪Accessories➪Communications➪Network Setup Wizard.**

   Another way to run the wizard is to choose Start➪Control Panel➪Network and Internet Connections and click the Network Setup Wizard link.

2. **Follow the wizard's directions. When it asks what you want to do, choose the option labeled "This computer connects through a residential gateway or through another computer on my network."**

   The "residential gateway" is your router. On the next page, the wizard asks you to name your computer, as shown in Figure 5-3.

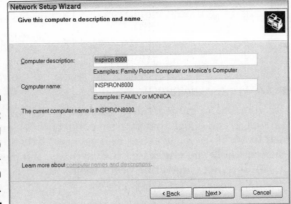

Figure 5-3: Configuring Windows to communicate on your LAN.

3. **When the wizard asks, give the computer a network name (such as "PLAYROOM," "OFFICE," or "JORDAN").**

4. **When the wizard asks for the *workgroup* name, use the *same* name for all the computers on your LAN.**

   We use "WORKGROUP" ourselves. Windows may suggest "MSHOME," which is fine too — just be consistent.)

If you connect a Mac to your LAN, it can probably see the LAN and work without your lifting a finger. If you do want (or need) to configure your network connection, and you use Mac OS 9 or earlier, choose Apple➪Control Panels➪TCP/IP to access the TCP/IP control panel. Or, run the Internet Setup Assistant by choosing your hard disk, then the Internet folder, and then Internet Setup Assistant. In Mac OS X, your network software is called Open Transport. To configure it, open the System folder, then the Control Panels folder, and then the TCP/IP control panel.

For more details on setting up your LAN, see *Home Networking For Dummies*, 3rd Edition, by Kathy Ivens (published by Wiley Publishing, Inc.).

Forget the Wires! Go WiFi

If you have computers in more than one room in the house, it's easier (though the hardware comes at a higher price) to use WiFi than to snake wires through the walls or basement.

Many laptop PCs have WiFi built in. For computers that don't, you can get WiFi PC cards, WiFi doozits with USB cables, and (less often) WiFi add-in cards. WiFi makers do a remarkably good job of adhering to industry standards; you can expect anyone's .11b or .11g WiFi equipment to work with anyone else's. The main practical difference among them is range; WiFi components have one standard feature in common: laughably optimistic estimates of how far away they can be from other WiFi equipment and still work. Bigger antennas get you more range — as does (sadly) more expensive equipment. WiFi's radio waves are in the same band as 2.4GHz cordless phones, so you can expect roughly the same range. Like a cordless phone, your WiFi connection will probably work in most parts of your house, but not down to the end of your driveway. If you have a normal-sized house, normal WiFi works fine. If you live in a $900,000 mansion, you might have to spring for the $100 WiFi card rather than the $50 one.

What can talk WiFi, and why A, B, and G aren't all that different

The engineers who design network equipment really enjoy making improvements. So it's no wonder that there's more than one flavor of wireless network. Network standards are set by a professional organization called the IEEE (the Institute of Electrical and Electronics Engineers, at ieee.org), in its standards group 802. (Yes, there really were 801 other groups ahead of it.) Group 802 has splintered into about two dozen subgroups, of which the most relevant are 802.3, which handles wired Ethernet and 802.11, which is wireless Ethernet. The .11 group assigns letters to projects as they're set up, so 802.11b is the original 11 megabit (millions of bits per second) WiFi that became popular around 2000, and 802.11g is a faster 54 megabit version which is most common now. Fortunately, .11b and .11g can talk to each other at the slower .11b rate, which is plenty fast for normal people. Avoid .11a, which came out *after* .11b (it started first but took longer to finish) — it's faster than .11b but not compatible with it. All versions of .11 can be called *WiFi,* so when you get WiFi equipment, be sure that it says *802.11b* or *802.11g* on the box to be sure it'll work with all the other the WiFi equipment you're likely to encounter.

Set a password, for Pete's sake!

It would be obvious if a random stranger walked into your house and plugged into your wired network. However, if you have a WiFi network and a stranger is out on the street with a laptop scanning the area for unprotected wireless access points (a practice known as "wardriving"), he can connect to your WiFi network and you can't easily tell. Some people don't care — at least until they realize that wardrivers can see *all* the shared files and printers on your LAN. You may well be able to hop onto your neighbors' WiFi networks, and they onto yours, which may or may not be okay, depending on how much you like your neighbors.

Fortunately, all WiFi systems have optional passwords. Cryptographers laugh derisively at the poor security of WiFi passwords, but they're adequate to make wardrivers and nosy neighbors go bother someone else. If you have serious secrets on your network, don't depend on WiFi passwords. A bad guy using a laptop and one of the widely available WiFi password-cracker programs can gather enough data from your network to break any password in under a week. If you need better cryptographic protection, it's available, but it's not exactly a do-it-yourself project to set up.

Windows Internet Connection Sharing? Get a router

Not only Windows XP, but several earlier editions (Windows 98 Second Edition, Me, and 2000), come with Internet Connection Sharing (ICS) — adequate built-in router software — but there's not much point in using it: You'll need a hub or router to connect your computers into a LAN anyway.

If you insist on using Internet Connection Sharing, be sure that the computer you plan to use is connected both to your cable or DSL modem and to the LAN, and that you leave the computer on all the time (it can't act like a router when it's turned off). What you do next depends on which version of Windows that computer is running:

✓ **Windows XP:** Choose Start⇨All Programs⇨ Communications⇨New Connection Wizard (the same Wizard used to set up your Internet connection) and choose Set Up a Home or Small Office Network. The Wizard steps you through the configuration of the *ICS server* (the computer that connects to the Internet) and the *ICS clients* (the rest of the computers).

✓ **Windows Me:** Choose Start⇨ Programs⇨ Accessories⇨Communications⇨Home Networking Wizard (you may need to click the little arrows at the bottom of the Communications menu to reveal all the commands).

Either way, if you have an Internet connection that requires you to log on, then (with luck) your ICS server will log you on automatically when someone on the LAN wants to connect to the Internet. Otherwise you'll have to use the ICS client program to poke the router awake before you log on. If you have always-on broadband, the Internet will just be there when you need it.

Those creative WiFi engineers created several flavors of passwords, too. The most widely used are called *WEP,* a term that allegedly means *Wired Equivalent Privacy* (which it's not). WEP passwords come in two sizes: 64 and 128 bits. Use 128 unless you have old equipment that can only handle 64, in which case, 64 will do. (Your entire network has to use the same size.) The password can be represented as either a text string or a hexadecimal (base-16) number — we leave it to you to guess which would be easier for you to type and remember. If you use 64-bit WEP, your password (in text format) must be exactly 7 characters long. For 128-bit WEP, you need a 13-character password. If you want to use a shorter password, pad it out with digits or punctuation.

Newer WiFi equipment uses a more secure password scheme called WPA (WiFi Protected Access). If all your WiFi equipment can handle it, use WPA instead of WEP. WPA passwords can be almost any length — you aren't limited to exactly 7 or exactly 13 characters.

The easiest way to set the password is to set it up at the same time you set up your network, as described in the next section.

Making the WiFi connection

To create a WiFi system, follow these steps:

1. **Get your router set up and then set up your computers to connect to it.**

   See the section "Setting up a router," earlier in this chapter.

2. **Use your Web browser to display the router's control page (usually at 192.168.0.1) so you can configure the router.**

3. **Give your network a name. Every WiFi network has a name.**

   With typical machine imagination, your router suggests something like linksys (a router manufacturer) or default. We suggest something like FredsHouse so any neighbors who happen on it will know it's you.

4. **Turn on WiFi passwords and set one, as described in the preceding section.**

   Your router probably has lots of other options — such as MAC cloning (less fruit-related than it sounds, and nothing to do with Macintosh computers) — all of which you can ignore.

   When your router is up and running and your PC (or Mac) can see the Internet (that is, you can display Web pages), you are done configuring the router for your WiFi network.

   Now, at last, you can cut the cord and go wireless. On each PC, you need to tell it which network to use and what the password is. If you are using Windows XP, particularly XP SP2, this process is fairly painless:

5. **Choose Start⇨Connect To⇨Wireless Network Connection.**

6. **After your PC sniffs the airwaves for a moment, Windows shows you a list of available networks, which should include the one you just set up.**

   If you have neighbors with WiFi networks, it may show them, too, but don't use your neighbors' networks unless they've given you permission.

7. **Select your network's name and then click the Connect button at the bottom.**

8. **Windows asks you to type the password twice. Enter the password, whether text or hexadecimal, exactly as you did on the router.**

9. **Click OK and you should be online.**

Windows remembers the wireless setup; in the future it will connect automatically.

Using Your Laptop at Home and Away

The whole point of having a laptop computer is to take it with you when you travel — and what fun is traveling with a computer if you can't use it to check your e-mail 17 times a day? After you've set up your laptop on a home WiFi network, following the instructions earlier in this chapter, you've already learned most of what you need to know to use it on other networks when you travel.

Home and office setup

Lots of people have laptops they take back and forth between home and the office. A lot of variables are involved in doing this successfully, depending not only on your particular laptop, but also on the networks you use at home and at the office. In general, however, this is how the various setups should work:

✔ If both home and the office have wired networks, your computer should work when it's plugged into either network. If your computer doesn't connect at work, talk to your network administrator.

✔ If your office has local shared files and printers and your house doesn't, or vice versa, Windows complains and sulks if it can't find them, but as long as you don't try to print to a printer that's at the other place, you can go online just fine.

✔ If both the home and office networks are wireless, or one is wireless and the other is wired, set each one up as described earlier in this chapter, and your PC should automatically recognize whichever is available — wireless or wired.

Snoops at the coffee shop

Although we think that a lot of concerns about Internet network security are overblown, one place it's a real issue is on public WiFi networks like the ones in hotels and coffee shops. Those networks frequently have no passwords, which means that *anyone on that network can snoop on your network connection.* Even if everyone in the coffee shop seems nice, a snoop might be sitting in a car out by the curb. And in a hotel, of course, you have no idea who's in all the nearby rooms.

Fortunately, a few simple precautions will keep you safe. When visiting Web sites, make sure that any site where you type in a password or other private info uses SSL encryption; so the address should start with `https://` and the little lock in the corner should be locked. If the site doesn't have SSL encryption, wait until you get home. For advice on securing your mail program, see "The mail problem" at the end of this chapter.

Getting WiFi with your latte

In olden days, people would go to a coffee shop, order cups of coffee (of which there was a maximum of two kinds, regular and decaf), and then chat with people sitting *right next to them.* Now, of course, that's hopelessly out of date. We cruise into the coffee shop with our laptops, order a half-caf-decaf mocha cappuccino grande with two-percent milk, cocoa drizzle, hold the sprinkles, put on our headphones, and talk or exchange messages with people thousands of miles away, utterly ignoring the losers at the next table. The magic of WiFi makes this possible, as coffee shops install WiFi *hotspots* — public areas with WiFi Internet access — to which customers can connect.

The amount of effort needed to get online at your coffee shop varies from none to way too much. At some places, the management has enough confidence in their product to figure that if they can get you to stick around, you'll keep buying coffee, so WiFi is free to the customers. (The coffee shop where John is sometimes found is in this category.) You turn on your computer; choose the Start⇨Connect To menu — if your computer doesn't look for a WiFi network by itself — click the name of the shop's network when it appears; tell it that, yes, you really want to connect to that insecure network; and you're on. The next time you come back, your computer remembers the network and connects automatically.

Other places are less confident. A typical large chain — let's call it *Ahab's* — made the WiFi a profit center so you have to pay by the hour. This adds an extra annoying step to the connection process, the one where you pay. After your computer is turned on, fire up your Web browser. No matter what your home page is, the network is set up so your browser shows *their* home page, which allows you to make payment arrangements.

There are about as many ways to pay for WiFi access as there are flavors of coffee. Maybe you buy or are given a ticket at the counter with a code number to enter. More likely the coffee shop made a deal with one of the large national mobile phone providers, T-Mobile or Cingular, who make a sideline of WiFi. In this case, you pay with a credit card, either by the hour (at about $6 an hour) or by buying a package of hours, signing up via your Web browser. The WiFi network lets you connect to the signup page for free (see Figure 5-4), but you have to sign up and pay to do anything else. If you plan to drink a great deal of coffee, you can sign up for a monthly flat-rate plan. It's not hard to get into the WiFi café biz, so you'll also find lots of tiny little providers. Many of the providers have reciprocal agreements and alliances, such that (for example) if you sign up with someone who belongs to a group called Ipass, you can use another Ipass member's WiFi hotspot.

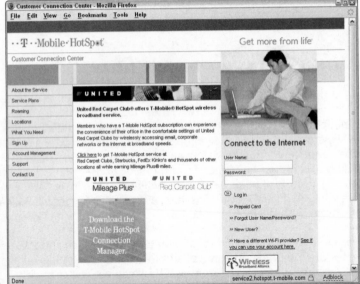

Figure 5-4: Logging on from the road.

Airports, hotels, and beyond

Coffee shops are hardly the only places that offer WiFi. If you spend much time in airports (John does because he's on a lot of advisory boards), you'll find lots of WiFi — with about the same options as in the coffee shops. The same two providers dominate (Figure 5-4 shows T-Mobile in an airline club in Chicago), with a lot of little local ones as well. After a while, frequent travelers learn WiFi folklore — say, that there's free WiFi in the airline club on the third level of the Pittsburgh airport, and even if you're not a member, you can use it if you sit in one of the chairs near the door.

Hotels, like cafés, either treat WiFi as a service — like the ice machine on each floor — or as a profit center — like your room's minibar-full-of-over-priced-beer. Some hotels still offer wired Ethernet (in which case there's a cable on the desk in your room that plugs into your computer), others go WiFi. If you're at an ice-machine-style hotel, you may be able to just turn on your computer and go online with no fuss, or you may have to sign in through your browser, even though you don't have to pay. Some hotels with WiFi give you a slip of paper with a login code when you register, to deter visitors who'd otherwise sit in the lobby and use it for free. In minibar-style hotels, you have to log in through your browser. Most hotels put the charge on the room bill; some want your credit card number so they can bill you separately. The typical charge is $10 per day, noon to noon, but we've seen hourly rates, lower rates, and higher ones.

If you encounter a problem with a hotel's Internet service, there is rarely anyone at the hotel who knows anything about it, but they should be able to give you an 800 number you can call to talk to someone at the company that actually provides the service.

The mail problem

WiFi connections in coffee shops, airports, and hotels sure are convenient, but remember: *They aren't private.* This is a particular problem when you send and receive e-mail, both because you usually want your mail to be private, and because your computer needs to send your network login and password over the Internet back to your mail server to pick up your mail. With a modest amount of advance planning, it shouldn't be hard to get your mail working securely on the road.

The simplest approach is Web mail — a secure Web site that you log into to read and send mail. It's worth checking to see if your mail system offers optional Web mail. If so, even if you don't use it at home, you might want to use it on the road, particularly if the Web mail offers a secure server. Check out Chapter 13 to discover how Web-based mail works and how you can make it work for you.

If you want to use your mail program, there is a fairly painful one-time process you have to slog through to set up secure mail. Because it involves adjusting the setup of your mail program, we cover it in Chapter 14, so flip ahead and check it out.

Part III
Web Mania

The 5th Wave — By Rich Tennant

"Since we began online shopping, I just don't know where the money's going."

In this part . . .

No doubt about it, the Web's *the* happenin' place. For many people, the World Wide Web *is* the Internet. We explain what the Web is and how to get around, along with great tips about how to actually find stuff you're looking for among the millions of clamoring Web pages. We also tell you about Web shopping and Web banking so you can confidently spend and save your money online, then relax and listen to lots of online music.

Chapter 6

Welcome to the Wild, Wonderful, Wacky Web

People talk about the *Web* today more than they talk about the *Net.* The World Wide Web and the Internet are not the same thing — the World Wide Web (which we call the Web because we're lazy typists) lives "on top of" the Internet. The Internet's network is at the core of the Web, and the Web is like a benevolent parasite that requires the Net for survival.

This chapter explains what the Web is, where it came from, how to install and use the Firefox browser, and how to use your Web browser to display Web pages. If you are already comfortable using the Web — and you've switched to the Firefox browser, then skip ahead to Chapter 7.

What Is the Web?

So what is the Web already? The Web is a bunch of "pages" of information connected to each other around the globe. Each page can be a combination of text, pictures, audio clips, video clips, animations, and other stuff. (We're vague about naming the other stuff because webmasters add new types of other stuff every day.) What makes Web pages interesting is that they contain *hyperlinks,* usually called just *links* because the Net already has plenty of hype. Each link points to another Web page, and, when you click a link, your *browser* fetches the page the link connects to. (Stay calm — we talk about browsers in a couple pages. Your browser is the program that shows you the Web.)

The other important thing about the Web is that the information in it is searchable. For example, in about ten seconds, you can get a list of Web pages that contain the phrase *domestic poultry,* or your own name, or the name of a book you want to find out about. You can follow links to see each page on the list to find the information you want. See the next chapter for how to use a *search engine* to search the Web.

Linking Web pages up

Each page your browser gets for you can have more links that take you to other places. Pages can be linked to other pages anywhere in the world so that when you're on the Web, you can end up looking at pages from Singapore to Calgary, from Sydney to Buenos Aires, all faster than you can say "Bob's your uncle," usually. Give or take network delays, you're only seconds away from any site, anywhere in the world.

This system of interlinked documents is known as *hypertext.* Figure 6-1 shows a Web page (our Web page, in fact). Each underlined phrase is a link to another Web page.

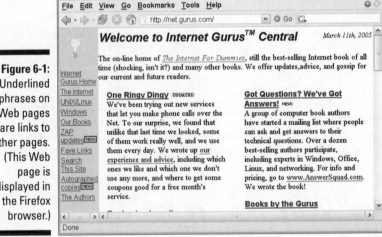

Figure 6-1: Underlined phrases on Web pages are links to other pages. (This Web page is displayed in the Firefox browser.)

Hypertext, the buzzword that makes the Web go, is one of those simple ideas that turns out to have a much bigger effect than you would think. With a hypertext system, people can create connections among pieces of information that let you go directly to related information. As you draw connections among the pieces of information, you can begin to envision the Web created by the links between the pieces. What's so remarkable about the Web is that it connects pieces of information from all around the *planet,* on different computers and in different databases, all fairly seamlessly (a feat you would be hard pressed to match with a card catalog in a brick-and-mortar library). We sometimes think of the Web as an extremely large but friendly alien centipede made of information.

Where did the Web come from?

The World Wide Web was invented in 1989 at the European Particle Physics Lab in Geneva, Switzerland, an unlikely spot for a revolution in computing. The inventor is a British researcher named Sir Tim Berners-Lee, who is now the director of the World Wide Web Consortium (W3C) in Cambridge, Massachusetts, the organization that sets standards and loosely oversees the development of the Web. Tim is terrifically smart and hard working and is the nicest guy you would ever want to meet. (Margy met him through Sunday school — is that wholesome or what?)

Tim invented *HTTP* (HyperText Transport Protocol), the way Web browsers communicate with Web servers; *HTML* (HyperText Markup Language), the language in which Web pages are written; and *URLs* (Uniform Resource Locators), the codes used to identify Web pages and most other information on the Net. He envisioned the Web as a way for everyone to both publish and read information on the Net. Early Web browsers had editors that let you create Web pages almost as easily as you could read them.

For more information about the development of the Web and the work of the World Wide Web Consortium, visit its Web site, at www.w3.org. You can also read Tim's book, *Weaving the Web* (HarperSanFrancisco, 1999). Tim was knighted in 2004, so now he's Sir Tim.

Name that page

Before you dive in and hit the Web (boing-g-g, that metaphor needs work), you need one more basic concept. Every Web page has a name attached to it so that browsers, and you, can find it. Great figures in the world of software engineering (well, okay, it was Tim) named this name *URL,* or *Uniform Resource Locator.* Every Web page has a URL, a series of characters that usually begins with http://. (How do you say "URL"? Everyone we know pronounces each letter, *U-R-L* — no one says *earl.*) Now you know enough to go browsing. For more entirely optional details about URLs, see the sidebar, "Duke of URL."

Browsing Off for Points Unknown

It's time to check the Web out for yourself. To do this, you need a *browser,* the software that gets Web pages and displays them on your screen. Fortunately, if you have Windows 95 or later (98, 2000, NT, Me, or XP), any recent Mac, or any computer with Internet access, you probably already have one. Also, one may have come from your Internet service provider (ISP) if you installed its Internet software.

Here are the two most popular browsers:

✔ **Internet Explorer (IE)** is the browser that Microsoft has built into every version of Windows since Windows 98. In fact, Microsoft insists that it's an integral part of Windows itself. (If it is, how can there be a standalone version for the Mac? Hmm.) Microsoft now has versions for Windows and the Mac. IE comes with Outlook Express, Microsoft's e-mail and newsgroup program, which we cover in Chapter 13. The latest version is 6.0, which comes with Windows XP and is available as a free download for Windows 98, Me, and 2000. IE 5.5, which came with Windows Me and 2000, looks a little different but works almost the same. IE 7.0 is due out any minute, and is reported to work similarly to 6.0.

✔ **Firefox** is the latest browser from the open-source Mozilla project at www.mozilla.org. It's related to the Mozilla and Netscape browsers, but Firefox is the latest and greatest. You can download Firefox for free for Windows, Macs, and Linux computers. Firefox runs faster than Internet Explorer and is much, much less susceptible to spyware. See the sidebar "Why you should switch from Internet Explorer to Firefox" for our opinion about whether to use Firefox or Internet Explorer on your computer.

Why you should switch from Internet Explorer to Firefox

Both programs are free and downloadable from the Internet, but beyond that, there are some important differences.

The advantages of Firefox

✔ Firefox runs faster. It's smaller and quicker.

✔ Firefox doesn't use ActiveX controls, a feature of Internet Explorer that spyware uses to infect your computer.

✔ Firefox has a built-in pop-up blocker.

✔ Firefox has some spiffy features like tabbed browser windows that Internet Explorer doesn't.

The advantages of Internet Explorer

✔ Some Web sites (mainly sites run by Microsoft itself) require Internet Explorer, because they use ActiveX controls.

✔ If you use Windows, you've already got Internet Explorer, because it comes bundled with Windows. (Some say that this bundling is illegal because Microsoft promised back in the 1990s not to bundle programs with Windows, but Microsoft won this case in the courts.)

✔ A few add-ins (such as the Google toolbar) work only with Internet Explorer.

Both IE and Firefox work fine for displaying and printing Web pages — don't get us wrong. However, we think that the security issue — avoiding spyware — trumps all other considerations hands down, and we recommend that you install Firefox and use it except for the few Web sites that require Internet Explorer. You can have both browsers installed at the same time — you can even have both running at the same time — so switching to Firefox doesn't mean that you can never use Internet Explorer again.

When you do decide to try Firefox, you can choose Help➪For Internet Explorer Users to see a pageful of helpful information.

We describe both Internet Explorer and Firefox in detail in this book. If you don't have a browser, or you want to try a different one, see the section "Getting and Installing a Browser" later in this chapter.

Surfing with Your Browser

When you start Firefox, you see a screen similar to the one shown earlier in Figure 6-1. The Internet Explorer 6 window looks like the one shown in Figure 6-2. Internet Explorer 5.0 and 5.5 look a little different, but they have almost identical menu choices and toolbar buttons. Which page your browser displays depends on how it's set up. Many ISPs arrange for your browser to display their home pages; otherwise, until you choose a home page of your own, Internet Explorer tends to display a Microsoft page, and Firefox usually shows a Mozilla page.

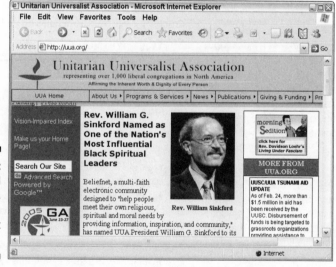

Figure 6-2:
Your typical
Web page,
viewed in
Internet
Explorer 6.

At the top of the window are a bunch of buttons and the Address box, which contains the URL for the current page. Remember that URLs are an important part of Web lore because they're the secret codes that name all the pages on the Web. (For details, see the sidebar, "Duke of URL.")

The main section of the browser window is taken up by the Web page that you're looking it. After all, that's what the browser is *for* — displaying a Web page! The buttons, bars, and menus around the edge help you find your way around the Web and do things like print and save pages.

Duke of URL

Part of the plan of the World Wide Web is to link together all the information in the known universe, starting with all the stuff on the Internet. (This statement may be a slight exaggeration, but not by much.)

One key to global domination is to give everything (at least everything that could be a Web resource) a name so that no matter what a hypertext link refers to, a Web browser can find it and know what to do with it.

Look at this typical URL, the one for the Web page shown in Figure 6-1:

```
http://net.gurus.com/index.phtml
```

The first item in a URL, the letters that appear before the colon, is the *scheme,* which describes the way a browser can get to the resource. Although ten schemes are defined, the most common by far is HTTP, which is the HyperText Transfer Protocol that is the Web's native transfer technique. (Don't confuse HTTP, which is the way pages are sent over the Internet, with HTML, which is the system of formatting codes in Web pages.)

Although the details of the rest of the URL depend on the scheme, most schemes look similar. Following the colon are two slashes (always forward slashes, never backslashes) and the name of the host computer on which the resource lives; in this case, `net.gurus.com` (one of the many names of John's Internet host computer). Then comes another slash and a *path,* which gives the name of the resource on that host; in this case, a file named `index.phtml`.

Web URLs allow a few other optional parts. They can include a *port number,* which specifies, roughly speaking, which of several programs running on that host should handle the

request. The port number goes after a colon after the host name, like this:

```
http://net.gurus.com:80/index.
    phtml
```

The standard `http` port number is 80, so if that's the port you want (it usually is), you can leave it out. Finally, a Web URL can have a *search part* at the end, following a question mark, like this:

```
http://net.gurus.com:80/index.
    phtml?chickens
```

When a URL has a search part, it tells the host computer, uh, what to search for. (You rarely type a search part yourself — they're often constructed for you from fill-in fields on Web pages.)

When you type a URL into your Web browser, you can leave out the `http://` part, because the browser will add it for you. Lazy typists, unite!

Three other useful URL schemes are `mailto`, `ftp`, and `file`. A `mailto` URL looks like this:

```
mailto:internet10@gurus.com
```

That is, a `mailto` link is an e-mail address. Clicking a `mailto` URL runs your mail program and creates a new message addressed to the address in the link. `Mailto` URLs are commonly used for sending comments to the owner of a Web page.

A URL that starts with `ftp` lets you download files from a File Transfer Protocol (FTP) server on the Internet (see Chapter 12). An `ftp` URL looks like this:

```
ftp://ftp.netscape.com/pub/nets
    cape7/english/7.02/windows/
    win32/NSSetup.exe
```

The part after the two slashes is the name of the FTP server (`ftp.netscape.com`, in this case).

The rest of the URL is the pathname of the file you want to download.

The `file` URL specifies a file on your computer. It looks like this:

    file:///C|/www/index.htm

On a Windows or DOS computer, this line indicates a Web page stored in the file `C:\www\index.htm` on your own computer. The colon turns into a vertical bar (because colons in URLs mean something else), and the backslashes turn into forward slashes. File URLs are useful mostly for looking at graphics files with `.gif`, `.png`, and `.jpg` filename extensions and for looking at a Web page you just wrote and saved on your hard drive.

Getting around

You need two simple skills (if we can describe something as basic as a single mouse click as a skill) to get going on the Web. One is to move from page to page on the Web, and the other is to jump directly to a page when you know its URL. (For the latter, see the section, "Going places," later in this chapter.)

Moving from page to page is easy: Click any link that looks interesting. That's it. Underlined blue text and blue-bordered pictures are links. (Although links may be a color other than blue, depending on the look the Web page designer is going for, they are usually underlined or otherwise highlighted.) Anything that looks like a button is probably a link. You can tell when you're pointing to a link because the mouse pointer changes to a little hand. If you're not sure whether something is a link, click it anyway because if it isn't, clicking doesn't hurt anything. Clicking outside a link selects the text you click, as in most other programs. Sometimes, clicking a link moves to you a different place on the same page, rather than a new page.

Backward, ho!

Web browsers remember the last few pages you visited, so if you click a link and decide that you're not so crazy about the new page, you can easily go back to the preceding one. To go back, click the Back or Previous button on the toolbar (its icon is an arrow pointing to the left, and it's the leftmost button on the toolbar) or press Alt+←.

Sometimes, clicking a link opens the new page in a new browser window — your browser (IE or Firefox) can display more than one Web page at the same time, each in its own window. If a link opens a new windows, the Back button does nothing in that window.

Going places

These days, everyone and his dog has a home page. A *home page* is the main Web page for a person or organization. Chapter 17 shows you how to make one for yourself and your dog, children, hobby, or business. Companies advertise their home pages, and people send e-mail talking about cool sites. When you see a URL you want to check out, here's what you do:

1. **Click in the Address box near the top of the browser window.**

2. **Type the URL in the box.**

   The URL is something like `http://net.gurus.com` — you can just type **net.gurus.com**. Be sure to erase the URL that appeared before you started typing.

3. **Press Enter.**

If you receive URLs in electronic mail, instant messages, documents, Usenet newsgroup messages, or anywhere else on your computer, you can use the standard cut-and-paste techniques and avoid retyping:

1. **Highlight the URL in whichever program it appears.**

   That is, use your mouse to select the URL, so that the whole URL is highlighted.

2. **Press Ctrl+C (+C on the Mac) to copy the info to the Clipboard.**

3. **Click in the Address box to highlight whatever is in it.**

4. **Press Ctrl+V (+V on the Mac) to paste the URL into the box, and then press Enter.**

Most e-mail programs highlight URLs in e-mail messages, so that URLs appear in color (usually blue) and underlined. All you have to do is click the link, and your browser pops up and opens the Web page.

Bad guys can easily create mail messages where the URL that you click isn't the URL that you actually visit. Keep this in mind if you get mail that purports to be from your bank — if you click the link and enter your account number and password in the Web page that appears, you may be typing it into a Web site run by crooks rather than by your bank. See the section "Phishing for inphormation" in Chapter 2.

Where's the best place to start browsing?

You find out more about how to find things on the Web in Chapter 8, but for now, here's a good way to get started: Go to the Yahoo! page. (Yes, the name of the Web page includes an exclamation point — it's very excitable. But we leave out the exclamation point throughout the book because we find it annoying.) To get to Yahoo, type this URL in your browser's Address box and then press Enter:

```
www.yahoo.com
```

In the middle of the Yahoo page are links to directories of millions of Web pages by topic. Just nose around, clicking links that look interesting and clicking the Back button on the toolbar when you make a wrong turn. We guarantee that you'll find something interesting.

For updates to the very book you are holding, go to this URL: `net.gurus.com`. Follow the links to the page about our books or about the Internet, and then select the pages for readers of *The Internet For Dummies,* 10th Edition. If we have any late-breaking news about the Internet or updates and corrections to this book, you can find them there. If you find mistakes in this book or have other comments, by the way, please send e-mail to us at `internet10@gurus.com`.

This page looks funny

Sometimes a Web page gets garbled on the way in or you interrupt it (by clicking the Stop button on the toolbar or by pressing the Esc key). You can tell your browser to get the information on the page again: In Firefox, click the Reload button or press Ctrl+R; in Internet Explorer, click the Refresh button or press Ctrl+R or F5.

Get me outta here

Sooner or later, even the most dedicated Web surfer has to stop to eat or attend to other bodily needs. You leave your browser in the same way that you leave any other program: by choosing File⇨Exit (File⇨Close for Windows Internet Explorer) or pressing Alt+F4. You can also click the Close (X) button in the upper-right corner of the window. Or, just leave the program running and walk away from your computer.

Getting and Installing a Browser

With luck, a browser is already installed on your computer. (Microsoft's plan is for Internet Explorer to come preinstalled on every computer in the universe, as far as we can tell, and it's working.) Without luck, you don't have a browser, or you have a very old one that you ought to upgrade if you want to see all the newer features used in Web pages. If you use a version of Internet

Explorer older than 6.0 or Firefox older than 1.0.4, you're missing lots of new features. Fortunately, browser programs aren't difficult to get and install, and most are free.

Even if you already have a browser, new versions come out every 20 minutes or so, and it's worth knowing how to upgrade because occasionally the new versions fix some bugs so that they're better than the old versions. Microsoft gives away Internet Explorer, and the Mozilla project gives away Firefox, so you may as well upgrade to the current version. (One can complain about many aspects of Internet Explorer, but not its price, unless you worry about software monopolies, as do we and many others.)

Getting the program

To get or upgrade Firefox, go to www.mozilla.org. To get or upgrade Internet Explorer, go to www.microsoft.com/ie.

Use your browser to go to the page and then follow the instructions for finding and downloading the program. You may also want to consult Chapter 12 for more information about downloading files from the Internet.

If you're upgrading from an older version of your browser to a newer one, you can replace the old version with the new one. The installation program will be smart enough to remember some of your old settings and bookmarks (favorites).

Running a new browser for the first time

To run your new browser, click the browser's attractive new icon. If you use Windows XP, the default browser also appears at the top of the lefthand column of the Start menu, too.

Firefox asks whether you'd like to import your settings — including your bookmarks and favorites — from another browser program. If you've already been using the Web for a while and have built up a list of your favorite Web sites, take advantage of this opportunity to copy your list into Firefox, so you don't have to search for your favorite sites all over again.

The first time you run Internet Explorer, it may run the Internet or New Connection Wizard, which offers to help you get connected to the Internet. If you want Microsoft's advice on selecting an ISP, which you probably don't, follow the instructions on-screen. If you already have an Internet connection that works, you have a chance to tell it so.

Chapter 7

Taking Your Browser for a Spin

*I*f you've read Chapter 6, you are all set to browse the Web. But to be an efficient, downright clever Internaut, you'll want to know about some other browser features, like printing Web pages, displaying more than one Web page at the same time, and storing the addresses of Web pages that you like to visit often. You also need to know how to handle spyware, an Internet menace that we describe in Chapter 2. This chapter is your guide to these extra features and how you can make the most of them right away.

Saving Stuff from the Web

Frequently, you see something on a Web page that's worth saving for later. Sometimes it's interesting information, a picture or some other type of file, or even the entire Web page. Fortunately, saving stuff is easy.

Saving a Web page

When you save a Web page, you have to decide whether to save only the text that appears or the entire HTML version of the page, including the format codes. (For a glimpse of HTML, see Chapter 17).

If you want to save the Web page you're viewing, follow these steps:

1. **Choose File⇨Save As (in IE) or File⇨Save Page As (in Firefox) to save the current Web page in a file.**

   You see the standard Save As dialog box. (IE 6.0 calls it Save Web Page, but you get the idea.)

2. **Specify the name to save the incoming file as or use the filename that your browser suggests.**

3. **Click the Save as Type drop-down list to determine how to save the page.**

   Choose Text Files to save only the text of the page with little notes where pictures occur. Choose HTML, HTML Files, or Web Page Complete (depending on which browser and version you are using) to save the entire HTML file.

4. **Click the Save button.**

Saving an image

To save an image you see on a Web page, follow these steps:

1. **Right-click the image.**

2. **Choose Save Image As (in Firefox) or Save Picture As (in IE) from the menu that appears.**

3. **In the Save Image or Save Picture dialog box, move to the folder or directory in which you want to save the graphics file, type a filename in the File Name text box, and click the Save button.**

A note about copyright: Contrary to popular belief, almost all Web pages, along with almost everything else on the Internet, are copyrighted by their authors. If you save a Web page or a picture from a Web page, you don't have permission to use it any way you want. Before you reuse the text or pictures in any way, send an e-mail message to the owner of the site. If an address doesn't appear on the page, write for permission to webmaster@domain.com, replacing domain.com with the domain name part of the URL of the Web page. For permission to use information on the http://net.gurus.com/books.phtml page, for example, write to webmaster@gurus.com.

Printing Pages from the Web

For the first year that Web browsers existed, they all had print commands that didn't work. Eventually the programmers realized that normal people (like you) like to read things the old-fashioned way, on paper, from time to time, so now browsers have print commands that work.

To print a page, click the Print button on the toolbar, press Ctrl+P, or choose File➪Print. The browser has to reformat the page to print, which can take awhile, so remember that patience is a virtue. Fortunately, each browser displays a progress window to let you know how it's doing.

 If the page you want to print uses frames (a technique that divides the browser window into subareas that can scroll and update separately), click in the part of the window you want to print before printing. Otherwise, you may get only the outermost frame, which usually has just a title and some buttons.

Filling in Forms

In Web pages, a *form* is a page with boxes you can type in, check boxes you can select, and other clickable stuff that you can use to fill out the form. Then you click a Submit button (or a button with some other name) to send in what you entered. Figure 7-1 shows a typical form.

White boxes in a form are fill-in text boxes in which you type, in this case, your name and e-mail address. Little square boxes are *check boxes,* in which you check whichever ones apply (all of them, we hope, on our sample form). Little round buttons are *radio buttons,* which are similar to check boxes except that you can choose only one of them from each set. In Figure 7-1, you also see a *list box,* in which you can choose one of the possibilities in the box. In most cases, you see more entries than can fit in the box, so you scroll them up and down. Although you can usually choose only one entry, some list boxes let you choose more.

Forms also include buttons that determine what happens to the information you entered into the form. Most forms have two such buttons: one that clears the form fields to their initial state and sends nothing, and one, usually known as the *Submit* button, that sends the filled-out form back to the Web server for processing.

Check boxes   Radio buttons   White boxes

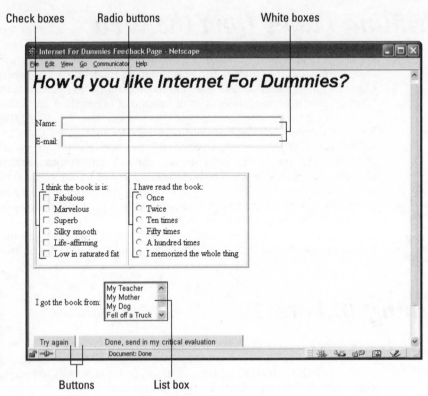

Figure 7-1:
Just fill out
a few forms.

Buttons   List box

Some Web pages have *search boxes,* which are one-line forms that let you type some text for which to search. Depending on the browser, a Submit button may be displayed to the right of the text area, or you may just press Enter to send the search words to the server. For example, the Google search page at www.google.com has a box into which you type a word or phrase; when you press Enter or click the Google Search button, the search begins. (See the next chapter to find out what happens!)

Using Secure Web Pages

When you fill out a form on a Web page, you may need to provide information that you'd prefer to keep private — your credit card number, for example. Not to worry! Browsers can *encrypt* the information you send and receive to and from a *secure Web server.* You can tell when a page is received encrypted from the Web server by a little padlock icon in the middle or right end of the status bar at the bottom of the browser window. If the padlock appears open or doesn't appear at all, the page is not encrypted. If the little lock is locked, encryption is on. To make it clearer, Firefox displays the padlock icon at the right end of the Address box, too, and shows the whole Address box in yellow.

Typed-in data in forms on secure pages are almost always sent encrypted as well, making it impossible for anyone to snoop on your secrets as they pass through the Net. Encrypted pages are nice, but in practice, it's unlikely that anyone is snooping on your Web session anyway, encrypted or otherwise. The real security problems are elsewhere (see Chapter 2).

Firefox and Internet Explorer have the habit of popping up little boxes to warn you about the dangers of what you are about to do. They display a box when you're about to switch from encrypted to nonencrypted (or back again) transmissions. Most of these warning boxes include a check box you can select to tell the program not to bother you with this type of warning again. Once you've read the warning, select the check box so that your browser can stop nagging you.

Letting Your Browser Keep Track of Your Passwords

Lots of Web sites ask you to enter a username and password. For instance, if you're buying something from an online store like Amazon.com, you create an account with a username and password that you enter each time you want to make a purchase. If you want to read *The New York Times* online at `http://nytimes.com`, you create an account with a password, too. (Accounts are free as of spring 2005, but this may change.) After you've used the Web for a while, you've probably piled up a heap of usernames and passwords. Who can remember them?

Firefox and Internet Explorer offer to remember your usernames and passwords for you. Using this feature can be dangerous if other people use your computer or if you use a computer in a public place, like a library or an Internet café. But if you are the only person who uses your computer, you may want to let your browser do the work of remembering some, if not all, of your usernames and passwords.

When you get to a Web page that asks for a username and password, your browser may pop up a little window offering to remember the username and password that you enter, as shown in Figure 7-2. If you click Yes, the next time you arrive at the same page, IE automagically types your password as soon as you type your username. Firefox enters both your username and password for you.

Figure 7-2:
Your
browser can
store your
Web site
passwords
for you.

You can control whether and how your browser stores these passwords. In Firefox, follow these steps:

1. **Choose Tools➪Options.**

   You see the Options dialog box, with a list of the categories of options down the left side.

2. **Click the Privacy category.**

3. **Click the Saved Passwords option.**

   Here you find the following options:

   • Select the Remember Password check box to clear the check mark if you want to turn this feature off (or click it again to turn it back on).

   • Click the View Saved Passwords button to review or delete usernames and passwords that Firefox is remembering for you.

   • Click the Set Master Password button to set a master password that you'll need to type only once, at the beginning of each Firefox session. (This option reduces the number of passwords you need to remember, while maintaining some security.)

4. **Click OK to exit the Options dialog box.**

In IE, remembering usernames and passwords is the job of the AutoComplete feature, which you set up by following these simple steps:

1. **Choose Tools➪Internet Options.**

   You see the Internet Options dialog box.

2. **Click the Content tab.**

   This tab contains sections for the IE Content Advisor (which can censor Internet pages for your kids), Certificates (which are used for secure Web pages), and Personal Information.

3. **In the Personal Information section, click the AutoComplete button.**

   You see the AutoComplete Settings dialog box.

4. **Click the check boxes to control what kinds of entries IE stores: web addresses, form entries, usernames, and passwords.**

   IE won't show you a list of the passwords you've saved, but you can turn the feature on and off by selecting the Prompt Me to Save Passwords check box.

5. **Click OK to exit the AutoComplete Settings dialog box, and OK again to exit the Internet Options dialog box.**

We let our browsers remember only passwords to accounts that don't involve spending money or revealing personal information. For example, if we have an account at a Harry Potter fan site that enables us to participate in online discussions, the danger of having someone break into this account is a lot less daunting than the thought of someone hacking into an online banking account. Don't let your browser remember passwords that have any real power.

Viewing Lots of Web Pages at the Same Time

Internet Explorer and Firefox can display several pages at once — a feature we love. When we're pointing and clicking from one place to another, we like to open a bunch of windows so that we can see where we've been and go back to a previous page just by switching to another window. Better yet, Firefox can display lots of Web pages in one window, by using tabs (explained in the section "Tab dancing" later in this chapter).You can also arrange windows side by side, which is a good way to, say, compare prices for *The Internet For Dummies,* 10th Edition, at various online bookstores. (The difference may be small, but when you're buying 100 copies for everyone on your Christmas list, those pennies can add up. Oh, you weren't planning to do that? Drat.)

Wild window mania

To display a page in a new Internet Explorer or Firefox window, click a link with the right mouse button and choose Open in New Window (or Open Link in New Window) from the menu that pops up. To close a window, click the Close (X) button at the top right of the window frame, or press Alt+F4, the standard close-window shortcut. Macs don't have a right mouse button, so hold down the button you use to get contextual menus (the default is the Control key). You close all Mac windows the same way — by clicking the button at the top left of the window. Users with three-button mice can open a link in a new window by clicking the middle button.

Short attention span tips

If you have a slow Internet connection, use at least two browser tabs or windows at the same time. While you're waiting for the next page to arrive in one tab or window, you can read the page that arrived a while ago in the other tab or window.

If you ask your browser to begin downloading a big file, it displays a small window in the corner of your screen. Internet Explorer and Firefox display a "thermometer" showing the download progress; Internet Explorer also shows tiny pages flying from one folder to another. Although some people consider watching the thermometer grow or the pages fly sufficiently entertaining (we do when we're tired enough), you can click back to the main browser window and continue surfing.

Warning: Doing two or three things at a time in your browser when you have a dialup Net connection is not unlike squeezing blood from a turnip — only so much blood can be squeezed. In this case, the blood is the amount of data your computer can pump through your modem. A single download task can keep your net connection close to 100 percent busy, and anything else you do shares the connection with the download process. When you do two things at a time, therefore, each one happens more slowly than it would by itself.

If one task is a big download and the other is perusing Web pages, everything usually works okay because you spend a fair amount of time looking at what the browser is displaying; the download can then run while you think. On the other hand, although browsers let you start two download tasks at a time (or a dozen, if you're so inclined), it's not much faster to do more than one at a time than one after another, and it can get confusing.

Some people hardly ever exit from their browsers, which probably isn't a good idea for their long-term mental stability. (Naturally, we're not talking abut anyone *we* know! Definitely not.) If you are such a person, however, remember that your browser *caches* pages — that is, your browser stores the pages temporarily on your hard disk for quick retrieval. Cached pages aren't normally reloaded from the Web (they're taken from your hard drive) until you reload them. For instance, if you are watching the page for an eBay auction that you have bid on (see Chapter 10 for how eBay works), someone might outbid you because you are looking at the version of the auction page that you loaded a few minutes ago, not a live page. If you want to make sure that you're seeing an up-to-date version of a page, reload it. Your browser is supposed to check whether a saved page has changed, but because the check sometimes doesn't work perfectly, we advise using an occasional Reload or Refresh command for pages that change frequently, such as stock prices or the weather report. Click the Reload or Refresh button on your browser's toolbar or press Ctrl+R.

You can also create a new window without following a link. Press Ctrl+N or choose File⇨New Window (in Firefox) or File⇨New⇨Window (in Internet Explorer). UNIX and Mac users should think "Alt" and "Apple" for "Ctrl" throughout this section.

Tab dancing

Firefox, like Netscape and Mozilla before it, has *tabs,* which are multiple pages that you can switch among in a window. Figure 7-3 shows a Firefox window with three tabs. Just click any of the tabs near the top of the window to show the different pages — the tabs are just above the top edge of the Web page, and below the browser's menu and toolbar(s). Choose File⇨New Tab or press Ctrl+T to make a new empty tab. Click the X at the right end to get rid of the current tab. As with multiple windows, you can have one tab loading in the background while you're reading another tab, and little rotating arrows in the tab bar show you which ones are loading and which are ready. For most purposes, we find tabs more convenient than windows. You can use both; if you open several windows in Firefox, each window can have several tabs.

Tabs

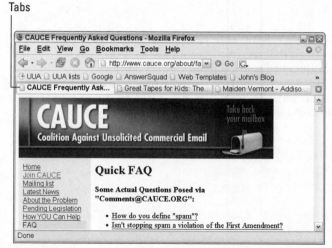

Figure 7-3:
A Firefox window with three tabs.

A Few of Your Favorite Things

The Web really does have cool places to visit. Some you will want to visit over and over again. (We've each visited the Google Web site thousands of times by now.) The makers of fine browsers have, fortunately, provided a handy way for you to remember those spots and not have to write down those nasty URLs just to have to type them again later.

Although the name varies, the idea is simple: Your browser lets you mark a Web page and adds its URL to a list. Later, when you want to go back, you just go to your list and pick the page you want. Firefox calls these saved Web addresses *bookmarks;* Internet Explorer calls them *favorites.*

Bookmarking with Firefox

Firefox has a Bookmarks choice on its menu that displays your current list of bookmarks. To bookmark a Web page — that is, to add the address of the page to your bookmarks — choose Bookmarks⇨Bookmark this Page, or press Ctrl+D, or drag the little icon at the left end of the Address box up to the Bookmarks menu item.

After you create a bookmark, it appears as an entry on the menu that you see when you choose Bookmarks on the menu bar. To go to one of the pages on your bookmark list, just choose its entry from the menu.

If you're like most users, your bookmark menu gets bigger and bigger and crawls down your screen and eventually ends up flopping down on the floor, which is both unattractive and unsanitary. Fortunately, you can smoosh (technical term) your menu into a more tractable form. Choose Bookmarks⇨ Manage Bookmarks or press Ctrl+B to display your Bookmarks window (as shown in Figure 7-4).

Figure 7-4:
The Firefox
Bookmarks
window
includes
commands
for moving,
editing, and
deleting
bookmarks.

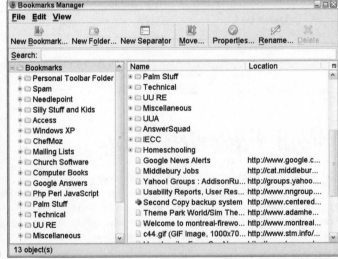

Because all these bookmarks are "live," you can go to any of them by double-clicking them. (You can leave this window open while you move around the Web in other browser windows.) You can also add separator lines and submenus to organize your bookmarks and make the individual menus less unwieldy. Submenus look like folders in the Bookmarks window.

In the Bookmarks window, click the New Separator button to add a separator line and the New Folder button to add a new submenu. After you create a folder, you can drag bookmarks, separators, and folders up and down to where you want them in the Bookmarks window. Drag an item to a folder to put it in that folder's submenu, and double-click a folder to display or hide that submenu. Because any changes you make in the Bookmarks window are reflected immediately on the Bookmarks menu, it's easy to fiddle with the bookmarks until you get them arranged as you like. Firefox starts out your bookmarks with pages the Firefox developers would like you to look at, but feel free to delete them if your tastes are different from theirs.

When you're done fooling with your bookmarks, choose File⇨Close or press Ctrl+W to close the Bookmarks window.

One-click bookmarks in Firefox

The Bookmarks toolbar is a row of buttons that usually appears just below the Address box. (If it isn't there, choose View⇨Toolbars⇨Bookmarks Toolbar to display it.) This row of buttons gives you one-button access to a bunch of Firefox developers' favorite Web sites. Wouldn't it be nice if your favorite Web sites appeared there instead? No problem! When you organize your bookmarks in the Bookmarks window, stick your top favorite sites in the Personal Toolbar Folder — any sites in this folder automagically appear on the Bookmarks toolbar. You can even add folders with bookmarks in them. We love this Firefox feature.

Storing favorites with IE

Internet Explorer uses a URL-saving system similar to Firefox's, although it calls the saved URLs *favorites* rather than bookmarks: You can add the current page to your Favorites folder and then look at and organize your Favorites folder. If you use Windows, this Favorites folder is shared with other programs on your computer. Other programs also can add things to your Favorites folder, so it's a jumble of Web pages, files, and other things. (Luckily, most people use favorites only for Web pages.)

To add the address of the current page to your Favorites folder, choose Favorites⇨Add to Favorites from the menu. The Add Favorite dialog box, shown in Figure 7-5, asks whether you want to be able to see the page when you are *offline* (that is, not connected to the Internet) — select this check box if you want to save the page on your computer's hard drive. (We usually don't.) Click the Create In button if you want to put the new favorite into a folder so that it appears in a submenu of your Favorites menu.

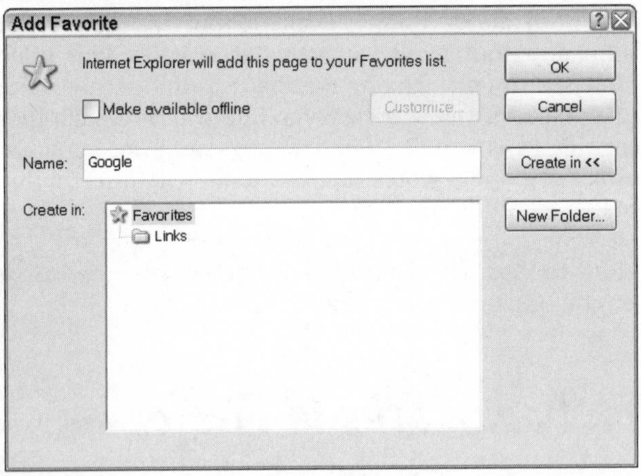

Figure 7-5:
Adding a Web page to your Internet Explorer favorites.

Internet Explorer has a Favorites button on the toolbar that displays your list of favorites down the left side of your Internet Explorer window — this list is called the *Favorites Explorer Bar* (there's a name for everything!). Click the Favorites button again to make the list go away. You can also press Ctrl+I to display or banish the Favorites Explorer Bar. When the list of favorites appears, click a favorite to go to it. Another way to go back to a Web site on your favorites list is to choose Favorites from the menu: Your favorites are at the bottom of the menu that appears.

If you want to reorganize your Favorites folder, choose Favorites⇨Organize Favorites. The Organize Favorites window lets you create folders for your favorites, move favorites around, edit them, and delete them. To see what's in a folder, click it. When you're done organizing your favorite items, click Close. You can also drag around favorites and folders directly on the Favorites Explorer Bar.

The folders you create in the Organize Favorites window appear on your Favorites menu, and the items you put in the folders appear on submenus. To return to a Web page you've added to your Favorites folder, just choose it from the Favorites menu.

In Internet Explorer 5.0 and up, you can make pages available when you're not connected to the Internet. In the Organize Favorites window, click the page and mark the Make Available Offline check box. Internet Explorer immediately fetches the page to your hard drive and refetches it from time to time when you're connected so that you can view the page when you click it while you're offline.

If you make a lot of pages available offline, your browser will spend a lot of time keeping them up to date. When you no longer need to browse a page offline, return to the Organize Favorites window and deselect the Make Available Offline check box or remove the page from your favorites altogether. We've found the offline pages system to be somewhat unstable. We would suggest using offline pages only if you are limited to going online once or a few times a day.

One-click bookmarks in Internet Explorer

Have you noticed the Links toolbar that usually appears just below or to the right of the Address box? (If it isn't there, choose View➪Toolbars➪Links to display it.) You might never want to visit any of the sites that appear by default on this toolbar, but you can put your favorite Web sites there instead! When you organize your favorites, drag your top favorite sites and folders into the Links folder — any sites in the Links folder automagically appear on the Links toolbar. Delete any sites in the Links folder that aren't your favorites. This feature is seriously handy for Web sites you visit often.

Customizing Your Browser

If you become a serious Internet user, you'll probably spend way, way too much time in front of your Web browser. To make your browsing experience as fun and efficient as possible, you can customize your browser to work the way you like.

Where do we start?

When you run your browser, it displays your _start page_. Firefox usually starts on a Mozilla Web page, and IE usually starts on a Microsoft page. But why not tell your browser to start where _you_ want to start?

In Firefox: When Firefox starts up, by default it loads the Firefox home page. After one or two times, beautiful though the page is, you will probably find that you can do without it. You can tell Firefox not to load any Web page, or a different page, when you start the program:

1. Choose Tools⇨Options.

You see the Options dialog box, as shown in Figure 7-6.

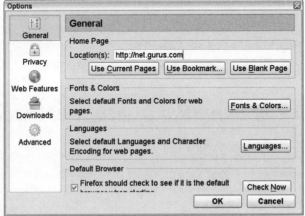

Figure 7-6:
The Options dialog box is where you can configure Firefox to start with your favorite Web site.

2. Click the General category icon in the upper left corner of the window, if it isn't already selected.

This category may already be selected, and its settings appear in the rest of the Options dialog box. The first setting is called Home Page — the Web page that Firefox displays on startup. (We think it ought to be called "Start Page," but no one asked us.)

3. To start with no page, click the Use Blank Page button.

To choose a page to start with, type the URL of a page into the Location(s) text box (how about `http://net.gurus.com`, which is our page?). To make the current page your home page, click (you guessed it!) the Use Current Pages button.

4. Click OK.

You can set Firefox to display a whole set of your favorite pages when it starts up, each on a separate tab. For example, you might want to have Firefox open a weather-reporting page (like Weather Underground at `www.wunderground.com`), the *New York Times* (`www.nytimes.com`), and Google (`www.google.com`)

each time you start Firefox. First, display the Web pages that you'd like to start with. Then choose Tools⇨Options, click General, and click Use Current Pages. Now starting Firefox (or clicking the Home button on its toolbar) opens all the pages you've currently got open.

In Internet Explorer: Internet Explorer usually starts by displaying the MSN home page or a Web page stored on your own hard drive, depending on which version of Internet Explorer you have. You can change that start page, or you can tell Internet Explorer to load a blank page. (Loading a home page from your hard drive is pretty fast, so we do that in preference to a blank page.) Follow these steps to change your start page:

1. **Display the Web page you want to use as your start page.**

   For example, you may want to start at the Yahoo page (www.yahoo.com), which we describe in Chapter 6; or Google (www.google.com); or our own Internet Gurus Central site at http://net.gurus.com.

2. **Choose Tools⇨Internet Options or View⇨Internet Options from the menu.**

   Which command you use depends on your version of Internet Explorer; use whichever appears on your menus. You see the Internet Options dialog box, as shown in Figure 7-7.

Figure 7-7:
The Internet Options dialog box has settings for Internet Explorer, including which Web page to display on startup.

3. **Click the General tab along the top of the dialog box.**

   Actually, it's probably already selected, but we say this in case you've been looking around at what's on the other tabs.

4. **In the Home Page section of the dialog box, click the Use Current button.**

   The URL of the current page appears in the Address text box. To start with no page at all, click the Use Blank button.

5. **Click OK.**

Choose a start page that doesn't have many pictures: By starting with a Web page that loads faster or with no start page, you don't have to wait long to start browsing.

Customizing your toolbar

The toolbar is the row of little icons just below your browser's menu bar (the line that says "File, Edit, View," and so forth). Browsers come with a suggested set of greatest-hits toolbar buttons, but you may find that you never use certain buttons, but you wish certain commands had toolbar buttons. You can customize your toolbar to include buttons for the commands you use the most.

To customize either the IE or Firefox toolbar (or the toolbar of many other programs, for that matter), right-click the toolbar anywhere except on the Back and Forward icons (the left- and right-pointing arrows, usually the two leftmost icons on the toolbar). Choose Customize from the menu that appears. You see a Customize Toolbar dialog box.

In Firefox, you can add a button to the toolbar by finding it in the Customize Toolbar dialog box and dragging it to the toolbar. To get rid of a toolbar button, drag the button back to the dialog box. Click Done when you're finished.

In IE, the Customize Toolbar dialog box shows two lists of buttons: all available buttons, and the buttons that are currently on your toolbar. Select a button from the Available Toolbar Buttons list and click Add to put it on your toolbar. Select a button from the Current Toolbar Buttons list and click Remove to get rid of it. Click Close when you're done.

If someone else uses your browser and your browser window ends up looking like worse for wear, you can easily put it back to normal:

✔ **If the whole top of the window is gone** — you have no window title bar or menu bar — you are in full screen mode. Press F11 to return to normal.

✔ **If some of your toolbars are missing,** choose View⇨Toolbars. If a check mark doesn't appear to the left of one of the toolbars, choose it to put a check mark back in front of it and to redisplay that window component. In IE, the toolbars are Standard Buttons, Address Bar, and Links. In Firefox, they are Navigation Toolbar and Bookmarks Toolbar.

✔ **If the buttons on your toolbar aren't the buttons you are used to,** right-click the toolbar anywhere except on the Back and Forward icons and choose Customize from the menu that appears. Click Reset (in IE) or Restore Default Set (in Firefox) and Close or Done.

✔ **If your browser, particularly IE, still looks strange,** especially if it's showing a lot of ads that you didn't ask for, your computer is probably infected with spyware. See Chapter 2 for a definition of spyware, and the section "Detecting spyware" in Chapter 4 for advice on getting rid of it.

Erasing history

Both IE and Firefox keep a *history list* of the Web sites you've been. No, your browser isn't spying on you; the history list remembers pages you went to earlier, even days ago, so you can find them again. Choose Go⇨History (in Firefox) or View⇨Explorer Bar⇨History (in IE) to see your history list. The list of sites you've visited appears on the left side of your browser window, arranged by day. Close the history list by clicking the X in its upper-right corner.

Your browser also uses the history list to provide a drop-down list of URLs that you've typed in. At the right end of the Address box is a little down-pointing arrow. When you click it, a list of recently visited URLs drops down. Some of our readers have asked us how to clear out that box, presumably because they meant to type www.disney.com, but their fingers slipped, and it came out www.hot-xxx-babes.com instead. (It could happen to anyone.) Because some of the requests sounded fairly urgent, here are the gruesome details:

✔ **In Firefox,** choose Tool⇨Options, click Privacy and click History. You can enter a number of days for Firefox to remember your Web sites, and you can click Clear to tell it to erase the current contents of the history list.

✔ **In IE,** choose Tools (or View)⇨Internet Options and click the General tab if it's not already selected. The History section of the Internet Options dialog box includes a box where you can type the number of days to keep the list of Web sites you've viewed. You can also find a Clear History button.

Controlling Cookies

To enhance your online experience, browser makers invented a type of special message that lets a Web site recognize you when you revisit that site. They thoughtfully store this info, called a *cookie,* on your very own machine. See "Cookies aren't so bad" in Chapter 2 for a full description of cookies, and how they compare to more serious security threats.

Luckily, both Firefox and IE provide ways that you can control which sites can store cookies on your computer. There are two ways that sites can set cookies:

- **First-party cookies:** These cookies come directly from the same server as the Web page you are viewing. These cookies are typically used to remember you if you signed up as a site member. The convenience is in not having to reenter your username and password every time.

- **Third-party cookies:** Many Web sites use specialty companies that deliver advertisements to their Web pages for them, and these third-party advertisements usually place cookies on your machine with the aim of gathering marketing data. Third-party cookies are useful only to the advertising companies, so we see no reason ever to accept them.

Controlling cookies in Firefox

Choose Tools⇨Options, click the Privacy category, and click Cookies. The options are shown in Figure 7-8:

- **Allow sites to set cookies:** Some sites won't work at all without cookies, including chat sites like Yahoo Groups (`groups.yahoo.com`).

- **For the originating web site only:** That is, accept first-party cookies but reject third-party. This is the setting we use.

- **Exceptions:** You can specify sites from which you want to block cookies, allow session cookies, or allow all cookies. Click Exceptions, type the Web address, and click Block, Allow for Session, or Allow.

- **View Cookies:** You can see a list of the cookies that Firefox has stored, along with the sites they came from and the data they contain. Most cookie values are unreadable codes. You can delete any cookies you don't like the looks of.

- **Keep cookies:** You can tell Firefox how long to store cookies on your computer: Until they expire (the usual setting), Until I close Firefox, or Ask me every time (too annoying to consider).

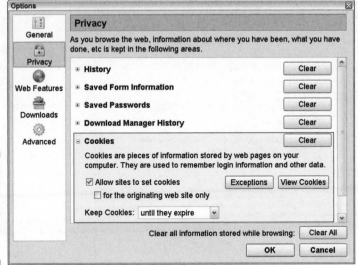

Figure 7-8:
Keeping
cookies
under
control in
Firefox.

Controlling cookies in IE

Use the Tools➪Internet Options command to display the Internet Options
dialog box. The cookie controls are on the Privacy tab (shown in Figure 7-9),
so click it. By default, Internet Explorer 6.0 manages cookies rather aggres-
sively, allowing cookies from the server you contacted, but not from *third-
party servers* (that is, ones other than the one that provided the page you're
viewing). Third-party servers usually deliver advertisements and those
annoying popup and pop-under ads. You can elect to manage them yourself
by clicking the Advanced button to see the Advanced Privacy Settings dialog
box, and then clicking the Override Automatic Cookie Handling check box.
The options are

- **First-party cookies:** You can choose to accept, block, or be prompted
  to choose, although this option gets tiresome very quickly if you
  encounter a lot of cookies. Some sites can store three or more cookies
  per page.

- **Third-party cookies:** Just say no to (that is, choose to block) third-party
  cookies.

- **Always allow session cookies:** This option lets all session cookies through;
  a session cookie is a type of cookie used to track a single instance of your
  visit to a Web site. These cookies are commonly used by shopping sites
  such as Amazon.com.

Figure 7-9:
Keeping
cookies
under
control in
Internet
Explorer.

If you use an old version of Internet Explorer (version 5.0 or 5.5), the cookie feature works a little differently. Use the Tools⇨Internet Options command to display the Internet Options dialog box. The cookie controls are on the Security tab, so click it. Click the Internet Web Content Zone (the colored globe) and then click the Custom Level button to see the Security Settings dialog box. Scroll down the list until you come to the Cookies section. You see two settings:

✔ **Allow cookies that are stored on your computer:** Some cookies are stored on your computer so that if you come back to the Web site tomorrow, the site can remember information about you. ("Welcome back, Tom! Here are your book recommendations for today.") You can turn these off (Disable), turn them on (Enable), or tell IE to ask you before storing each cookie (Prompt).

✔ **Allow per-session cookies (not stored):** Some cookies are stored only until you exit from Internet Explorer. For example, shopping cart systems (Web server programs that let you shop at a Web site and then "check out") may store temporarily information about what items you want to buy. You can choose Disable, Enable, or Prompt.

Blocking Popup Windows

Popup windows, as described in Chapter 2, are browser windows that open without you asking for them, usually at the command of the Web site you are viewing. Some Web sites display so many popups that your computer become unusable until you can close them all. If you've encountered these sites, you'll be glad to hear both Firefox and IE can block most (though not all) popup and pop-under windows.

No popups in Firefox

In Firefox, choose Tools⇨Options to open the Options window, click the Web Features category, and you'll see an option to block popup windows. (We leave it selected.)

Blocking all popups makes a few Web sites stop working. In particular, some shopping sites pop up small windows into which you have to type credit card verification information. Firefox thoughtfully includes an Allowed Sites button where you can specify Web sites whose popups are okay with you.

When a Web site tries to display a popup, you see a message at the top of the Web page, saying, "Firefox prevented this site from opening a popup window. Click here for options." If you want the popup, click the message and choose from the menu that appears:

- ✔ **Allow popups from *sitename*** puts this site on your Allowed list.

- ✔ **Enable Popup Blocker Options** displays the Allowed Sites dialog box so you can edit your list of sites.

- ✔ **Don't show this message when popups are blocked.** Instead, it will show a little red X in the lower-right corner of the Firefox window that you can click to see the popup options.

- ✔ **Show *address of popup window*** displays the popup that was just blocked, but keeps blocking other popups from this site.

Click the red X at the right end of the message to make the message go away.

Unfortunately, as quickly as browser makers add popup blockers, Web site creators come up with new ways to spawn popups. If you still see too many popups for your tastes, consider installing the free Adblock Firefox extension. Go to `www.mozilla.org/products/firefox` and click the Firefox Extensions link. (They keep redesigning this page, so we can't tell you exactly where it will be.) Look for the Adblock extension. When you find its page, click the Install Now link to download and install it into Firefox.

Blocking popups in IE

What about Internet Explorer? Microsoft finally added a popup blocker in response to Firefox's growing popularity. If you keep your Windows installation up-to-date with Windows Update, your IE includes the popup blocker. If not, go to `windowsupdate.microsoft.com` to get the latest version of IE.

IE's popup blocker also displays a message at the top of the Web page whenever it blocks a popup window, and clicking the message displays a similar set of options. You can tweak your popup blocking options any time by choosing Tools⇨Internet Options, clicking the Privacy tab, and looking at the Pop-up Blocker section at the bottom of the dialog box. The Block pop-ups check box controls whether the feature is enabled, and the Settings button shows the list of sites that are allowed to display popups.

Getting Plugged In with Plug-Ins

Web pages with pictures are old hat. Now, Web pages have to have pictures that sing and dance or ticker-style messages that move across the page, or they have to be able to play a good game of chess with you. Every month, new types of information appear on the Web, and browsers have to keep up. You can extend your browser's capabilities with *plug-ins* — add-on programs that glue themselves to the browser and add even more features. Internet Explorer can also extend itself by using things called *ActiveX* controls, which are another type of add-on program.

What're you to do when your browser encounters new kinds of information on a Web page? Get the plug-in program that handles that kind of information and glue it onto the browser program. *Star Trek* fans can think of plug-ins as friendly parasitic life forms that attach themselves to your browser and enhance its intelligence.

A parade of plug-ins

Here are just a few of the useful plug-ins out there:

- ✔ **Flash Player:** Plays both audio and video files as well as other types of animations. Widely used on Web pages. It's available at `http://macromedia.com/software/flashplayer`.

- ✔ **RealPlayer:** Plays *streaming* sound and video files while you download them. (Other programs have to wait until the entire file has downloaded before beginning to play.) A free player is available at `www.real.com`, along with more powerful players that cost money. You may have to browse around to find the free player, but the other players are also a good value (most cost less than $30). Real.com provides a list of sites that handle RealAudio sound files. Our favorite site is the National Public Radio Web site (`www.npr.org`), where you can hear recent NPR radio stories. Another favorite is the BBC at `www.bbc.co.uk` with news in 43 languages (really) and other BBC programs 24 hours a day.

- ✔ **QuickTime:** Plays video files as you download them. Available at `www.apple.com/quicktime/download`.

- ✔ **Adobe Acrobat:** Displays Acrobat files formatted exactly the way the author intended. Lots of useful Acrobat files are out there, including many U.S. tax forms (at `www.irs.ustreas.gov`). You can find Acrobat at `www.adobe.com` (or more precisely, at `www.adobe.com/products/acrobat/readstep.html` if you don't mind some extra typing).

How to use plug-ins

After you download a plug-in from the Net, run it (double-click its icon, or its filename in My Computer or Windows Explorer) to install it. Depending on what the plug-in does, you follow different steps to try it out — usually, you find a file that the plug-in can play and watch (or listen) as the plug-in plays it.

After you install the plug-in, you don't have to do anything to run it. The plug-in fires up automatically when you view a Web page that contains information that requires the plug-in.

Chapter 8

Needles and Haystacks: Finding Almost Anything on the Net

*O*kay, all this great stuff is out there on the Internet. How do I find it?" That's an excellent question and thanks for asking. Questions like that are what make this country strong and vibrant. We salute you and say, "Keep asking questions!" Next question, please.

Oh, you want an *answer* to your question. Fortunately, quite a bit of (technical term follows) stuff-finding stuff is on the Web. More particularly, free services called *search engines* and *directories* are available that cover most of the interesting material on the Web. There's even a free encyclopedia (more about that later in the chapter).

You can search in dozens or hundreds of different ways, depending on what you're looking for and how you prefer to search. (John has remarked that his ideal restaurant has only one item on the menu, but it's exactly what he wants. The Internet is about as far from that ideal as you can possibly imagine.)

To provide a smidgen of structure to this discussion, we describe several different sorts of searches:

✔ **Topics:** Places, things, ideas, companies — anything you want to find out more about

✔ **Built-in searches:** Topic searches that a browser does automatically, and why we're not always thrilled about that

✔ **People:** Actual human beings whom you may want to contact, find out more about, or spy on

✔ **Goods and services:** Stuff to buy or find out about, from mortgages to mouthwash

---

Search engine, directory — what's the difference?

When we talk about a *directory,* we mean a listing like an encyclopedia or a library's card catalog. (Well, like the computer system that *replaced* the card catalog.) It has named categories with entries assigned to them (partly or entirely) by human catalogers. You look things up by finding a category that you want and seeing what it contains. In this book, we think of the table of contents as a directory.

A s*earch engine,* on the other hand, periodically looks at every page it can find on the Internet, extracts keywords from them (by taking all the words except for *the, and,* and the like), and makes a big list. (Yes, that takes a lot of computers — and one search engine company, Google, owns over 100,000.) They then try to figure out which pages are most important (using factors such as how many other sites link to that page), and give each page a score. You use the search engine by specifying some words that

seem likely, and it finds all the entries that contain that word, ranking them by their score.

We think of the index in the back of the book as a hard-copy equivalent of a search engine; it has its advantages and disadvantages, as do directories (which are more like this book's table of contents). Directories are organized better, but search engines are easier to use and more comprehensive. Directories use consistent terminology, while search engines use whatever terms the underlying Web pages use. Directories contain fewer useless pages, but search engines are updated more often.

Some overlap exists between search engines and directories — Yahoo, the best-known Web-page directory, now includes a search engine; Google, which is mainly a search engine, includes a version of the Open Directory Project (ODP) directory.

To find topics, we use the various online search engines and directories, such as Google and Yahoo. To find people, however, we use directories of people — and those are (fortunately) different from directories of Web pages. Wondering what we're talking about? Read on!

Your Basic Search Strategy

When we look for topics on the Net, we always begin with a search engine, usually Google. (The word "google" has now been verbed, much to the dismay of Google's trademark lawyers.)

You use all search engines in more or less the same way:

1. **Start your Web browser, such as Firefox or Internet Explorer.**

2. Go to your favorite search engine's home page.

Many browsers now have search boxes that you can set to your favorite search engine. If not, tell your browser to go to the search engine's home page. You can try one of these URLs (Web addresses): `www.google.com`, `www.yahoo.com`, or `dmoz.org`. We list the URLs of other search sites later in this section.

3. Type some likely keywords in the Search box and click Search.

After a delay (usually brief, but after all, the Web *is* pretty big), the search engine returns a page with some links to pages that it thinks match your keywords. The full list of links that match your keywords may be way too long to deal with — say, 300,000 of them — but the search engine tries to put them in some reasonable order and lets you look at them a screen-full at a time.

4. Adjust and repeat your search until you find something you like.

One trick is to pick keywords that get at your topic from two or three different directions, like `ethopian restaurants trumansburg` or `war women song`. After some clicking around to get the hang of it, you find all sorts of good stuff.

5. If the search engine is producing results too scattered to be useful, and you can't think of any better keywords, try one of the directories: `dmoz.org` or `www.yahoo.com`.

When you see a list of links to topic areas, click a topic area of interest. In the "directory" approach, you begin at a general topic and get more and more specific. Each page has links to pages that get more and more specific until they link to actual pages that are likely to be of interest.

The lazy searcher's search page

You may feel a wee bit overwhelmed with all the search directories and search engines we discuss in this chapter. If it makes you feel any better, so do we.

To make a little sense of all this stuff, we made ourselves a search page that connects to all the directories and search engines we use — call it one-stop searching. You can use it, too. Give it a try at `net.gurus.com/search`.

In the not unlikely event that new search systems are created or some of the existing ones have moved or died, this page gives you our latest greatest list and lets you sign up for mailed updates when we change it.

Doing a Search-a-Roo

Once upon a time in an Internet far, far away, lots of search engines and directories all battled with each other to see which would be the favorite. There were Altavista and Dogpile and lots of other sites you can find in earlier editions of this book. Well, it seems that the first pan-galactic search war is pretty much over, with Google and Yahoo the victors — at least for now. However, Microsoft is trying to mount a new campaign and a new challenge is coming from the open source world, particularly the Open Directory Project and Wikipedia, the online encyclopedia. Visit `net.gurus.com/search` for all the exciting developments.

Google-oogle, our favorite search engine

Our favorite Web search engine is Google. It has little robots that spend their time merrily visiting Web pages all over the Net and reporting what they see. It makes a humongous index of which words occurred in which pages; when you search for something, it picks pages from the index that contain the words you asked for. Google uses a sophisticated ranking system, based on how many *other* Web sites refer to each one in the index; more often than not, Google's ranking puts the best pages first.

Using Google or any other search engine is an exercise in remote-control mind reading. You have to guess words that will appear on the pages you're looking for. Sometimes, that's easy — if you're looking for recipes for Key lime pie, `key lime pie` is a good set of search words because you know the name of what you're looking for. On the other hand, if you have forgotten that the capital of France is Paris, it's hard to tease a useful page out of a search engine because you don't know what words to look for. (If you try `France capital`, you find info about investment banking and Fort de France, which

---

The Number One reason a search doesn't find anything

Well, it may not be *your* Number One reason, but it's *our* Number One reason: One of the search words is spelled wrong or mistyped. John notes that his fingers insist on typing "Interent," which doesn't find much — other than Web pages from other people who can't spell or type. Google often catches spelling mistakes and helpfully suggests an alternative. We sometimes use a Google search to check the preferred spelling of words that haven't made it into the dictionary yet. (Thanks to our friend Jean Armour Polly, for reminding us about this problem.)

is the capital of the French overseas département of Martinique. If you use Google, though, it takes pity on you and tells you at the top: "Capital: Paris.")

Now that we have you all discouraged, try some Google searches. Direct your browser to www.google.com. You see a screen like the one shown in Figure 8-1.

Figure 8-1:
Google,
ready to roll.
(It was
National
Teacher's
Day.)

Type some search terms, and Google finds the pages that best match your terms. That's "*best* match," not "match" — if it can't match all the terms, it finds pages that match as well as possible. Google ignores words that occur too often to be usable as index terms, both the obvious (ones such as and, the, and of) and merely routine (terms such as internet and mail). These rules can sound somewhat discouraging, but in fact it's still not hard to get useful results from Google. You just have to think up good search terms. Try that recipe example by typing **key lime pie** and clicking the Search button. You get the response shown in Figure 8-2.

Your results won't look exactly like Figure 8-2 because Google will have updated its database since this book went to press. Most of the pages it found do, in fact, have something to do with Key lime pie — some have pretty good recipes. Google says it found 371,000 matches (yow!) but it takes pity on you and only will show you about 100 of them, 10 at a time. Although that's still probably more than you wanted to look at, you should at least look at the next couple of screens of matches if the first screen doesn't have what you want. Since the list includes a lot of restaurants with Key lime pie on the menu and some references to a movie called *Key Lime Pie,* you could just narrow the search by adding the keyword recipe. Search engines are pretty dumb; you have to add the intelligence. At the bottom of the Google screens are page numbers; click Next to go to the next page.

Figure 8-2:
Plenty of
pages
of pie.

The links in the right column are "sponsored" links, that is, paid ads, ranked by how much the advertiser was willing to pay. Often they're worth clicking, but remember that they're ads.

The "I'm Feeling Lucky" button searches and takes you directly to the first link, which works, well, when you're lucky.

Handy search engine targeting tips

Google makes it easy to refine your search more exactly to target the pages you want to find. After each search, your search terms appear in a box at the top of the page so that you can change them and try again. Here are some tips on how you may want to change your terms:

✔ Type most search words in lowercase. Type proper names with a single capital letter, such as `Elvis`. Don't type any words in all capital letters.

✔ If two or more words should appear together, put quotes around them, as in `"Elvis`

`Presley"`. You should do that with the pie search ("key lime pie") because, after all, that is what the pie is called, although in this example, Google is clever enough to realize that it's a common phrase and pretends you typed the quotes anyway.

✔ Use + and – to indicate words that must either appear or not appear, such as `+Elvis +Costello -Presley` if you're looking for the modern Elvis, not the classic one.

Even more Google options

Although Google looks very simple, it has plenty of other options that can be handy:

✔ **You can get there from here.** Type in a street address, and Google offers a link to a map. Type in a person's name and a full or partial address, at least the state abbreviation, and it'll give you addresses and phone numbers. Type in a phone number, and it'll often give you the name and address. (Try typing **202-456-1414**). The information is all collected from public sources, but if you find this a bit too creepy, look yourself up and if it finds you, it'll include a link to a page where you can have your info removed.

✔ **You can search Usenet for information.** *Usenet* is the giant collection of Internet *newsgroups* (online discussion groups) that's been around since before the Web. Simply click the Groups tab near the search box. If a topic has been discussed in the past 20 years on Usenet (as it seems most topics have), this technique is the best way to find the messages about that topic. It's a great place to find out how to fix computer problems — most likely, whatever question you have has been asked and answered on Usenet, and Google has all of it. (John found things there that he wrote in 1981.) For a description of Usenet, see net.gurus.com/usenet.

✔ **You can search for images as well as text.** Simply click the Image tab on any Google search page. Google has no idea what each image is but looks at the surrounding text and the filename of the image and does a remarkably good job of guessing. If you do an image search for "key lime pie," you will indeed see dozens of pictures of tasty pies. A "safe search" feature omits pictures of naked people and the like. If you turn off safe search, you can find some impressively unsafe pictures.

✔ **You can get the news.** Google News (click the News tab or start at news.google.com) shows a summary of current online news culled automatically from thousands of sources all over the world. *Warning:* If you are interested in current events, you can easily waste 12 hours a day following links from here.

✔ **You can limit your search to documents in a specific language.** No sense in finding pages in a language you can't read, although Google has a subsystem that can try, with mixed success, to translate pages from some other languages. Click the Language Tools link at the bottom of the Google window.

✔ **You can do painless arithmetic.** Google is even a calculator. Type in **2+2** and Google says "2 + 2 = 4." It knows units, so if you type **4 feet 8.5 inches**, Google says "4 feet 8.5 inches = 1.4351 meters."

> ✔ **You can find files fast on your own computer.** Google offers a program you can download to your PC called Google Desktop that lets you do Google-like searches (while getting Google-like ads) of the contents of you PC hard-drive. Carol finds it particularly useful for finding old files and e-mail she's convinced is somewhere on her computer.

Yahoo, ancient king of the directories

Yahoo (yes, you normally see it with an exclamation point, but we don't like to yell) is one of the oldest directories — and still a pretty good one. As with ODP, you can search for entries or click from category to category until you find something you like. We start our Yahoo visit at its directory page, `dir.yahoo.com` (at least the page name doesn't use an exclamation point), as shown in Figure 8-3. As with all Web pages, the exact design may have changed by the time you read this, but Yahoo's layout has remained pretty steady for years. You'll see a whole bunch of categories and subcategories listed; click any of them to see another page that has even more subcategories and links to actual Web pages. You can click a link to a page if you see one you like, or click a sub-subcategory, and so on.

Figure 8-3: Ready to Yahoo.

At the top of each Yahoo directory page is the list of categories, subcategories, and so on, separated by angle brackets that lead you to that page. If you want to back up a few levels and look at different subcategories, just click the place on that list to which you want to back up. After a little clicking up and down, it's second nature. Many pages appear in more than one place in the directory because they fall into more than one category. Web pages can have as many links referring to them as they want.

Although all categories in the Yahoo list have plenty of subcategories under them, some have many more than others. If you're looking for a business-related page, for instance, it helps to know that Yahoo sticks just about everything commercial under the category Business and Economy (as shown in Figure 8-4). If we were looking for Internet Gurus Central, for example (which we think people should look for several times a day, at least), we could click our way to it from the Yahoo home page by clicking Business and Economy on that page, clicking Shopping and Services, then Books, then Bookstores, then Computers, and then Internet; when you get to that page, you can link to pages with lots of Internet books, including ours.

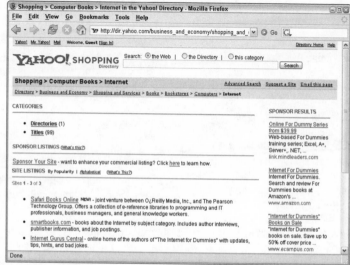

Figure 8-4:
A store-house of commercial information at Yahoo.

If you know in general but not in detail what you're looking for, clicking up and down through the Yahoo directory pages is a good way to narrow your search and find pages of interest.

Early on, it was easy to get a Web page into Yahoo simply by entering it into their Submissions page and waiting a week or so for their editors to look at the new page. Now that it's so popular that normal submissions take a long, long time before anyone on staff looks at them (months, maybe years), unless you pay them $299 a year for the "express" service. You can draw your own conclusions about how that affects what gets into Yahoo (and what doesn't), and why we like dmoz.org.

Searching through Yahoo

"Click Business And Economy, and then, on that page, click Shopping And Services, then Books, then Bookstores, then Computers, and then Internet? How the heck did they know which categories to click?" you're doubtless asking. We admit it. We cheated — we searched for the page instead.

The 404 blues

More often than we want to admit, when you click a link from a search results page, rather than get the promised page, you get a message such as `404 Not Found`. What did you do wrong? Nothing. Web pages come and go and move around with great velocity, and the various Web search engines were designed as delivery vehicles (not garbage trucks), so they do a lousy job of cleaning out links to old, dead pages that have gone away.

At least the search engines are a bit better in this regard than the manual directories. That's because search engines have software robots that revisit all the indexed pages every once in a while and note whether they still exist. Even so, many lonely months can pass between robot visits, and a great deal can happen to a page in the meantime. Google *caches* (stores) a copy of most pages it visits, so even if the original has gone away, you can click the Cache link at the end of a Google index entry and see a copy of the page as it was when Google last looked at it. Here are some other ways to chase down that tantalizing link that has wandered off into nowhere.

✔ The Internet Archive operates a nifty service — called the Wayback Machine — that can retrieve older versions of Web sites. Enter your broken link in their search box at `www.archive.org`. (Yes, they own a lot of computers too.)

✔ Sometimes Web sites try to tidy up a bit and move their files around in the process. If the broken link is a long one, say `www.frobliedoop.org/glompty-dompty/snrok/amazingtip.html`, try shorter versions, `www.frobliedoop.org/glompty-dompty/snrok`, or `www.frobliedoop.org/glompty-dompty` or even `www.frobliedoop.org` to find clues as to where they put that tip. Also try a Google search on just the file name, `amazingtip.html`. There may be a copy at another Web site.

✔ Finally, we should mention that Web sites sometimes shut down, either because of some equipment failure or for periodic maintenance (late nights, Sunday mornings, and major holidays are favorite times for the latter). Your 404'd link might magically just work tomorrow.

Bad links are all just part of life on the online frontier — the high-tech equivalent of riding your horse along the trail in the Old West and noticing that there sure are a lot of bleached-white cattle skulls lying around.

Yahoo also lets you search its index by keyword, which is the best way to use it if you have some idea of the title of the page you're looking for. Every Yahoo screen has near the top a search box in which you can type words you want to find in the Yahoo entry for pages of interest. For example, we typed **Internet for dummies**, clicked the Search button next to the type-in box, and got a page with lots of entries, starting with our publisher's Web site and our own.

With each entry Yahoo finds, it includes a link to the page's category if the page is in their directory. Even if the entry isn't quite right, if you click the category, you find other related pages, and some of them may well do the trick.

You can click the Advanced Search link near the top of the page to get to the slightly more advanced Yahoo search page. It lets you limit how far back you want to see pages, and you can tell it to look for either all the words or any of the words you typed.

Tons more at Yahoo

Although Yahoo was originally a directory of resources available on the Web, it's now a *portal,* which means it has lots of other databases available to encourage you to stick around inside Yahoo. Each has a link you can click (just under the box in which you would enter search terms). They add new databases about once a week; some popular ones include

- ✔ **My Yahoo:** A customized starting page just for you with headlines, stock prices, local weather, Weblogs, and just about every other source of information known to 21st-century humanity.
- ✔ **Mail:** A popular Web-mail system, which we prefer to Hotmail.
- ✔ **Yellow Pages:** A business directory.
- ✔ **People Search:** Finds addresses and phone numbers like a white pages directory (see the "Finding People" section).
- ✔ **Maps:** Gets a map of a street address you type.
- ✔ **Classifieds:** Here you can read and submit ads for automobiles, apartments, computers, and jobs.
- ✔ **Personals:** Here you can read and submit ads for dates in all (and we mean *all*) combinations.
- ✔ **Chat:** Gets you into online chat through the Web.
- ✔ **Auctions:** Web-based auctions, not unlike eBay.
- ✔ **TV:** Impressively complete TV, cable, and satellite listings, by area.
- ✔ **Travel:** A link to the Travelocity reservation system, as well as a variety of other resources. (See `airinfo.aero` for our opinions and suggestions about online travel services.)
- ✔ **Today's News, Stock Quotes, and Sports Scores:** News from a variety of wire services, newspapers, and other media.

ODP: It's open, it's big, and it's freeeeee

Wouldn't it be nice if there were a really big directory with as much stuff as a search engine? Sure, but who'd ever be able to pay people to build a directory that big? Nobody — but volunteers do it for free. Netscape started the Open Directory Project (ODP), a volunteer effort to create the world's biggest and best Web directory. Propelled by the same community spirit that built

---

You may already be an expert

The Open Directory Project depends on volunteers to manage a category. If you search for something, look at what's in the category, and think, "Sheesh, I could do better than that," perhaps it's time to volunteer and do so. The time commitment for a single category is modest — just a few minutes a week to see what's been suggested, and edit, add, or reject it.

To volunteer, click the Become an Editor link near the top of any dmoz.org window. There's a small questionnaire that asks who you are, why you're interested, and what entries you would like to add to your category. If you're accepted (most people are if they have some new pages to suggest for the category), you can start editing in a day or two. There are tutorials and mailing lists for editors, so you don't have to do it all by yourself.

John edits the categories for *compilers,* a kind of software that's a professional interest from his grad-school days, as well as the one for Unitarian church camps because he was looking for one camp, saw the category, and thought "Sheesh, I could . . . oh, right." Margy edits topics about e-mail mailing lists and restaurants in Vermont. Carol is trying to get a life.

Linux, Mozilla Firefox, and Wikipedia, ODP has indeed become a killer Web directory. Because ODP is available for anyone to use for free, dozens of search engines provide ODP along with their own index information. For example, Google's version is at `www.google.com/dirhp`.

ODP lives at `www.dmoz.org`, (*dmoz* stands, more or less, for *D*irectory *M*ozilla). The directory is a set of categories, subcategories, sub-subcategories, and so on down to an impressive level of detail. Each category can — and usually does — contain a bunch of Web pages. You can either start at the top directory level and click your way through the categories, or search within the directory to find pages and then look at the categories that include interesting pages. Because those pages have all been at least glanced at by a person, they're probably of higher quality than the mechanically collected ones in the general Google list. You see not only the relevant Web pages, but also links to related categories. There are so many categories in ODP that you often have to click around to find the exact subcategory you want — but when you find it, you generally find some interesting links. (If you don't, see the sidebar "You may already be an expert".)

For real facts, try Wikipedia first

TIP

Wikipedia, `www.wikipedia.org`, is an encyclopedia that you can use for free over the Internet. *Wiki* means fast in Hawaiian (actually, "wikiwiki" does) and Wikipedia has earned its name. The Wikipedia project, which started in 2001, has grown to over half a million articles in English, covering almost every conceivable topic, from the `Battle of Dunkirk` to `Dummies books`, and, yes, there's even a `Key lime pie` article, where we discover that "Proper

Key lime pie is made with canned sweetened condensed milk, for fresh milk was not a common commodity in the Florida Keys before modern refrigerated distribution methods."

If you are looking for the scoop on most topics, Wikipedia is a great place to start. You can search on both article titles and article text. Words in the article body that are highlighted blue link to other articles in Wikipedia. Many articles also have links to external Web sites that have more information on the topic. Articles are created and edited by a volunteer team of over 6,000 active contributors. There are Wikipedias in dozens of other languages as well (check out is.wikipedia.org if you ever wondered what Icelandic looks like).

Anyone can edit a Wikipedia article any time they wish. That might seem a prescription for chaos, but most articles are watched over by interested volunteers and inappropriate edits are quickly reversed, so the overall quality remains remarkably high.

If the idea of editing encyclopedia articles on your favorite subjects sounds appealing, talk to your family first. Wikipedia can be very addictive.

Articles are supposed to reflect a neutral point of view (NPOV in WikiSpeak), but a few topics, like abortion, creationism, and Middle East politics are constantly debated. Wikipedia is not as authoritative as conventional works like *Encyclopædia Britannica*, but its articles are usually up to date and to the point, with side issues dealt with by links to other articles. One particularly cool thing

Who pays for all this stuff?

You may be wondering who pays for all these wonderful search systems. Advertising supports all except two of them. On every page of most search systems, you see lots and lots of ads. It used to be that ad revenue was pretty skimpy, hence the dotcom bust of 2000, but then the search sites discovered an important secret: When you enter key words, you are telling the search site something about your interests at the moment. That turns out to be *very* valuable information to advertisers. An automobile company might pay a lot to have its ad near the top of the results page when you search on automobile dealer Kansas. Some sites (notably Google) auction off prime ad placement. Google marks all such ads as "sponsored links." Usually they are on the left of the results page, but sometimes they are on top with a colored background (surprise — these cost more). Other search sites may not be so scrupulous. Advertisers pay Google when you click their links.

The exceptions are the Open Directory Project and Wikipedia, which work on the open-source model. The vast majority of contributors are unpaid volunteers with a small amount of support for the ODP site provided by AOL's Netscape subsidiary.

Visit net.gurus.com/search for the latest details.

on Wikipedia is its collection of comprehensive lists, en.wikipedia.org/wiki/Category:Lists, on all sorts of arcane subjects. List of countries with mains power plugs, voltages & frequencies is one of our favorites.

If you do a Google search on a topic, there is a good chance a Wikipedia article will show up as one of the links Google returns. That link might be a good place to start reading.

Here ends our survey of Key lime pies. Just a minute while we run down to the kitchen and have another piece.

The Usual Suspects: Other Useful Search Engines

After you surf around Yahoo, Google, and ODP for a while, you may want to check out the competition.

Amazon's A9.com

www.a9.com

Amazon.com, the giant online books-and-everything-else store, has its own search engine that shows results in a multi-column form: one column is for Google search, a second shows books (from Amazon, of course) on the topic, and other columns show results from other sources. If you have an Amazon account and sign in, it remembers previous searches and can tell you what's new since last time. We think it's kind of cluttered, but sometimes its results can be interesting.

About.com

www.about.com

About is a directory with several hundred semiprofessional "guides" who manage the topic areas. The guides vary from okay to very good — Margy knows a couple of the very good ones — so if you're looking for in-depth information on a topic, it's worth checking About.com to see what the guide has to say. About.com was purchased by *The New York Times* in 2005.

The ten-minute challenge

Our friend Doug Hacker (his real name) claims to be able to find the answer to any factual query on the Net in less than ten minutes. Carol challenged him to find a quote she vaguely knew from the liner notes of a Duke Ellington album whose title she couldn't remember. He had the complete quote in about an hour but spent less than five minutes himself actually searching. How? He found a mailing list about Duke Ellington, subscribed, and asked the question. Several members replied in short order. The more time you spend finding your way around the Net, the more you know where to go for the information you need.

Bytedog

www.bytedog.com

Bytedog assembles the results of searches at other search engines and presents them in a ranked list with cute dog graphics (cuter than Microsoft's, if you ask us). It takes a few extra seconds to respond, but that's because it's filtering out bad links before you have to deal with them. Bytedog is a project of a couple of students at the University of Waterloo, Ontario.

Microsoft search

www.msn.com

Microsoft sees Google as a threat and is not about to cede the lucrative search business without a fight. Right now their search technology is unremarkable, but the folks at Redmond have money to burn. And, surprise, MSN is the default search engine in Internet Explorer.

Other Web guides

ODP has a directory of several hundred other guides: See dmoz.org/Computers/Internet/Searching for links to them.

Yellow pages

www.superpages.com
www.smartpages.com
www.infousa.com

Quite a few "yellow pages" business directories, both national and local, are on the Net. The directories in this list are some of the national ones. InfoUSA even offers credit reports and other unpleasantly intrusive information.

Finding People

Finding people on the Internet is surprisingly easy. It's so easy that, indeed, sometimes it's creepy. Two overlapping categories of people-finders are available: those that look for people on the Net with e-mail and Web addresses, and those that look for people in real life with phone numbers and street addresses.

In real life

Directories of addresses that you can send paper mail to and numbers that will ring actual telephones are compiled mostly from telephone directories. If you haven't had a listed phone number in the past few years, you probably aren't in any of these directories.

www.superpages.com
www.smartpages.com

Superpages and Smartpages are run by Verizon and SBC respectively, the two largest phone companies in the United States, and have very up-to-date listings for their own service areas. They also have Yellow Pages business directories (see the sidebar.)

On the Net

The process of finding e-mail and Web addresses is somewhat hit-and-miss. Because no online equivalent to the official phone book that the telephone company produces has ever existed, directories of e-mail addresses are collected from the addresses used in Web pages, Usenet messages, mailing lists, and other more-or-less public places on the Net. Because the different directories use different sources, if you don't find someone in one directory, you can try another.

Because the e-mail directories are incomplete, there's no substitute for calling someone up and asking, "What's your e-mail address?"

Googling for people

Type in someone's name and address to Google (for the address, use at least the state abbreviation, but more is better), and it'll show you matches from phone-book listings.

If you're wondering whether someone has a Web page, use Google or Yahoo to search for just the person's name. If you're wondering whether you're famous, use Google or Yahoo to search for your own name and see how many people mention you or link to your Web pages. If you get e-mail from someone you don't know, search Google for the e-mail address — unless the message was spam, the address is bound to appear on a Web page somewhere.

Yahoo People Search (Four-eleven)

people.yahoo.com

You can search for addresses and phone numbers and e-mail addresses. If you don't like your own listing, you can add, update, or delete it.

WhoWhere

www.whowhere.lycos.com

WhoWhere is another e-mail address directory. Although Yahoo usually gives better results, some people are listed in WhoWhere who aren't listed in other places.

Canada 411

www.canada411.com

Canada 411 is a complete Canadian telephone book, sponsored by the major Canadian telephone companies. Aussi disponible en français, eh? For several years the listings for Alberta and Saskatchewan were missing, leading to concern that the two provinces were too boring to bother with, but they're all there now, proving that they're just as gnarly as everyone else.

Mail, one more time

Mailing lists are another important resource. Most lists (but not all — check before you ask) welcome concrete, politely phrased questions related to the list's topic. See Chapter 16 to find more information about mailing lists, including how to look for lists of particular topics of interest to you.

We're from Your Browser, and We're Here to Help You

Microsoft and Mozilla keep trying to crowbar their way into the search-engine market. (Who? Us? Opinionated?) Both take you directly to their respective preferred search system if you give them half a chance. These search systems aren't awful, but unless you are the kind of person who turns on the TV and watches whatever is on the first channel you come to, you'll probably find that you prefer to choose your own search engine.

The Firefox and Safari search box

Firefox and Safari (Apple's browser for Macs) have a useful built-in search box to the right of the address box. Just type your search words in the search box and hit Enter. Your words are sent to a search engine and the results appear on-screen. Firefox and Safari come with their default search engines set to Google. You can select a different search site in Firefox by clicking the search-engine logo (usually Google's "G" icon), and selecting another site from the drop-down list. Safari seems fixated on Google.

Microsoft's Autosearch

In Internet Explorer, if you type keywords into the Address box, Internet Explorer sends them to MSN Search, an adequate Web directory, along with a lot of links that look suspiciously like advertisements.

Internet Explorer (IE) also has the Search Bar. If you click the Search button on the toolbar, a Search Companion pane appears to the left of your IE window with a small search engine page. In IE 6, the Web search lets you use one or more search engines — and combines the results. Click the Change Preferences button to tell it which engines you like. Of the options they offer, Google is the one of choice.

Getting the goods on goods and services

All the commercial directories and search engines now put shopping information somewhere on their home page to help get your credit card closer to the Web faster. You can find department stores and catalogs from all over, offering every conceivable item (and some inconceivable items). We tell you all the dos, don'ts, and how-tos in Chapter 10.

While you're at it, you can get rid of the annoying Search Doggie, turn off the useless balloon tips, and otherwise make your browser act more like a tool for you and less like an ad for Microsoft. Clicking the Change Preferences button in the Search Companion pane displays these options (among others):

- **Without an Animated Search Character:** Click it to make the search pooch leave. Click With a Different Character to change the doggie to a red dot, a robot, a Windows logo, or other equally, um, adorable icons.

- **Change Internet Search Behavior:** Click it to choose whether or not you want the Search Companion pane to appear, and to choose which search engine to use.

- **Don't Show Balloon Tips:** Click it to disable the little thought-bubbles that Windows sometimes displays.

IE's search box confusingly mixes Web searches with file searches on your own computer; the options called Indexing Service and Files or Folders affect only the way that Windows searches the disk on your own computer, not the Net.

If you use IE, despite our advice to the contrary and your heightened risk of spyware, and you like to use Google for your searches, Google has a nice little IE add-in that among other things has a Google search box. Visit `toolbar.google.com` for more info and to download and install it.

More search magic

Microsoft and Firefox are in frantic competition for users, so by the time you read this, there will doubtless be even more search features in each browser. Drop by our Web site at `net.gurus.com/search` to find out what's new.

Chapter 9

Music and Video on the Web

A thousand years ago, when we wrote the first edition of *Internet For Dummies*, Internet content consisted almost of entirely of text. (It was 1993, but it sure *feels* like a thousand years ago.) You could download a few archives of pictures, and there was this weird thing called the World Wide Web that could mix pictures and text together, but for the most part, it was text. Connections were so slow, downloading pictures took so long, and computer screens were so fuzzy, that we stuck to text. The pictures you could download were single images, like cartoons or snapshots. Audio was nearly unheard of (so to speak), and video files were so bulky that even if you could find a clip and wait a week for it to download, it wouldn't fit on your computer's disk. By the late 1990s, Internet connections sped up enough and screens had improved enough that pictures were normal fare — and audio was entering the mainstream enough that we put a sample voice message on our Web site in case any of our readers had sound cards. (It's still there, at `net.gurus.com/ngc.wav`.)

Things have advanced a little since then. Ordinary users now have Net connections that run at a several million bits per second — faster than the main backbones of the early '90s — and computer disks have gotten enormous beyond imagining. Passing around audio and video over the Net has become practical and widespread. In fact, the amounts of audio and video out there now are so vast that you could spend your entire life looking at online commercials without ever getting to anything worth watching. So this chapter will try to help bring a little order to the vast wasteland of online media.

To avoid writing "audio and/or video" a hundred more times in this chapter, henceforth we use the concise (albeit imprecise) term *media* to refer to them.

Five Ways to Get Media and One Way Not To

There are approximately ten zillion different programs and formats in which you can get your media fix. Fortunately, they fall into a modest number of categories: free, streaming, rented, purchased, shared, and outright stolen.

Getting it as a gift

The simplest approach is to download media offered for free and then play it. Visit www.nasa.gov/multimedia, where NASA has lots of free little movies on topics ranging from dust storms on Mars to how a roller coaster ride feels like taking off in the Space Shuttle. You can also find independent movies and videos from producers more interested in letting people see their work than charging for it. Visit epitonic.com for an eclectic collection of music that artists, some well-known and some obscure, released so that people can listen to and make their own mixes.

Borrowing it

Even on a broadband connection, downloading a whole media clip can take a while. Rather than download first and play later, *streaming* media downloads and plays at the same time, thereby recreating (in a complex digital manner) the way that radio and TV have worked since the 1920s. As with TV and radio, once it's streamed, it's gone — and if you want to play it again, you have to stream it again. Streaming audio can work over a dialup connection, but streaming video needs a broadband connection.

Most streaming media is provided *on demand* — that is, you click a link and they send you whatever it is, sort of like a jukebox. Alternatively, some streaming media is a single program to which you can listen in and hear what's playing at any moment. Not surprisingly, this is called *Internet radio,* and in many cases these audio streams are actual radio programs, such as our local public radio stations at wrvo.fm (click Listen Live) in upstate New York and www.vpr.net (Listen Online) in Vermont. We say more about I-radio in the section "Internet Radio" later in this chapter.

Renting it

A great deal of music isn't available for free, but it's available for cheap. Services such as Real Networks' Rhapsody (www.real.com/rhapsody) offer monthly subscriptions that let you listen to large libraries of recorded music. You pay them a fixed monthly fee, and they let you click songs from their catalog to play them, and to make and share playlists of your favorites. But you can only listen online; to download for keeps or to copy to CD or to an iPod, you have to buy it.

These rental services have enormous catalogs of music, with each one claiming to be the largest. They really *are* large; while checking out Rhapsody, we were finally able to do a side-by-side comparison of Desi Arnaz's muscular late-1940s version of "Babalu" and his mentor Xavier Cugat's more elegant 1941 recording. (You'll just have to decide for yourself which one you like better.)

Buying it

Apple's iTunes offers a remarkable and innovative approach to online music. Go to www.apple.com/itunes and you can listen to the first little bit of any song in the catalog. If you like it, you can buy your own permanent copy (for 99 cents) that you can copy to your iPod or burn on a CD. You don't have to be a Mac user to like iTunes; you can play the tunes using a Windows version of the iTunes program (see the section "Organizing your music with iTunes" later in this chapter). It's no surprise that people buy in droves, making iTunes the biggest online store. Likewise, many more Web sites sell music either through a Web store or as an add-on to a rental service, most for about the same price as iTunes.

Sharing it

Napster (at www.napster.com) was the first well-known music-exchange service, allowing members to download MP3 music files from each other for free. The system was the first large-scale *peer-to-peer (P2P)* information exchange, where people exchange files with each other instead of downloading them from a central library. Eventually, the big record labels sued and shut it down because most of what people exchanged was in flagrant violation of the music's copyright. Napster was later reincarnated as a music rental system.

Downloads for the post-literate

Not all downloadable audio files contain music. There is a thriving niche market in what used to be called "talking books." You can download books, magazines, and just about anything that you might otherwise read, as well as radio programs you might have missed. Although listening to downloaded books on your computer works fine — and it can be an essential tool for the visually impaired — it's kind of pointless if you can read the actual book faster than you could listen to it (and kick back on the patio while you're at it). But if you drive to work or go jogging, a talking book on CD in the car player (or copied to the MP3 player or iPod on your belt) is just the ticket.

The largest source of talking books is Audible.com (www.audible.com). You can buy individual books for book-like prices, or you can subscribe and get one or two books a month cheaper than you could by paying individually. Either way, the books you buy are yours to keep. They provide a reasonably nice program you can download and install to keep track of the files for the books you've bought and burn them onto CDs (*lots of* CDs — about 15 for a full-length book). They have also made deals with many other media programs, so there's an Audible plug-in for iTunes that lets you copy your books to an iPod, as well as a plug-in for Windows Media Player for all the MP3 devices it handles, and so forth.

Audible usually offers a trial subscription with a couple of free books, and their catalog includes public-interest stuff like presidential inaugural speeches available for free if you want to try it out. *Warning:* John tried it out and ended up inventing errands that involved driving to faraway stores so he could listen to the last CD of *The Da Vinci Code*. On the other hand, Margy's husband survives a long commute thanks to his Audible subscription.

A currently popular peer-to-peer system is KaZaA (www.kazaa.com), which has so far resisted legal attacks by having no central index site like Napster did and by being headquartered in an obscure Pacific island that's sort of part of Australia. We don't recommend you use KaZaA, partly because there's still an awful lot of pirated stuff, but mostly because KaZaA comes packaged with really annoying adware that pops up ads all over your screen. (At least, they say that's all it does.) Fortunately, one P2P system, BitTorrent is open source and free of junkware, so you can use it safely — see "Peering at Peer-to-Peer" later in this chapter.

Stealing it — um, no

There's still plenty of pirated stuff on the Net, and probably always will be. We expect our readers, being of good moral character, wouldn't want to look for it, but if you do, you'll have to do so without our help.

What Are You Listening With?

The three most popular programs used for playing Web-based online media are Windows Media Player, Real Player, and Apple QuickTime. Each includes a separate player program and plug-ins for Web browsers so Web pages can embed little windows that show movies or play music. Some give you your choice of which player to use, some only use one or two. You'll eventually have to install all three if you want to handle all the links you click. All three work pretty well, although we give QuickTime the nod for its combination of smooth performance and the fewest annoying ads.

RealPlayer

www.real.com

The most popular system for playing streaming media files, the kind that you borrow or rent, is RealPlayer, as shown in Figure 9-1. Files in Real's format have the extension .ra or .ram. To play RealAudio files, you need the RealPlayer program, which you can download from www.real.com. The RealAudio player also handles RealVideo, which shows smallish moving pictures to go with your sound.

You have to download and install the player before you can use it. The installation process is a pain because Real desperately wants you to fill out registration info so they can add you to their marketing lists, and you'll see a variety of ominous warnings if you decline to register (or even turn off the "message center" that pops up from time to time to show ads, helpful hints, ads, update info, and ads). Just say no; it works fine with no registration and no popups.

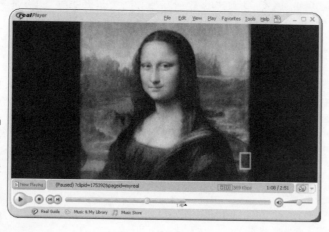

Figure 9-1:
Catching up on the latest media with RealPlayer.

If you start RealPlayer directly, it includes a Web browser (really Internet Explorer) that opens a media-guide page with lots of stuff you can listen to or watch and — they hope — buy.

Windows Media Player

www.microsoft.com/windows/windowsmedia

Microsoft decided to create its own streaming audio format and to bundle a player for it with newer versions of Windows. You can play files in Advanced Streaming Format (with extensions .asf or .asx) with the Windows Media Player (WMP; see Figure 9-2) program, as well as most other formats. More recent versions added useful new features, so if you don't have Media Player 10, it's worth visiting Windows Update or the Media Player site to download it.

Figure 9-2:
Staying up
to date with
Windows
Media
Player.

WMP comes with built-in links to an odd set of online media stores, ranging from Wal-Mart (cheap downloadable music) to Major League Baseball (current and past games) to Court TV (the truth, the whole truth . . .). You're not limited to those stores; they're just the ones that paid Microsoft to get built-in links.

Apple QuickTime

www.apple.com/quicktime

The third popular streaming format is Apple's QuickTime. QuickTime supports streaming video (see Figure 9-3) as well as audio in most popular formats. The necessary software is standard on Macintoshes and is available free for Windows at www.apple.com/quicktime. Apple would like to sell you the more capable Pro version, but the free version is fine for dealing with media downloads.

Figure 9-3: Some guy from Apple in QuickTime.

Okay, How About Some Real Music?

One of the hottest activities on the Internet is downloading and exchanging music files with your friends in the MP3 file format. MP3 stands for MPEG level 3 (acronyms within acronyms — how techoid) and is simply the soundtrack format used with MPEG movies. Because that format is widely available and does a pretty good job of compressing music down to a reasonable size for downloading, it has been adopted by music lovers on the Net. Many Web sites devoted to the MP3 format (such as www.mp3.com), have sprung up almost overnight. They're good places to look for the software you need to play MP3 files and even record your own music. You can play MP3 files with many different programs, including Windows Media Player (which comes with Windows), RealPlayer, and iTunes (which has QuickTime built in, as described in the next section).

Naturally, Microsoft has a competing file format called WMA, with the extension .wma. Windows Media Player can *rip* (copy) tracks from music CDs to your computer's hard disk in WMA format and can burn (record) tracks onto CD-R (blank, writable CDs) if you have a CD writer. RealPlayer can also handle WMA.

Organizing your music with iTunes

Apple's iTunes (www.apple.com/itunes) lets you buy legal downloaded songs for the fairly reasonable price of 99 cents each. Both Mac and Windows users can buy and play songs from iTunes by downloading the free iTunes program, which is excellent for keeping your songs organized. Although iTunes handles MP3 perfectly well, it creates files in newer MPEG-4 audio formats that sound better. The songs you buy come in m4p (*MPEG level 4, purchased* — which means copy-protected) format, while songs from CDs or other unprotected sources are in AAC (Advanced Audio Coding, the audio part of mp4). Figure 9-4 shows iTunes running on Windows.

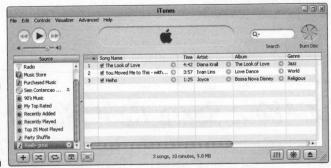

Figure 9-4:
A collection of classics in iTunes.

RealPlayer can also download music for 99 cents a track, or you can subscribe to its Rhapsody service, which offers unlimited online listening to their large catalog and downloads for 89 cents apiece, for $10 a month. Several of the built-in links in Windows Media Player are for other music rental and download services with similar prices.

If this blizzard of audio file types seems baffling, you're right — it is. Fortunately, most programs can read each other's formats, so you don't have to worry too much about which is which for typical downloads. We suggest you experiment with a few programs and then use the one you like best. We like iTunes.

Playing music after you've got it

If you want to listen to music while you're sitting in front of your computer, you're all set — fire up one of the media programs and listen. But we hear that some people actually have a life and would like to listen to music in other places.

MP3 is so popular that several manufacturers now offer portable MP3 players that store hundreds or thousands of MP3 cuts, so you can listen while you jog, travel, or just hang out. It's like a Walkman, but you don't need tapes or CDs. You hook your MP3 player up to your computer whenever you want to download new tunes. The latest players can hold *weeks* of music. The most popular is the ubiquitous Apple iPod, but lots of other players are cheaper and work fine. Only iPods can play m4p (copy-protected) music, and only for files to which you own a license.

Programs called *rippers* let you transfer music from your CDs to your computer disk in MP3 format. RealPlayer, iTunes, and Windows Media Player can all rip from CDs, and can burn new CDs of music you've ripped and downloaded.

More threats and promises

Folks ripping their favorite tunes from CDs and e-mailing them to their 50 closest friends are a hideous threat to the recording industry, not to mention a violation of copyright law. (The previous hideous threats, for those old enough to remember, were cassette tapes and home VCRs, which totally destroyed the music and movie industries. What, they didn't? Uh, well *this* time it's different because, um, just because it is.) The industry's efforts to shut down Web sites that offer ripped songs for free download has been moderately successful, but private e-mail is hard to stop.

The recording industry came up with a music file format of its own, called SDMI, for the Secure Digital Music Initiative, intended to let you download but not share music. It flopped, partly because it had technical defects quickly analyzed and reported by enterprising college professors and students, and partly because nobody wanted crippleware music. The recording industry has been filing lawsuits against the most visible music sharers, on the peculiar theory that if they threaten and sue their customers, the customers' attitude will improve and they will buy more stuff. Maybe someday they'll figure out, as Apple did, that if they sell decent music at a reasonable price and let the customers listen to it the way they want to, people will pay for it.

There're CDs, and then there're CDs

Although all CDs look the same, they don't all play the same. Normal audio CDs contain a maximum of about 74 minutes of music and work on every CD player ever made. When you burn a CD-R (the kind of CD you can only write once), you're making a normal audio CD. Since blank CD-Rs are so cheap (about 15 cents apiece if you buy them in quantity), the main disadvantage of this approach is that you end up with large stacks of CDs.

MP3 files are much smaller than audio CD files, so if you burn a CD full of MP3's, you can put about ten hours of music on each disc. DVD players and many recent CD players can play MP3 CDs. If you're not sure whether your player can handle MP3 CDs, just make one on your computer and try it in your player. It won't hurt your player, although you may see some odd error messages. Although rewritable CD-RWs don't work in normal CD players, players that can handle MP3 CDs can usually handle CD-RWs as well. Again, if you're not sure, try it; it won't hurt anything if it doesn't work.

Getting music onto your player or CDs

All media programs have some provision for creating CDs and copying music to portable players. But be sure your player matches your program. If you want to use an Apple iPod, the program has to be iTunes. Most other programs can handle most other players, but if there's a program you prefer, better check before you buy a new player.

Most programs let you copy only music you've ripped or bought. One exception is the new Napster (www.napster.com) which lets you copy any music from their rental catalog to players so long as you keep your subscription active — that is, the music in the player is copy-protected. Naturally, you have to use a player that works with *their* copy protection, but if you want to select and listen to 24 hours of different music every day, it's worth a look.

Internet Radio

If you like to listen to music while you work, check out Internet radio stations. Like real radio stations, they offer a mix of music, talk, and sometimes commercials. Unlike real radio stations, they're extremely cheap to set up, so lots and lots of people do — providing lots of quirky little niche stations run by people all over the world. You listen to them with a streaming program, usually RealPlayer or Windows Media. Most are available for free, some require a subscription, or have a subscription option to make the ads go away.

To get started, here are some directories of Internet radio stations:

✔ `launch.yahoo.com`: Yahoo's Launchcast.

✔ `shoutcast.com`: AOL's Shoutcast works best with their free Winamp media program.

✔ `radio.msn.com`: Microsoft's MSN Radio comes in a free version and a higher-quality paid version.

Peering at Peer-to-Peer

Our favorite peer-to-peer program is BitTorrent because it's adware-free, you have a lot of control over what your computer shares, and there is a relatively large amount of legal material available.

To start, download and install a BitTorrent client program. The original one, which works fine, is at `www.bittorrent.com`. Click the button for the kind of computer you have, probably Windows or Mac OS X. Because BitTorrent is open-source, the programs are free — although Bram Cohen (who invented and maintains BitTorrent) wouldn't mind a donation.

Although it's possible to start BitTorrent directly, it's much easier to start it via Web links to `.torrent` files. Just click a link, and BitTorrent starts up and starts torrenting away. As your file downloads, the program reports both a download rate and an upload rate. That's the peer-to-peer part. Each file is divided into chunks, and your computer starts downloading chunks from other computers. When your computer has a chunk, it then makes that chunk available to others. The result is that you can download large files very quickly (it can download several chunks at once), and at the same time, you're providing the chunks to other people who want the same file. Polite BitTorrent users (you, for example) leave their BitTorrent program running for a while after the download is complete so their computers can continue to offer the file to others.

So now that you're all set up for torrents of data, here are some places to start:

✔ `www.legaltorrents.com`: An eclectic (a nice way of saying "miscellaneous") collection of music, movies, and the occasional talking book, all with permission to distribute.

✔ `bt.etree.org`: Mostly concert recordings of "trade-friendly" musicians who permit concert recordings. If you like Phish or the Grateful Dead (and everyone does), there's lots of both.

✔ `litezone.com`: A directory of BitTorrent directories, some more legal than others. Some contain pornographic material, but those are clearly marked so you can avoid them if you want.

Movies on the Net

The original standard digital-movie format is called *Moving Picture Experts Group (MPEG)*. MPEG was designed by a committee down the hall from the JPEG committee that defined file formats for scanned photos, and — practically unprecedented in the history of standards efforts — it was designed based on earlier work. MPEG files have the extension `.mpeg` or `.mpg`.

Microsoft, responding to the challenge of emerging standards that it didn't control, created its own formats. Audio/Visual Interleave (AVI) format is for nonstreaming video, with the extension `.avi`. Advanced Streaming Format (with extensions `.asf` or `.asx`) is for both streaming audio and video data.

Getting movies

Web browsers themselves can't play any of these video formats — you need to get a player program. You also need a reasonably fast computer to display movies in anything close to real time. RealPlayer, Windows Media Player, and QuickTime all handle movies (and are described earlier in this chapter). Macromedia's Shockwave is also occasionally used for movies; if it's not already loaded on your computer, you can get a free player at `www.macromedia.com/software/shockwave`.

If you want to try watching movies online, go to `www.bmwfilms.com` to see some 10-minute action-adventure flicks that (not surprisingly) feature a lot of car chases with fancy German cars. You can either download whole movies or stream them.

Also visit `www.ifilm.com` which has a large collection of short independent movies and trailers. All their movies are streamed, which means that they show in a little window on your screen. The Net just isn't fast enough to stream full-screen video, at least not yet.

Watching real movies

If you can plan your movie viewing a little ahead of time, Movielink (`www.movielink.com`) may be for you. They rent full-length full-screen movies you can watch on your computer screen or, if your computer has a TV adapter (as many recent ones do), on your TV. To start, you have to sign up and install their player program. Then pick the movie you want and tell them to download it, at which point they charge your credit card about $3 and start the download, which takes about an hour. When the download is done (or even partly done if you're in a hurry), you can watch it. It's sort of like turning your computer into a VCR or TiVo. You can watch the movie any time during the month after you download it — but once you start watching it, you have to finish within 24 hours.

Chapter 10

More Shopping, Less Dropping

In This Chapter

▶ Discovering the pros and cons of shopping online

▶ Using your credit card online without fear

▶ Shopping step-by-step

▶ Finding airline tickets, mutual funds, books, clothes, computers, and food online

The Internet is the world's latest bazaar, with stores that carry everything from books to blouses, DVDs to prescription drugs, mutual funds to musical instruments, plane tickets to, uh, specialized personal products (don't read too much into that). Shopping online is convenient — no parking or standing in line — and allows you to compare prices easily. But is online shopping safe? Well, we've bought all kinds of products online, and we're still alive to tell the tale.

Shopping Online: Pros and Cons

Here are some reasons for shopping on the Net:

✔ Online stores are convenient, open all night, and don't mind if you aren't wearing shoes or if you window-shop for a week before you buy something.

✔ Prices are often lower online, and you can compare prices at several online establishments in a matter of minutes. Even if you eventually make your purchase in a brick-and-mortar store, what you find out online can save you money. Shipping and handling is similar to what you'd pay for mail order, and you don't have to drive or park.

✔ Online stores can sometimes offer a better selection. They usually ship from a central warehouse rather than having to keep stock on the shelf at dozens of branches. If you're looking for something hard to find — for example, a part for that vintage toaster oven you're repairing — the Web can save you weeks of searching.

✔ Sometimes stuff just isn't available locally. (Two of the three authors of this book live in small rural towns. Trumansburg, New York, is a wonderful place, but if you want to buy a book other than the three days a year the library has its book sale, you're out of luck. And Margy couldn't find a harmonium anywhere in the Champlain Valley.)

✔ Unlike malls, online stores don't have Muzak. (A few Web sites play background music, but we don't linger on those sites.)

On the other hand, here are some reasons why you shouldn't buy everything on the Net:

✔ You can't physically look at or try on stuff before you buy it, and in most cases, you have to wait for it to be shipped to you. (We haven't had much luck buying shoes online, f'rinstance.)

✔ Your local stores deserve support.

✔ You can't flirt with the staff at a Web store or find out about the latest town gossip.

The Credit Card Question

How do you pay for stuff you buy online? Most often you pay by credit card, the same way you pay for anything else. Isn't it incredibly, awfully dangerous to give out your credit card number online, though? Well, no.

For one thing, most online stores encrypt the message between your computer and the store's server. (An encrypted connection is indicated in your Web browser by a closed lock icon in the bottom-left corner of the window). Even if a site doesn't encrypt communications between you and their server, the chances of a bad guy listening in are infinitesimal.

Credit cards and debit cards look the same and spend the same, but credit cards bill you at the end of the month while debit cards take the money right out of your bank account. In the United States, consumer protection laws work differently for credit and debit cards, and they're much stronger for credit cards. The important difference is that in case of a disputed transaction, *you* have the money if you used a credit card, but *they* have it if you used a debit card. We suggest using a credit card to get the better protection and then pay the bill at the end of the month so you don't owe interest.

Real fake credit cards you can use

One of the cleverer innovations in online banking is the *virtual credit card.* If you want to place an online credit card order with a merchant you don't entirely trust not to overcharge you, first visit your bank's Web site, tell the bank how much the order will cost, and on the spot, it concocts a brand new card number. Then you return to the merchant's site and order with that card number rather than your regular number. As soon as the merchant places the charge, your bank links the new number to the merchant, so even if the merchant leaks the number, it's no good to anyone else. The number's credit limit is the amount you set when you created it, so if the merchant tries to overcharge you, the bank will say no. You can also create virtual numbers good for a set number of charges, for subscriptions that require regular payments.

Different banks use different names for this service. Citibank and Discover call it virtual numbers. MBNA calls it ShopSafe. Ask your bank whether it offers this service.

John found that virtual numbers also work for phone orders, mail orders, and any charge where you don't use the physical card. Because he's paranoid, he uses virtual numbers for everything from his electric bill to his college alumni association. However, don't use them for buying plane tickets; you may have to show a real card with the matching number at the airport.

When you use plastic at a restaurant, you give your physical card with your physical signature to the wait staff, who takes it to the back room, does who knows what with it, and then brings it back. Compared with that, the risk of sending your number to an online store is pretty small. A friend of ours used to run a restaurant and later ran an online store and assures us that there's no comparison: The online store had none of the credit card problems that the restaurant did.

If, after this harangue, you still don't want to send your credit card number over the Internet, most online stores are happy to have you call in your card number over the phone (though, likely as not, an operator halfway around the globe will then enter your credit card number by using the Internet). If you're one of those fiscally responsible holdouts who don't do plastic, send a check or money order. (You can also use PayPal — see the sidebar, "E-mail cash to anyone," elsewhere in this chapter.)

Paying at the Store

Stores on the Web work in two general ways: with or without virtual *shopping carts.* In stores without carts, you either order one item at a time or fill out a big order form with a check box for everything the store offers. In stores with carts, as you look at the items the store has for sale, you can add items to your cart and then visit the virtual checkout line when you're done, where you provide your payment and delivery information. Until you check out, you can add and remove items from your cart whenever you want, just like in the real world — except that you don't have to put unwanted items back on the shelf.

Simple cart-less shopping

For an example of simple shopping, our randomly chosen site happens to sell books written by one of us authors. (Us? Venal? Naah.) Follow the Autographed Copies link from our site net.gurus.com, and in one click, you arrive at the order page shown in Figure 10-1. It shows the selected item and has an order form ready for your details.

In the form, you enter the same information you would put on a paper order form. Most forms have a place for typing a credit card number; if you're not comfortable entering it there (see the section "The Credit Card Question," earlier in this chapter), leave that blank — the store invariably has a way you can call the number in. Click the Prepare Order button, and you'll see an order review page (as shown in Figure 10-2) where you can check that the details are correct. Click the Place Order button, and your order is on its way.

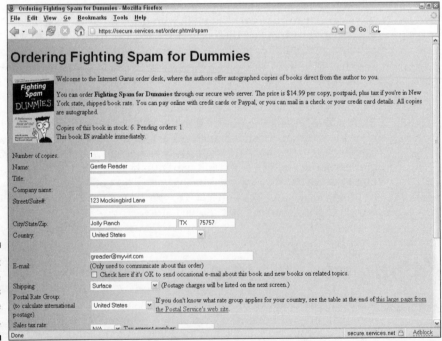

Figure 10-1: Welcome to John's secure online store.

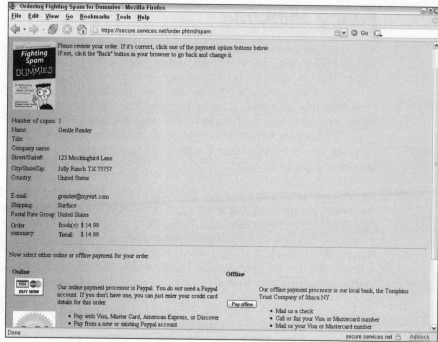

Figure 10-2:
Ready to
order some
quality
literature.

You generally get an e-mail message confirming the details of your order and frequently get e-mail updates if any problems or delays occur.

TIP

Cookie alert

You may have heard horrible stories about things called *cookies* that Web sites reputedly use to spy on you, steal your data, ravage your computer, inject cellulite into your hips while you sleep, and otherwise make your life miserable. After extensive investigation, we have found that most cookies aren't bad; when you're shopping online, they can even be quite helpful. (See the section "Cookies aren't so bad" in Chapter 2 for more on cookies.)

A *cookie* is no more than a little chunk of text a Web site sends to a PC with a request (not a command) to send the cookie back during future visits

to the same Web site. The cookie is stored on your computer in the form of a tiny snippet of text. That's all it is. For online shopping carts, cookies let the Web server track the items you have selected but not yet bought, even if you log out and turn off your computer in the interim. Stores can also use cookies to keep track of the last time you visited and what you bought, but the stores can keep that data on their own computers, so what's the big deal? (If you really don't want Web sites to store cookies on your computer, you can prevent them; see how in Chapter 7.)

Fancy shopping

Although a simple store works okay for stores that don't have many different items in their catalogs or for businesses where you buy one thing at a time, this method is hopeless for stores with large catalogs, so they use a *shopping cart* instead Margy runs a little online kids' videotape store called Great Tapes for Kids at www.greattapes.com. Originally, there was a single order page with an order form listing every tape in her rapidly expanding catalog. When the Great Tapes order form got hopelessly large, John reprogrammed it to provide a shopping cart to help track the items people order. (John will do practically anything to avoid writing.)

As you click your way around a site, you can toss items into your cart, adding and removing them as you want by clicking a button labeled something like Add Item to Your Shopping Cart. Then, when you have the items you want, you visit the virtual checkout line and buy the items in your cart. Until you visit the checkout, you can always take the items out of your cart if you decide that you don't want them, and at online stores, they don't get shopworn, no matter how often you do that.

Figure 10-3 shows the Great Tapes for Kids shopping cart with two items in it. When you click the Proceed to Checkout button, the next page asks for the rest of your order details, much like the form shown earlier in Figure 10-1.

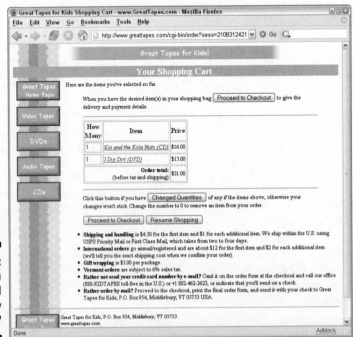

Figure 10-3:
Have you finished your holiday shopping?

Some stores even have the online equivalents of layaway plans and gift registries. For example, some Web shopping sites let you add items to a wish list that you can share with your friend, so you or someone else can buy the item for you later. Some sites offer gift certificates, too, for shopping online.

Up, Up, and Away

We buy lots of airline tickets online. Although the online travel sites aren't as good as the best human travel agents, the sites are now better than most agents and vastly better than bad travel agents. Even if you have a good agent, online sites let you look around to see what your options are before you get on the phone. Often airlines themselves offer cheap fares online that aren't available any other way. They know that it costs them much less to let the Web do the work, and they pay you (in the form of a hefty discount) to use the Web.

Understanding the theory of airline tickets

Four giant airline computer systems in the United States called Sabre, Galileo, Worldspan, and Amadeus handle nearly all the airline reservations in the country. (They're known as *CRS,* for computer reservations systems, or *GDS,* for Global Distribution Systems.) Although each airline has a "home" GDS, the systems are all interlinked so that you can, with few exceptions, buy tickets for any airline from any GDS. Some of the low-price, start-up airlines are available via GDS, but others, notably Southwest and Jet Blue, don't participate in any of these systems but have their own Web sites where you can check flights and buy tickets.

In theory, all the systems show the same data; in practice, however, they get a little out of sync with each other. If you're looking for seats on a sold-out flight, an airline's home system is most likely to have that last, elusive seat. If you're looking for the lowest fare to somewhere, check all four systems (using different travel Web sites) because a fare that's marked as sold out on one system often mysteriously reappears on another system. Also check Orbitz (www.orbitz.com) which has direct connect access to many airlines, bypassing GDS altogether.

Some categories of fares are visible only to travel agents and don't appear on any of the Web sites, particularly if you aren't staying over a weekend, so check with a good agent before buying. On the other hand, many airlines offer some special deals that are *only* on their Web sites and that agents often don't know about. Confused? You should be. We were.

The confusion is even worse if you want to fly internationally. Official fares to most countries are set via a cartel called the IATA, so computer systems usually list only IATA fares for international flights. It's easy to find entirely legal *consolidator* tickets sold for considerably less than the official price, however, so an online or offline agent is extremely useful for getting the best price.

Here's our distilled wisdom about buying tickets online:

✔ Check the online systems to see what flights are available and for an idea of the price ranges. Check sites that use different GDS. (We list some sites at the end of this section.)

✔ After you've found a likely airline, check that airline's site to see whether it has any special Web-only deals. If a low-fare airline flies the route, be sure to check that one, too.

✔ Check prices on flights serving all nearby airports. An extra 45 minutes of driving time can save you hundreds of dollars.

✔ Check with a travel agent (by phone, e-mail, or the agent's Web site) to see whether he can beat the online price, and buy your tickets from the agent unless the online deal is better.

✔ For international tickets, do everything in this list, and check both online and with your agent for consolidator tickets, particularly if you don't qualify for the lowest published fare. For complex international trips such as around-the-world, agents can invariably find routes and prices that the automated systems can't.

✔ If you bid on airline tickets at a travel auction Web site, make sure that you already know the price at which you can buy the ticket, so you don't bid more.

If you hate flying or would rather take the train, Amtrak and Via Rail Canada offer online reservations (www.amtrak.com and www.viarail.ca). If you're visiting Europe, you can buy your Eurailpass online at www.raileurope.com.

Major airline ticket sites, other than individual airlines, include

✔ **Expedia:** Microsoft's entry into the travel biz, now a part of the Interactive media empire (www.expedia.com).

✔ **Hotwire:** Multi-airline site offering discounted leftover tickets (www.hotwire.com).

✔ **Orbitz:** The high-tech entry into the travel biz, now part of the Cendant travel empire, with most airlines' weekly Web specials (www.orbitz.com).

✔ **Travelocity:** Sabre's entry into the travel biz (www.travelocity.com). Yahoo Travel and AOL's travel section are both Travelocity underneath.

More about online airlines

Because the online airline situation changes weekly, anything more we printed here would be out of date before you read it. One of the authors of this book is an air travel nerd in his spare time; to get his current list of online airline Web sites, Web specials, and online travel agents, visit his Web site, at `airinfo.aero`.

Even More Places to Shop

Here are a few other places for you to shop on the Web. We have even bought stuff from most of them.

Books, music, and more

You can't flip through the books in an online bookstore as easily as you can in person (although Amazon.com comes pretty close by offering a selection of pages from many books). However, if you know what you want, you can get good deals.

Here are some of the top sites:

✔ **Advanced Book Exchange** (`www.abebooks.com`): ABE offers the combined catalogs of thousands of second-hand booksellers. You'll pay the same as you would in the used bookshop (plus shipping, of course), and you'll save hours of searching. Whether you're looking for a favorite book from your childhood or a rare, first-edition *For Dummies* book, this site is worth visiting.

✔ **AddALL** (`www.addall.com`): AddALL is another good used-book site offering titles from thousands of used-book stores as well as a price comparison service for new books.

✔ **Amazon.com** (`www.amazon.com`): Amazon.com is one of online commerce's great success stories, springing up from nothing (if you call several million dollars of seed money nothing) to one of the Net's biggest online stores. Amazon has an enormous catalog of books, CDs, and a growing variety of other junk, much of which it can get to you in a few days. It also has an "affiliates" program in which other Web sites can refer you to their favorite books for sale at Amazon, creating sort of a virtual

virtual bookstore. For an example, see our Web site, at `net.gurus.com`, where we have links to Amazon for every book we have written in case, because of an oversight, you don't already have them all. Amazon sells most books at less than list price. They also have used books, DVDs, and just about everything else from pogo sticks to underwear.

✔ **Powell's Books** (`www.powellbooks.com`): Powell's Books is the country's largest independent (nonchain) bookstore and has a correspondingly large Web site offering new and used books. We like their e-mail newsletter with new and rediscovered books and author interviews.

✔ **Barnesandnoble.com** (`www.bn.com`): Barnes & Noble is the biggest bookstore chain in the United States, and its online bookstore is big, complete, and well done. You can even return online purchases at any of its stores. It also has a large selection of music.

✔ **J&R Music World** (`www.jr.com`): The online presence of one of New York's largest music stores has a huge selection of music CDs. You can also buy a stereo to listen to your new CDs and a refrigerator to keep appropriate beverages at hand.

Clothes

This section points out a few familiar clothing merchants with online stores. Directories such as Open Directory Project (ODP) and Yahoo have hundreds of other stores both familiar and obscure.

✔ **Lands' End** (`www.landsend.com`): Most of this catalog is online, and you can order anything you find in any of its individual printed catalogs along with online-only discounted overstocks. It also has plenty of the folksy blather that encourages you to think of the company in terms of a few folks in the cornfields of Wisconsin rather than a corporate mail-order colossus belonging to Sears Roebuck. (It's both, actually.) Moderately cool 3-D virtual models attempt to show what the clothes you're ordering look like on a cyborg with chunky hips just like yours.

✔ **REI** (`www.rei.com`): This large sports equipment and outdoor-wear co-op is headquartered in Seattle. Members get a small rebate on purchases. The whole catalog is online, and you can find occasional online specials and discounts.

✔ **The Gap** (`www.gap.com`): This site has the same stuff you find in the stores, but for people of unusual vertical or horizontal dimension, it also has jeans in sizes the stores don't stock, and the rotating pants in the pictures are pretty cool.

An online shopper's checklist

Here are some questions to keep in mind when you're shopping online. An astute shopper will notice that these are the same questions to keep in mind wherever you're shopping:

✔ Are the descriptions clear enough to know what you're ordering?

✔ Are the prices competitive, both with other online stores and with mail order and regular retail?

✔ Does the store have the products in stock, or does it offer a firm shipping date?

✔ Does the store have a good reputation?

✔ Does the store have a clearly written privacy policy that limits what it may do with the data it collects from you?

✔ Can you ask questions about your order?

✔ How can you return unsatisfactory goods?

Computers

When you're shopping for computer hardware online, be sure that the vendor you're considering offers both a good return policy (in case the computer doesn't work when it arrives) and a long warranty.

Here are a few well-known vendors:

✔ **Dell Computers** (`www.dell.com`): This site has an extensive catalog with online ordering and custom computer system configurations.

✔ **Apple Computer** (`store.apple.com`): The Apple site has lots of information about Macintosh computers, and now it offers online purchasing of iPods, too.

✔ **PC Connection and Mac Connection** (`www.pcconnection.com` and `www.macconnection.com`): For computer hardware, software, and accessories, PC and Mac Connection is one of the oldest and most reliable online sources. And you can get overnight delivery within the continental United States even if you order as late as 2 a.m.!

Auctions and used stuff

You can participate in online auctions of everything from computers and computer parts to antiques to vacation packages. Online auctions are like any other kind of auction in at least one respect: If you know what you're looking for and know what it's worth, you can get some great values; if you don't, you can easily overpay for junk. When someone swiped our car phone handset, at eBay we found an exact replacement phone for $31, rather than the $150 the manufacturer charged for just the handset.

Many auctions, notably eBay (as shown in Figure 10-4), also allow you to list your own stuff for sale, which can be a way to get rid of some of your household clutter a little more discreetly than in a yard sale. A service called *PayPal* (www.paypal.com), now owned by eBay, lets you accept credit card payment from the high bidder via e-mail. (See the sidebar, "E-mail cash to anyone.")

TIP

E-mail cash to anyone

Credit cards are easy to use — if you're *spending* money. But until recently, *receiving* payments by credit card has been all but impossible for individuals. Even small businesses found it expensive and time consuming to accept credit card payments. PayPal (www.paypal.com) has changed all that.

To send money, you have to have a PayPal account, but they're easy to open. Individual accounts are free, but you can't accept credit card payments. (PayPal doesn't put any limit on payments sent from bank accounts.) Premier accounts have no such limit but are charged a small fee on each payment they receive. After you open an account, you can send money to anyone who can receive e-mail. If the recipient doesn't already have a PayPal account, he will open one when he "cashes" your e-mail.

PayPal encourages you to give it your bank account number so it can take money for payments directly without having to pay the credit card companies, and so you can move money you receive into your account. PayPal verifies that it's really your account by making two random deposits of less than a dollar. You then have to tell PayPal the amount of the deposits to complete your registration.

Some green-eyed monster purporting to be PayPal has been sending out notices claiming to be from PayPal, soliciting your account number and password. PayPal will never, ever ask you for your password or account information in an e-mail message. Forward the fraudulent e-mail to PayPal; go to www.paypal.com and click the Security Center link.

PayPal is a boon to individuals who sell at auction sites like eBay, but it has many other uses, too. PayPal makes starting a small business on the Web easy; small organizations can use PayPal to collect payments for events like dinners and amateur theater, and it's just about the only way to make payments to individuals in other countries without paying a service charge larger than the amount you're paying. If you're thinking of accepting PayPal for things you sell, be sure to heed PayPal's warnings to ship only to verified addresses. Be sure to carefully comply with all the fine print to protect yourself against fraud. Most first-time sellers find out the hard way that it's they who pay the cost of fraud and even the cost of their customers' innocent errors. PayPal's fraud rate is lower than most credit-card fraud, but it's a case of *merchant beware* — know your customer and take appropriate steps to safeguard your transactions.

Figure 10-4:
You can find just about anything for sale on eBay.

Online auction sites include

- ✔ **eBay** (www.ebay.com): This is the most popular auction site on the Web, and people flock here to sell all sorts of stuff, from baby clothes and toys to computer parts to cars to the occasional tropical island. You can sell stuff, too, by registering as a seller. eBay charges a small commission for auctions, which the seller pays. Searching the auctions at eBay is also a terrific way to find out what something is worth. If you were thinking of selling that rare Beanie Baby, search the completed auctions for the bad news that it's worth slightly less than it was when it was new. Many sellers also offer "Buy it now" fixed price sales. See *eBay For Dummies*, 4th Edition by Marsha Collier (Wiley Publishing, Inc.) for more.

- ✔ **Yahoo Auctions** (auctions.yahoo.com): eBay was such a big hit that Yahoo decided to hold auctions, too.

- ✔ **priceline.com** (www.priceline.com): This site sells airline tickets, hotel rooms, new cars, prepaid long distance phone service, and a grab bag of other items. It's not exactly an auction; you specify a price for what you want and Priceline accepts or rejects it.

Food

To show the range of edibles available online, here are some of our favorite places to point, click, and chow down:

- **Cabot Creamery** (`www.cabotcheese.com`): This site sells the best cheese in Vermont.

- **Bobolink Dairy** (`www.cowsoutside.com`): A recovering software nerd and his family in rural New Jersey make and sell their own cheese — a rich, gooey, French-style cheese. You can even order cheese made from yak milk in Tibet. The URL refers to cows out in the pasture rather than tied up in the barn.

- **Gimme Coffee** (`www.gimmecoffee.com`): Highly opinionated coffee from the wilds of upstate New York. Online orders handled through PayPal; follow the Visit Our Stores link to find pictures of the place John goes when in need of literary inspiration, also know as *caffeine*.

- **Gaspar's** (`www.linguica.com`): If you weren't aware that Portuguese garlic sausage is one of the four basic food groups, this site will fix that problem. Oddly, online orders incur steep shipping charges, but phone or fax orders are shipped free, so we print and fax the order form.

- **Peapod** (`www.peapod.com`): Peapod lets you shop for groceries online and then delivers them to your home. You have to live in an area that the parent grocery chains serve. If you live somewhere else, Netgrocer (`www.netgrocer.com`) delivers nonperishables by rather pricey overnight express.

The Shopping Update

Like everything else on the Net, shopping changes day by day as new businesses appear and old ones change. For the latest updates, see our update pages at `net.gurus.com/shopping`.

Chapter 11

Banking, Bill-Paying, and Investing Online

* *

In This Chapter

▶ Managing your checking and savings accounts online

▶ Looking at your credit card statements online

▶ E-mailing payments with PayPal

▶ Managing your investments online

* *

*O*nce upon a time, money was substantial stuff that glinted in the sun and clinked when you dropped it on the table. Investments were engraved certificates that you kept in your safety deposit box if they worked out, and used as bathroom wallpaper if not. Well, that was then. Now money and investments are mere electronic blips scampering from computer to computer, and if you do any banking or investing, one of the computers they scamper through might as well be yours.

You can do just about any banking online that doesn't require physically handling pieces of paper, which means everything except depositing checks and withdrawing cash. For those, you have to use an ATM, or, for the truly retro, you can actually visit a bank branch and talk to a human being. But we'll help you avoid that last one as much as possible.

Going to the Bank without Ever Leaving Home

Nearly every bank in the country now offers online banking. They don't do it to be cool; they do it because online banking is vastly cheaper for them than ATMs or tellers. Because both you and your bank have a strong interest in making sure that the person messing around online with your accounts is *you,* the signup process is usually a bit complicated — with the bank calling you to verify that you signed up, or mailing you a paper letter with your password. After you're signed up, you visit the bank's Web site and log in with your new username or number and password. Each bank's Web site is different, but they all show you an account statement along the lines of the one from John's bank in Figure 11-1.

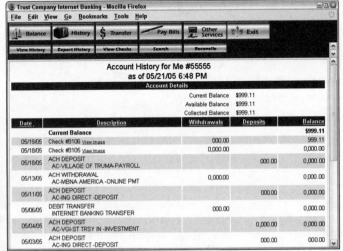

Figure 11-1:
A week of bank stuff, give or take a few details.

As you can see, deposits and withdrawals look similar to a conventional printed statement that you would receive in the mail. If you click the *View image* link next to a check number, it shows you a picture of the cancelled check. The ACH lines are for Automated Clearing House, described in a nearby sidebar.

If you use an accounting program like Quicken or Microsoft Money, banks invariably offer a way to download your account info into your program. Look for a link called Download or Export. In Figure 11-1, it's the small Export History button near the top left.

Details differ, but beyond the capability to check your statement, banks all offer roughly the same services, including transfers and bill-paying.

ACH! It's better than a check!

For the past 150 years or so, the usual way to get money from one person's account at one bank to a second person's account at another bank has been for the first person to write a check and give it to the second person, who takes it to her bank and deposits it. (At least, that's the system in the U.S. — in Europe, the first person writes out a bank transfer and gives it to his bank to initiate the payment.) Now that we're in the computer age, we have a high-tech replacement for this process called *Automated Clearing House transfers,* or ACH for short.

ACH transfers can do anything a check can do. Rather than print payroll checks, companies can use ACH to deposit the money directly into employees' bank accounts. The U.S. Government uses ACH to make social security payments. You can use ACH to pay bills or to move money between accounts at different banks. For most purposes, ACH is better than paper checks because it's faster and more reliable.

To identify the account to use for an ACH transfer, you need to provide the *routing number* that identifies the bank and the account number at that bank. The easiest way to find the numbers for your own checking account is to look at the line of funny-looking numbers printed along the bottom of one of your checks. The routing number is nine digits, usually printed at the left end of the line. The account number also appears on that line, and a check number (which ACH doesn't use) may appear, too. Savings accounts work for ACH transfers, too; to get the routing number, look at a check on the same bank or call the bank and ask.

You may be wondering "Can anyone who knows my account number suck money out of my account using ACH?" Yes, but when you get your statement, you can challenge any bogus ACH transaction just as you'd challenge a forged check and get your money back. In practice, ACH is safe and reliable and we use it for our own accounts all the time.

Transferring money between bank accounts

If you have more than one account at a bank, a checking and savings account, some CDs, or a mortgage, you can usually move money from one account to another. In the account in Figure 11-1, the line that says INTERNET BANKING TRANSFER indicates that money has been transferred from the checking account to a mortgage account to make the monthly mortgage payment. To get a better idea of how this works, here are the steps for transferring money from a checking account to a mortgage account (note again that the specific steps vary from bank to bank):

1. **Click the Transfer button (or whatever your bank's Web site calls it).**

2. **Enter the amount you want to transfer in the box called something like Amount.**

3. **Select the account the transferred money's coming from, generally from a list of possible "from" accounts.**

4. **Select the account number the transferred money's going to, generally from a list of possible "to" accounts.**

5. **Click the button called something like Transfer or Do It — and it's done.**

It's that easy. Most banks handle transfers within the same bank the same day; at John's bank, you can enter a transfer as late as 7:00 p.m., which is handy when you remember at dinnertime that the mortgage is due today.

Many banks also let you make transfers to and from accounts at *other* banks, using ACH. To set up the transfers, you provide the other bank's routing number and account number. Depending on the bank, they may want a voided check from that account, they may verify that the account name is the same as your account name, or they may just believe the numbers you enter. After you set up a transfer, it's like a transfer within your own bank: you specify the accounts and the amount and click. You can also do transfers between your bank and your mutual fund or brokerage account. In Figure 11-1, for example, the ACH deposits from ING DIRECT are from another bank, and the ACH deposit from VGI-ST TRSY is from a Vanguard mutual fund.

Transfers to other banks have two important differences: time and price. Even though the transfer is handled entirely electronically, it takes anywhere from two days to a week for the money to show up at the other end, depending on the other bank. The time it takes for any particular bank is pretty consistent, so if they took three days last time, expect it to take three days next time — but if you really need the money to be there so you can write checks on it, allow a week, and keep an eye on your balances until you've done enough transfers to know how long they take.

The price for transfers varies from two bucks down to zero, with no consistency among banks. A transfer can be started from either the sending or receiving end; often a bank charges you $1 if you tell them to *send* money to bank B, but if (instead) you tell bank B to *receive* the exact same money from bank A, it's free.

One handy and increasingly common way to do online transfers is through PayPal (described later in this chapter). With PayPal, you can move money from just about any bank account to any other bank account for free.

Paying bills online

Writing checks is *so* 20th-century. Now you can pay most of your bills online. In many cases, companies to whom you make monthly payments can arrange for automatic payments from your bank account. (In Figure 11-1, MBNA AMERICA is the MasterCard bill.) We've arranged for payments for credit cards, the electric and gas company, and mobile phones — a pretty typical mix. Each of these companies has its own procedure. Let's use the electric company in an example to show how this usually works. You send the electric company a voided check on your bank account, or sometimes you just enter the routing number and account number that ACH needs (see the sidebar "ACH! It's better than a check!"). After your payment is set up, the payee (the electric company, here) pays the bill from your bank account on the bill's due date.

If you want to automate all of your bill-paying, most banks can accommodate you with a *bill-pay* service. Most banks use one of a handful of specialized companies in this field (CheckFree is the best known). Usually there are two levels of service: one only lets you pay bills from a list of about 300 large companies that want to send you your bill electronically; the other lets you pay anyone. The first version is available for free on the Web sites of most of the companies you can pay, through banks that resell the service, or directly. (CheckFree's is at www.mycheckfree.com.)

Figure 11-2 shows the free version of CheckFree offered by MBNA, a large credit-card bank. To set it up, you pick the companies to pay and then enter your account number and some other info from the bill to be sure they get the right bill. You have the option of *electronic presentment,* which means you get your bill on the Web rather than by paper mail. You also tell the system which bank account you want to pay the bills from by entering the ACH info. (See the sidebar, "ACH! It's better than a check!") Then, to pay your bills each month, you just visit the Web site and enter the amount to pay and the date. They automatically move the money out of your account on that date.

The 300 companies that participate in Checkfree's free service all accept ACH payments. For the paid service, if your payee doesn't want ACH, they print out an old-fashioned paper check on your account and mail it.

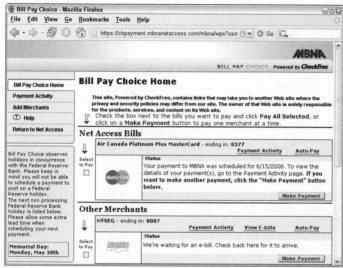

Figure 11-2:
Ready to
pay some
bills.

Other online bank services

Since doing business over the Web is so much cheaper than doing it in person, banks are putting all sorts of other services online. Visit your bank's Web site and see what it offers. Among some of the services we've seen offered are

- ✓ Loan applications
- ✓ Retirement accounts
- ✓ Checkbook-balancing calculators

A few recommended banks

These days, any bank you pass while driving down the street offers online banking, but there are also specialist banks that do everything online. To give you a flavor of what's available, here are two banks that we've used and recommend:

ING Bank

www.ingdirect.com

ING is a very large Dutch bank with subsidiaries all over the world. In the U.S., their subsidiary is a savings bank that offers online accounts with better interest rates than most competitors (and no minimum balances) by reducing expensive human-to-human transactions as far as possible: You do everything online. (They have an office in Wilmington, Delaware, that we walked past one time but we didn't see any reason to go in.)

To open an account, you fill out a form on the Web site, including the ACH info about a checking account you link to your new ING account. When it's set up, you can move money back and forth between the accounts as needed, with the restriction that money you put into your ING account has to stay there for a week before you can get it back; it's a savings account, not a checking account. They also offer certificates of deposit, mortgages, home-equity loans, and retirement accounts.

Waterhouse Bank

www.waterhousebank.com

Later on in this chapter, we discuss the discount stockbroker TD Waterhouse. Down the virtual hall from the broker is the TD Waterhouse bank — which offers bank accounts with all the usual features — checks, ATM cards, overdraft protection, online bill payments to anyone, and the like — with nearly everything being free if you have a brokerage account. Most online brokers

How safe are these banks, anyway?

When you open a bank account in person, you visit the bank and look around and see that the bank looks like a bank, with tellers, people in suits, and a vault, which is good, or you see a couple of people in a Winnebago with some card tables and money in cooler chests, which is bad. When you visit a bank's Web site, it's hard to tell a good one from a bad one. But it's not hard to do a little research.

Every real bank in the United States is a member of the Federal Deposit Insurance Corporation (FDIC). The FDIC has a nice Web site at www. fdic.gov that, among other things, offers detailed reports on each member bank. On the home page, click the DEPOSIT INSURANCE link near the top left, then click Is My Bank Insured. On that page, you can search by name or by location. For example, to check out ING Bank,

enter its full name (**ING bank, fsb**, as it says on their home page) and search. (For this particular bank, an alternative route to this same information is to click the FDIC icon on the bank's home page.) Either way, you get a reassuring page saying, yes, it's insured. For more info, click Financial Information and see their latest balance sheets. In ING Bank's case, it says that the bank has $43 billion in assets and $4 billion in capital. Sounds like a bank to us.

If you do business with a credit union (not a bad idea if you're eligible for one), they're insured by the National Credit Union Association at www. ncua.gov. Click Credit Union Data in the pane down the left side of the screen and then click the Find a Credit Union link near the middle of the page that appears.

offer bank accounts to their customers; this one is typical. (If you don't have a brokerage account, you have to open your bank account in person at their office in beautiful Jersey City, New Jersey, so let's assume you already have an account.) Since you probably don't get to their ATM in Jersey City very often, they rebate a dollar every time you use another bank's ATM to cover the other bank's fee. You can transfer money online between your bank account and your brokerage account. Because there's no minimum required either in your checking account or the brokerage account to which it is linked, this kind of account is a very good deal if you have any investments at all with an online broker.

They also offer some more exotic services, notably telephone transfer to and from accounts at their Canadian affiliate TD Canada Trust at favorable exchange rates, for people who travel to Canada enough to have a bank account there.

Dealing with Credit Cards

Just about every credit card in the country offers online access for the same reason that bank accounts do — online transactions are a lot cheaper for them than if you call their 800 number.

Online credit-card services start with applying for the card. Search Google for "credit cards" and you will find a myriad of offers. They change daily, but you can look for various goodies — no annual fee, bonuses and rebates, and low interest rates. Most of the sites that appear to compare cards are in fact selling one bank's cards, so treat their claims of unique and superior features with skepticism.

After you have your card, typical online conveniences include these:

- Checking your balance and recent transactions
- Paying your bill from your checking account, using CheckFree or a similar service
- Applying for a credit line increase
- Asking for copies of sales slips for charges you don't recognize or challenging ones you think are bogus
- Downloading account information into Quicken and other personal finance programs
- Creating single-use card numbers for online shopping. (See Chapter 10.)

Different credit-card-issuing banks have somewhat different versions of these services, but it's difficult to compare them without getting the credit card first. For example, if you have a Bank of America credit card, you can set up automatic payments to pay each bill in full on the due date, getting the maximum use of your money without paying interest. But if your card is from MBNA, you have to visit its Web site each month to schedule the month's payment. On the other hand, MBNA has single-use card numbers and Bank of America doesn't. We'd make a list of features, but it'd be out of date before it was printed, so you'll have to visit the Web sites of banks of interest and see what they're offering.

Paying Your Pals with PayPal

Credit cards are easy to use — if you're *spending* money. But until recently, it has been all but impossible for individuals (rather than companies) to *receive* payments by credit card. Even small businesses found it expensive and time-consuming to accept credit-card payments. PayPal (www.paypal.com) has changed all that, as well as providing an easy way to move money among accounts at different banks.

PayPal is a boon to individuals who sell at auction sites like eBay (which owns PayPal), but it has many other uses, too. PayPal makes it easy to start a small business on the Web. Small organizations can use PayPal to collect payments for events like dinners and amateur theater, non-profits can accept donations, and it's just about the only way to make payments to individuals in other countries without paying a service charge larger than the amount you're paying.

If you plan to accept PayPal for your business, be sure to heed PayPal's warnings regarding shipping *only to verified buyer addresses*. Be sure to comply carefully with all the fine print to protect yourself against fraud. Most first-time sellers learn the hard way that it's they who pay the cost of fraud — and even the cost of their customers' innocent errors. PayPal's fraud rate is lower than that of most credit-card fraud, but it's a case of *merchant beware* — know your customer and take appropriate steps to safeguard your transactions.

PayPal offers the following services, but there are a few rules to observe:

- ✔ To send money, you have to have a PayPal account, but an account is easy to open.

- ✔ After you open an account, you can send money to anyone who can receive e-mail. If that person doesn't already have a PayPal account, he or she will open one when "cashing" your e-mail. The money you send can come from the balance in your PayPal account, or from a bank account or credit card you link to your Paypal account.

- ✔ Once there's money in your account, you can use it to pay other people, move it to your linked bank account, or spend it with a debit card linked to your Paypal account.

- ✔ Individual accounts are free, but you can't accept credit-card payments. (There's no limit on accepting payments sent from bank accounts, though.)

- ✔ Premier accounts have no such limit on accepting payments, but are charged a commission on each payment they receive.

The folks at PayPal encourage you to provide them with your bank account number so that when somebody pays you, PayPal can take the money directly. That way they don't have to pay the credit-card companies, and you can move any money you receive into your account with minimum hassle.

Be careful about giving your bank-account information to *anyone*. A variety of criminals send out huge numbers of notices, claiming to be from PayPal, claiming that you "must" provide them with your account number and password right away to clear up an account problem. Don't fall for it. PayPal will *never*, *ever* ask you for your password or account information in an e-mail message — or anywhere other than on their Web site (at `https://www.paypal.com`). Help take a "byte" out of crime: Forward any such fraudulent e-mail to PayPal. Just go to PayPal's Web site and click the Security Center link.

When you first tell Paypal to link your account to a bank account, PayPal verifies your bank account number by making two random deposits of less than a dollar. You then have to tell PayPal the amount of the deposits to complete your registration. You can link several bank accounts to your PayPal account, then move money out of one account into PayPal, wait a few days for the transaction to be complete, and then move the money out of PayPal into a different account — all for free.

If you leave money in your PayPal account, it pays interest at a decent rate — but since PayPal isn't a bank, your money is safer in your bank account. (Most U.S. bank accounts are insured; PayPal accounts are not.) We recommend that you only leave money in PayPal that you're planning to use within a few days. ING Direct (described earlier in the chapter) is a real bank and generally pays a higher interest rate than PayPal. You can easily open an account at ING Direct and link your PayPal account to it, as well as linking your PayPal account to your main bank account.

Investing Your Money Online

If you invest in mutual funds or the stock market (something that's difficult to avoid these days unless you anticipate dying at an early age), you can find a remarkable range of resources online. An enormous amount of stock information is also available, providing Net users with research resources as good as professional analysts had before the advent of online investing.

The most important thing to remember about *all* online financial resources is that everyone has an ax to grind — and wants to get paid somehow. In most cases, the situation is straightforward; for example, a mutual-fund manager wants you to invest with her funds, and a stockbroker wants you to buy and sell stocks with him. Some other sites are less obvious: Some are supported by advertising, and others push certain special kinds of investments. Just consider the source (and any vested interests they may have) when you're considering that source's advice.

Mutual funds

Mutual funds are definitely the investment of the Baby Boomer generation. The world now has more mutual funds than it has stocks for the funds to buy. (Kind of makes you wonder, doesn't it?) Most fund managers have at least descriptions of the funds and prospectuses online, and many now provide online access so you can check your account, move money from one fund to another within a fund group, and buy and sell funds — all with the money coming from and going to your bank account via ACH.

Well-known fund groups include

- ✔ **Fidelity Investments** (`www.fidelity.com`): This 500-pound gorilla of mutual funds specializes in actively managed funds.

- ✔ **Vanguard Group** (`www.vanguard.com`): The other 500-pound gorilla specializes in low-cost and index funds.

- ✔ **American Century** (`www.americancentury.com`): This company offers another broad group of funds.

Many online brokers listed in the following section also let you buy and sell mutual funds, although it almost always costs less to do that if you deal directly with a fund manager. The Open Directory Project has a long list of funds and fund groups at `dmoz.org/Business/Investing/Mutual_Funds`.

Stockbrokers

Most well-known, full-service brokerage firms have jumped onto the Web, along with a new generation of low-cost online brokers that offer remarkably cheap stock trading. A trade that may cost $100 with a full-service firm can cost as little as $8 with a low-cost broker. The main difference is that the cheap firms don't offer investment advice and don't assign you to a specific broker. For people who do their own research and don't want advice from a broker, the low-cost firms work well. For people who do need some advice, the partial- or full-service firms often offer lower-cost trades online, and they let you get a complete view of your account whenever you want. The number of extra services the brokerages offer (such as retirement accounts, dividend reinvestment, and automatic transfers to and from your checking account) varies widely.

Online brokers include

- ✔ **Charles Schwab** (`www.schwab.com`): One of the oldest discount brokers.

- ✔ **TD Ameritrade** (`www.ameritrade.com`): A low-cost, limited-advice broker, affiliated with Toronto-Dominion bank, one of the largest Canadian banks. If you open an account, also consider a bank account at Waterhouse Bank, described earlier in the chapter.

- ✔ **E*TRADE** (`www.etrade.com`): Another low-cost, no-advice broker, which also offers bank accounts, credit cards, boat loans, and just about every other financial service known to humankind.

- ✔ **Smith Barney** (`www.smithbarney.com`): A full-service broker with online access to accounts and research info, and a subsidiary of Citigroup, one of the largest banks in the world.

Most fund groups, including the ones in the preceding list, have brokerage departments — which can be a good choice if you want to hold both individual stocks and funds.

Tracking your portfolio

Several services let you track your portfolio online. You enter the number of shares of each fund and stock you own, and the service can tell you — at any time — exactly how much they're worth and how much money you lost today. Some of them send a daily e-mail portfolio report, if you want. These reports are handy if you have mutual funds from more than one group or both funds and stocks. All the tracking services are either supported by advertising or run by a brokerage that hopes to get your trading business.

- ✔ **My Yahoo** (my.yahoo.com): You can enter multiple portfolios and customize your screens with related company and general news reports. You can also get lots of company and industry news, including some access to sites that otherwise require paid subscriptions. It's advertiser-supported, comprehensive, and easy to use.

- ✔ **Smart Money** (www.smartmoney.com): The online face of *Smart Money* magazine. Track portfolios and read news stories. Although they'd really like you to subscribe to the magazines, the free portfolio tracker isn't bad.

- ✔ **MSN MoneyCentral** (moneycentral.msn.com): This service also has portfolios and lots of information, although we find it cumbersome to set up and more of a pain to use than My Yahoo.

Chapter 12

Swiping Files from the Net

- -

In This Chapter

▶ Using your Web browser to download files

▶ Uploading your Web pages to Web servers

▶ Sharing files with other Netizens

▶ Installing software you've swiped from the Net

- -

*T*he Internet is chock-full of computers, and those computers are chock-full of files. What's in those files? Programs, pictures, sounds, movies, documents, spreadsheets, recipes, *Anne of Green Gables* (the entire book and several of the sequels), you name it. Some of the computers are set up so that you can copy some of the files they contain to your own computer, usually for free. In this chapter, we tell you how to find some of those files and how to copy and use them.

What Is Downloading?

Downloading means copying files from a computer Up There On The Internet "down" to the computer sitting on or under your desk. *Uploading* is the reverse — copying a file from your computer "up" to a computer on the Internet.

You probably won't be surprised to hear that there are at least three different ways to download and upload files:

- ✔ **Click a link on a Web page.** Web browsers can download files, too. In fact, they do it all time when they download Web pages so you can see them.

- ✔ **Participate in a file-sharing service.** Since these are of dubious legality, and tend to install spyware on your computer, we don't recommend most of them. (See Chapter 9 for more details.)

- ✔ **Run a file-transfer program.** *FTP* stands for File Transfer Protocol, an older (but still very popular) way that computers transfer files across the Internet.

You can also transfer files by attaching them to e-mail messages sent to other e-mail users, which we discuss in Chapter 15.

By far the easiest way to download files is by using your Web browser — clicking links is our favorite method of finding and downloading files.

How you download a file and what you do with it once you have it also depends on what's in the file. This chapter describes how to download pictures, programs, and other files. If you want to download music and video, see Chapter 9.

Downloading Pictures

To download a picture from the Web, follow these steps:

1. **Display the picture in your Web browser.**

2. **Right-click the picture.**

   A menu of commands appears. A small number of Web sites disable right-clicking pictures to prevent you from saving them. Oh, well!

3. **Choose Save Image As (in Firefox) or Save Picture As (in Internet Explorer).**

4. **In the Save Image or Save Picture dialog box that appears, tell your browser where to save the picture on your computer.**

   You can choose the folder where you want to put it, and the filename to use.

5. **Click Save.**

That's all it takes!

Graphics files have special filename extensions that identify what graphics format the file is in. When you download a picture, you can change the name of the file but *don't* change the extension. Common extensions are GIF, JPG, and TIF. (See the section "For the Artistically Inclined" in Chapter 20 for a roundup of graphic file formats.)

Art ain't free

As plentiful as art is on the Internet, consider: Somebody had to work to create every one of those images. Some of the artists want to control what happens to their work, or even get paid for it (what a concept) . . . .

Just because a picture is on a Web page doesn't mean that no one owns it. Nearly all graphics on Web pages are copyrighted, and it's not legal to use the picture without getting permission from the copyright owner. No one is going to sue you for storing a picture on your computer (so far as we know — we're not lawyers) but don't plan on using downloaded graphics in your own Web site or publication without getting permission. Unless a picture comes from a site that specifically offers pictures as reusable *clipart* (that is, art you can clip and use), you have to get permission to reuse the picture for most purposes — even to upload it to your own noncommercial Web page.

To find clipart sources, search for "clip art" or "clipart" — and include a word or phrase describing what you need a picture of. Some of what you're shown is free, and some requires a subscription or payment per picture. We like www.clipart.com, which requires a subscription fee but offers a mountain of clipart and photos you can legally download and reuse.

Sharing pictures

We love sharing our family photos with other people, and the Web makes it easy. Also, sharing via the Web saves you the cost of making extra prints of your snapshots, and it's quick. Several Web sites enable you to upload your digital pictures to the site and share them with your friends and family. These photo-sharing sites make their money by selling prints — once your family sees that gorgeous shot of little Mary finger-painting with pudding, they'll *have* to have a copy for the fridge!

Here are a few good photo-sharing sites:

✔ Kodak's www.kodakgallery.com, which (not surprisingly) offers Kodak prints. This site used to be called Ofoto, and typing www.ofoto.com takes you to the same site.

✔ Snapfish, at www.snapfish.com. Hewlett-Packard now owns the site.

Downloading Programs

Lots of the programs that this book recommends can be downloaded from the Web, often for free. This section describes the process for downloading programs and getting them running.

The plan: download, install, and run

When you download a program, you transfer a file from a computer on the Internet to your computer. But the program is still trapped inside the file — you usually need to take some additional steps to let it out. The file you download is usually an installation program, which you run to install the actual program. While you are at it, you'd be wise to scan the program for viruses before running it.

All these steps are described in the following pages — just keep reading!

Finding programs to download

The first step in downloading a program is to find it. In some cases, you already know the Web address where the file is available for download. For example, in Chapter 6 we recommend that you stop using Internet Explorer as your Web browser, because it is a target for viruses and spyware. (Chapter 2 describes what we mean by viruses and spyware.) We suggest that you switch to Firefox, which is a free download from the Web site getfirefox.com or www.mozilla.org/products/firefox.

In other cases, you may hear about a program, but you don't know where to find it. Google is your friend — search for the program's name and you will probably find its source.

Programs may or may not be free

Some software is free — it's called *freeware*. Freeware is available for download for free with no strings attached. Firefox is freeware, as are some of the programs at www.download.com.

However, some downloadable software isn't totally free. When the authors ask for a donation if you like the program — on the honor system — it's called *shareware*. You can download and install the program for free (just like freeware), but if you keep using it, you should feel honor-bound to make a donation to the author. (If you don't, then don't expect the program to be updated in the long run!) The site from which you download shareware should indicate what

the requested donation is. You can usually also choose Help from the program's menu to find out how to make a donation.

Finally, some downloaded programs are *trial versions* or *crippleware*, which are time-limited or otherwise-limited versions of the program. You can use the downloaded program for free, but if you want the real, complete program, you'll need to pay for it. The program itself will tell you what the limitations are, what the price is, and how to pay. Some programs don't limit the features, but they display ads unless you pay — a reasonable tradeoff, in our opinion.

Other good sources for downloadable programs are software libraries like
these:

✔ www.download.com includes reviews of the downloadable programs

✔ www.shareware.com is a great source for shareware (that is, programs
that you can use for free, but for which you should really make a donation if you use it often)

✔ www.tucows.com (The Ultimate Collection Of Windows Software, which
now also includes Mac programs) is a large, well-organized collection
with user ratings, one cow to five.

Downloading a program

Before you start downloading, make a folder to store all your downloaded
files. In Windows, we make a folder in our My Documents folder, and we
name it something like Downloaded Files or Downloads. (To create a folder
in My Documents, launch Windows Explorer or My Computer, select the
My Documents folder, and choose File➪New➪Folder from the menu.)

Downloading a program file over the Web is easy — you click a link to it, frequently a link that says either *Download* or the name of the program. Your
Web browser stops and asks you what to do with the file. If it's a program
(in Windows, a file with the extension .exe or .com) or a ZIP file (with the
extension .zip), the most reasonable thing for you to do is to save it to disk
(in your Downloads folder) so you can deal with it later.

If you're interested in downloading an Internet program, for example, you may
go to TUCOWS, The Ultimate Collection of Windows (and Mac) Software, at
www.tucows.com. After you're at the site, click links to choose the operating
system you use, choose a site near you, and choose the type of programs you
want to download. TUCOWS displays a list of programs available for downloading. Alternatively, type a program name into the Search box to find programs
by that name. When you find the page about the program, you can download
its program file; just click the name of the program, or the Download Now
button, or another appropriate-sounding link.

Uncompressing and unzipping

Most downloadable software on the Internet is in a compressed format to save
both storage space on the server and transmission time when you download
the file. Most software is *self-installing* — the file is (or contains) a program that
does the necessary uncompressing and installing. Self-installing Windows files
have the extension .exe, and non-self-installing compressed files have the
extension .zip.

Viruses and spyware can be contained in .exe files, too, so don't run an executable file unless you are sure that you know what's in it! Stick with the software libraries we recommend in this chapter because they scan their files for viruses and spyware. Or download programs directly from the software organization (for example, get Firefox from www.mozilla.org).

To install a self-installing file, just double-click the file to run it. The file should open itself and walk you through a wizard-style set of windows to collect any needed setup info — and then install itself.

If a file is compressed, you need a program to deal open and uncompress it. Files with the file extension .zip identify compressed files (these files are called, amazingly, *ZIP files*). If you use Windows XP, its Compressed Folders feature (which is normally turned on) lets you open ZIP files right in Windows Explorer windows. Just double-click the ZIP file to see what's inside it.

If you don't use Windows XP, programs like WinZip (downloadable from www.winzip.com) can both unzip and zip things for you. We also like ZipMagic (available from www.allume.com/win/zipmagic), which makes ZIP files look like Windows folders, just like Windows XP's Compressed Folders. (Mac users, see the sidebar "Mac users say StuffIt" in this chapter.)

If you use Windows XP or you already have WinZip (which is also available through the mail or from various shareware outlets), skip the next section.

Getting and running WinZip

To get WinZip from the Web, go to www.winzip.com. Click Download or Download Evaluation to get to the download page. On that page, click the link for your version of Windows, tell Windows where you want to store the WinZip program (your Downloads folder), and wait for it to download.

To install WinZip, follow these steps:

1. **Run the file you just downloaded.**

   The file is named something like Winzip90.exe, depending on the version.

2. **Follow the installation instructions WinZip gives you.**

   Although you have a bunch of options, you can accept the suggested defaults for all of them.

Give it a try! Double-click that icon! WinZip looks like Figure 12-1.

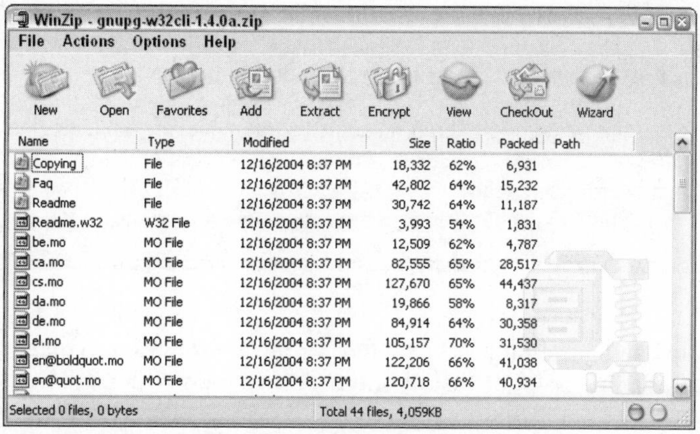

Figure 12-1:
WinZip is
ready to
deal with
your ZIP
files.

Zipping and unzipping with WinZip

To open a ZIP file (which the WinZip folks call an *archive*), click the Open button and choose the directory and filename for the ZIP file. Poof! WinZip displays a list of the files in the archive, with their dates and sizes.

If you want to use a file from a ZIP file, you have to open the ZIP file and *extract* it — that is, you ask WinZip to uncompress it and store it in a new file. To extract a file, follow these steps:

1. **Choose the file from the list of files.**

   You can choose a group of files that are listed together by clicking the first one and then Shift+clicking the last one. To select an additional file, Ctrl+click it.

2. **Click the Extract button.**

   A dialog box asks in which directory you want to put the extracted files, and whether you want to extract all the files in the archive or just the one you selected.

3. **Select the directory in which you want to store the unzipped files.**

4. **Click OK.**

   WinZip unzips the file and puts its contents in your chosen directory. The ZIP file is unchanged, and now you have the uncompressed file (or files) that was in it as well.

Mac users say StuffIt

Mac users can get programs named ZipIt, Unzip, or MindExpander from www.macorchard.com. The most popular is a shareware program, by Raymond Lau, known as StuffIt Expander. StuffIt comes in many flavors, including a shareware version and a commercial version from www.stuffit.com. StuffIt files of all varieties generally end with the extension .sit.

If WinZip can figure out that a ZIP file contains a program to install, it will often offer a Checkout or Install button. Checkout extracts all the files and then makes a menu window where you can easily click whichever extracted file(s) you want to open or run. Install runs a self-installing ZIP file for you.

Although WinZip can do a bunch of other things, too, such as add files to a ZIP file and create your own ZIP file, you don't have to know how to perform these tasks in order to swipe software from the Net, so we skip them. (We bet that you can figure them out just by looking at the buttons on the WinZip toolbar.) WinZip is shareware, so if you use it much, please register it and send Mr. WinZip his fee so he can afford to eat and keep developing new versions.

Scanning for viruses

We warn you about viruses in Chapter 2, and encourage you to install a virus-checker in Chapter 4. Chapter 14 describes how to configure your virus-checker, and how to tell your e-mail program not to run programs that you receive by e-mail. As you can tell, we take viruses seriously, and we think you should, too.

We all know that you practice safe software: You check every new program you get to make sure that it doesn't contain any hidden software viruses that may display obnoxious messages, or trash your hard drive. If that's true of you (no fibbing, now), then you can skip this section.

For the rest of you — make that all of us, these days — it's a good idea to run a virus-scanning program at regular intervals, and keep it updated. You never know what naughty piece of code you may otherwise unwittingly download to your defenseless computer!

Run your virus checker after you have obtained and run *any* new piece of software. Although the Web and FTP servers on the Internet make every effort to keep their software archives virus-free, nobody is perfect.

If you use WinZip, you can configure it to run your virus checker before you even unzip the ZIP file containing a program. Choose Options⇨Configuration from the menu, click the Program Locations tab, and in the Scan program box, type the pathname of your virus-checker program.

Installing the program

Okay, now you have the downloaded program file, and you know that it's safe to proceed. However, most downloaded programs are still trapped in an installation file — they aren't ready to use yet. For example, when you download Firefox, you get a file with a name like Firefox Setup 1.2.6.exe. (The .exe at the end tells you that it's a program; it's short for *executable*.) That's not Firefox; it's the Firefox Setup program, which *contains* Firefox.

To install the program, double-click the name of the setup program in Windows Explorer or My Computer. The setup program probably creates an icon for the program on your desktop. In Windows, it may also add the program to your Start menu.

Some simple programs don't come with an installation program — you just get the program itself, and after it's unzipped, you need only run the program you extracted from the ZIP file. To make the program easy to run, you need an icon for it. You can create your own icon or menu item for the program. In Windows, follow these steps:

1. **Run either My Computer or Windows Explorer and select the program file (the file with the extension .exe, or occasionally .com or .msi).**

2. **Use your right mouse button to drag the filename out on the desktop or into an open folder on the desktop.**

   An icon for the program appears.

Another method is to choose Start⇨Programs or Start⇨All Programs, find the menu choice for the program, hold down the Shift key, drag the menu choice to the desktop, and release the Shift key. Windows copies the menu choice as an icon on the desktop.

To run your new program, you can just click or double-click the icon (depending on how you have Windows configured — try clicking first, and if nothing happens, double-click). Cool!

Configuring the program

Now you can run the program. Hooray!

You may have to tell the program, however, about your Internet address or your computer or who knows what before it can do its job. Refer to the text files (if any) that came with the program — or choose Help from the program's menu bar — to get more information about how to configure and run your new program. The Web site from which you got the program may have some explanations, too.

Downloading Other Types of Files

If you want to download some other type of file — like a Word document, a spreadsheet, a database, or some other kind of file — you can use the same general steps:

1. **Find the file on the Web.**

   Search the Web for it.

2. **Follow the instructions on the Web page to download the file.**

   This step usually just means clicking a Download button.

3. **When your browser displays a Save or Save As dialog box, choose where to put the file.**

   If you have created a Downloads or Downloaded Files folder, put it there. Or put it in the folder where you want the file to end up.

4. **Check the file for viruses.**

   See the section "Scanning for viruses" earlier in this chapter for details.

5. **Unzip the file if necessary.**

   If the file is large, or you're downloading a group of files, the file(s) may be compressed into a ZIP file. See the "Uncompressing and unzipping" section (earlier in this chapter) for how to uncompress the file.

6. **Open the file with its matching program.**

   If you downloaded a Word document, open it in Word. (Duh!) If you aren't sure what kind of file you've got, or what program opens it, display the filename in My Computer or Windows Explorer and double-click the filename. If you have a program installed that can open the file, Windows should run the program and open the file automatically.

Your files are ready to use!

Downloading the old-fashioned way with FTP

Back before the Web was even invented, the Internet was up and running. (And yes, Al Gore was a major player in getting the funding that made the Internet possible.) When you wanted to download a file, you used an FTP program — File Transfer Protocol. You needed to know the name of the server on which the file was stored, and what folder it was stored in.

If you want the retro FTP experience, see `net.gurus.com/ftp` for how FTP used to work — and still does.

Web browsers can download files by FTP automatically; if you see a URL that starts `ftp://`, that's an FTP download, which works just like any other Web download.

About Face! Uploading You Go!

Okay, you know how to retrieve files from other computers by downloading —
so how about copying the other way and *up*loading? The main reason that you
might need to upload files is that you have your own Web site. If you do, you'll
need to upload your Web pages to your Web server.

You can upload files to a server only if you have permission to store files on
that server. If you have a Web site, you have a username and password on the
Web server that enable you to log on to your account, and which give you permission to store files there. You can't just upload files to any old server on the
Internet — other servers won't let you. For that reason, we'll talk about uploading Web pages (and the graphic files that appear on your Web pages, if any)
in this chapter.

Uploading with your Web-page editor

A good Web page editor (the software, that is) includes a file-transfer (FTP)
program so those awesome Web pages you create can have a destination:
You can upload them to a Web server. For example, in Dreamweaver (a popular Web page editor), you can click the Put button on the toolbar to upload
the Web page you are editing to your Web server. See Chapter 17 for details
on how to create and upload Web pages.

Uploading with your browser

Strangely, Firefox doesn't have an upload feature. In Internet Explorer, you
can log on to the Web server as yourself by using an FTP URL, something
like this:

```
ftp://yourid@www.yourprovider.com/
```

In this example, `yourid` and `yourprovider` are placeholders we use to stand
for (respectively) your logon ID and the name of your Web server. The server
name usually starts with www, followed by the ISP's name or Web server company's name; sometimes it may start with something else (such as `ftp.www.
fargle.net`) but look for the friendly www. (Ask your Web server administra-
tor if this info isn't in the sign-up packet it gave you.)

The browser asks for your password. If you are using your ISP's Web server,
use the same password you use when you dial in. If this password works,
you see your home Web directory listed on-screen. If you want to upload
files to a different directory, click that directory's name so that you see that
directory.

After you have the directory you want on-screen, just drag the file from where it is to where you want it. Doing so uploads the file from any other program (such as Windows Explorer) into the browser window. Poof! The file is now uploaded. (It may be a slow p-o-o-f, depending on how big the file is.)

Uploading with an FTP program

FTP may have been around for a while, but it's still good technology. You can use FTP programs to upload or download files — that's what they're for. Our Web page at net.gurus.com/ftp contains instructions.

Part IV
E-Mail, Chat, and Other Ways to Hang Out Online

The 5th Wave   By Rich Tennant

"You know, I liked you a whole lot more on the Internet."

In this part . . .

You've found out all about the Web, which is very, very slightly like TV because you're mostly looking at stuff that other people created. Now we turn to the part of the Internet that's very, very, slightly like talking on the phone, because you're talking (or typing or waving) to other people. We start with e-mail, just about the oldest but still the most useful Net service, both for one-to-one conversations and discussions among larger e-mail communities. You'll find advice about how to use e-mail and how to keep safe from e-mail-borne spam and viruses. We finish with faster-paced modern alternatives, such as instant messages, and online chat.

Chapter 13

It's in the Mail: Sending and Receiving E-Mail

*E*lectronic mail, or *e-mail,* is without a doubt the most popular Internet service, even though it's one of the oldest and least glitzy. Although e-mail isn't as glitzy as the World Wide Web, more people use it. Every system on the Net supports some sort of mail service, which means that no matter what kind of computer you're using, if it's on the Internet, you can send and receive mail. Even some systems that aren't technically on the Internet — think cellphones and PDAs (a personal digital assistant, such as a Palm Pilot or a BlackBerry) — can do e-mail.

What's My Address?

Everyone with e-mail access to the Internet has at least one *e-mail address,* which is the cyberspace equivalent of a postal address or a phone number. When you send an e-mail message, you type in the address(es) of the recipient(s) so that the computer knows where to send it.

Before you can do much mailing, you have to figure out your e-mail address so that you can give it to people who want to get in touch with you. You also have to figure out some of their addresses so that you can write to them. (If you have no friends or plan to send only anonymous hate mail, you can skip this section.)

E-mail addresses have two parts, separated by an @ (the *at* sign). The part before the @ is the *username* or *mailbox,* which is (roughly speaking) your personal name. The part after that is the *domain,* usually the name of your Internet service provider (ISP), such as `aol.com` or `gurus.com`.

The username part

Your *username* is the name your ISP assigns to your account. If you're lucky, you get to choose your username; in other cases, ISPs standardize usernames, and you get what you get. You may choose (or be assigned) your first name as your username — or your last name, your initials, your first name and last initial, your first initial and last name, or a completely made-up name. Over the years, for example, John has had the usernames `john`, `john1`, `jrl`, `jlevine`, `jlevine3` (must have been at least three `jlevine`s there), and even `q0246`; Carol has been `carol`, `carolb`, `cbaroudi`, and `carol377` (the provider threw in a random number); Margy tries to stick with `margy` but has ended up with `margy1` or `73727,2305` on occasion. A few ISPs assign names such as `usd31516`. (Ugh.)

For example, you can write to the President of the United States. at `president@whitehouse.gov`. The President's username is `president`, and the domain that stores his mailbox is `whitehouse.gov` — reasonable enough.

Back when many fewer e-mail users were around and most users of any particular system knew each other directly, figuring out who had what username wasn't all that difficult. These days, many organizations assign usernames in a consistent format for all users, most often by using the your first and last name with a dot (`.`) between them, or your first initial followed by the first seven letters of your last name. In these schemes, your username may be something like `elvis.presley@bluesuede.org` or `epresley@bluesuede.org`. (If your name isn't Elvis Presley, adjust this example suitably. On the other hand, if your name *is* Elvis Presley, please contact us immediately. We know some people who are looking for you.)

The domain part

A domain name for an ISP in the U.S. usually ends with a dot and a two- or three-letter code (called the *Top-Level Domain,* or TLD) that gives you a clue to what kind of outfit owns the domain name. The following is a brief explanation of what type of organization owns domains with what TLD codes:

✔ **Commercial organizations** typically own domain names ending in `.com`. which includes both providers such as America Online (AOL) and MSN and many companies that aren't public providers but that are commercial entities, such as `www.aa.com` (AMR Corporation, better known as American Airlines), `www.greattapes.com` (Margy's online video store), and `www.taugh.com` (John's hard-to-pronounce Taughannock Networks).

✔ **U.S. colleges and universities** typically own domain names ending in `.edu` (such as `www.yale.edu`). Elementary, middle, and high schools don't get to use `.edu`, only institutions of higher learning.

✔ **Networking organizations** typically end with `.net`. These include both ISPs and companies that provide network services.

✔ **Government organizations** in the U.S. typically own domain names ending in `.gov`. For example, the National Do Not Call Registry run by the Federal Trade Commission is at `donotcall.gov`.

✔ **U.S. military organizations** typically own domain names ending in `.mil`.

✔ **Nonprofits** and **special interest groups** typically own domain names ending in `.org`. For example, the Unitarian Universalist Association (where Margy works) is at `uua.org`.

✔ **Organizations in specific countries** frequently own domain names ending in a two-letter country code, such as `.fr` for France or `.zm` for Zambia. See our Web site (at `http://net.gurus.com/countries`) for a listing of country TLD codes. Small businesses, local governments, and K-12 schools in the U.S. usually end with the two-letter state abbreviation followed by `.us` (such as John's community Web site at `www.trumansburg.ny.us`).

In 1997, an international group (the Internet Corporation For Assigned Names and Numbers, or ICANN, at `icann.org`) proposed adding some extra, generic domains such as `.firm`, `.arts`, and `.web`. After a lengthy detour through a maze of international intellectual-property politics, the first new domains (`.biz` and `.info`) appeared in 2001. The result is confusion that practically guarantees that, more often than not, `whatever.biz` and `whatever.info` are owned by the same group that owns `whatever.com`, and when they are owned by someone else, they're usually sleazy knockoffs. ICANN has since added these domain extensions:

✔ `.name`: Personal vanity domains

✔ `.pro`: Licensed professional doctors, lawyers, and accountants

✔ `.coop`: Co-ops

✔ `.museum`: Museums

✔ `.aero`: Air travel

✔ `.jobs`: Job offers

✔ `.travel`: Travel in general

✔ `.mobi`: Services for people using cell phones and other mobile devices

✔ `.xxx`: All porn all the time

None is widely used. We'll put any late-breaking updates on the Web at `http://net.gurus.com/domains`.

Where is your mailbox?

When you sign up with an ISP, the provider creates a mailbox for each of your usernames. Although some ISPs offer only one username with each Internet account, many ISPs offer up to five mailboxes with five different usernames for a single account. These mailboxes usually live on your ISP's mail server.

If you don't have an ISP (say, you connect from the public library), all is not lost. Many Web sites provide free mailboxes for you to use — try Hotmail at `www.hotmail.com`, Mail.com at `www.mail.com`, or Yahoo Mail at `http://mail.yahoo.com`. Yahoo and Hotmail use the Web site's domain name (`yahoo.com` or `hotmail.com`) as the second part of your e-mail address, whereas Mail.com offers a long list of "vanity" domains like `www.tokyo.com` or `www.doctor.com`. Google has been testing Gmail, its own free mail service, for several years; it's at `www.gmail.com` although (as of Summer 2005), you need an invitation to get an account.

Putting it all together

Whenever you set up a mail program, you need to enter information about your e-mail mailbox. People switch mail programs from time to time (new versions often come out with swell new features), so write your e-mail address and other info that your ISP provided when you set up your account in Table 13-1 (and fold down the corner of this page, so you can find it again later). Capitalization never matters in domains and rarely matters in mailbox names. To make it easy on your eyes, therefore, most domain and mailbox names in this book are shown in lowercase. (Don't worry about the parts of the table you don't understand right away — we explain what *servers* are later in this chapter.)

Whaddaya mean, you don't know your own address?

It happens frequently — you know what e-mail address you requested for your new account, but you're not absolutely positive that you got it. Before you give out your address to everyone you know, test it out by sending a message to a friend or two. Tell them to reply to your message when they get it and to let you know what address your message came from. Or you can write to us at `internet10@gurus.com` and see what address our reply is addressed to.

Table 13-1	Information Your E-Mail Program Needs to Know	
	Description	*Example*
Your e-mail address	Your username followed by an @ and the domain name	`internet10@ gurus.com`
Your e-mail password	The password for your e-mail mailbox (usually the same as the password for your account)	`dum3my`
Your incoming (POP3 or IMAP) mail server	The name of the computer that receives your e-mail messages (Get this name from your ISP; skip it if you use Web-based mail or AOL.)	`pop.gurus.com`
Is your incoming mail server POP3 or IMAP? __ POP __ IMAP __ Web mail __ AOL	Which protocol your server uses, and which your e-mail program needs to use to get your mail; doesn't apply to Web mail or AOL	
Your outgoing (SMTP) mail server	The name of the computer that distributes your outgoing mail to the rest of the Internet (often the same as the POP3 or IMAP server); doesn't apply to Web mail or AOL	`smtp.gurus.com`

If you're sending a message to another user in your domain (an account on the same ISP), you can often leave out the domain part altogether when you type the address. If you and a friend both use AOL, for example, you can leave out the @aol.com part of the address when you're writing to each other.

If you don't know what your e-mail address is, a good approach is to send yourself a message and use your e-mail login name as the mailbox name. Then examine the return address on the message. Or you can send a message to *Internet For Dummies* Mail Central, at internet10@gurus.com, and a friendly robot will send back a message with your address. (While you're at it, tell us whether you like this book because we authors read that mail and write back when time permits.) If you're planning on testing your e-mail many times and don't care whether we read your message, send it to test@gurus.com.

My Mail Is Where?

If you're the sort of person who lies awake at night worrying about obscure questions, it may have occurred to you that your computer can receive e-mail only while it's connected to the Internet — so what happens to mail that people send during the 23 hours a day you're engaged in real life? (If your computer is permanently connected to the Internet with a DSL (Digital Subscriber Line), cable Internet, or office connection, this question may never have occurred to you.)

When your mail arrives, the mail doesn't get delivered to your computer automatically. Mail gets delivered instead to an *incoming mail server,* which holds onto the mail until you connect to the Net and run your mail program, which then picks up the mail. Two types of incoming mail servers are common:

> ✔ **POP:** Also known as *POP3,* for Post Office Protocol version 3
>
> ✔ **IMAP:** Internet Mail Access Protocol

To send mail, your *e-mail program* has to take mail to the post office — your *outgoing mail server* (or *SMTP server,* for the badly misnamed Simple Mail Transfer Protocol). It's sort of like having a post office box rather than home delivery — you have to pick it up at the post office and also deliver your outgoing mail there. (Strange but true: Margy and Carol, because they're normal, get their e-mail via a mail server and have their paper ("snail") mail delivered to their homes; John, who's abnormal, has his e-mail delivered directly to his home computer but walks to the post office every day, often in the freezing drizzle, to get his paper mail.)

Unless you use your Web browser to read your e-mail, you have to set up your e-mail program with the name of your incoming and outgoing mail servers. When your e-mail program picks up the mail, it sucks your mail from the incoming mail server to your PC or Mac at top speed. After you download your mail to your own computer — if you dial in to the Net — you can disconnect your Internet connection, thus freeing up your phone line. Then you can read and respond to your mail while you're *offline.* After you're ready to send your responses or new messages, you can reconnect and transmit your outgoing mail to the outgoing mail server — again at top network speed.

Write the names of your incoming (POP3 or IMAP) and outgoing (SMTP) mail servers in Table 13-1. If you don't know what to write, ask your ISP or whatever organization hosts your e-mail mailbox. With luck, your mail program has the server names set automatically, but when (note we don't say "if") the setup gets screwed up, you'll be glad you know what to restore the settings to.

AOL has its own mail system, so AOL users don't use a POP, IMAP, or SMTP server when you are using AOL's own software. However, AOL provides an IMAP server (imap.aol.com) in case you want to use some other e-mail program. MSN uses Hotmail for its mail system, so it doesn't do POP, IMAP, or SMTP either. Yahoo Mail provides Web-based accounts, but if you sign up for its premium service at $20 U.S. per year, it also provides a POP server in case you'd like to use an e-mail program instead of your browser to read your mail.

After you send a piece of e-mail, you can't cancel it! Some e-mail programs keep outgoing messages in a holding area to be sent in batches. However after your messages go to the outgoing mail server, you can't call them back. (Note to AOL users: When you send a message to another AOL address, rather than the Internet, you can cancel the message up until the moment that the other AOL user opens and read it.)

So Many E-Mail Programs to Choose From

It's time for some hand-to-hand combat with your e-mail system. The bad news is that countless slightly different and slightly incompatible e-mail programs exist — programs that read and write electronic-mail messages. (So many of them exist that none of us felt up to the task of counting them.) You've got your freeware, you've got your shareware and your commercial stuff, and even more programs probably came with your computer. They all do more or less the same thing; they're all e-mail programs, after all.

E-mail programs of the world

Here's a quick rundown of types of e-mail accounts and the programs you can use with each:

- **Windows PC or Mac with a dialup or broadband Internet account:** You can use any of a long list of e-mail programs, including Thunderbird, Outlook, Outlook Express, Eudora, Pegasus, Mailapp, and Entourage. See the next section for advice on choosing one and setting it up.

- **Corporate account:** If you use e-mail at work, your organization may use a different type of mail server, called Microsoft Exchange. In addition to providing mail services, Exchange also provides shared calendars, to-do lists, and other nifty features. The most popular program that works with all of Exchange's features is Microsoft Outlook, so your organization probably insists that you use it, despite its security flaws. Outlook works somewhat like Outlook Express, which is described in the next section. To read about Outlook, get *Outlook 2003 For Dummies*, by Bill Dyszel (Wiley Publishing, Inc.). IBM Lotus Notes is the main competitor to Exchange, with its own set of fancy features.

✔ **America Online:** At long last, AOL now provides an IMAP server, so you can use standard mail programs to read your AOL mail! You now have three options for managing mail sent through AOL servers:

  • *AOL's e-mail program:* Most AOL users read and send e-mail from the same AOL program that they use to connect to their account. Click the Read icon on the toolbar or any little mailbox icon you can find.

  • *Another e-mail program:* You can use any Windows or Mac e-mail program that handles IMAP, which is nearly all of them. These e-mail programs tend to have better features for filtering spam (junk e-mail) and filing messages. We recommend that you use Thunderbird, which we describe in the next section of this chapter.

  • *Your Web browser:* Your third option is to do mail from the AOL Web site at www.aol.com, which has the advantage that you can use any Web browser from any computer.

✔ **Web mail:** Many Web sites offer free e-mail accounts that you can access using your browser. The best known are Hotmail at www.hotmail.com, Mail.com at www.mail.com, and Yahoo Mail at http://mail.yahoo.com. You use your browser to read and send mail (see Chapter 7 if you need help using a browser).

✔ **UNIX shell accounts:** If you don't know what a UNIX shell account is, don't worry — you don't have one. But if you do, we recommend the simple but sturdy Pine e-mail program; if your ISP doesn't have it, demand it. For a description of Pine, see our page about it at http://net.gurus.com/shell/pine.phtml.

Regardless of which type of mail you're using, the basics of reading, sending, addressing, and filing mail work in pretty much the same way, so it's worth looking through this chapter even if you're not using any of the mail programs we describe here.

You can use your browser for e-mail

Even if you normally use an e-mail program like Thunderbird or Outlook Express to read your messages, you might want to find out whether your ISP or other mailbox provider has a Web-based mail system. With a Web mail system, you can read your mail from any computer on the Internet, including computers at your friends' houses, public libraries, and Internet cafés. For example, if you have an account with EarthLink, you can use its Web site to read and send messages at any computer on the Net; go to `earthlink.net` and click the `Web Mail` link.

To find out whether your ISP provides Web mail, go to its Web site and look around or write to its support e-mail address. Most ISPs have `Web Mail` or similar links on its home pages. You log in with the same mailbox name and password that you jot down in Table 13-1.

Setting Up Your E-Mail Program

After you understand what an e-mail program is supposed to do, it's much easier to figure out how to make a specific e-mail program do what you want. We've picked the two most popular e-mail programs to show you the ropes:

- **Thunderbird:** The people who created Firefox, the Web browser that we describe in Chapter 7, have also written an excellent, free e-mail program called Thunderbird. Thunderbird works with regular Internet accounts as well as with AOL accounts. See Chapter 12 to find out how to get hold of Thunderbird.

- **Outlook Express:** Windows 98 and later versions come with some version of *Outlook Express*, Microsoft's free e-mail program. When you get a copy of the Microsoft Web browser, Internet Explorer, you get Outlook Express, too. We describe Outlook Express 6.0, which comes with Windows XP, with Internet Explorer 6.0, or as a download from `www.microsoft.com`. A similar version of Outlook Express is available for Macs. *Note:* Despite the similar name, Outlook Express is unrelated to Outlook 97, 98, 2000, XP, or 2003; those are full-featured commercial programs that are included in various versions of the Microsoft Office package.

To round out our discussion, we also describe a Web-based mail system, Yahoo Mail, which is on the Web at `http://mail.yahoo.com`. Microsoft's Hotmail (`www.hotmail.com`) is similar. Our instructions for Yahoo Mail have to be a bit vague because (like all Web sites) it could have been completely redesigned twice since we wrote this book (even if you get the first copy off the press.)

Before you can use your e-mail program, you need to tell it two things:

- **Where your mailbox is stored** (usually on a mail server at your ISP)

- **Where to send outgoing mail** (usually to the same or another mail server at your ISP)

Avoid Outlook Express and Outlook, if possible

Outlook Express (because Microsoft includes it with Windows) and Outlook (because it comes with Microsoft Office) are slowly taking over the world of e-mail programs. Both for that reason and because they're riddled with security flaws, many viruses specifically target Outlook Express. So if you use Outlook Express, you need to do a few things to protect yourself:

✔ **Never open an attachment or run a program that someone sends you, even if you know the sender.** Open an attachment only after you check with the sender that he or she actually *meant* to send you the attachment. Many viruses spread when people open infected messages that contain a program that then launches itself and sends infected messages to everybody in your Outlook Express address book — all without you knowing it. If you get e-mail from someone you don't know, it's best to delete it without ever opening it.

✔ **Check the Microsoft Web site frequently (say, once a week) for security reports.** Go to

`http://windowsupdate.microsoft.com` for the latest security updates, including *patches* (corrections) for both Outlook Express and Internet Explorer. You need to use Internet Explorer to view this Web site because the site and the program are both from Microsoft. Be sure to download and install all the security updates in the Critical Updates section.

✔ **Tell Outlook Express to be careful.** If you don't expect to receive attached files, choose Tools➪Options, click the Security tab, and select the Do Not Allow Attachments to Be Saved or Opened That Could Potentially Be a Virus check box. (Maybe Microsoft needs to run its check-box names through the grammar checker!) Also select the Warn Me When Other Applications Try to Send Mail as Me check box — this setting may prevent a virus from surreptitiously spreading itself.

Better yet, switch to a safer e-mail program.

For Yahoo Mail and other Web-based e-mail servers, you have to create a mailbox for yourself, but you don't have to input information about your mail server. Web-based e-mail already knows! Follow the instructions in the following sections to get up and running. Later sections describe how to send and receive mail using each program.

Thunderbird

The Mozilla Foundation, which creates free, open-source software, has written Thunderbird to complement its excellent Firefox browser. Mozilla Foundation also offers a browser called *Mozilla* that combines a browser like Firefox, an e-mail program like Thunderbird, and a Web editor that is described in Chapter 17. AOL's version of Mozilla, Netscape 8, combines versions of these same programs.

Chapter 12 describes how to download and install programs; follow its procedures to download and install Thunderbird from `www.mozilla.org/ products/thunderbird`.

 Start Thunderbird by clicking the desktop icon or choosing Start⇨All Programs⇨Mozilla Thunderbird⇨Mozilla Thunderbird. If you use Mozilla or Netscape and have the mail module of the program installed, you can switch from the browser window to the mail window (which is very similar to Thunderbird) by choosing Window⇨Mail & Newsgroups. The first time you run Thunderbird, the Account Wizard runs, asking for your name, the type of e-mail account you have (POP or IMAP), your e-mail address, and your mail servers (incoming and outgoing), as described in section "My Mail Is Where?" earlier in this chapter.

If you need to change your e-mail account information later or set up Thunderbird to work with a different e-mail account, choose Tools⇨Account Settings. To run the Account Wizard again, click New Account. To change the settings for an existing account, choose the account, click the categories of settings below the account name, and change the settings that appear. Type your name, e-mail address, incoming mail server, and outgoing server, copying the information from Table 13-1. When you're done, you see your new account in the Account Settings window, which you can close.

The Thunderbird window looks like Figure 13-1. A list of your mailboxes (mail Folders) appears at upper left. To the right are a list of the messages in that mailbox and the text of the selected message.

Figure 13-1:
Thunderbird
displays
your mail
Folders to
the left,
messages
at upper
right, and
the selected
message at
lower right.

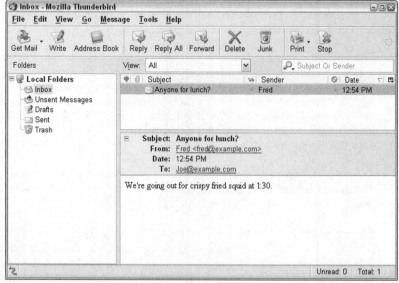

If more than one person will use Thunderbird on the same account on one computer, each can have his or her own setup so everyone can read his or her own mail, rather than each other's. Choose Start➪All Programs➪Mozilla Thunderbird➪Profile Manager to create a new profile for each person. If your computer runs Windows XP and you give people separate Windows accounts, each account has its own Thunderbird profile automatically.

Outlook Express

If you have Windows, you don't have to install Outlook Express — it's just there. In fact, we don't know of any way to truly get rid of it. (Microsoft claims that Internet Explorer is an integral part of Windows, and maybe Microsoft is getting ready to make the same claim about Outlook Express.)

To run Outlook Express

- **In Windows XP**: Choose Start➪E-mail Outlook Express or Start➪All Programs➪Outlook Express.

- **In other versions of Windows:** choose either

    • Start➪Programs➪Outlook Express

    or

    • Start➪Programs➪Internet Explorer➪Outlook Express

You're bound to find it in one of those places.

Or double-click the Outlook Express icon on your desktop (It's an envelope with blue arrows around it.)

The first time you run Outlook Express, the Internet Connection Wizard wakes up and asks some questions: Most of the answers you should already have written in Table 13-1. When prompted, type your name, your e-mail address, your incoming (POP or IMAP) mail server, your outgoing (SMTP) mail server, your username, and your password. Click Next after filling in the information that the wizard requests, and then click Finish when the Wizard says that you may leave.

At long last, you see the Outlook Express window, as shown in Figure 13-2. The layout is similar to Thunderbird's, displaying the Folders and Contacts lists, a message list, and the selected message.

If you need to add or change your e-mail accounts later, choose Tools➪ Accounts from the Outlook Express menu. Click the Mail tab if it's not already selected. You can edit an account by clicking it and clicking the Properties button. Add an e-mail account (mailbox) by clicking the Add button.

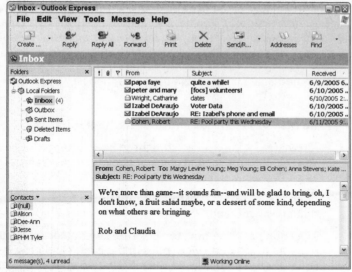

Figure 13-2:
The Outlook
Express
window is
divided into
three
sections:
Folders and
Contacts, a
list of
messages in
the selected
folder, and
the text of
the selected
message.

Hotmail, Yahoo Mail, and other Web mail

Years ago, some genius had the idea of creating a Web site where you can
sign up for an e-mail account and then log in to read and send messages.
Your e-mail mailbox lives on the Web site's mail servers, and you use your
browser, rather than a regular e-mail program, to read and send messages.
The first such *Web mail* system was Hotmail (at www.hotmail.com, later
bought by Microsoft). Other popular Web mail systems are Yahoo Mail (at
mail.yahoo.com) and Mail.com (at www.mail.com). Google Mail, or Gmail,
is at www.gmail.com, but as of this writing, you still need an invitation to
get an account.

Yahoo Mail is our favorite Web-based mail service because of its wide range
of features. After you set up a free Yahoo ID, you get a mailbox, a Web site at
http://geocities.com, and an ID you can use when buying and selling in
Yahoo's online stores and auctions. Your Yahoo ID works when using Yahoo
Messenger for instant messages, voice conferencing, or video conferencing
(see Chapter 16). The exact services (as well as the exact instructions for setting up and using a Yahoo Mail mailbox) vary from week to week as the Yahoo
people change their Web site, but we can give you a general idea. Currently,
the account is free as long as you check your mail at least every four months
and as long as you don't mind using your browser to read your mail. If you
sign up for a paid account, you get extra bells and whistles, including the ability to use an e-mail program to access your messages.

Hotmail, Mail.com, and Gmail work similarly to Yahoo Mail — just read the Web sites for instructions. If you have an account with an ISP that also provides Web mail, these instructions should give you a general idea of how the Web site works for sending and receiving messages.

To set up a Yahoo Mail mailbox, sign up for a Yahoo ID. (Don't worry, it's free). Two steps do the job:

1. **Go to `www.yahoo.com` and click the Mail icon.**

   Alternatively, you can go straight to `http://mail.yahoo.com`. You see links for signing in if you already have a Yahoo ID as well as a `Sign Up Now` link.

2. **Click the `Sign Up Now` link and fill in the forms with information about yourself.**

   They don't ask anything too nosy. Be sure to click the links to read the terms of service (rules of the game) and privacy policy (what they plan to do with the information you give them).

In Table 13-1, you need to write only your e-mail address, which is your Yahoo ID followed by `@yahoo.com`. You don't need to fill in any other information. You're ready!

To access your Yahoo Mail mailbox, go to the Web site and log in:

1. **Go to `http://mail.yahoo.com`.**

   (Or click the Mail icon at `www.yahoo.com`.)

2. **Sign in with your new Yahoo ID and password.**

   You see a Web page with links for sending and reading e-mail, as shown in Figure 13-3.

Figure 13-3: Yahoo Mail is a Web mail system that enables you to read and send e-mail from your Web browser.

A cool thing about Web mail systems like Yahoo Mail and Hotmail is that you can read and send messages from any computer on the Net. Your mailbox is stored on Yahoo's mail servers, and any computer with a Web browser can access it. Of course, no one can read your messages, or send messages as you, without typing your password. In this chapter and Chapter 15, when we tell you how to send and receive mail with Yahoo Mail, keep in mind that you don't have to be at your own computer — you can check your mail from a friend's computer or from the computer at the public library. One downside is that reading and sending messages tends to be slower with Web mail than with an e-mail program because you have to wait for a new Web page to arrive every time you click a new message.

Sending Mail Is Easy

Sending mail (whether through an e-mail program or through Web-based e-mail) is easy enough that we show you a few examples rather than waste time explaining the theory.

Sending e-mail with Thunderbird

Here's how to send an e-mail message using Thunderbird:

1. **In Thunderbird, click the Write icon on the toolbar or press Ctrl+M.**

   Yet another window (the Compose window) opens with a blank message.

2. **Fill in the recipient's address (or recipients' addresses) in the To box.**

   If you want to send the same message to more than one person at a time, press Enter (instead of Tab). You can send this message to as many people as you want by pressing Enter after each address. When you're done including everybody in the To box, press Tab to move to the Subject box. If you want a recipient to be Cc'ed or Bcc'ed, click the To: next to the address and select Cc: or Bcc: from the list that drops down.

3. **Type the subject in the Subject box.**

   Make it specific. If you want help, don't type **Help!** as the subject. Type **Need help getting my cat not to spit out his pills.**

   Press Tab to move to the message box.

4. **Type the message in the big box.**

   The cursor should be blinking in the *message area*, the large empty box where the actual message goes.

CC and BCC

The term *carbon copy* should be familiar to those of you who were born before 1960 and remember the ancient practice of putting sheets of carbon-coated paper between sheets of regular paper to make extra copies when using a typewriter. (Please don't ask us what a typewriter is.) In e-mail, a *carbon copy* is simply a copy of the message you send. All recipients, on both the To and Cc lines see who's getting the message — unless a recipient's e-mail address is typed in the *Bcc* field instead. *Blind carbon copies* (Bccs) are copies sent to people without putting their names on the message so that the other recipients are none the wiser. *You* can figure out why you may want to send a copy to someone but not want everyone to know you sent it.

5. **Click the Send icon on the toolbar to send the message.**

   If you are connected to the Internet, the message wings its way to your ISP and on to the addressee. If you're not online, Thunderbird stores your message in the Unsent Messages folder.

6. **If you compose messages offline, when you next connect to the Internet, choose File⇨Send Unsent Messages.**

When you send a message in which you use formatting (such as boldface or italics, using the toolbar buttons in the Compose window), Thunderbird may ask you whether you really want to send the message using formatting. See the sidebar "To format or not to format" later in this chapter for when to send formatted messages.

You can tell Thunderbird to check the spelling in your message before you send it. To use spell checker, follow these steps:

1. **Choose Tools⇨Options.**

2. **Click Composition in the left-hand list and select the Check Spelling Before Sending check box.**

   Each time you click Send to send a message, Thunderbird asks you about each word that it doesn't recognize.

Sending e-mail with Outlook Express

Here's how to send an e-mail message using Outlook Express:

1. **In Outlook Express, click the Create icon on the toolbar or press Ctrl+N.**

You see a New Message window with boxes to fill in to address the message.

2. **In the To box, type the address to which to send the message and then press Tab to move to the Cc box.**

   If you want to send a message to more than one address, type the addresses separated by commas or semicolons.

3. **If you want to send a copy of the message to someone, type that person's address in the Cc box. Then press Tab.**

   If you want to send Bcc copies, choose View➪All Headers in the New Message window.

4. **In the Subject box, type a succinct summary of the message. Then press Tab again.**

5. **In the large, empty box, type the text of the message.**

   When you have type your message, you can press F7 or choose Tools➪ Spelling to check its spelling.

6. **To send the message, click the Send icon on the toolbar or press Alt+S (not Ctrl+S, which means Save).**

   Outlook Express sticks the message in your Outbox folder, waiting to be sent. If you're connected to the Internet, Outlook Express may be configured to send the message immediately.

7. **Connect to your Internet provider if you're not already connected.**

   To send the message, you have to climb on the Net.

8. **Click the Send/Receive icon on the toolbar or press Ctrl+M.**

   Your message is on its way.

To tell Outlook Express to check the spelling in your message, click the Spelling button at the top of the New Message window.

If you use formatting commands to choose fonts and colors when you compose your message, some people may have trouble reading the message — specifically, people with older e-mail programs. If you get complaints, choose Format➪Plain Text in the New Message window when you are composing the message. See the sidebar, "To format or not to format," later in this chapter for when to send formatted messages.

To format or not to format

A few years ago, someone got tired of e-mail's plain, unformatted appearance. After all, now that almost all computers can display boldface, italics, different fonts, and different font sizes, why not use them in e-mail? And formatted e-mail was born.

One problem is that not all e-mail programs can display formatted e-mail. Both Thunderbird and Outlook Express can. The formatting usually takes one of two forms: MIME (in which the formatted text is sent like an attached file with the message) and HTML (in which Web page formatting codes are included in the text). If your mail program can't display formatted mail and you receive a formatted message, you see all kinds of gobbledygook mixed in with the text of the message, rendering it unreadable.

Another problem is that any HTML-formatted mail can potentially contain viruses, hostile Web pages that take over the screen, and other annoying or dangerous content. Some people turn off HTML mail, both nice mail like yours and the nasty kind, to avoid having to deal with the nasty kind.

If you know that the person to whom you are writing uses an e-mail interface that can handle formatted e-mail, go ahead and use it. Boldface, italics, and color can add emphasis and interest to your messages although they're no substitute for clear, concise writing. If you receive formatted messages from someone, you can send him formatted messages, too. However, if you don't know whether your recipient's mail program can display formatted messages, don't use it. And when sending messages to a mailing list (which we discuss in Chapter 16), don't use formatting — you never know who's on the list, who will receive your message, and what fonts their programs support.

Sending e-mail with Web mail, like Yahoo Mail and Hotmail

After you have a Yahoo ID and Yahoo Mail mailbox, follow these steps (more or less — the Yahoo Mail Web site may have changed ten times since we wrote this). Other Web mail sites work similarly.

Here's how to send an e-mail message using Yahoo Web mail:

1. **Sign in.**

   Go to `mail.yahoo.com` (or click the Mail icon at `www.yahoo.com`) and sign in with your Yahoo ID and password.

2. **Click the Compose button (or any link about writing and sending a message).**

   Your browser displays a form with boxes for To (the address), Subject, and a large, unlabeled box for the text of the message.

3. **Type one or more addresses in the To box.**

   If you want to send your message to more than one address, separate each address with a comma.

4. **Type a subject line in the Subject box.**

5. **Type your message in the big box.**

6. **Scroll down and click the Send button.**

   If you want to check your spelling first, which is the polite thing to do, click the Spell Check button before clicking Send. That's all it takes!

Mail Coming Your Way

If you send e-mail (and in most cases even if you don't) you most likely receive it. The arrival of e-mail is always exciting, even when you get 200 messages a day. (Exciting in a depressing kind of way, sometimes.)

You can do much of what you do with mail while you're not connected to your account. On the other hand, when you want to check your mailbox for your most current messages, you have to connect to the Internet.

You can tell your computer to connect to the Internet automagically when you tell your e-mail program to send or fetch your mail. To configure Windows to dial the Internet automatically, see Chapter 4.

Reading mail with your e-mail program

To check your e-mail with Thunderbird, Outlook Express, or almost any other e-mail program, follow these steps:

1. **Make your Internet connection.**

   You can skip this step if your computer is always connected to the Internet or if it dials automatically whenever you need it to.

2. **Start your e-mail program if it's not already running.**

3. **If your program doesn't retrieve mail automatically, select the Check Mail or Send/Receive button on the toolbar to retrieve your mail.**

   If you have a full-time Internet connection, your e-mail program may retrieve your mail automatically, in which case you only have to start the program to get your mail. In addition, if you leave your e-mail program running, even hidden at the bottom of your screen as an icon, it may automatically check for new mail every once in a while. Most e-mail programs can even pick up mail while you're reading or sending other messages.

The program may play a tune, display a message, or show you a cute picture of a mailman delivering a letter when you receive messages. The mail appears in your inbox (usually in a window or folder called *In* or *Inbox*), showing one line per message. If you don't see it, double-click the In or Inbox mailbox in the list of mailboxes that usually appears at the left side of the window.

4. **To see a message, double-click the line or click the line and press Enter.**

   You see the text of the message, along with buttons for replying, forwarding, and deleting the message.

5. **To stop looking at a message, click the Close (X) button in the upper-right corner of the message window (the standard way to get rid of a window), or press Ctrl+W or Ctrl+F4.**

Here are some tips for displaying your Inbox in specific e-mail programs:

- ✔ **Thunderbird:** To display your Inbox, click your e-mail address, account name, or Inbox in the Mail Folders list.

- ✔ **Outlook Express:** If you don't see your Inbox, double-click the Local Folders item in the Folders list.

Reading mail with Web mail

To check your mail at Yahoo Mail, Hotmail, or any other Web mail system, try this:

1. **Make your Internet connection.**

   You can skip this step if your computer is always connected to the Internet or if it dials automatically whenever you need it to.

2. **Start your Web browser if it's not already running.**

3. **Go to the Web mail site and log in to your Web mail account with your username and password.**

   If the browser offers to remember your password for you, and you are using a public computer, someone else's computer, or a computer that you share with other people, decline its kind offer, to prevent others from getting into your mailbox.

4. **Click the Check Mail, Inbox, or other promising-looking button.**

   You see a list of the messages in your inbox.

5. **Click a message.**

   The Web mail system displays the text of the message, along with buttons for replying, forwarding, and deleting the message.

One-click surfing

Most e-mail programs display Web addresses as links. That is, if the text of a message includes a Web address (like `http://net.gurus.com`), the address appears underlined, and perhaps in blue. Just click the link to display the page in your browser.

When you send messages, you don't have to do anything special to display a Web address as a link — the recipient's e-mail program should do this automatically.

Be sure to log out from the Web mail site when you are done reading and sending mail, especially if you are using a friend's computer or a computer in a public place. Otherwise, someone else can come along and read or send messages using your account.

When you use Web mail, rather than download mail to your own computer, you're managing your mail back on the server at headquarters. If you have more than one mail folder, you can use the same folders whether you move messages among folders in the mail program or on the Web.

Deleting messages from the message list

You don't have to read every single message before you delete it; sometimes you can guess from the sender's name or the subject line that reading the message would be a waste of time. Buttons on the e-mail program's toolbar at the top of its window let you dispose of your mail. First, click once to highlight the message. Then, (in most e-mail programs), click the Trash or Delete button on the toolbar to discard the message. You can do lots of other things with messages (such as replying, saving, and forwarding), which we discuss in Chapter 15.

In Web mail, on the Web page that displays each message there's some kind of Delete button. Some Web mail systems have a check box on the Web page that lists all the messages in your inbox folder, and a Delete button at the bottom of the list. To delete a bunch of messages, select their check boxes and then click Delete.

A Few Words from the Etiquette Ladies

Sadly, the Great Ladies of Etiquette, such as Emily Post and Amy Vanderbilt, died before the invention of e-mail. Here's what they may have suggested about what to say and, more important, what *not* to say in electronic mail.

E-mail is a funny hybrid, something between a phone call (or voice mail) and a letter. On one hand, it's quick and usually informal; on the other hand, because e-mail is written rather than spoken, you don't see a person's facial expressions or hear her tone of voice.

A few words of advice:

- ✔ When you send a message, watch the tone of your language.
- ✔ Don't use all capital letters — it looks like you're SHOUTING.
- ✔ If someone sends you an incredibly obnoxious and offensive message, as likely as not, it's a mistake or a joke gone awry. In particular, be on the lookout for failed sarcasm.

Flame off!

Pointless and excessive outrage in electronic mail is so common that it has a name of its own: *flaming*. Don't flame. It makes you look like a jerk.

When you get a message so offensive that you just *have* to reply, stick it back in your electronic inbox for a while and wait until after lunch. Then . . . don't flame back. The sender probably didn't realize how the message would look. In about 20 years of using electronic mail, we can testify that we have never, ever, regretted *not* sending an angry message (although we *have* regretted sending a few — ouch).

When you're sending mail, keep in mind that the person reading it will have no idea of what you *intended* to say — just what you *did* say. Subtle sarcasm and irony are almost impossible to use in e-mail and usually come across as annoying or dumb instead. (If you're an extremely superb writer, you can disregard this advice — but don't say that we didn't warn you.)

Another possibility to keep in the back of your mind is that it is technically easy to forge e-mail return addresses. If you get a totally off-the-wall message that seems out of character for the person that sent it, somebody else may have forged it as a prank. (No, we're not going to tell you how to forge e-mail. How dumb do you think we are?)

Smile!

Sometimes it helps to put in a :-) (called a *smiley* or *emoticon*), which means, "This is a joke." (Try tilting your head to the left if you don't see why it's a smile.) In some communities, <g> or <grin> serves the same purpose. Here's a typical example:

People who don't believe that we are all part of a warm,
caring community who love and support each other are no better
than rabid dogs and should be hunted down and shot. :-)

We feel that any joke that needs a smiley probably wasn't worth making, but
tastes differ.

For more guidance about online etiquette, see our `http://net.gurus.com/
netiquette` Web page.

How Private Is E-Mail?

Relatively, but not totally. Any recipient of your mail may forward it to
other people. Some mail addresses are actually mailing lists that redistribute
messages to many other people. We've gotten misrouted mail in our
`internet10@gurus.com` mailbox with details of our correspondents' lives
and anatomy that they probably would rather we forget. (So we did.)

If you send mail from work or to someone at work, your mail is not private,
since companies have the right to read all the employee e-mail that passes
through their systems. You and your friend may work for companies of the
highest integrity whose employees would never dream of reading private
e-mail. When push comes to shove, however, and someone is accusing your
company of leaking confidential information and the corporate lawyer says,
"Examine the e-mail," someone reads all the e-mail. (This situation happened
to a friend of ours who was none too pleased to find that all his intimate cor-
respondence with his fiancée had been read.) E-mail you send and receive is
stored on your disk, and most companies back up their disks regularly. If anybody really wants to read your mail, it's not hard to do. The usual rule is not
to send anything you wouldn't want to see posted next to the water cooler or
perhaps scribbled next to a pay phone.

If you really care about someone other than your intended recipient reading
the content of your mail, you must *encrypt* it. The latest e-mail systems
include encryption features that make the privacy situation somewhat better
by scrambling a message so that anyone who doesn't know the keyword can't
decode it.

Here are some of the most common tools for encrypted mail:

- ✔ **S/MIME:** Secure Multipurpose Internet Mail Extension is a standard
  encryption system that Thunderbird and Outlook Express both support.

- ✔ **PGP:** Pretty Good Privacy is one of the most widely used encryption programs, both in the United States and abroad. Many experts think it's so
  strong that even the National Security Agency can't crack it. We don't
  know about that, but if the NSA wants to read your mail, you have more
  complicated problems than we can help you solve.

BTW, what does IMHO mean? RTFM!

E-mail users are often lazy typists, and abbreviations are common. Here are some of the most widely used:

Abbreviation	What It Means
AFAIK	As far as I know
BTW	By the way
IANAL	I am not a lawyer, (but. . . .)
IMHO	In my humble opinion
ROTFL	Rolling on the floor laughing

RSN	Real soon now (that is, any time in the next century)
RTFM	Read the manual — you could have and should have looked it up yourself
TIA	Thanks in advance
TLA	Three-letter acronym (for a three-letter acronym)
YMMV	Your mileage may vary

PGP is available for free on the Net. To find more information about privacy and security issues, including how to get started with PGP and S/MIME, point your browser to `http://net.gurus.com/pgp`.

To Whom Do I Write?

As you probably have figured out, one teensy detail is keeping you from sending e-mail to all your friends: You don't know their addresses. In this chapter, you find out lots of different ways to look for addresses. Start out with the easiest, most reliable way to find out people's e-mail addresses:

> Call them on the phone and ask them.

Pretty low-tech, huh? For some reason, this technique seems to be absolutely the last thing people want to do (see the sidebar, "Top ten reasons *not* to call someone to get an e-mail address"). Try it first. If you know or can find out the phone number, this method is much easier than any of the others.

Another way to find a person's e-mail address is by using an online directory. Wouldn't it be cool if some online directory listed everybody's e-mail address? Maybe, but the Internet doesn't have one. For one thing, nothing says that somebody's e-mail address has any connection to her name. For another, not everybody wants everybody else to know his e-mail address.

Although lots of directories attempt to accumulate e-mail addresses, none of them are complete, most are somewhat out of date, and many work only if people voluntarily list themselves with the service.

This situation reiterates, of course, our point that the best way to find someone's e-mail address is to ask. When that method isn't an option, try Yahoo People Search at `http://people.yahoo.com`, which enables you to search by name and state. However, it's far from a complete database of addresses.

Another approach is to go to a search engine like Google (`www.google.com`) or Yahoo Search (`www.yahoo.com`) and type the person's full name, enclosed in quotes. You'll see a list of pages that include the name — of course, there may be many people with the same name if your friend is called Allen Johnson or Bob Smith. Try searching for your own name and see what you find!

Top ten reasons *not* to call someone to get an e-mail address

10. You want to surprise a long-lost friend.

9. You want to surprise a long-lost *ex*-friend who owes you a large amount of money and thinks that she has given you the slip.

8. Your friend doesn't speak English. (That happens — a majority of Internauts are outside the U.S.)

7. You don't (or your friend doesn't) speak at all. (That happens, too — networks offer a uniquely friendly place for most people with handicaps; nobody has to know or care whether a someone has a disability.)

6. It's 3 a.m. and you need to send a message right now or else you'll never get to sleep.

5. You don't know the phone number, and because of an unfortunate childhood experience, you have a deathly fear of calling directory assistance.

4. The phone takes only quarters; nobody around can break your $100 bill.

3. Your company has installed a new phone system, no one has figured out how to use it, and no matter what you dial, you always end up with Dial-a-Prayer.

2. You inadvertently spilled an entire can of soda into the phone and can't wait for it to dry out to make the call.

1. You called yesterday, didn't write down the answer, and forgot it. Oops.

Chapter 14

Safe Mail: Viruses, Spam, and Secure Mail over WiFi

In This Chapter

▶ Protecting yourself from viruses by mail

▶ Dealing with spam (it's not just for breakfast anymore)

▶ Getting your e-mail safely via WiFi

*O*kay, now you know how to send and receive e-mail. It's time to have a little chat about e-mail safety. If you've used e-mail, you probably have already seen *spam* and maybe even *viruses.* Take a look back at Chapter 2 for definitions of these e-mail-borne menaces. This chapter describes how to protect yourself from them. Listen up.

I Think I've Got a Virus

A virus arrives on your computer as an attachment to an e-mail message. (See the section "Viruses arrive via e-mail" in Chapter 2 for a description of how viruses work.) In most e-mail programs (including Thunderbird), programs contained in attachments don't run until you click them — so *don't* open programs that come from people you don't know. Don't even open attachments from people you *do* know if you weren't expecting to receive them. Many successful viruses replicate themselves by sending copies of themselves to the first 50 people in an address book. Many viruses look like they come from someone who knows you.

In addition to taking care not to run viruses by opening, you should set up your virus checker and e-mail program to catch as many viruses as possible and not to run them inadvertently. The following sections explain how.

Configuring your virus checker

In Chapter 4, we told you to install a virus checker as soon as you connect your computer to the Internet, but this is so important that we are going to tell you again. You'll need to pay for a virus checker — we don't know of a good free one — and you'll need to pay annually to keep your subscription current for updates to the list of viruses that the checker checks for. Here are three of the many good virus checkers that are available:

- **McAfee VirusScan,** www.mcafee.com
- **Norton AntiVirus,** at www.symantec.com
- **F-Prot,** at www.f-prot.com (a good deal if you have several computers because you have to pay for only one license to run the program on all the computers in your house)

Once your virus checker is installed, look at its configuration settings to make sure that the program downloads updates regularly. You can set up the program to connect to the Internet and download updates automatically. Most programs check for updates at least weekly. If you have an always-on Internet connection and you leave your computer on all the time, you can configure your program to check in the middle of the night, so it never disturbs you during the day. If you turn your computer off when you're not using it, or if you have a dial-up Internet account, you'll need to remember to run the program's update function regularly.

Most virus checkers look for viruses in two ways:

- Checking e-mail messages as they arrive
- Scanning your whole computer (that is, your hard disk) for viruses

We recommend that you turn on both of these options.

Virus checkers give you a variety of ways to handle the viruses that they find. We recommend that you set your virus checker to delete virus files. Infected files are unlikely to contain anything that you want, and we can't see any reason to leave them lying around your hard disk.

Configuring Thunderbird not to run viruses

Thunderbird was designed to resist viruses: It doesn't use Internet Explorer to display formatted e-mail messages (as some other e-mail programs do), and it doesn't automatically open attachments. There are just a few settings you might want to check, by following these steps:

1. **In Thunderbird, choose Tools⇨Options to display the Options dialog box.**

   It has a list of option categories down the left side, as shown in Figure 14-1.

2. **Click the Advanced category.**

   You see a list of the advanced types of settings, with Privacy heading the list.

3. **If there's a plus box to the left of the Privacy heading, click it.**

   Now you see the privacy-related settings.

4. **If a check appears in the Enable JavaScript in Mail Messages check box, click it to clear the check mark.**

   JavaScript is a programming language used in Web pages, and it's safer to turn it off in e-mail messages. Few messages contain JavaScript, anyway.

Figure 14-1:
You can tell Thunderbird not to run JavaScript programs or display images from unknown senders.

5. **While you are in there, click Block Loading of Remote Images in Mail Messages, if it's not selected, as well as Allow Remote Images If the Sender Is in My Personal Address Book.**

   These settings tell Thunderbird not to display pictures that appear in e-mail messages because they may be web bugs (described in

Chapter 2). Okay, this isn't really about viruses, but it's a good setting to check, just the same. When you receive messages that contain pictures, you can tell Thunderbird to display the images if you recognize the source of the messages (like, for example, pictures in your daily e-mail newsletter from the *New York Times*).

6. **Click OK.**

Configuring Outlook Express not to run viruses

If you use Microsoft's Outlook Express 5.0 or later, or Outlook 97 or later, the situation is dire. Some versions of Outlook (which comes with Microsoft Office) open attachments as soon as you view the message. Outlook Express (which comes with Windows) provides a *preview pane* that displays a file and its attachments before you click it at all. Early versions of Outlook Express 5.0 and Outlook 97, 98, and 2000 allowed attached programs to do all kinds of horrible things to your PC. Luckily, Microsoft has changed the default settings on more recent versions of Outlook Express and Outlook.

Keeping Windows and Outlook Express updated

Outlook Express users should install Microsoft's Service Pack 2 (SP2), a free upgrade, and enable the automatic software update feature that comes with it.

We say this with trepidation. We recommend that before you install Service Pack 2, you do a complete backup of your system so that you can go back if need be. We know people for whom installing Service Pack 2 was a disaster. If you know a computer geek, keep that person close by. Also be sure to check Microsoft's www.windowsupdate.com weekly for the latest bug fixes.

Checking Outlook Express's security settings

Outlook Express users should also check the program's configuration. Here's how:

1. **In Outlook Express, choose Tools⇨Options.**

   You see the Options dialog box shown in Figure 14-2.

2. **Click the Security tab.**

   The Virus Protection and Download Images sections both deserve your attention.

3. **Set the Internet Explorer Security Zone to Restricted Sites Zone.**

If you work in a corporation and expect to receive programs from co-workers, you may need to change this setting; talk to your system administrator. For the rest of us, this is the safe setting.

4. **Make sure that the Warn Me When Other Applications Try to Send Mail as Me check box is selected (click it if it doesn't contain a check mark).**

   If your computer is infected with a spyware or virus program that tries to use your computer as a spam-sending machine, this setting may prevent it.

5. **Select the Do Not Allow Attachments To Be Saved or Opened That Could Potentially Be a Virus check box.**

   If you expect to receive programs, Excel spreadsheets, Word documents, or Access databases, you may need to turn this setting off because all of these types of files can contain viruses. But start out with it turned on.

6. **Select the Block Images and Other External Content in HTML E-mail check box.**

   Images in e-mail may be web bugs, which are described in Chapter 2. Web bugs aren't viruses, but we don't like them anyway.

7. **Click OK.**

Figure 14-2:
Outlook Express also has virus protection settings.

Chain letters: Arrrrrgggghhh!

One of the most obnoxious things you can do with e-mail is pass around chain letters. Because all mail programs have forwarding commands, you can send a chain letter along to hundreds of other people with only a few keystrokes. Don't do it. Chain letters are cute for about two seconds, and then they're just annoying. After 20 years of using e-mail, we've *never* received a chain letter worth passing along. That's **NEVER!** (Please excuse the shouting.) So don't you pass them along either, okay? No, they don't destroy your computer, but they are just *annoying*.

A few chain letters just keep coming around and around, despite our best efforts to stamp them out:

✔ **Make big bucks with a chain letter:** These letters usually contain lots of testimonials from people who are now rolling in dough, and tell you to send $5 to the name at the top of the list, put your name at the bottom, and send the message to a zillion other suckers. Don't even think about it. These chain letters are illegal in the U.S. even when they say that they aren't, and, besides, they don't even work. (Why send any money? Why not just add your name and send it on? Heck, why not just replace all the names on the list with yours?) Think of them as gullibility viruses. For more info, see the Postal Service Web site at www. usps.com/cpim/ftp/pubs/pub300a_print.htm, which explains in detail why chain letters, even ones that claim to not be chain letters, are illegal and don't work.

✔ **Big company will send you cash for reading e-mail:** This one has circulated with both Disney and Microsoft as the designated corporation. The message claims that the company is conducting a marketing test and that you can get big bucks or a trip to Disney World for sending the message along. Some claim that a sick child will receive 1 cent for each person you forward the message to. Yeah, right. A variation says that something interesting but unspecified will happen when you forward it; we suppose that's true if having all your friends find out how gullible you are counts as interesting. This chain letter isn't dangerous, it's just a waste of time — yours and everyone to whom you send it.

✔ **Hideous virus will wreck your computer:** Occasionally these are true; generally they're not, and when they are true, they tend to be about viruses that have been around since 1992. If you run software that's subject to viruses (Microsoft Outlook Express and Outlook are particularly vulnerable), look at the vendor's Web site and at the sites belonging to antivirus software makers for some more credible reports, downloadable updates, and antivirus advice. Some of the apparent virus warnings are themselves viruses. If a message shows up saying "Install this patch from Microsoft immediately to keep viruses out," it's not a patch; it's a virus.

Get This Spam Outta Here!

Spam is defined as unsolicited bulk e-mail, and we describe its history and sources in detail in Chapter 2. But you probably don't care about details — you just want it to go away.

One approach to spam is to ask your computer to figure out which messages are spam and either trash them or put them in a separate folder so you can trash them yourself. This seems like the perfect solution. The problem is how to get your computer to know what is spam and what is not. Many techniques are available, but none are perfect. Here are a few of the most common:

- **Blackhole lists:** A number of organizations circulate lists of Internet addresses that they consider to be sources of spam. Most ISPs subscribe to one or more of these blackhole lists and block all messages from listed sites. These ISPs block spam for you, at least the spam that comes from these Internet addresses. That's not all spam, but it's a start. The best and most widely used lists are from the Spamhaus Project in England.

- **Content-based filters:** These spam identifiers look for words or phrases in the e-mail that are common in spam. They also note certain formatting errors that spammers seem to make often. Each text match earns a score. If a message scores above a certain threshold, it gets trashed. For example, messages with the word "Viagra" or the phrase "mortgage rate" are much more likely to be spam than other messages.

- **Bayesian filters:** Tom Bayes was a mathematician who died 208 years before the Internet was born, but his groundbreaking work in statistics now helps computers figure out what is spam by being shown examples of messages that are spam along with others that are not. Many e-mail programs have built-in Bayesian filters. In your e-mail program, you might have noticed a button or menu option that says something like This Is Junk. As you read your e-mail, you tell it which messages are spam. After a while, the program starts guessing based on the examples you've given it, and redirects suspected spam into a Junk or Trash mailbox so you don't have to read it. However, you do need to check the spam mailbox from time to time, since Bayesian filters are not infallible and sometimes junk good mail.

All these methods make mistakes that let some spam through and block the occasional legit message. To reduce the latter problem, some e-mail systems *whitelist* senders listed in your e-mail address book, telling the filters you always want to see messages from those senders, perhaps your boss or your significant other. Whitelists won't help you get messages from long lost friends or people who just changed e-mail addresses because their ISP got bought out.

Filtering spam in Thunderbird

Thunderbird contains a Bayesian filer that works pretty well once you've given it some examples of what your spam looks like.

Telling Thunderbird to start filtering

First, set up your spam-filtering configuration settings, like this:

1. **Choose Tools⇨Junk Mail Controls.**

   You see the Junk Mail Controls dialog box shown in Figure 14-3.

2. **Click the Settings tab if it's not already selected.**

3. **Click the White Lists check box (the one about not marking messages as junk mail if the sender is in your address book) if it doesn't already contain a check mark in it.**

   Presumably, people you know won't spam you.

4. **Click the Move Incoming Messages Determined To Be Junk Mail To check box if it doesn't already contain a check mark. Choose where to move your spam.**

   The default setting is a Junk folder, which sounds good to us.

5. **Clear any check mark from the Automatically Delete Junk Messages Older Than ___ Days from This Folder check box.**

   Don't let Thunderbird delete suspected spam before you have a chance to review it. It's terribly embarrassing to tell someone that you threw away an important message because your program thought it was spam.

6. **Click the When I Manually Mark Messages as Junk check box if it doesn't already a check mark. Choose Delete Them.**

   Your other option is to move them to your Junk folder, but if you've already decided that they are junk, why not just get rid of them?

7. **Click the When Displaying HTML Messages Marked as Junk Sanitize Them check box if it doesn't already contain check mark.**

   When you go through your junk messages to make sure that no good messages are mistakenly trashed, Thunderbird might as well make sure that no suspicious HTML code from these messages is run on your computer.

8. **Click OK.**

Now Thunderbird is ready to learn to tell the spam from the ham — the bad messages from the good. As you read the messages in your Inbox folder, each time you receive a spam message, click the Junk button on the toolbar. The message vanishes from your Inbox, and Thunderbird analyzes the words in the message and makes a note that they are likely to appear in spam. The more spam messages you mark with the Junk button, the more Thunderbird knows about what spam looks like.

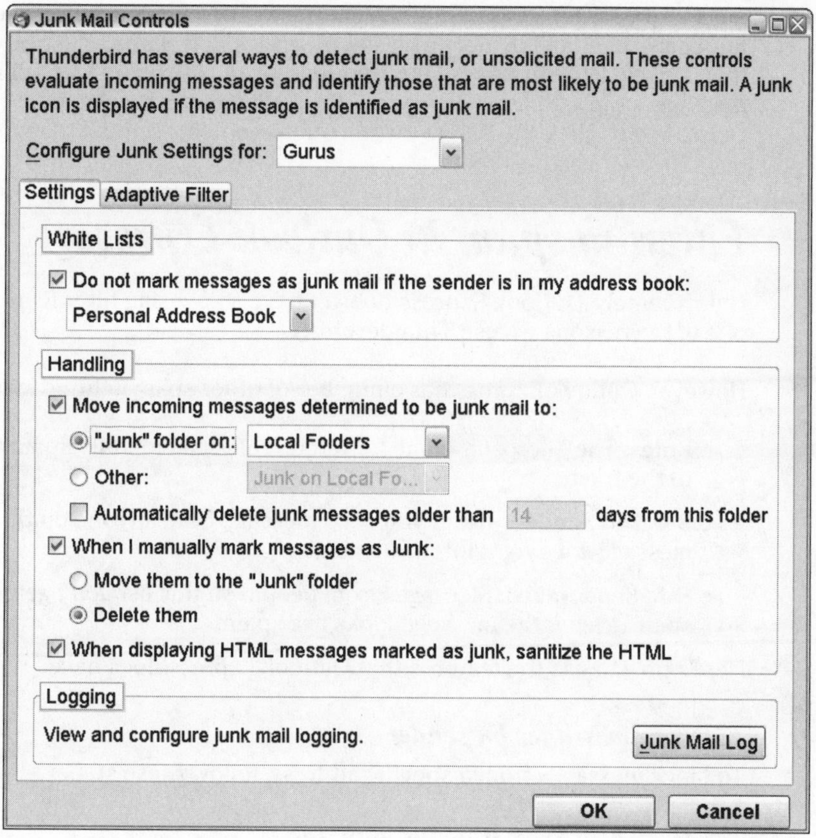

Figure 14-3:
Configuring
Thunderbird
to can your
spam.

Checking your Junk folder for ham

From time to time (every week or so), open the Junk Mail folder (or whatever folder you told Thunderbird to put suspected spam into in Step 4 of the "Telling Thunderbird to start filtering" section in this chapter). The Junk Mail folder appears on your list of folders, below your Inbox, Templates (that is, form letters), and Sent Message folders. Click the Junk folder to see the list of messages. You don't need to open each message — reviewing the sender names and subjects is usually enough to reveal whether any good messages are mixed in there.

If you see a good message in your Junk folder, select it and click the Not Junk button on the toolbar (it's where the Junk button usually is — the button turns into Not Junk when you open the Junk folder). This button tells Thunderbird to look at the words in this message and to make a note that they appear in a good message ("ham," not spam). Then drag the message back into your Inbox. When you're sure that all the messages in your Junk folder are indeed junk, delete all the messages in it. The easiest way to do this is to click the first message, and then scroll down and Shift+click the last message — now all the messages in the Junk folder are selected. Press the Delete key or click the Delete button on the toolbar to trash them.

Filtering spam in Outlook Express

Unfortunately, Outlook Express doesn't have a Bayesian filter feature. (That's one of the reasons we use Thunderbird.)

However, Outlook Express has a number of other spam-fighting features:

✔ **Rules:** The Microsoft name for filters, rules can identify spam and send it to the trash.

✔ **Blocked Senders list:** If you get a message from anyone on this list, the message goes right into the trash.

✔ **Safe Senders list:** Messages from people on this list *don't* get marked as spam, even if the message looks like spam.

Here's how to use the features that Outlook Express does have.

Blocking messages by sender

To block messages from a specific address, follow these steps:

1. **Open a message from the address.**

2. **In the window that displays the message, choose Message⇨Block Sender.**

   You may see a message confirming that the address has been added to your Blocked Senders list.

3. **If you see a confirmation message, click OK.**

   The message you opened is still in your Inbox; the program will block *future* messages, but doesn't do anything about this one. Just delete it!

Viewing your Blocked Senders list

You can look at or edit the Blocked Senders list later, in case you add a friend accidentally or you want to type a bunch of spammer addresses. Choose Tools⇨Message Rules⇨Blocked Senders List from the menu bar in the main Outlook Express window. You see the Message Rules dialog box with the Blocked Senders tab selected, as shown in Figure 14-4.

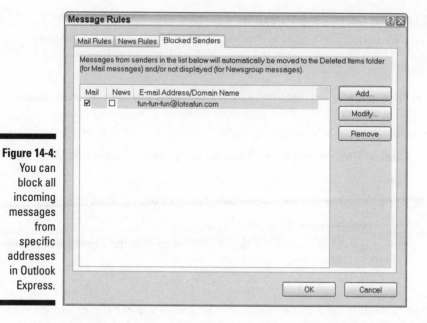

Figure 14-4:
You can
block all
incoming
messages
from
specific
addresses
in Outlook
Express.

Messages from any addresses on your Blocked Senders list are shunted straight to your Deleted Items folder.

You can add more addresses to your Blocks Senders list by clicking Add and typing or pasting the address in the dialog box that appears. If you decide to accept messages from an address after all, you can delete it from the list by choosing the address and clicking Remove.

Blocking messages from entire domains

The Blocked Senders list can include entire domains (a *domain* is the part of an e-mail address after the @). For example, if you don't want to receive *any* mail from the White House, you could block all messages that come from `anything@whitehouse.gov`. Follow these steps to block all messages from an entire domain:

1. **Display the Blocked Senders list, as described in the preceding section.**

2. **Click the Add button.**

   You see the Add Sender dialog box.

3. **Type the domain name and click OK.**

   Leave the Mail Messages radio button selected. When you click OK, the new entry appears on your Blocked Senders list.

Creating a folder for your spam

If you are going to use rules to filter spam out of your Inbox, you need to create a folder named Suspected Spam into which your rules can put suspected spam messages. Follow these steps:

1. **On the folder list, select the folder in which you want to store this new folder.**

   We usually select Local Folders.

2. **Choose File⇨New⇨Folder from the menu bar, or press Ctrl+Shift+E.**

   You see the Create Folder dialog box.

3. **Type the name for your new folder in the Folder Name box.**

   How about Suspected Spam?

4. **Select Local Folders on the list of folders so that the new folder is contained in that folder.**

5. **Click OK.**

Your new folder appears on the folder list. To see what is in it (nothing yet), click it. If you decide later to remove or rename it, right-click it and choose Delete or Rename from the menu that appears.

Creating Outlook Express rules to trash spam

You can create a bunch of *rules* that tell Outlook Express what a particular spam message looks like and what to do with it — mainly, to get it the heck out of your Inbox! The e-mail program applies each rule to each message as it arrives in your Inbox; and, by creating rules that match the headers or text of spam messages, you can deflect spam from your Inbox into another folder.

 Rules don't work with Web-based mailboxes, like Hotmail. Rules don't work with IMAP-based mailboxes either (these mailboxes, used mainly in large organizations, allow you to read mail on the mail server without downloading it for storage on your computer).

You can make pretty fancy rules. For example, you can specify that if a message contains the phrase *low-interest mortgage* or *debt reduction* and it's *not* from your bank, it should be deleted. You can make lots of rules, one for each type of spam you get. Spammers mutate their messages so fast that you'll never make enough rules to keep up with them, but the rules are better than nothing. Rules are also quite useful for sorting wanted mail into mailboxes, such as mail from frequent correspondents or mailing lists.

Creating a new rule in Outlook Express

To work with rules, choose Tools⇨Message Rules⇨Mail to display the Message Rules dialog box, as shown in Figure 14-5. If you haven't created any rules yet, Outlook Express displays the New Mail Rule dialog box, as shown in Figure 14-6. From the Message Rules dialog box, click the New button to create a new rule.

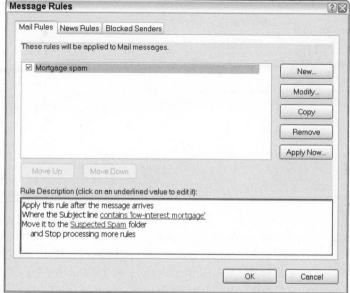

Figure 14-5: You can create, modify, and delete mail-filtering rules in Outlook Express.

The New Mail Rule dialog box contains four boxes in which you specify information about the rule:

- **Select The Conditions For Your Rule:** You specify which parts of the message Outlook Express should look at in determining to which messages to apply the rule. You can select the From line, Subject line, message body, To line, CC line, priority, mail account, size, attachment, and security setting. Or, you can choose to apply the rule to all messages. Strangely, you don't specify the text, address, or other information here; you provide this information in Box 3. Go figure.

- **Select The Actions For Your Rule:** You specify what Outlook Express should do when a message matches a condition. You can move a message to a folder, copy it to a folder, delete it, forward it, reply to it, or mark it as highlighted, flagged, read, or unread. You can also tell Outlook Express not to download the message from your mail server or to delete it from the mail server without downloading it.

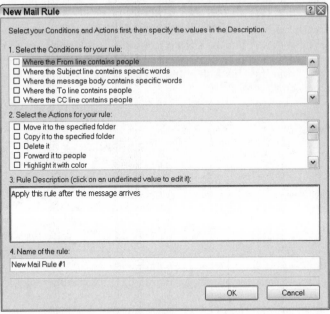

Figure 14-6:
To create a
mail-filtering
rule, you tell
Outlook
Express the
conditions
that
messages
must match
and what
you want
the program
to do with
matching
messages.

✔ **Rule Description:** This box shows the rule as you create it. You specify details about the rule, such as what text to look for or which folder to move messages to, by clicking underlined links in the description.

✔ **Name Of The Rule:** You can name the rule. (If you don't, Outlook Express comes up with creative names, like New Mail Rule #1.)

Follow these steps to create a rule to filter out spam:

1. **In Box 1, Select The Conditions For Your Rule, select the check box for the part of the message that identifies the message as spam.**

   For example, if you want to block all messages that contain the phrase *low-interest mortgage* on the Subject line, select the second check box, Where The Subject Line Contains Specific Words.

2. **In Box 2, Select The Actions For Your Rule, select the first check box, Move It To The Specified Folder.**

   Box 3 now shows text based on your choice in Boxes 1 and 2. For example, if you selected the Subject Line check box in Box 1, Box 3 says

   ```
   Apply this rule after this message arrives
   when the Subject line contains specific words
   move it to the specified folder
   ```

3. **In Box 3, Rule Description, click the Contains Specified Words link to specify the word or phrase to match.**

   You see the Type Specific Words dialog box.

4. **Type the word or phrase that appears in the spam you want to trash. Click the Add button.**

   For example, type **low-interest** in the box. When you click the Add button, the Words box shows the words you're looking for.

5. **If you want the rule to look for another phrase too, repeat Step 4.**

   You may want the same rule to look for other loan and mortgage spam messages, so you can type **debt reduction** and click the Add button and then type **reduced interest** and click Add again. The Words box shows the whole list of words and phrases you want the rule to match.

6. **Click OK to return to the New Mail Rule dialog box.**

   Box 3 shows the list of phrases the rule matches. But you still haven't told the rule what to do with messages that contain these phrases on the Subject line.

7. **Click the Specified link in Box 3.**

   Outlook Express displays the Move dialog box, showing a list of your folders.

8. **Select the folder and click OK.**

   We like to move spam to a Suspected Spam folder, which we look through from time to time, to check for good messages that may have been misidentified as spam. Your other option is to move the messages directly into the Deleted Items folder.

9. **Click to select the Stop Processing More Rules check box in Box 2 (Select The Actions For Your Rule).**

   You'll need to scroll down the list of actions to find this one. When you select it, the phrase *and stop processing more rules* appears at the end of your rules description, telling Outlook Express that, after it has moved a message once, it's done applying rules to that message; it's time to go on to the next message.

10. **In Box 4, Name Of The Rule, type a name for this rule.**

    You can use any name; you're the only person who sees it. Type something that makes finding the rule easy if you decide to change it later, such as **loan spams**.

11. **Click OK.**

    Outlook Express stores the rule and you return to the Message Rules dialog box.

Sneaky ways spammers evade filters

Spammers are smart — if they weren't, outraged Internet users would have shut them down long ago. Every time spam filterers come up with another way to spot spam, spammers change what they send out. It's like a sped-up version of e-mail evolution.

Here are some tricks that spammers use to prevent your filters from catching their junk messages:

✔ **Funky capitalization:** Most mail filter programs look for the exact capitalization you specify. If your filter looks for `spammers rus.com` on the From line, you don't catch messages from `SpammersRus.com` or `spaMmersruS.com`.

✔ **No text:** Many spam messages contain almost no text, just a graphical image of text. By sending the text as a graphical image, filters can't read the text to spot the phrases you're looking for.

✔ **Wrods Speled w.r.0.n.g:** People are remarkably good at making sense of garbled text, so it's not hard to garble text enough to defeat filters and remain legible to people.

✔ **Hidden bogus codes:** E-mail messages can contain HTML formatting codes, which are enclosed in <angle brackets>. These formatting codes can create bold (with the <b> code) and italics (with <i>) text in your messages. However, lots of codes have no meaning in HTML, like <m> and <n>, so your e-mail program ignores them when displaying messages. However, if these meaningless codes are sprinkled in your messages, your filters are prevented from finding the words you have flagged. For example, a filter that's looking for `make money` doesn't match a message that contains `ma<m>ke mon<n>ey`.

Some spam-tagging programs add a header to each message that indicates whether the message is spam. If your ISP, or a third-party spam-filtering program, adds these tags, you can create a rule that spots these messages and moves them into your Suspected Spam folder.

Reviewing your spam

From time to time, be sure to look through the messages that your rules identify as spam. Perfectly innocent messages sometimes are mislabeled as spam.

To look in your Suspected Spam folder (or whatever folder you shunt spam into), double-click it on the folder list. The list of messages in that folder appears. Scroll through the messages; the unread messages appear in bold. (All spam you never saw should appear in bold.)

If you see any good messages, drag them into your Inbox folder. Then look at the message and at your message rules to figure out how it got tagged as spam, and fix your rules.

Getting a spam-filtering program

If you use Thunderbird, you've got a very capable Bayesian spam filter built right in — for free. You don't need another spam-filtering program. If you use Outlook Express (or many other e-mail programs), you don't have a spam filter. Outlook Express users, as well as people who use other programs, aren't out of luck, though. You can buy and install spam filters that work with your e-mail program.

Here are some spam-filtering programs that work with your e-mail program, many of them for free:

- **Death2Spam, at** death2spam.com: You can try this program for free for 30 days, and then it's a modest $35 a year.

- **K9, at** www.keir.net/k9.html: This free program uses Bayesian filters and doesn't work with Web-based e-mail accounts.

- **MailWasher and MailWasher Pro at** www.mailwasher.net: There are free and paid versions. The paid version supports Hotmail accounts.

- **POPfile, at** popfile.sourceforge.net: This free program retrieves your mail and tags it using a Bayesian filter. It doesn't work with Web-based e-mail accounts.

- **Spamihilator, at** www.spamihilator.com: This free program uses Bayesian filters.

- **SpamPal, at** www.spampal.org: This free program uses blacklists to determine what's spam.

For more information about many, many more spam filters, see About.com's list of spam filters at email.about.com/od/windowsspamfightingtools. For instructions for how to install and use spam filters, and lots of information about spam in general, get *Fighting Spam For Dummies*, John Levine, Margaret Levine Young, and Ray Everett-Church (hey, that's two out three of the same authors as this book!), by Wiley Publishing, Inc.

What else can I do?

The Internet grew from a need for the easy and free flow of information, and everyone using it should strive to keep it that way. Check out these Web sites for information about spam and how to fight it, technically, socially, and legally:

- spamabuse.net (a spam overview)

- www.cauce.org (antispam laws)

- www.abuse.net (a complaint forwarding service for e-mail abuse)

One-click surfing, but no phishing

Most e-mail programs convert URLs (Web site addresses) in your e-mail messages into links to the actual Web site. You don't have to type these addresses into your browser. All you have to do is click the highlighted link in the e-mail message and — poof — your browser opens and you're at the Web site. If your e-mail program has this feature (all the programs mentioned in this chapter do), URLs in e-mail messages appear underlined and blue — a nice feature.

Unfortunately, this feature is abused by phishers. Phishing is sending faked e-mail that claims to be from your bank or other official organization to trick you into revealing personal information, and it's described in Chapter 2. If you do click one of these links and it takes you to a Web site that asks for a password, credit card number, or the like, don't give them any information!

We believe that spam is not just a technical problem, and only a combination of technical, social, and legal solutions will work in the long run. In the meantime, every ISP now does at least some spam filtering on incoming mail, and many let you "tune" the filters. Check with your ISP for the specific services it provides.

Secure That Mail

If you have a laptop and you use it to read your e-mail in public WiFi hotspots, you may have a security problem. (See Chapter 5 for what we mean by "WiFi" and "hotspot.") Public WiFi setups allow anyone connected to the same hotspot (that is, anyone in the same café or area of the airport) to eavesdrop on what you type, including potentially seeing your e-mail username and password.

Fortunately, most mail programs and mail servers let you use a secure connection, the same kind that secure web pages use, for incoming and outgoing mail. Setting up the secure connection can be a little tricky, but you only have to do it once.

Secure mail with Thunderbird

To set up secure mail in Thunderbird:

1. **Select Tools⇨Account Settings.**

   You'll see the Account Settings window, with a list of your mail accounts on the left.

2. **Click Server Settings under your incoming mail account.**

   You may have to click the little + sign next to your account's name to see the Server Settings option.

3. **Check Use Secure Connection (SSL).**

4. **Now click Outgoing Server (SMTP) at the bottom of the left column.**

   If you have several accounts set up, you may have to scroll down to find it.

5. **Under Use Secure Connection, click TLS.**

6. **Click OK.**

Now check your mail, and try sending yourself a message. If it doesn't work, your mail provider may not offer secure mail, or may offer it in a nonstandard way, and you'll have to call for help.

Secure mail with Outlook Express

To set up secure mail in Outlook Express:

1. **Select Tools⇨Accounts.**

2. **Click the name of your mail account in the window that opens, and then click Properties.**

3. **In the window that opens, click the Advanced tab.**

   There's a Security tab, but that's not what you want here.

4. **Check the boxes for "This server requires a secure connection (SSL)" for both incoming and outgoing mail.**

5. **Click OK.**

Now check your mail and try sending yourself a message, clicking the Send/Recv button to make Outlook Express connect to the server. If it doesn't work, your mail provider may not offer secure mail, or may offer it in a non-standard way, and you'll have to call for help.

Chapter 15

Putting Your Mail in Its Place

· ·

· ·

*A*fter you get used to using e-mail, you'll start sending and receiving enough messages that you'd better keep it organized. This chapter describes how to delete, reply, forward, and file messages in Thunderbird, Outlook Express, and Web mail systems such as Yahoo Mail. (See Chapter 13 for how to get started using these programs.)

After you see an e-mail message, you can do a bunch of different things with it (much the same as with paper mail). Here are your usual choices:

✔ Throw it away.

✔ Reply to it.

✔ Forward it to other people.

✔ File it.

You can do any or all these things with each message. If you don't tell your mail program what to do with a message, the message usually stays in your mailbox for later perusal.

Deleting Mail

When you first begin to get e-mail, the feeling is so exciting that it's difficult to imagine just throwing away the message. Eventually, however, you *have* to know how to get rid of messages, or else your computer will run out of room. Start early. Delete often.

Throwing away mail is easy enough that you probably have figured out how to do it already. In Thunderbird and Outlook Express (and in most other e-mail programs, for that matter), the process goes like this:

Display the message or select it from the list of messages in a folder. Then click the trashcan, big *X*, or other trashy-looking icon on the toolbar, or press Ctrl+D or Del (on the Mac, press +D or Delete). In Yahoo Mail or other Web mail systems, click the Inbox or Check Mail link to see a list of your messages. Then select the check box by the message and click the Delete button at the bottom of the list. When you're looking at a message in Web mail, you can click an X or Delete button, too.

You can delete mail without even reading it. If you subscribe to mailing lists (which we describe in Chapter 16), certain topics may not interest you. After you see the subject line, you may want to delete the message without reading it. If you're the type of person who reads everything Ed McMahon sends to you, you may have problems managing junk e-mail, too. Consider getting professional help.

When you delete a message, most e-mail programs don't throw it away immediately. Instead, they file the message in your Trash or Deleted Messages mailbox or mail folder, or just mark it as deleted. From time to time (usually whenever you exit the e-mail program), the program empties your trash, truly deleting the messages.

Back to You, Sam: Replying to Mail

Replying to mail is easy: Choose Message⇨Reply in Thunderbird, or Message⇨ Reply to Sender in Outlook Express. Or, click the Reply button on the toolbar or press Ctrl+R (Cmd+R on the Mac). In Web mail, you usually see a Reply button.

When you have the reply message open, ask yourself two particular questions:

✔ **To whom does the reply go?** Look carefully at the To line, which your e-mail program has filled out for you. Is that who you thought you were addressing? If the reply is addressed to a mailing list, did you really intend to send a message to the entire list, or is your reply of a more personal nature, intended only for the individual who sent the message? Did you mean to reply to a group? Are all the addresses that you think you're replying to included on the To list? If the To list isn't correct, move the cursor to it and edit it as necessary.

Occasionally you may receive a message that has been sent to a zillion people, and their addresses appear in dozens of lines in the To section of the message. If you reply to a message like this, look at the To section of your reply to make sure it isn't addressed to the entire list of recipients.

Some e-mail programs have a separate Reply To All command or button that addresses your reply to both the people that the message was from and the people who received copies of the message (that is, to "To" people and the "Cc" people). Thunderbird and Outlook Express both have a Reply All button on the toolbar,

✔ **Do you want to include the content of the message to which you're replying?** Most e-mail programs include the content of the message to which you're replying, usually formatted to show that it's a *quotation* or *quoted text*. Edit the quoted text to include just the relevant material. If you don't give some context to people who get a great deal of e-mail, your reply makes no sense. If you're answering a question, include the question in the response. You needn't include the entire text, but give your reader a break. She may have read 50 messages since she sent you mail and may not have a clue what you're talking about unless you remind her.

When you reply to a message, most mail programs fill in the Subject field with the letters *Re:* (short for *regarding*) and the Subject field contents of the message to which you're replying.

Keeping Track of Your Friends

After you begin using e-mail, you quickly find that you have enough regular correspondents that keeping track of their e-mail addresses is a pain. Fortunately, every popular e-mail program provides an *address book* in which you can save your friends' addresses so that you can send mail to Mom, for example, and have it automatically addressed to chairman@exec.hq.giant corp.com. You can also create address lists so that you can send mail to family, for example, and it goes to Mom, Dad, your brother, both sisters, and your dog, all of whom have e-mail addresses.

All address books let you do the same things:

✔ Save in your address book the address from a message you have just read

✔ Use addresses you have saved for outgoing messages

✔ Edit your address book

The Thunderbird address book

Thunderbird has a good address book, and adding people to it is easy. Display the Address Book window by clicking the Address Book button on the toolbar, pressing Ctrl+2 (Cmd+2 on the Mac), or choosing Tools⇨Address Book — you see a window that looks like Figure 15-1. You can add a new person to your address book by clicking New Card and filling out the form. To edit an entry, select it and click the Properties button on the toolbar. You can also create a *list* — that is, an address book entry that sends a message to a bunch of people (for example, the members of a committee or of your family). Click New List to create one.

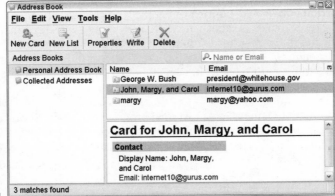

Figure 15-1:
Thunder-
bird's
address
book.

To use the address book while you're composing a message, just start typing the person's name in your new message. As soon as Thunderbird sees a name that begins with the same letters as an address book entry, it displays the person's name. If more than one entry matches, you see a list you can choose from.

To create a mailing list, click the New List button, which creates an empty list, and then type the addresses you want.

When you're reading a message in Thunderbird, you can add the sender's address to your address book by clicking the sender's name or address in the From line and choosing Add to Address Book from the menu that pops up. This opens a New Card window in which you can enter additional information about the person. Then click OK to add it to the address book.

The Outlook Express address book

To display and edit the address book, click the Addresses button on the tool-bar. (You may need to widen the Outlook Express window to see it — it's near the right end of the toolbar in some versions.) Add a new person by clicking the New button on the Address Book window's toolbar and choosing New Contact from the menu that appears. To change someone's entry, select the entry and click Properties on the toolbar.

The process of copying a correspondent's address into the address book is easy: Right-click the person's name in the list of messages, and choose Add Sender to Address Book from the menu that appears.

After you add some entries to your address book, you use them while you're creating a new message by clicking the little book icon to the left of the To or Cc line in the New Message window. In the Select Recipients window that appears, double-click the address book entry or entries you want to use — they appear in the Message Recipients list. Then click OK.

Web mail address books

Most Web mail systems (which we describe in detail in Chapter 13) include an address book — it's just too useful a feature to leave out. After you log into your mail account by using your browser, click the Addresses or Address Book link to display your address book. Click the Add Contact or similar button to add someone. Fill out the form that appears, and be sure to enter a *nickname* for the person: You can type the nickname when addressing an e-mail message instead of typing the person's whole e-mail address. The form may include fields for the person's postal address and phone numbers, but you can leave them blank. Then click the Save or Save Contact button. (These instructions are approximate, because Web mail sites change their buttons' names all the time.)

Web mail systems provide several ways to address a message to someone in your address book. When composing a message, try typing the person's nick-name to see whether a matching entry appears. In Yahoo Mail, you can click the To or Insert Addresses link to see a popup window of address book entries. Click the To, Cc, or Bcc box by the person's name and then click Insert Checked Contacts, as shown in Figure 15-2.

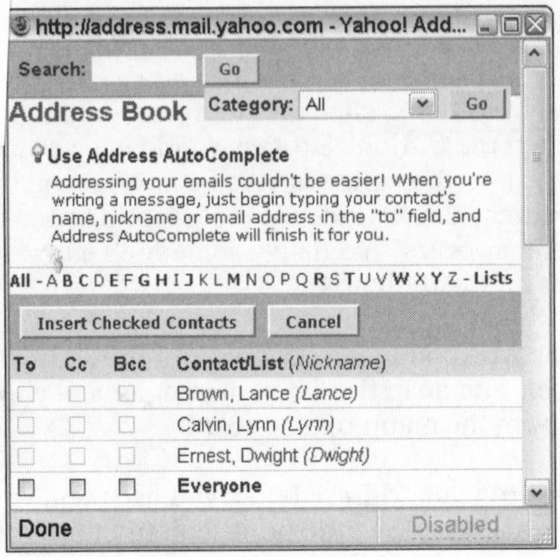

Figure 15-2:
Yahoo Mail,
like most
Web mail
systems,
includes an
address
book.

Hot Potatoes: Forwarding Mail

You can forward e-mail to someone else. It's easy. It's cheap. Forwarding is one of the best things about e-mail and at the same time one of the worst. It's good because you can easily pass along messages to people who need to know about them. It's bad because you (not *you* personally, but, um, people around you — that's it) can just as easily send out floods of messages to recipients who would just as soon not hear *another* press release from the local Ministry of Truth (or another joke that's making the rounds). Think about whether you will enhance someone's quality of life by forwarding a message to him. If a message says "forward this to everyone you know," do everyone you know a favor and delete it instead.

What's usually called *forwarding* a message involves wrapping the message in a new message of your own, sort of like putting sticky notes all over a copy of it and mailing the copy and notes to someone else.

- Forwarding mail is almost as easy as replying to it: Select the message and click the Forward button on the toolbar, or choose Message⇨Forward. Pressing Ctrl+L (Cmd+L on the Mac) also works in Thunderbird, and Ctrl+F forwards in Outlook Express. In Yahoo Mail and other Web mail systems, a Forward button usually appears when you view a message. The mail program composes a message that contains the text of the message you want to forward; all you have to do is address the message, add a few snappy comments, and send it.

The text of the original message appears at the top or bottom of the message, usually formatted as quoted text and preceded by a line that says who the original message was from, and when. You then get to edit the message and add your own comments. (See the sidebar "Fast forward" in this chapter for tips about pruning forwarded mail.) In Yahoo Mail, clicking Forward sends the original messages as <u>an attachment</u> to your new message. If you want the original text right in your message, you can click in the box to the right of the Forward button and click As Inline Text.

Fast forward

Whenever you're forwarding mail, be sure to delete uninteresting parts. All the glop in the message header is frequently included automatically in the forwarded message, and almost none of it is comprehensible, much less interesting, so get rid of it.

The tricky part is editing the text. If the message is short (a screenful or so), you probably should leave it alone:

```
>Is there a lot of demand for
    fruit pizza?
>
I checked with our research
    department and found that
    the favorite pizza toppings
    in the 18-34 age group are
    pepperoni, sausage, ham,
    pineapple, olives, peppers,
    sauerkraut, hamburger, and
    broccoli. I specifically
    asked about prunes, and
    they found no statistically
    significant response.
```

If the message is really long and only part of it is relevant, you should, as a courtesy to the reader, cut it down to the interesting part. We can tell you from experience that people pay much more attention to a concise, one-line e-mail message than they do to 12 pages of quoted stuff followed by a two-line question.

Sometimes it makes sense to edit material even more, particularly to emphasize one specific

part. When you do so, of course, be sure not to edit to the point where you put words in the original author's mouth or garble the sense of the message, as in the following reply:

```
>I checked with
>our research department and
    found that the
>favorite pizza toppings ...
    and they
>found no statistically
    significant
>response.
```

This version of the original message is totally misleading — it twists the original text. Sometimes, it makes sense to paraphrase a little — in that case, put the paraphrased part in square brackets, like this:

```
>[When asked about prunes on
    pizza, research]
>found no statistically signif-
    icant response.
```

People disagree about whether paraphrasing to shorten quotes is a good idea. On one hand, if you do it well, it saves everyone time. On the other hand, if you do it badly and someone takes offense, you're in for a week of accusations and apologies that will wipe out whatever time you may have saved. The decision is up to you.

Cold Potatoes: Saving Mail

Saving e-mail for later reference is similar to putting potatoes in the fridge for later. (Don't knock it if you haven't tried it — day-old boiled potatoes are yummy with enough butter or sour cream.) Lots of your e-mail is worth saving, just as lots of your paper mail is worth saving. Lots of it *isn't,* of course, but we covered that subject earlier in this chapter.

You can save e-mail in a few different ways:

✔ Save it in a folder full of messages.

✔ Save it in a regular text file.

✔ Print it and put it in a file cabinet with paper mail. (Spare a tree; don't use this method.)

The easiest method usually is to stick messages in a folder. E-mail programs usually come with folders called In (or Inbox), Outbox, Sent, and Trash, and perhaps some others. But you can also make your own folders.

People use two general approaches in filing mail: by sender and by topic. Whether you use one or the other or both is mostly a matter of taste. For filing by topic, it's entirely up to you to come up with folder names. The most difficult part is coming up with memorable names. If you aren't careful, you end up with four folders with slightly different names, each with a quarter of the messages about a particular topic. Try to come up with names that are obvious, and don't abbreviate. If the topic is accounting, call the folder `Accounting` because if you abbreviate, you'll never remember whether it's called `Acctng`, `acct`, or `Acnthg`.

You can save all or part of a message by copying it into a text file or word-processing document. Select the text of the message by using your mouse. Press Ctrl+C (+C on a Mac) or choose Edit⇨Copy to copy the text to the Clipboard. Switch to your word processor (or whatever program into which you want to copy the text) and press Ctrl+V (+V on the Mac) or choose Edit⇨Paste to make the message appear where the cursor is.

Filing with Thunderbird

Thunderbird lists your mail folders down the left side of the window, starting with Inbox. Thunderbird provides folders named Inbox, Unsent Messages, Drafts, Sent, and Trash, but you can create your own folders. If you have a *lot* of messages to file, you can even create folders within folders to keep things organized. To make a new folder, follow these steps:

1. **Choose File➪New➪New Folder.**

   You see the New Folder dialog box.

2. **Type a name for the folder in the Name text box.**

   Make one called Personal, just to give it a try.

3. **Set the Create As A Subfolder Of drop-down box to the folder name in which you want the new folder to live.**

   Usually, you want your folder to be a subfolder of Local Folders, so set it to Local Folders and click Choose This For The Parent. Or choose another folder; for example, you could have a folder called Personal, and inside that could be a folder for each friend you get messages from.

4. **Click OK.**

The new folder appears on the list of folders on the left side of the Thunderbird window. You can see the list of message headers for any folder by clicking the folder name.

You can save a message in a folder by dragging the message to the folder name — easy enough. Or, right-click the message, choose Move To from the menu that appears, and choose the folder from the list that appears.

To save a message or several messages in a text file, select the message or messages and choose File➪Save As➪File (or press Ctrl+S). Type a filename and click the Save button.

When you compose a message, you can tell Thunderbird to save a copy of your message in a folder. While writing the message, choose Options➪Send A Copy To and then choose a folder.

Filing with Outlook Express

You start out with folders named Inbox, Outbox, Sent Items, Drafts, and Deleted Items. To make a new folder, choose File➪Folder➪New or File➪New➪Folder, give the folder a name, and choose which folder to put this new folder into. (Like Thunderbird, Outlook Express can have folders within folders — very convenient.)

Move messages into a folder by clicking a message header and dragging it over to the folder name, right-clicking the message on the message list and choosing Move To Folder, or choosing Edit➪Move To Folder.

You can save the text of a message in a text file by clicking the message and choosing File➪Save As, clicking in the Save As Type box and choosing Text Files (*.txt), typing a filename, and clicking the Save button.

Filing with Web mail systems

To save a message in a folder in Yahoo Mail, click the Move button and choose the folder where you want the message. To create a new folder, choose New Folder from the list of folders and click Move. Yahoo Mail asks you for a name for the folder.

Your folders appear in the list of folders down the left side of your browser window, under the My Folders heading. Your folders include Inbox, Sent, Draft, and Bulk (where Yahoo files stuff that looks like spam to them). Click a folder name to see the messages in that folder.

Exotic Mail and Mail Attachments

Sooner or later, just plain, old, everyday e-mail isn't good enough for you. Someone's gonna send you a picture you just have to see, or you're gonna want to send a video clip of Fluffy to your new best friend in Paris. To send stuff other than text through the mail, a message uses special file formats. Sometimes, the entire message is in a special format, and sometimes people *attach* things to their plain text mail. The most widely used format for attaching files to messages is called MIME (Multipurpose Internet Mail Extensions). The programs we describe in this chapter can send and receive files attached with MIME, as do most e-mail programs on the planet — only a few, very old e-mail programs still can't.

Corresponding with a robot

Not every mail address has an actual person behind it. Some are mailing lists (which we talk about in Chapter 16), and some are robots, programs that automatically reply to messages. Mail robots have become popular as a way to query databases and retrieve files because setting up a connection for electronic mail is much easier than setting up one that handles the more standard file transfer. You send a message to the robot (usually referred to as a mailbot or mail server), it takes some action based on the contents of your message, and then the robot sends back a response. If you send a message to internet10@gurus.com, for example, you receive a response telling you your e-mail address.

When you receive a file that's attached to an e-mail message, your mail program is responsible for noticing the attached file and doing something intelligent with it. Most of the time, your program saves the attached file as a separate file in the folder you specify. After the file has been saved, you can use it just like you use any other file.

You can send the following types of files as attachments:

✔ Pictures, in image files

✔ Word-processing documents

✔ Sounds, in audio files

✔ Movies, in video files

✔ Programs, in executable files

✔ Compressed files, such as ZIP files

E-mail viruses usually show up as attachments. If you get a message with an unexpected attachment, even from someone you know, **DON'T OPEN IT** until you check with the sender to make sure he or she sent it deliberately. Viruses often suck all the addresses from a victim's address book so the virus can mail itself to the victim's friends. Some kinds of attachments can't carry viruses, notably GIF and JPG images. See Chapter 14 for details.

Your ISP or Web-based mail service may place a limit on the size of your mailbox (the place on their server where your messages are stored until you pick them up). Gmail, Google's invitation-only Web-mail system, has a high limit (at least 1GB), so other mail systems have been increasing their limits to match, but you may still run into a size limit if someone sends you a truly gigantic file (for example, a video file). One way to shrink the size of attached files is to ZIP them first, using Windows XP's Compressed Folders feature or a separate program like WinZip. See the section "Uncompressing and unzipping" in Chapter 12 if you receive a ZIPped file (with file extension .zip).

Thunderbird attachments

To attach a file to the message you're composing, click the Attach button or choose File➪Attach. Then select the file you want to send. You can also insert a picture right into the text of the message by positioning your cursor where you want the picture appear, choosing Insert➪Image, and specifying the filename.

For incoming mail, Thunderbird displays any attachments that it is able to display itself (Web pages and GIF and JPEG image files). For other types of attachments, it displays a little description of the file, which you can click. Thunderbird then runs an appropriate display program — if it knows of one — or asks you whether to save the attachment to a file or to configure a display program, which Thunderbird then runs in order to display the attachment.

Outlook Express attachments

In Outlook Express, create a new message and then attach a file to a message by choosing Insert⇨File Attachment or by clicking the Attach button. (The Attach button might be off the right side of the toolbar — make the Composition window wider to display it.) Then select the file to attach. Or just drag the file into the message composition window. Then send the message as usual.

When an incoming message contains an attachment, a paper-clip icon appears in the message on your list of incoming messages and in the message header when you view the message. Click the paper clip to see the filename — double-click, and you may be able to see the attachment.

Microsoft has "solved" some of Outlook Express's chronic security problems by making it refuse to show you many attachments, including a lot of benign ones such as attached text messages and PDF files. You can sort of fix this by choosing Tools⇨Options in the main Outlook Express window, clicking the Security tab, and then deselecting the *Do Not Allow Attachments to Be Saved or Opened That Could Potentially Be a Virus* check box. Then Outlook Express lets you open your attachments, although of course when someone *does* send you a virus, Outlook Express cheerfully opens that, too.

Web mail attachments

To attach stuff with Yahoo Mail, compose a message as usual. Then click the Attach File button and specify up to five files to attach. Click the Browse button to find the file on your computer. (You may need to change the Files of Type box in the File Upload dialog box to All Files to see all your files.) Then click the Open button. When you've chosen all the files to attach, click Attach Files again. Your Web browser, amazing beast that it is, copies the file right off your hard drive and sends it to the Yahoo Mail system to include in your message. Your browser even scans the file for viruses just in case. Click Continue To Message to return to the Yahoo Mail page where you're composing your message — the filename appears just below the subject line. Send the message as usual.

When you get a message with attachments, a box appears at the bottom of the message, displaying the filename and size of the attachment. Click the Download File button to get the file onto your computer.

Your Own Personal Mail Manager

After you begin sending e-mail, you probably will find that you receive quite a bit of it, particularly if you put yourself on some mailing lists (see Chapter 16). Your incoming mail becomes a trickle, and then a stream, and then a torrent, and pretty soon you can't walk past your keyboard without getting soaking wet, metaphorically speaking.

Fortunately, most mail systems provide ways for you to manage the flow and avoid ruining your clothes (enough of this metaphor already). Thunderbird can create *filters* that can automatically check incoming messages against a list of senders and subjects and file them in appropriate folders. Outlook Express has the Inbox Assistant, which can sort your mail automatically. Most other mail programs (and a few Web mail systems) have similar filtering features. If you sort mail into separate mailboxes for each mailing list or other category, you can deal with it a lot more efficiently.

For example, you can create filters that tell your mail program, "Any message that comes from the CHICKENS-L mailing list should be automatically filed in the Cluck mail folder." Figure 15-3 shows such a filter in Thunderbird.

Figure 15-3:
Moving poultry-related messages to a separate folder for immediate attention.

Filter Rules		✕
Filter name: Chicken list		

For incoming messages that:
○ Match all of the following   ● Match any of the following

Sender	contains	chickens-l@

More   Fewer

Perform these actions:
☑ Move to folder: Cluck on Local Folders   ∨   New Folder...
☐ Copy to folder: Local Folders   ∨   New Folder...

OK   Cancel

You can create filters to highlight messages from particularly interesting friends, or delete certain messages (you know the ones we mean) so you never have to see them. Here's how for the main e-mail programs we discuss in the book:

- **Thunderbird:** Choose Tools⇨Message Filters to display the Message Filters window, where you can see, create, edit, and delete filters. Click New to create a new filter, and then specify a filter name (for your own reference), how Thunderbird can match incoming messages to this filter, and what to do with messages that match. Or click the To or From address in a message and choose Create Filter from Message to make a filter for mail sent to or from that address.

- **Outlook Express:** Tell the Inbox Assistant how to sort your mail into folders by choosing Tools⇨Message Rules⇨Mail. See Chapter 14 for details.

- **Yahoo Mail:** Click the `Mail Options` link on the Yahoo Mail Web page, and then click the Filters heading. You can create, edit, or delete your filters.

All this automatic-sorting nonsense may seem like overkill, and if you get only five or ten messages a day, it is. After the mail really gets flowing, however, dealing with it takes much more of your time than it used to. Keep those automated tools in mind — if not for now, then for later.

Chapter 16

Typing and Talking on the Net

In This Chapter

▶ Typing to one friend at a time with instant messaging

▶ Typing to a lot of friends at a time with chat rooms and mailing lists

▶ Talking to friends old and new, with a webcam

▶ Using telephones over the Net

*I*nternet e-mail is pretty fast, usually arriving in less than a minute. But sometimes that's just not fast enough. Instant-message (IM) systems let you pop up a message on a friend's screen in a matter of seconds. They also have Buddy Lists that watch to see when one of your buddies comes online so you know the instant you can instantiate an instant message to them. (Excuse us, this gives us a headache. Just a moment while we get some instant coffee. Ahh, that's better.)

The good thing about instant messages is that you can stay in touch with people as fast as by talking to them on the phone. The bad thing about instant messages is that they also offer an unparalleled range of ways to annoy people. AOL Instant Messenger (discussed later in this chapter) has about two features to send and receive messages, and about 12 features to reject, denounce, erase, and otherwise deal with unwanted messages. (This may say more about AOL users than the technology, of course.)

Gregarious people can chat with a whole bunch of people at once, either typing at the same time like a party line, or sending messages to each other by e-mail or Web forums.

Of course, even better than typing messages to another person is talking right out loud. If your computer has a microphone and speakers, you can use IM systems to talk to people over the Net — even groups of people — with no toll charges. If you connect a digital video camera (or *webcam*) to your computer, your friends can even see you as you talk or type. It's not hard to do!

TIP

Which instant message system should I use?

Unfortunately, the instant-messaging systems don't talk to one another. Because the goal of all of these systems is to help you stay in touch with your friends, use whichever one they use. If you're not sure who your friends are, AOL Instant Messenger is a good bet because it's easy to set up and works automatically with any AOL user; it's the same system that AOL uses internally. We like Yahoo Messenger because it's free, supports text, voice, and video, and allows more than two people to chat. (We've held meetings on Yahoo Messenger with six people on voice, two on video, and everyone typing snide comments at the same time.) If you have Windows XP, you already have Windows Messenger, which comes pre-installed.

If you're really message-mad, you can run more than one system at the same time. While we were writing this chapter, we had Windows Messenger, AOL Instant Messenger, and Yahoo! Messenger all running at once. It was an awful lot of blinking and flashing, but it did work. We also like an open source program called Gaim at `gaim.sourceforge.net` that handles every IM system you ever heard of simultaneously.

Other IM programs also exist including ICQ (described in the sidebar "Where did IM come from?").

The Next Best Thing to Being There

Instant Messaging (IM) lets you type short messages that appear in a window on someone else's computer. It's faster than e-mail, but slightly less intrusive than a phone call, and so far few people have their secretaries screen their IMs.

This chapter describes how to use the most popular IM systems: AOL Instant Messenger, Windows or MSN Messenger, and Yahoo Messenger.

TIP

Instant message programs open a new window when one of your buddies sends you a message. If you have a program that blocks popup windows in your browser, IM windows aren't affected. This is because popup-blockers block only Web browser popups.

AOL Instant Messenger (AIM)

AOL Instant Messenger (*AIM* for short) is one of the simplest chat systems around. All it does is let you type messages back and forth. This section describes AIM version 5. If you use AOL, you can either use the separate AIM program we describe here or the AIM part of the regular AOL program (which does the same things although the windows are a little different).

Taking AIM

If you're an AOL user, you're already set up for instant messages. If not, you have to install the AIM program. AOL subscribers can also run the AIM program and use their AOL screen names when they're logged in to another kind of Internet account.

AOL, being the hyper-aggressive marketing organization it is, has arranged for AIM to be bundled in with a lot of other packages. If you don't have it, visit www.aim.com and follow the directions on the Web page to download it. Before you can download the program, you have to choose a screen name — which can be up to 16 letters long (be creative so yours won't collide with one of the 30 million names already in use) — and a password. You also have to enter your e-mail address. AOL, refreshingly, doesn't want any more personal information. The e-mail address you give does have to be real; AOL sends a confirmation message to that address, and you must reply or your screen name is deleted.

 Save the downloaded file somewhere on your computer. (C:\Windows\Temp is an okay place if you don't have another folder you use for downloads.) Then run the downloaded program (which is called Install_aim.exe last we looked) to install AIM. Normally AIM runs in the background whenever you're online. If it's not running, click the AIM icon on your desktop.

The first time you use AIM, you have to enter your AIM or AOL screen name, as in the left part of Figure 16-1. Type your screen name and password and click Sign On. If you want to use AIM every time you're online, check the Save Password and Auto-login boxes before signing on, and AIM will sign you on automatically in the future. After you sign in, you see the AIM window shown in the middle of Figure 16-1. You also see a big window full of news, ads, and links to AOL's Web site — just close it.

Figure 16-1:
Signing on to AIM, the AIM window, and the Buddy List Setup window.

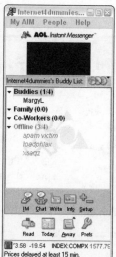

AIM may run the New User Wizard, which offers help getting started. Follow its instructions, or click Cancel to go it alone (you can always return to the wizard by choosing Help⇨New User Wizard from the AIM menu). A stock ticker runs along the bottom of the AIM window (for you serious investors); click the button on its left edge to see news details or to customize the ticker.

Getting your buddies organized

First you create your Buddy List, and then you can send messages.

When AIM opens, you see your *Buddy List*, that is, other AIM users who you like to chat with. The window shows which of your many buddies are currently online (everyone who's not currently listed in the Offline category). What? None of your pals appears? You need to add your friend's AOL or AIM screen names to your Buddy List.

 In the AIM window, click the Setup or Edit Buddy List button to display the Buddy List Setup window shown on the right side of Figure 16-1. It lists all your groups of buddies. AOL provides three groups: Buddies, Family, and Co-Workers. (You can make other groups, too, using the Add Group button.) Click the group to which you want to add it, click the Add Buddy button, type the buddy's screen name, and press Enter. If you know the e-mail address but not the screen name, return to the AIM window and choose People⇨Find a Buddy Wizard. Doing so starts a wizard that looks for that address and helps you add any screen names that match. You can drag a buddy around (from one group to another in the Buddy List Setup window), or get rid of a buddy (by clicking the buddy and then clicking the Delete button).

After you select your buddies, click the Return to Buddy List button, which closes the Buddy List Setup window and returns you to the AIM window. You see your Buddy List with offline folks' names in pale gray and everyone else organized by group.

Where did IM come from?

ICQ (pronounced *I seek you*) was the original instant messenger and still has many million users, especially outside the United States. It's available from their Web site at www.icq.com. ICQ comes in 18 languages and has about a quadrillion different features and options, but basically, you download and install ICQ and set it up to get an ICQ#, sort of like a phone number, that identifies you. Then you identify some buddies and start sending them instant messages and chatting with them. The ICQ program runs on Windows (all versions, starting with 3.1), Macs, Palm Pilots, and, for all we know, certain espresso machines.

AOL bought ICQ many years ago, and we expected that they'd integrate it with AIM, but it seems that ICQ and AIM will stay separate systems.

Getting buddy-buddy online

To send a message to someone, double-click the buddy's name to open a message window, type the message, and click the Send button. AIM pops up a window (shown in the left part of Figure 16-2) on the recipient's machine, plays a little song, and you and your buddy can type back and forth. When done, close the message window.

Unless you are a very fast typist or your friend lives in Mongolia, a highly effective thing to type is "What's your phone number?" and call the person on the phone — or follow the instructions in the next section.

Figure 16-2: Chatting using AIM.

Making noise with AIM

After you establish a conversation using AIM, you can switch to voice (assuming that both parties have computers equipped with microphones and speakers). Click the Talk button and click Connect. Your friend sees a window asking whether (s)he wants to make a direct connection with you. Clicking Accept in that window displays the Talk With window shown in the right part of Figure 16-2. Click Disconnect when you are done talking.

Buzz off

AOL evidently has a lot of ill-mannered users, because AIM has a system for warning and blocking users you don't like. If someone sends you an annoying message, you can click the Warn button. With enough warnings (about five), a user is blocked from sending instant messages for a while. If you find a sender to be totally objectionable, click the Block button to refuse all messages from that person.

You can fine-tune who you let send messages to you: Click the Prefs button to display the AOL Instant Messenger Preferences window, then the Privacy category. You can limit messages to people on your Buddy List, permit specific people access, or block specific people. You can also add or delete people from your Block list. We recommend choosing Allow Only Users on My Buddy List unless you like being contacted by total strangers at inconvenient moments.

Some obvious rules of messaging conduct

Sending someone an instant message is the online equivalent of walking up to someone on the street and starting a conversation. If it's someone you know, it's one thing; if not, it's usually an intrusion.

Unless you have a compelling reason, don't send instant messages to people you don't know who haven't invited you to do so. Don't say anything that you wouldn't say in an analogous situation on the street.

For some reason, AOL is plagued with childish users who now and then send rude instant messages to strangers or unwilling acquaintances, which is why AIM has its Warn and Block buttons. Not only is it rude to do that, it's silly: AOL has chat rooms full of people eager to converse on all sorts of topics, rude or otherwise.

Most instant-message programs allow you to send and receive files. Leave the file feature off except when you have a specific file you need to send or receive. Unsolicited files from people you don't know are generally spam, viruses, or both. Most virus-checkers don't monitor file transfers via an IM program.

The messages that you send with AIM and other chat programs may appear to be ephemeral, but it's easy for anyone in the conversation to store the messages. Most IM programs have a "log" feature that saves the series of messages in a text file, which may be embarrassing later.

Finally: If someone tells you to give a series of commands, or download and install a program, don't do it. And never tell anyone any of your passwords.

There is no escape

When you exit from AIM by clicking its Big Red X, the program usually doesn't stop running. Instead, it changes into a tiny icon in your Windows notification area, on the right end of the Windows Taskbar, near the clock. AIM continues to run so that if one of your buddies wants to contact you, it can respond and pop up the incoming message. You can sign off or exit from the program by right-clicking the icon and choose Sign Off or Exit.

Windows Messenger, alias MSN Messenger

Windows XP comes with the latest instant messaging program, called Windows Messenger. Microsoft noticed that this was a niche in which they didn't have the dominant program, and so decided to issue everyone a copy of theirs. Windows XP nags you to sign up for a Microsoft .NET Passport, a free account that you use to log in to Windows Messenger, the Hotmail Web site, and other Microsoft Web sites. We don't see the advantage of Windows Messenger over the other instant message programs: It has far fewer neat features than Yahoo Messenger. It does support voice and video, but only with one person at a time.

Versions are available for Windows 95 and newer Windows versions, as well as for Macs. Unless all your friends use MSN Messenger there's little reason to use it — but if they do (and you want to), there's more info on our Web site at net.gurus.com/msnmessenger.

Yahoo Messenger

Yahoo, the popular Web site, has its own instant message program called Yahoo Messenger. It's our favorite, because not only can you type messages and talk using a microphone, you can also see each other if you have web-cams. Better yet, more than three people can join in the conversation. We've held six-person voice-and-video conference calls using Yahoo Messenger for a total cost of $0.

To get the program, go to messenger.yahoo.com and follow the directions to download and install the program. Yahoo Messenger is available in many versions including versions for Windows 95/98/Me/2000/XP, Macs, UNIX, Palm Pilots, and a version that runs as a Java applet in your Web browser — on *any* system that has a Java-enabled browser. It can also exchange messages with mobile phone users; see the sidebar "IM by phone."

When you download the program, it installs automatically. To log in, you create a free Yahoo ID for yourself. Go to the messenger.yahoo.com Web site and click the Sign In link if you already have a Yahoo ID, or click the Sign Up link if you don't.

Adding Voices and Faces

If you don't want to talk with or see people while you chat — that is, if you don't mind being limited to typing back and forth with your friends — skip this section. If you do want the audiovisual goodies, read on.

Say what? — Hooking the sound up

Almost every computer comes with speakers, which are connected to a *sound board* inside the computer. These speakers are what make the various noises that your programs make (like the "You've got mail!" announcement of AOL). Most sound boards also have a jack for a microphone. (Check your computer manual or ask almost any teenager for help with this.) If you don't have a microphone, you can get one that works with almost any computer. A mike should cost less than $20 at your local computer store or at online at stores like PC Connection (www.pcconnection.com).

To test your mike and speakers on a Windows machine, run the Sound Recorder program; try recording yourself and playing it back.

1. **Choose Start⇨All Programs⇨Accessories⇨Entertainment⇨Sound Recorder in Windows XP or Me.**

2. **Click the red Record button to start recording, and the square Stop button to stop.**

   Talk, sing, or make other noises in between your Start and Stop clicks.

3. **Then click the triangular Play button to hear what you just recorded.**

   Click Record again to add onto the end of your recording. Choose File⇨ New to start over and throw away what you recorded.

4. **Choose File⇨Save to save it as a .WAV (audio) file.**

   We like to make .WAV recordings of our kids saying silly things and e-mail them — the recordings, not the kids — to their grandparents.

You can adjust the volume of your microphone (for the sound coming into the computer) and your speakers or headphones (for the sound coming out) by choosing Start⇨All Programs⇨Accessories⇨Entertainment⇨Volume Control. If a volume control for your microphone doesn't appear, choose Options⇨Properties, click the Microsoft check box so that a check mark appears, and click OK.

If you want to test how voices from the Net sound on your computer, type the URL net.gurus.com/ngc.wav into your browser and see what happens. You may need to click an Open or Open with Default Application button after it downloads. (Yes, that's John's mellifluous voice.)

If you can record yourself and hear the recording when you play it back, you're ready for Internet-based phone calls or chats!

I see you!

If you want other people to be able to see you during online conversations, consider getting a *webcam*. This is a small digital-video camera that can connect to a computer. Webcams come in many sizes and shapes, and prices run from $50 to $500. More expensive webcams send higher-quality images at higher speeds, and come with better software. On the other hand, we've had great luck with a $60 webcam for chatting with friends and participating in videoconferences.

Most webcams connect to your computer's USB port, a little rectangular plug on the back of the computer. Older computers don't have USB ports. The better cameras connect to special video-capture cards, which you have to open your computer to install.

If you own a digital video camera for taking video of your family and friends, you may be able to connect it to your computer for use as a webcam. Check the manual that came with the camera.

For news and reviews about webcams, see the WebCam.com site at www.webcam.com.

Around the Virtual Town Pump

Typing or talking to one person is fun and interesting, but for really good gossip, you need more than two people. Fortunately, the Internet offers limitless opportunities to find like-minded people and discuss anything you can imagine. Clubs, churches, and other groups use the Internet to hold meetings. Hobbyists and fans talk about an amazing variety of topics, from knitting to *American Idol* and everything in between. People with medical problems support each other and exchange tips. You get the idea — anything that people might want to talk about is currently under intense discussion somewhere on the Net.

You can talk with groups of people on the Internet in lots of ways, including these:

- ✔ E-mail mailing lists, in which you exchange messages via e-mail
- ✔ Web-based message boards, where messages appear on a Web page
- ✔ Usenet newsgroups (the original Internet discussions groups), which you read with a *newsreading program*

This section tells you how to participate in Internet-based discussions using e-mail mailing lists and Web message boards. For a description of Usenet newsgroups and how to read them, see our Web site at net.gurus.com/usenet.

For the full story on Internet-based communities, get our book, *Poor Richard's Building Online Communities,* published by Top Floor Publishing.

Mailing lists: Are you sure that this isn't junk mail?

An e-mail mailing list is quite different from a snail-mail mailing list. Yes, both distribute messages to the people on the list, but with most e-mail mailing lists, the messages contain a discussion among the subscribers rather than junk mail and catalogs.

Here's how an e-mail mailing list works. The list has its own special e-mail address, and anything someone sends to that address is sent to all the people on the list. Because these people in turn often respond to the messages, the result is a running conversation. For example, if the authors of this book hosted a discussion about the use and abuse of chocolate called *chocolate-lovers*, and if the list-server program ran at `lists.gurus.com`, the list of the address would be `chocolate-lovers@lists.gurus.com`. (We do actually run a bunch of lists, but not one about chocolate. Yet.)

Different lists have different styles. Some are relatively formal, hewing closely to the official topic of the list. Others tend to go flying off into outer space, topicwise. You have to read them for a while to be able to tell which list works which way.

Mailing lists fall into three categories:

- **Discussion:** Every subscriber can post a message. These lists lead to freewheeling discussions and can include a certain number of off-topic messages.

- **Moderated:** A moderator reviews each message before it gets distributed. The moderator can stop unrelated, redundant, or clueless postings from wasting everyone's time.

- **Announcement-only:** Only the moderator posts messages. Announcement mailing lists are essentially online newsletters.

Getting on and off mailing lists

Something or somebody has got to take on the job of keeping track of who's on the mailing list and distributing messages to all the subscribers. This job is *way* too boring for a human being to handle, so programs usually do the job. (A few lists are still run by human beings, and we pity them!) Most lists are run by programs called *list servers* or *mailing-list managers*. Popular list-server programs include LISTSERV, Majordomo, ListProc, MailMan, and many others, as well as Web-based systems such as Yahoo Groups.

Talking to the human being in charge

Someone is in charge of every mailing list: the *list manager*. The list manager is in charge of helping people on and off the list, answering questions about the list, and hosting the discussion. If you have a problem with a list, write a *nice* message to the list manager. Remember, most list managers are volunteers who sometimes eat, sleep, and work regular jobs as well as maintain mailing lists. If it takes longer than you want, be patient. *Don't* send cranky follow-ups — they just cheese off the list manager.

The list manager's address is usually the same as the list address with the addition of *owner-* at the beginning or *-request* right before the @. For example, the manager of the `chocoloate-lovers@gurus.com` list would be `chocoloate-lovers-request@gurus.com`.

Getting on lists

To find out how to subscribe to a list, or how to unsubscribe to the list, take a look at the instructions that (with luck) came with whatever information you received about the mailing list.

Subscribing from the Web

Newer list-server programs allow you to subscribe, unsubscribe, and change your subscription settings from the Web. So don't be surprised if the instructions for a mailing list tell you to go to a Web page and fill out a form. Generally you enter your e-mail address in a box on a Web page, click a Send or Subscribe button, and you're on the list. (Figure 16-3 shows the list signup page for our site.) This is often more convenient than sending a command by e-mail.

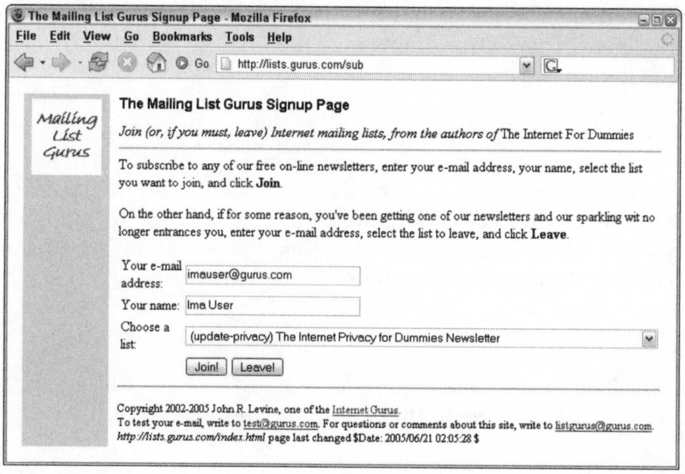

Figure 16-3:
Signing up
for quality
lists.

Before you subscribe, be sure there is some way to get *off* the list (an option that some marketing-oriented outfits neglect to provide).

Subscribing by mail

Before the Web was popular, the usual signup method was to send a mail message to the list-server program that ran a particular list. That method is still in use in some online places: Because a program is reading the message, the message has to be spelled and formatted exactly right, and sent to the *list-server address* (or *administrative address*), which is the name of the program (for example, LISTSERV or Majordomo) followed by @ and the computer on which the list server runs. For example, we host lists on our lists.gurus.com computer using the Majordomo list server program, so you could send commands to majordomo@lists.gurus.com. To join, send a command like this to the list-server address:

```
subscribe listname
```

Refer to the instructions that came with the list — some require your name after the list name; others don't work if you include it (so much for consistency). Replace the `listname` placeholder shown here with the name of the list. Type the command as the first line of the message, not the subject line.

Whether you sign up by mail or on the Web, you should get back a chatty, machine-generated welcoming message telling you that you have joined the list, along with a description of some commands you can use to fiddle with your mailing-list membership. Usually, this message includes a request to confirm that you received this message and that it was really you who wanted to subscribe. Follow the instructions by clicking a link or replying to this message, or whatever else the instructions say to do. Confirmation helps lists ensure that they aren't mailing into the void, and keeps people from sticking you onto lists without your knowledge. If you don't provide this confirmation, you don't get on the list.

Don't delete the chatty, informative welcome message that tells you about all the commands you can use when you're dealing with the list. For one thing, it tells you how to get *off* the mailing list if it's not to your liking. We have in our mail program a folder called Mailing Lists in which we store the welcome messages from all the mailing lists we join, so we don't have to embarrass ourselves by asking for help with unsubscribing later.

Getting off lists

To get off a list, you again visit the Web page or write to the list-server address, this time sending this line in the text of the message (not the subject line):

```
signoff listname
```

or

```
unsubscribe listname
```

(Use the actual name of the list in place of *listname*.) You don't have to give your name again because after you're off the list, the list software has no more interest in you, and forgets that you ever existed.

Stupid mailing-list tricks

Most list servers know some other commands, including commands to hold your mail for a while, send you a daily message that includes all the postings for the day, and see a subscriber list. Refer to the instructions that you received when you subscribed to the list for the exact commands, which vary depending on the list server software. (You did save the welcome message, didn't you?)

For more about mailing lists, including lots of list server commands, see our Web site at lists.gurus.com.

Sending messages to mailing lists

Okay, you're signed up on a mailing list. Now what? First, wait a week or so to see what sort of messages arrive from the list — that way, you can get an idea of what you should or should not send to it. When you think that you have seen enough to avoid embarrassing yourself, try sending something in. That's easy: You mail a message to the list address, which is the same as the name of the list — chocolate-lovers@lists.gurus.com or dandruff-l@bluesuede.org or whatever. Keep in mind that because hundreds or thousands of people will be reading your pearls of wisdom, you should at least try to spell things correctly. (You may have thought that this advice is obvious, but you would be sadly mistaken.) On popular lists, you may begin to get back responses within a few minutes of sending a message.

Some lists encourage new subscribers to send in a message introducing themselves and saying briefly what their interests are. Others don't. Don't send anything until you have something to say. After you watch the flow of messages on a list for a while, all of this stuff becomes obvious.

Urrp! Computers digest messages!

Some mailing lists are *digested*. No, they're not dripping with digital gastric juices — they're digested more in the sense of *Reader's Digest*. All the messages over a particular period (usually a day or two) are gathered into one big message with a table of contents added at the front. Many people find this method more convenient than getting messages separately, because you can easily look at all the messages on the topic at one time.

We prefer to get our messages individually, and to tell our e-mail program to sort our incoming messages into separate folders, one for each mailing list we subscribe to. Thunderbird, Outlook Express, and many other e-mail programs can sort your messages.

Boing!

Computer accounts are created and deleted often enough and mail addresses change often enough that a large list always contains, at any given moment, some addresses that are no longer valid. If you send a message to the list, your message is forwarded to these invalid addresses — and a return message (reporting a bad address) is generated for each of them. Mailing-list managers (both human and computer) normally try to deflect the error messages over to the list owner, who can do something about them, rather than to you. As often as not, however, a persistently dumb mail system sends one of these failure messages directly to you. Just ignore it because you can't do anything about it.

Sometimes you may get an "I'm away on vacation" message or a "click here if you're not a spammer" message in response to list messages you send. *Don't respond to those either* — vacation and anti-spam programs shouldn't be responding to list mail at all — but do forward them to the list manager so he or she can suspend those recipients' subscriptions until they get their software under control.

Some mailing lists have rules about who is allowed to send messages, meaning that just because you're on the list doesn't automatically mean that any messages you send appear on the list. Some lists are *moderated:* Any message you send in gets sent to a human *moderator* who decides what goes to the list and what doesn't. Although this process may sound sort of fascist, moderation can make a list about 50 times more interesting than it would be otherwise because a good moderator can filter out the boring and irrelevant messages and keep the list on track. Indeed, the people who complain the loudest about moderator censorship are usually the ones whose messages most urgently need to be filtered out.

Another rule that sometimes causes trouble is that many lists allow messages to be sent only from people whose addresses appear on the list, to prevent the list from getting overrun with spam. If your mailing address changes, you have to resubscribe or you can't post anything.

The fine points of replying to mailing-list messages

Often, you receive an interesting message from a list and want to respond to it. When you send your answer, does it go *just* to the person who sent the original message, or does it go to the *entire list?* It depends on how the list manager set up the list. About half the list managers set things up so replies go automatically to just the person who sent the original message, on the theory that your response is likely to be of interest only to the original author. The other half set things up so replies go to the entire list, on the theory that the list is a running public discussion. In messages coming from the list, the mailing-list software automatically sets the Reply-To header line to the address to which replies should be sent.

Fortunately, you're in charge of that feature. When you start to create a reply, your mail program should show you the address to which it's replying. If you don't like the address it's using, change the address. Check the To and Cc fields to make sure that you're sending your message where you want. Don't run the risk of sending a message such as, "I agree with you — aren't the rest of these people idiots?" to the whole list if you intend it only for one person.

While you're fixing the recipient's address, you may also want to fix the Subject line. After a few rounds of replies to replies to replies, the topic of discussion often wanders away from the original topic, so change the subject to better describe what is really under discussion, as a favor to the other folks trying to follow the discussion.

How to avoid looking like an idiot

After you subscribe to a list, don't send anything to it until you read it for a week. Trust us — the list has been getting along without your insights since it began, and it can get along without them for one more week.

You can learn what topics people really discuss, the tone of the list, and so on. It also gives you a fair idea about which topics people are tired of. The classic newcomer gaffe is to subscribe to a list and immediately send a message asking a dumb question that isn't really germane to the topic and that was beaten to death three days earlier.

The number-two newcomer gaffe is to send a message directly to the list asking to subscribe or unsubscribe. This type of message should go to the list manager or list server program, *not* to the list itself, where all the other subscribers can see that you screwed up.

One last thing not to do: If you don't like what another person is posting (for example, some newbie is posting blank messages or "unsubscribe me" messages or is ranting interminably about a topic), don't waste everyone's time by posting a response on the list. The only thing stupider than a stupid posting is a response complaining about it. Instead, e-mail the person *privately* and ask him to stop, or e-mail the list manager and ask that person to intervene.

Posting to message boards

Mailing lists are great if you want to receive messages by e-mail, but for some people, it's more convenient to read online community messages on the Web. These folks are in luck: *message boards* are Web-based discussion groups that post messages on a Web site. They are also called *discussion boards*, *forums*, or *communities*. Like mailing lists, some message boards are readable only by subscribers, some allow only subscribers to post, and some are moderated (that is, a moderator must approve messages before they appear on the message board). Other message boards are more like bulletin boards — anyone can post anytime, and there's no continuity to the messages or feeling of community among the people who post.

Many Web sites include message boards. Some Web sites are dedicated to hosting message boards on lots of different topics. Some sites host message boards that can also send the messages to you by e-mail, so they work as message boards and mailing lists rolled into one.

Great Web-based discussion sites

Here are some of our favorites:

About.com, at www.about.com

About.com hired experts in a wide variety of fields to host sites about each field. For example, the knitting site at `knitting.about.com` is run by a world-class knitter who posts articles and patterns and hosts one or more message boards about knitting. Figure 16-4 shows a discussion of knitting techniques.

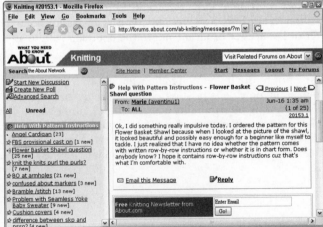

Figure 16-4: About.com hosts sites about hundreds (thousands?) of topics, each with a message board.

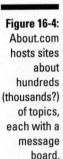

MSN Groups, at groups.msn.com

MSN Groups include message boards, live chat rooms, and other information. You can browse lists of groups by topic, or search for groups with a particular word or phrase in its name. To join a group, you need to sign up for a free .NET Passport (described in the section "Windows Messenger, alias MSN Messenger" earlier in this chapter).

Yahoo Groups, at groups.yahoo.com

Yahoo Groups include message boards and file libraries, and you can read the messages either on the Web site or by e-mail — your choice when you join a group. Yahoo Groups also feature calendars for group events and real-time chats right on the Web site. To join, you must first sign up for a free Yahoo ID, which also gets you a mailbox and free Web space — what a deal! You can also create your own Yahoo Group by clicking links — either a public group for all to join or a private group for your club or family.

Subscribing and participating

To subscribe to a community on one of these Web sites, just follow the instructions on the site. Some community Web sites let you read the messages posted to their lists without actually subscribing — you can click links to display the messages in your Web browser.

Finding interesting online communities

Tens of thousands of communities — in the form of mailing lists, message boards, and hybrids of the two — reside on the Internet, but there's no central directory of them. This is partly because so many lists are intended only for specific groups of people, like members of the Board of Directors of the First Parish Church of Podunk or students in Economics 101 at Tech State.

You can find some communities by searching the Web (as described in Chapter 8) and including the word or phrase, mailing list, community, forum, or message board. Or start at about.com, groups.yahoo.com, groups.msn.com, or tile.net/lists and search for your topic.

Online chat lets you communicate with other people who are at their computers and connected to the Internet by typing messages back and forth to each other. Chat may seem like just a version of instant messaging, but it is really a very different experience. Unlike e-mail or IM, chat often takes place among groups of strangers in chat rooms. Though kids sometimes use chat to talk to friends from school, one important aspect of chat is the ability to converse with someone new and maybe interesting, any time you feel like it.

Chat has led to marriages and divorces, to new friendships and occasionally to ugly incidents that make lurid headlines in the tabloid newspapers. Does chat sound intriguing? We'll tell you how it works — and suggest some tips to help you avoid trouble.

You can set up your own mailing lists or message boards, too. It's free because the sites display ads on their Web pages, and may even tack ads onto the postings on the list. If you have an unusual hobby, job, interest, or ailment, you may want to create a list to discuss it. Or set up a list for a committee or family group to use for online discussions.

Look Who's Chatting

Online chat is similar to talking on an old-fashioned party line (or CB radio). In the infancy of the telephone system, people usually shared their phone lines with other families because stringing telephone lines was expensive. Everyone on the party line could join in any conversation, offering hours of nosy fun for people with nothing better to do.

You begin chatting by entering an area of the Internet called an electronic *chat room* or *channel.* After you join a room, you can read on-screen what people are saying, and then add your own comments just by typing them and clicking Send. Although several people participating in the chat can type at the same time, each person's contribution is presented on-screen in order received. Whatever people type appears in the general conversation window and is identified by their screen names. On some chat systems, such as AOL, each participant can select a personal type font and color for his or her comments.

If one of the people in a chat room seems like someone you'd like to know better, you can ask to establish a *private room* or *direct connection,* which is a private conversation between you and the other person and not much different from instant messaging. And, of course, you might get such an invitation from someone else. It's not uncommon for someone to be in a chat room and be holding several direct conversations at the same time, though it's considered rude (not to mention confusing!) to overdo this.

You might also get asked to join a private chat room with several other people. We're not really sure just what goes on in those rooms because we've never been invited.

Who are those guys I'm talking to?

Which groups of people you can chat with depends on which chat system you connect to. If you use America Online, you can chat with other AOL users. MSN Groups (at groups.msn.com) and Yahoo Groups (at groups.yahoo.com) include a chat room for each group. Many web-based chat sites provide chat rooms that anyone with access to the Web can use. An older system called IRC (Internet Relay Chat) is available to anyone with Internet access and is still popular but harder to use — see "Chatting via IRC" later in this chapter. Chatting is pretty much the same from system to system, though the participants vary. This section gives a sense of the essence of chat no matter where you go to do it. Because AOL is by far the chattiest chat, we use it for our examples.

Each chat room has a name; with luck, the name is an indication of what the chatters there are talking about or what they have in common. Some channels have names such as *lobby,* and the people there are probably just being sociable.

Who am I?

No matter which chat facility you use, each participant has a *screen name,* or *nickname,* often chosen to be unique, colorful, or clever and used as a mask. Chatters sometimes change their screen names. This anonymity makes a chat room a place where you need to be careful. On the other hand, one of the attractions of chatting is meeting new and interesting people. Many warm and wonderful friendships have evolved from a chance meeting in a chat room.

When you join a group and begin chatting, you see the screen names of the people who are already there and a window in which the current conversation goes flying by. If the group is friendly, somebody may even send you a welcome message.

As in real life, in a room full of strangers you're likely to encounter people you don't like much. Because it's possible to be fairly anonymous on the Internet, some people act boorish, vulgar, or crude. If you're new to chat, sooner or later you'll visit some disgusting places, although you'll find out how to avoid them and find rooms that have useful, friendly, and supportive conversations. So be very careful about letting children chat unsupervised (see Chapter 3). Even in chat rooms that are designed for young people and provide some supervision, there can be unwholesome goings-on.

Ways to chat

The original chat rooms consisted entirely of people typing messages to each other. Newer chat systems include *voice chat* (which requires you to have a microphone and speakers on your computer) and even video (which requires a webcam if you want other people to be able to see you).

Your First Chat Room

Your first time in a chat room can seem stupid or daunting or both. Here are some things you can do to get through your first encounters:

- Remember that when you enter a chat room, a conversation is probably already in progress. You don't know what went on before you arrived.

- Wait a minute or two to see a page full of exchanges so you can understand some of the context before you start writing.

- Start by following the comments of a single screen name. Then follow the people that person mentions or who reply to that person. After you can follow one conversation, known in cyberspace as a *thread,* try picking up another. Getting the hang of it takes practice.

- AOL (and many Web-based programs) can highlight messages from selected people. This can make things easier to follow.

- You can also indicate people to ignore. Messages from these chatters no longer appear on your screen, although other members' replies to them do appear. This is usually the best way to deal with obnoxious chatters. You may also be able to get your chat program not to display the many system messages, which announce when people arrive, leave, or are ejected forcefully from the chat room.

- Scroll up to see older messages if you have to, but remember that on most systems, after you have scrolled up, no new messages appear until you scroll back down.

Online etiquette

Chatting etiquette is not that much different from e-mail etiquette, and common sense is your best guide. Here are some additional chatting tips:

- The first rule of chatting is not to hurt anyone. A real person with real feelings is at the other end of the computer-chat connection.

- The second rule is to be cautious. You really have no idea who the other people are. Remember, too, that there might be people hanging out in a chat room quietly collecting information ,and you might not notice them because they never say anything. (See the next section, "Safety first.")

- Read messages for a while to figure out what is happening before sending a message to a chat group. (Reading without saying anything is known as *lurking.* When you finally venture to say something, you're *de-lurking.*) Lurking isn't necessarily a bad thing, but be aware that you might not always have the privacy you think you have.

- ✔ Keep your messages short and to the point.

- ✔ Don't insult people, don't use foul language, and don't respond to people who do.

- ✔ Create a profile with selected information about yourself. Most chat systems have provisions for creating profiles (personal information) that other members can access.

Don't give out your last name, phone number, or address. Extra caution is necessary for kids: They should never enter their age, hometown, school, last name, phone number, or address. This is a rule on AOL. Parents should insist on it always. Although you don't have to tell everything about yourself in your profile, what you do say should be truthful. The one exception is role-playing chat where everyone is acting out a fantasy character.

- ✔ If you want to talk to someone in private, send a message saying hi, who you are, and what you want.

- ✔ If the tone of conversation in one chat room offends or bores you, try another. As in real life, you'll run into lots of people in chat rooms you *don't* want to meet — and you don't have to stay there.

Safety first

As in society at large, online chat involves some contact with strangers. Most encounters are with more-or-less reasonable folks. For the rest, common sense dictates that you keep our wits about you — and your private information private.

Here are some guidelines for conducting safe and healthy chats:

- ✔ Many people in chat groups lie about their occupation, age, locality, and (yes) even gender. Some think they're just being cute, some are exploring their own fantasies, and some are really sick.

- ✔ Be careful about revealing information that enables someone to find you personally — such as where you live or work, where you go to school, the name of your teacher or team, or your phone number. This information includes your last name, mailing address, and place of worship.

- ✔ Never give your password to anyone. *No one should ever ask you for it.* If someone does, don't respond, but do tell your service provider about the request.

- ✔ If your chat service offers profiles and a person without a profile wants to chat with you, be extra cautious.

✔ Kids: Never, *ever* meet someone without your parents. Do not give out personal information about yourself or any member of your family, even when you're offered some sort of prize for filling out a form.

✔ Parents, realize that if your children use chat, others may try to meet them. Review the guidelines in this list with your kids before they log on. Have your kids show you how to log on and try the chat rooms they use for yourself.

If you're a grown-up and choose to meet an online friend in person, use at least the same caution that you would use in meeting someone through a newspaper ad:

✔ Don't arrange a meeting until you have talked to a person a number of times, including conversations at length by telephone over the course of days or weeks.

✔ Meet in a well-lit public place with other people around, such as a restaurant.

✔ Bring a friend along if you can. If not, at least let someone know what you're doing and agree to call that person at a certain time (for example, a half-hour) after the planned meeting time.

✔ Arrange to stay in a hotel if you travel a long distance to meet someone. Don't commit yourself to staying at that person's home. And don't invite the person to stay with you.

Chat abbreviations and smileys

Many chat abbreviations are the same as those used in e-mail. Because chat is live, however, some are unique. We've also listed some common emoticons (sometimes called *smileys*) — funky combinations of punctuation used to depict the emotional inflection of the sender. If at first you don't see what they are, try tilting your head down to the left. Table 16-1 shows you a short list of chat abbreviations and emoticons.

Table 16-1		Chat Shorthand	
Abbreviation	*What It Means*	*Abbreviation*	*What It Means*
AFK	Away from keyboard	RL	Real life (opposite of RP)
A/S/L	Age/sex/location (response may be 35/f/LA)	ROTFL	Rolling on the floor laughing

Abbreviation	What It Means	Abbreviation	What It Means
BAK	Back at keyboard	RP	Role playing (acting out a character)
BBIAF	Be back in a flash	TOS	Terms of service (the AOL member contract)
BBL	Be back later	TTFN	Ta-ta for now!
BRB	Be right back	WB	Welcome back
CYBER	A chat conversation of a prurient nature (short for *cybersex*)	WTG	Way to go!
GMTA	Great minds think alike	:) or :-)	A smile
FTF or F2F	Face to face	;)	A wink
IC	In character (playing a role)	{{{{bob}}}}	A hug for Bob
IGGIE	To set the Ignore feature, as in "I've iggied SmartMouthSam"	:(or :-(	Frown
IM	Instant message	:'(	Crying
J/K	Just kidding	0:)	Angel
LTNS	Long time no see	}:>	Devil
LOL	Laughing out loud	:P	Sticking out tongue
NP	No problem	*** or xox	Kisses
OOC	Out of character (an RL aside during RP)	<----	Action marker that appears before a phrase indicating what you are doing (<----eating pizza, for example)
PM	Private message (same as IM)		

In addition to the abbreviations in the table, chatters sometimes use simple shorthand abbreviations, as in "If u cn rd ths ur rdy 2 chat."

Let's Chat

Chat service is one of AOL's major attractions. Goodness knows no one goes there for the advertising. In this section, we cover chatting with AOL, Web-based chat, and chatting using IRC.

Chatting on AOL

When you chat on AOL, you have a conversation with other AOL users. Only AOL members can participate in the AOL chat rooms. Because AOL can — and does — eject unruly chatters, its chat rooms are a bit more civilized than those of many other chat services. The popularity of AOL chat may be why AOL is the largest value-added provider.

 You get started chatting in America Online by clicking the Chat icon on the toolbar (or by going to the **chat** keyword) to see the AOL People Connection window. Then click the Chat Room Listings icon to display the Find a Chat window.

Click a category from the listings, click the View Chats button in the middle of the window, and look at the list that appears on the right. Then click a likely-looking topic and click the Go Chat button. You see a chat window something like the one in Figure 16-5.

In a chat window, the large box on the left shows the ongoing conversation. (We like the way that AOL shows different people's messages in different colors and typefaces to help keep track of who is saying what.) The People Here box shows the AOL screen names of the folks in the chat room.

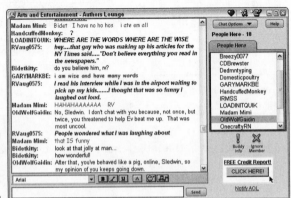

Figure 16-5: Authors are chatting!

To send a message, click in the white box at the bottom of the window, type your message, and either press Enter or click Send. Your message appears in the conversation box. When you are done chatting, just close the chat window.

Identifying others

If you want to know something about the other occupants of the room, double-click one of their names in the People Here window. A window pops up with the person's profile (if there is one), which may include name, location, marital status, and other information, but which rarely does. This window also enables you to send the person e-mail or an IM message, block e-mail or IM messages from this person, or add the person to your AOL address book or AIM Buddy List. If you don't want to see chat-room messages from this person, click the screen name and click the Ignore Member button. This technique is a good way to stop receiving messages from annoying people.

Identifying yourself

You're identified by your screen name, which, if you do nothing, is the *master screen name,* the one you used when you first signed on to AOL. Many people use, for privacy reasons, a different screen name when they're chatting. AOL lets each account use as many as seven different screen names, as long as no other AOL user is already using them. One of the screen names is the master screen name, which can never be changed. If you want to add or change other screen names, you must log on to AOL under the master screen name. After you've established other screen names and passwords, you can log on to AOL by using the alternative name. Each screen name has a separate mailbox. You can use screen names for either different family members or different personalities (for example, your business self and your private self).

Stop bothering me!

While you chat on AOL, you might find that an instant message pops up about every 30 seconds from someone with a screen name like `sexygirl2546787`, with whom you are not interested in chatting. (At least Margy isn't.) To put an end to this annoyance, follow these easy steps:

1. **In the Settings toolbar menu, click Preferences.**

2. **In the Preferences window, click Privacy.**

3. **Choose Allow Only People on my Buddy List, Block All Others.**

4. **Click Save and close the Preferences window.**

Member-created rooms

In the Find a Chat window (which you display by clicking Chat on the toolbar and then Chat Room Listings), you can create your own chat room. Click the Create a Chat button, and then choose to create a Member Chat (open to all) or a Private Chat (only for people you invite). Then choose which category you want your room to be in, type a name for your chat room, and click Go Chat. Now all you have to do is wait for people to join you, or you can IM people and invite them to come in.

Private chats

The names of private rooms, unlike those of public or member rooms, are not revealed. To join one, you have to know its name — that is, someone must invite you to join. When you click the Enter a Private Chat button in the Find a Chat window, you're asked to name the room you want to join. If it doesn't exist, one is created, and you're the sole occupant (at least at first).

Private rooms enable people to talk more intimately — there's little danger of a stranger popping in. Two (or more) people can agree to create a private room and meet there.

Private rooms have a somewhat sleazy reputation. If you get invited to one, you should be careful about guarding your privacy. Remember that what the other people are saying about themselves may not be true. If you enter a private chat room with someone you don't know, don't be surprised if the talk gets real rude real fast.

Calling the AOL cops

A link in the lower-right corner of the chat window is labeled Notify AOL. If you think that someone is violating the AOL terms of service (TOS) by asking you for your password or credit-card number, using abusive language, or otherwise behaving badly, you can *and should* report that person to AOL. When you click the Notify AOL link, a window pops up to help you gather all the information you want to report — for example, the chat category and room you were in, the offensive chat dialog pasted into a window, and the offender's screen name. You can then send the report to AOL by clicking Send.

Because of this policing and the power of AOL to terminate (permanently) the accounts of people who play without the rules, the AOL chat rooms have a deserved reputation for safety and for being a good place to play. The fact that AOL has so many subscribers who like chat means you have a good chance of finding a chat room that meets your needs.

Chatting on the Web

Although AOL limits chatting to its paid members, many Web sites enable you to chat with nothing more than your browser. These sites have Java-based chat programs that your browser can download and run automatically. Some other Web chat sites require that you download a plug-in or ActiveX control to add chat capability to your browser (see Chapter 7 for information on how to use plug-ins).

Most Web-based chat programs look a lot like AOL's chat screen. A large window displays the ongoing conversation, a smaller window displays the screen names of the participants, and a text area gives you a place to type your messages and find a Send button.

Some Web chat sites include

 ✔ Yahoo! Chat at `chat.yahoo.com`
 ✔ MSN Groups at `groups.msn.com`

Many other Web sites have chats on the specific topic of the site. Search for *Chat* at `www.dmoz.org` for a variety of chat venues.

Chatting via IRC

IRC (Internet Relay Chat), the classic form of chat, is available from most Internet providers as well as from AOL. To use IRC, you have to install an *IRC client* program on your computer. An IRC client (or just *IRC program*) is another Internet program, like your Web browser or e-mail program, and freeware and shareware programs are available for you to download from the Net. The most popular shareware IRC programs include

 ✔ **mIRC** for Windows
 ✔ **ircii** for Linux and Unix (freeware)
 ✔ **Ircle** for the Macintosh

You can find these IRC programs, along with others, at shareware Web sites, such as TUCOWS (`www.tucows.com`) or at the IRC Help page (`www.irchelp.org`).

Chatting on IRC is not so very different from chatting on AOL, but you can use it to chat with people who aren't AOL members. IRC uses networks of servers all over the world, with tens of thousands of people usually chatting at once.

For the full story on IRC, see our Web page about it at net.gurus.com/irc.

Networking Communities

Several Web sites have set themselves up as virtual town squares in the Internet's global village. You sign up on any of them, then locate other people who've signed up that you know — who might (in turn) connect you to friends of friends and so forth, on out to everyone on the planet. Each site tells you how many people are in your network; if it's under a million you're not very popular. Although the sites all do generally the same thing, they definitely feel different. Here are some we've used:

www.friendster.com is popular among 20-somethings who want to stay in touch and meet new people socially.

www.orkut.com is part of the Google empire, you have to be invited by an existing member to join. Originally it was for extremely cool friends-of-friends-of-cool-people who knew someone at Google, where *everyone* is very cool (just ask them.) But now it has an awful lot of Brazilian teenagers as the saying goes; it's so crowded that nobody goes there any more.

The hype about Skype

Skype is a freeware VoIP package from Luxembourg, a tiny country in Europe whose main attraction is that it's not anywhere else. You download and install Skype on your computer from www.skype.com, set up a free account, and start using it to talk to other Skype users. You need a headset with headphones and a microphone, or a handset (which is like a phone handset) plugged into your computer. Skype's voice quality over most broadband is very good, much better than that of a normal phone.

Skype isn't limited to talking to other Skype users. You can set up a SkypeOut account to which you add money — from credit card or as a bonus included with some computer headsets — and you can then call any normal phone in the world and pay by the minute. Rates are quite low, about 2¢/minute for the United States, Canada, or Europe, and do not depend on where you're using Skype, only where you're calling. John once called home using his laptop via a WiFi connection in a hotel lobby in Argentina for 2 cents rather than the dollar a minute it would have cost from a payphone. They also offer SkypeIn — a real phone number for your Skype phone so people can call you — for a monthly fee.

Skype lets you have conference calls of up to five people, any combination of Skype users and SkypeOut calls to regular phones. And it has its own version of chat with Skype Me. You set up a profile, set your online status to SkypeMe, and you've invited people to call. Skype users live all over the world, so with luck, you may make some new faraway friends.

www.linkedin.com is intended for professional businesspeople to make useful contacts; it's stayed pretty businesslike.

www.spoke.com is the same general idea as linkedin, but designed more as a sales prospecting tool than for general networking.

Internet Phones and Voice Chat

For about a decade, Internet phones were just around the corner. If you have a broadband net connection, they're here. No Internet phenomenon would be complete without an arcane abbreviation, so this one is *VoIP* for *Voice over Internet Protocol*.

Some kinds of VoIP use a microphone and headphones plugged into your computer, but most people prefer the variety that use regular phones plugged into a *terminal adapter* or TA. (See the sidebar "The hype about Skype" for the main exception.)

Signing up

You can get VoIP service from large familiar companies like AT&T and Verizon, semi-familiar companies like Lingo which is part of Primus, a large Canadian long-distance company, and VoIP startups like Vonage and Broadvoice. Compare prices, see whether you can get a local phone number in the place you want (which can be either where you live, or anywhere you want people to be able to call you as a local call), and check out how big the local calling area they provide is — as well as whether they offer real 911 service (important if your VoIP phone is your main phone.)

Different VoIP companies vary a lot, with local calling areas ranging from a single U.S. state to all of North America and Europe. Calls to other customers of the same VoIP company are always free, so you might want to get the same one your friends have. See our Web site at net.gurus.com/phone for our latest suggestions.

If you have a cable modem, your cable company may also offer VoIP, which you should consider since the quality of service is better than what you'd get with third-party VoIP providers.

When you sign up, the VoIP company will send you a TA. If you don't have a router on your broadband connection, the TA connects between your cable or DSL modem and your computer. If you do have a router, it may connect between the modem and the router; some plug into the router like a PC. Once it's plugged in, plug it into the power, plug a phone into the TA, and as soon as the TA initializes itself, your phone is like any other phone, only cheaper.

Using your VoIP phone

It's a phone. When it rings, answer it. If you want to call someone, pick up the phone and dial. Most VoIP companies offer a full suite of phone features like voice mail, call forwarding, and caller-ID, usually controlled via a Web page rather than through the phone itself.

Part V
Advanced Internet Activities

The 5th Wave   By Rich Tennant

©RICHTENNANT

"Ooo-wait! That's perfect for the clinic's home page. Just stretch it out a little further... little more..."

In this part . . .

A few topics don't fit anywhere else but are too important to leave out, so here they are. We describe the essentials of setting up your own Web site — your homestead in the global village — and how to use weblogs (blogs for short) to manage and/or contribute to the Web's information overload.

Chapter 17

Setting Up a Web Site

· ·

· ·

After you've used the Internet and browsed the Web for a while, you've probably thought of putting your own material on the Web. Hey, you've got interesting things to say, probably more interesting than a lot of Web sites that are out there! You can create a Web site for yourself — consisting of one or a number of pages — with your own domain name.

Although creating Web pages is not difficult, it may seem complicated for a new user. But if you can use a word processor like Microsoft Word to type a letter, you can create at least a simple Web page. (Indeed, you can use Word or most any other word processor to do so.) For better-looking Web pages with more features, you'll want to use a program specifically designed for creating Web pages — a *Web-page editor* or *Web editor*.

Creating a Web Site: The Big Picture

If you want to share information, news, or opinion with the world, you can create a Web site, which involves choosing a place to store your Web pages, designing and creating the pages, and doing a little publicity so people will find your new pages.

Do you need a home page, or more?

Although a Web site can consist of many Web pages, the main page of a site — the front door, or the table-of-contents page — is generally known as its *home page*. People have home pages, companies have home pages, and groups of highly talented authors and speakers have home pages. (You can check out Carol's at `www.carolbaroudi.com`, John's at `www.johnlevine.com`, Margy's at `gurus.com/margy`, and Internet Gurus Central at `net.gurus.com`.)

If you have only one page of information to put on the Web, you can make a home page. If you have more to say, or information on several different topics, you should make more than just a home page. Your home page can be the front page from which people can find your other pages. For example, if you have written an essay on the current political situation (and who hasn't?), you have a collection of pictures of your chickens, and you have a killer recipe for Key lime pie you should make four pages:

- ✔ Your home page, with links to the other three pages
- ✔ A page with your political essay
- ✔ A page with your chicken pix
- ✔ A page with your Key lime pie recipe

When you have a pretty good idea of what page(s) you might want to put on the Web, you need to know how Web pages and Web servers work.

Don't assume that every visitor will start at your home page. People may arrive at your Web site by following a link from a Google or other search, and may jump directly to a page that contains the word or phrase they were searching for. So consider *every* page as a potential front door; include your Web site's title and other information about the site on every page.

Web pages on Web servers

The basic steps to creating a Web site are pretty simple:

1. **Write some Web pages.**

   One page is plenty to start with. You can use any text editor or word processor, but spiffy Web-page authoring programs designed for this purpose are available — and many are free — so you may as well use one. Save the pages in files on your computer's hard drive.

2. **Test your Web pages by using your own browser.**

Before you make your pages visible to everyone, make sure they look good! Using your browser, open the pages (press Ctrl+O and specify the name of the file that contains your page). Ideally, check how they look in recent versions of both Internet Explorer and Firefox.

3. **Publish your Web pages on your Internet service provider's (ISP's) system.**

   The rest of the world can't see Web pages that are stored in files on your disk. You have to copy them to your ISP's computer so that their *Web server* (the big computer where Web pages live) can offer them to the world. You don't have to use your ISP's Web server, but most Internet accounts come with free Web space, so why not?

Many Web-editing programs have a Publish, Upload, or Remote Save command on the File menu that sends your creation to your provider's system. If your program doesn't have this command, you can use File Transfer Protocol (FTP), a type of program we discuss in more detail on our Web page at net.gurus.com/ftp. In either case, you need to know these details:

- ✔ **The name of the computer to which you upload your files:** This isn't always the same as the name of the Web server. At one of our local ISPs, for example, the Web server is www.lightlink.com, whereas the FTP upload server is ftp.lightlink.com.

- ✔ **The username and password to use for FTP:** Usually this is the same as the name and password you use to connect in the first place and to pick up your e-mail.

- ✔ **The name of the folder on the server to which you upload the pages:** For example, it might be /www/*username*.

- ✔ **The filename to use for your home page:** Usually this is index.html or index.htm. (You can call your Web pages anything you want, but this is the page that people see first.)

- ✔ **The URL where your pages will appear:** It's usually http://www.*yourisp*.com/~*username* or http://www.*yourisp*.com/*username*.

You can usually find this info on your ISP's Web site or (in the worst case) you can call or e-mail your ISP and ask.

If you don't want to use your ISP's Web server, lots of Web-hosting companies will be happy to let you use their servers. Some are even free, if you don't mind their advertisements appearing on your Web pages. Two of the best-known free Web-hosting sites are Yahoo's Geocities at geocities.yahoo.com, Tripod at www.tripod.lycos.com, and Angelfire at www.angelfire.lycos.com. Reputable paid, ad-free Web-hosting companies are Pair Networks (www.pair.com) and Go Daddy (www.godaddy.com).

Why you don't care (much) about HTML

Just so that you know what *HTML* is, in case someone asks, it stands for *HyperText Markup Language,* and it's the language native to the World Wide Web. Web pages are made up of text and pictures that are stuck together and formatted by using HTML tags (short codes, like "<b>" for bold type). Fortunately, you have waited until now to get started creating a Web page, when clever programs are available that let you create your pages and write the HTML tags for you automatically, so you don't have to write the codes yourself.

If you find you want to write a lot of Web pages, you should eventually master some HTML. Although complex interactive pages require a fair amount of programming, the basics aren't all that complicated. For example, the HTML for **"complicated"** is <b>complicated</b> (that's <b> for bold type), and the tag to insert a picture is "<img source="kidsplaying.jpg"> ("img" stands for *image* and the source is the name of the file that contains the picture). In case you decide that you want to be in the Web-page creation business, entire books have been written about how to do it. Stick to recent titles because extensions to HTML are evolving at a furious pace and the books go out of date in less than a year. We recommend *HTML 4 For Dummies,* Fifth Edition, by Ed Tittel and Mary Burmeister (Wiley Publishing, Inc.) for the basics and *Web Design in a Nutshell* (by Jennifer Niederst and published by O'Reilly & Associates) for more advanced information.

Picking your Web editor

The two general approaches to creating Web pages are the geek approach (write all the HTML code yourself), and the WYSIWYG approach (you get a program that writes the code for you). If you were an HTML geek, we figure you wouldn't be reading this chapter, so we're not going to discuss that at all. The more (ahem) normal approach is to use one of the WYSIWYG Web editors.

WYSIWYG, pronounced *whiz*-ee-wig, stands for *what you see is what you get.* In the case of Web editors, it means that as you create your page, instead of seeing rather unattractive HTML codes, you see roughly what it will look like in a browser. HTML purists point out that WYSIWYG editors churn out less-than-elegant HTML code, but the pages they make generally look fine. If you're planning to create a large, complex Web site, WYSIWYG editors will run out of steam, but for a page or three, they're great.

A number of free and cheap Web editors are available. You can choose one yourself by starting at www.download.com, clicking Developer Tools, check Web Page Creation, and then HTML Editors. Many of these programs have free demos, but if you want to continue to use the program you have to pay for it — which usually costs from $20 to $70 dollars, as shown in the Download.com listing.

Serious Web developers use more expensive programs, mainly Dreamweaver (from Macromedia, at `www.macromedia.com/software/dreamweaver`). Another excellent, more advanced program is called GoLive (from Adobe, at `www.adobe.com/products/golive`). But before you shell out several hundred dollars, try a cheap program first.

In this chapter, we use Mozilla Composer, which comes for free with the Mozilla browser. Mozilla is the predecessor to the Firefox browser that we've been telling you to use whenever you want to browse the Web. Mozilla is a package that includes a browser that's very much like Firefox (described in Chapter 6), an e-mail program that's amazingly similar to Thunderbird (described in Chapter 13), a chat program, and a Web editor, of all things.

 You probably already have a Web editor — your own word processor. Both Microsoft Word (versions 97 and later) and WordPerfect (versions 8 and later) have capable Web-editing features built right in. Web page authoring tools are usually more convenient, have more advanced features, and produce more efficient pages. Microsoft Word creates pages that contain large numbers of extra codes that make the pages take longer to download and view. If you use Microsoft Excel (a spreadsheet program) or Access (a database program), you can export reports as Web pages, too.

Getting Mozilla Composer

You can use a free Web editor like Mozilla Composer to create Web pages and upload them to a Web server. (If you have Netscape 7.0 or later, which is another, similar Web browser, it also includes Composer, and you can use most of the same commands shown in this chapter.)

Installing and configuring Mozilla Composer

To download Mozilla, go to `www.mozilla.org` and look for Mozilla or Mozilla Suite, which includes Mozilla Composer. If you don't see it on the home page, click the Products tab or the All Products link and look around. Click the Download or Download Now link and make a note of where you store the file. (See Chapter 12 for more information about downloading and installing programs.)

Next, run the file that you just downloaded. Answer the configuration questions. If you already have your e-mail set up in another program, you may want to uncheck the option for including Mail & Newsgroups, since you won't be using them. You can also uncheck options for Chatzilla (a chat program).

When Mozilla is installed, the installation program offers to run it for you — why not? If it asks you to create a profile, type your name as the profile name.

When Mozilla is up and running, it looks uncannily like the Firefox browser — in fact, you don't need its browser if you already have Firefox. It you don't have Firefox, however, start using Mozilla as your browser — it beats the pants off of Internet Explorer when it comes to avoiding popups and spyware.

Opening up Composer for a look

The whole point of this exercise, though, is to run a Web editor. No problem — choose Windows➪Composer from the menu. You see a screen like Figure 17-1.

Creates a new Web page

Uploads your page to a Web server

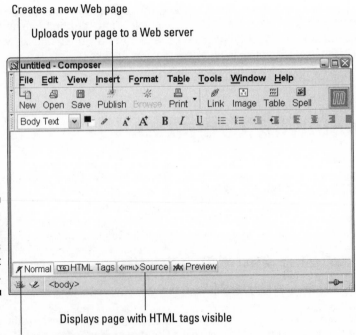

Figure 17-1:
Mozilla Composer is ready to edit a Web page.

Displays page with HTML tags visible

Displays WYSIWYG version of the page

If you want Mozilla to start up with Composer running (instead of the browser), choose Edit➪Preferences to display the Preferences dialog box, which contains oodles of configuration options. In the Category list at the left, click Appearance. In the settings that appear is a setting called "When Mozilla starts up, open." You can uncheck Navigator (the browser) and check Composer (the Web editor) by clicking each one. Then click OK.

Getting Word to create smaller Web page files

If you use Microsoft Word to create Web pages, the pages are enormous and bloated. Word not only saves the Web page's HTML tags, but it also saves a zillion invisible codes that allow the page to be read back into Word later. Luckily, you can download a small program from Microsoft that teaches Word (and the other programs that make up Microsoft Office) to save only the HTML tags — the codes that a Web browser can understand.

The Office 2000 HTML Filter is available to download for free. As of this writing, a version is available for Office 2000, but not Office XP or 2003. To find the version that works with your version of office, start at www.google.com and search for

    microsoft office html filter

Click a link that starts with office.microsoft.com — don't download it from any other source, just to be sure that you're getting the real Microsoft deal. See Chapter 12 for more information.

Making Your First Web Page

A Web page is a file — just like a word-processing document or a spreadsheet. You create it and save it, and then open it and edit it some more, just as you would any other document.

Naming your page

The name of the file becomes part of the Web page's address once you've uploaded it to your Web server, so choose a filename that makes sense. Filenames for Web pages end with the extension .html or .htm. For example, if you are making a page about your cats, name it something like mycats.html or cats.html. Don't use spaces, punctuation, or capital letters in your filenames — if you must, you can use underscores (_) or hyphens (-) to make them readable.

You should generally call your home page — the one you want people to see first — index.html. If someone goes to your Web address without specifying a filename (such as www.iecc.com/~elvis/), what appears on-screen (by universal convention) is the page named index.html or index.htm. If you don't have a page by that name, the server may or may not know what to do: Some Web servers construct a page with a directory listing of the files in your site; others display an error page. If you make an index.html page and it doesn't appear automagically when you type the URL without a filename, consult your ISP; ask whether it uses a different default filename.

Picking up your pen

You begin by creating your Web pages directly on your hard disk. You can see how they look by telling your browser to view them from your hard disk. (Browsers are happy to accept filenames to display rather than URLs.) Edit and view the pages until you have something you like, and then upload them to your ISP to impress the world.

Making your page

Here's our step-by-step approach to using Microsoft Word (versions 97 or later) or Mozilla (or Netscape 7 or later) Composer. If you'd rather use another program, feel free, although the commands are a little different.

1. **Start up Mozilla (or Netscape). If you would rather use your own word processor, skip this step.**

   See "Getting Mozilla Composer" earlier in this chapter for how to download and install Mozilla if you don't have it installed already.

2. **Run Mozilla Composer or your word processor.**

   To work with Netscape or Mozilla Composer (as shown in Figure 17-1), run Mozilla and then choose Window⇨Composer from the menu (or press Ctrl+4).

3. **Open a new or existing Web page.**

   If you want to edit an existing Web page that you have stored on your hard disk, click Open, choose File⇨Open, or press Ctrl+O to open it), and then choose the file.

   If you want to edit a page that's on your Web site, you can display it in Mozilla Navigator (the browser). Choose Window⇨Navigator, browse to the page, and choose File⇨Edit Page (or press Ctrl+E).

   If you started Word, you see your usual word-processing window. If you want to edit an existing page, open it the way you would an ordinary Word file.

4. **Create a new Web page or edit the one you opened.**

   In Mozilla Composer: You're face to face with a big, empty page. Go ahead — make your page the same way you would in a word processor, by entering headings and paragraphs of text. Stuck for ideas and where to start? Make a page about your favorite hobby, author, or musician!

   In Word: Choose File⇨New from the menu bar, click the Web Page tab or link in the dialog box or task pane that appears. In some versions of Word, you can choose a template (try the Web Page Wizard, a template that talks you through making a Web page).

When asked for a filename, call the document `index.html` if it's going to be your home page. This name is the one that most Web servers use.

5. Save your work.

When you've done enough work that you wouldn't want to have to start over from scratch if your computer suddenly crashes, choose File⇨Save from the menu bar or press Ctrl+S. In principle, when you're done with your page, you save it, but dismal experience has taught us to save early, save often.

The first time you save a page in Mozilla Composer, it prompts for a title for the page, as shown in Figure 17-2. Type a title (we like to capitalize the first letter of each word) and click OK. When you see the Save Page As dialog box, Composer suggests this same title as the filename. Don't take its suggestion! Instead, type the filename you want to use (such as **index.html** or **chickens.html**) with no spaces or capital letters. In Word, choose File⇨Save As, set the Save As Type to Web Page (not Single File Web Page), type a name, and click Save.

Figure 17-2: Give your page a title, which appears in the title page of the browser.

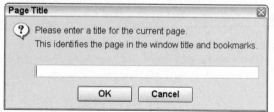

Creating your first Web page is pretty easy. Choosing what you put on your page, however, is harder. What is the page for? What kind of person do you want to see it? Is it for you and your family and friends and potential friends across the world, or are you advertising your business online? If your page is a personal page, don't include your home address or phone number unless you want random people who see the page potentially calling you up. If it's a business page, by all means include your address and phone number. The content of your first page isn't all that important — we just want you to get the feel of putting it out there. You can always add to it and pretty it up, and you don't have to tell anybody about your site until you're happy with it.

Be extremely careful about putting identifying information about your children on your Web page. We each have kids whom we love dearly, but you won't read much about them on our home pages. Just knowing your hobbies and your kids' names and where they go to school may be enough for some no-good-nik to pose as a friend of the family and pick them up after school.

Pictures to Go: Adding Images to Your Web Page

Most Web pages contain graphics of some sort. Each picture that appears on a Web page is stored in a separate file. To add an image to a Web page, you add an HTML *tag* (command) that includes the name of the file that contains the picture, the size of the picture as it should appear on the screen, a caption for the visually impaired, and positioning information (whether you want the pictures to the left, center, or right, and whether text should flow around it).

Picture formats

Pictures come in dozens of formats. Fortunately, only three picture formats are in common use on the Web: GIF, PNG, and JPEG. Many lengthy . . . er, *free* and *frank* discussions have occurred on the Internet concerning the relative merits of these formats. John, who is an Official Graphics Format Expert (by virtue of having persuaded two otherwise-reputable publishers to publish his books on the topic), suggests that photographs work better as JPEG, while clip art, icons, and cartoons are better as PNG or GIF. JPEG files are smaller, and download faster. PNG is a superior, new replacement for GIF, with its only disadvantage being that people with very old browsers (Netscape 3.0 and older, for example) can't easily view PNG files.

If you have a picture in any other format, such as BMP or PCX, you must convert it to GIF, PNG, or JPEG before you can use it on a Web page. Windows comes with a program called Paint, which you can run by choosing Start⇨ All Programs⇨Accessories⇨Paint. Or check out Tucows (at tucows.com/ downloads/Windows) or Download.com for graphics programs that can do conversions. For the Mac, consider GraphicConverter at www.lemkesoft.de/ en/graphcon.htm.

Where do the pictures come from?

That's a good question. You can draw them by using a paint program, scan in photographs, or use that fancy digital camera you got for Christmas. Then use Paint or some better graphics editor to crop your pictures, fix the red-eye, and generally spiff up your pix.

If you need graphics that you can't produce yourself, you can find lots of sources of graphical material:

✔ Plenty of freeware, shareware, and commercial clipart are available on the Net. Try the Clip Art page at our favorite Web directory, the Open Directory Project list, at `www.dmoz.org/Computers/Graphics/Clip_Art`.

✔ If you see an image you want to use on a Web page, write to the page's owner and ask for permission to use it. More likely than not, the owner will let you use the image.

✔ Lots of regular old software programs totally unrelated to the Internet — such as paint and draw programs, presentation programs, and even word processors — come with clipart collections.

✔ You can buy CD-ROMs full of clipart, which tends to be of higher quality than the free stuff. These aren't all that expensive, particularly considering how many images fit on one CD-ROM.

✔ If you need a lot of clipart, you can subscribe to an online clipart library that has the material organized and has already gotten permission for you to use it. We like `www.clipart.com`.

Clipart, like any art, is protected by copyright laws. Whether it's already been used on a Web page or whether a copyright notice appears on or near the image doesn't matter — it's all copyrighted. If you use someone else's copyrighted art, you must get permission to do so. Whether your use is educational, personal, or noncommercial is irrelevant. If you fail to secure permission, you run the risk of anything from a crabby phone call from the owner's lawyer to winding up on the losing end of a lawsuit.

Most people are quite reasonable whenever you ask for permission to use something. If an image you want to use doesn't already come with permission to use it, check with the owner before you decide to add it to your own Web page.

Adding a picture to your page

After you've got the graphics file you want to use, you can include it on your Web page. In Mozilla Composer, follow these steps:

1. **With your cursor at the place in the page where you want the picture to appear, click the Image button on the toolbar.**

2. **In the Image Properties dialog box, on the Location tab (shown in Figure 17-3), type the filename in the Image Location box or click Choose File to find the file on your hard drive.**

3. Type a caption in the Alternate Text box.

The Alternate Text doesn't appear below the picture, like a regular caption. Instead, it appears when the user's mouse points to the picture. The screen-reading programs used by blind and vision-impaired people read the Alternate Text out loud, to give the person an idea of what the picture is of.

4. Make any other formatting changes you want.

If you want the image to display larger or smaller than its actual size, click the Dimensions tab and set the size. Click the Appearance tab if you want to add space around your picture or change the way it aligns with adjacent text.

5. Then click OK to finish specifying your image.

You can also drag the file from a My Computer window into Composer and then right-click and select Image Properties if you want to change its size or appearance.

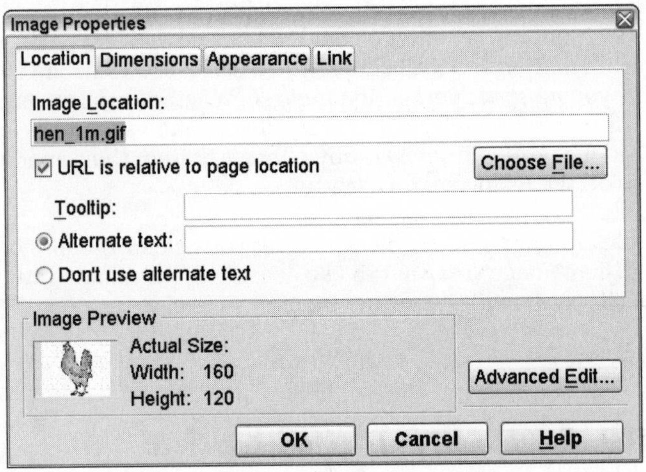

Figure 17-3:
Adding a
chicken to
your Web
page.

Image Properties	⊠

| Location | Dimensions | Appearance | Link |

Image Location:

hen_1m.gif

☑ URL is relative to page location   Choose File...

Tooltip:

⦿ Alternate text:

○ Don't use alternate text

Image Preview

Actual Size:
Width: 160
Height: 120   Advanced Edit...

OK   Cancel   Help

In Word, choose Insert➪Picture➪From File, specify the picture, and click Insert.

After you insert the picture, it may look terrible — it may be the wrong size, or push the text out of the way in an unattractive manner. Delete the picture (by clicking in it and pressing Del), edit it with a graphics editor, and reinsert it. If the size is wrong, use Paint, Paint Shop Pro (our favorite), or some other program to resize it. In Paint, open the picture file by choosing File➪Open, and then chose Image⇨Stretch and Skew (which sounds unnecessarily violent to us). Enter a percentage to shrink or expand the picture, using the same number for the Horizontal and Vertical percentages if you don't want to warp the picture.

You can control the way that text flows around a picture. In Mozilla, right-click the picture and choose Image Properties from the menu that appears. Click the Appearance tab and change the Align Text to Image setting — try different settings until you find one you like. In Word, right-click the picture and choose Format⇨Picture. Then select the Layout tab, where you have a few options for how you want the text to wrap.

Making an online photo album

If you want to put pictures on the Web for your far-flung family and friends to see, you don't need to create your own site. Instead, you can create a free account on one of a number of photo-sharing sites. (No, they aren't for sharing *that kind* of photos!) Try Kodak EasyShare Gallery at www.kodakgallery.com (formerly Ofoto at www.ofoto.com) or Snapfish at www.snapfish.com.

Once you've created an account at Kodak Gallery or Snapfish, you can upload photos into online photo albums by filling out forms on the site (see the figure below for Kodak's EasyShare Gallery). Then you can share your albums with your friends. Photos on these sites are not visible to general public — only to the people with whom you share the album.

You (and your friends) can also order prints of your uploaded photos — that's how these sites make their money. But the prices for prints are reasonable, and we find these systems very convenient.

Linking to Other Pages

The *hyper* in hypertext is the thing that makes the Web so cool. A *hyperlink* (or just *link*) is the thing on the page that lets you "surf" the Web — go from page to page just by clicking the link. A Web page is hardly a page if it doesn't link somewhere else.

The immense richness of the Web comes from the links that Web page authors place on their pages. Contribute to this richness by including links to places you know of that the people who visit your page may also be interested in. Try to avoid including links to places that everyone already knows about and has in their bookmarks. For example, everyone knows where to find Google and Yahoo, so leave them off. If your home page mentions your interest in one of your hobbies, however, such as canoeing or volleyball or birding or your alma mater, include some links to related sites you know that are interesting.

To make a link on your Web page, follow these instructions:

- ✔ **Mozilla Composer:** Highlight the text that you want to be a link and click the Link button on the toolbar. In the Link Properties dialog box, type the exact URL into the Link Location box, or click the Choose File button to choose another Web page you've created. (Rather than typing a URL, consider cutting-and-pasting from the Address or Location box of your browser; it avoids typos.) Then click OK.

- ✔ **Word:** First, select the text that you want to be a link. Then issue the command to make the link. Choose Insert⇨Hyperlink (or press Ctrl+K) and type the exact URL into the Address box. (In earlier versions of Word, this box is called Type the File or Web Page Name.)

If you create multiple pages, you can put links among your pages; be sure to upload all the pages.

Good Page Design

After you put together a basic Web page, use the tips in this section to avoid some mistakes that novice Websters often make.

Fonts and styles

Don't overformat your text with too many fonts, too many colors, or too much emphasis with **bold**, *italics,* underlining, or some ***combination***. Experienced designers disparage it as "ransom note" text. Blinking text universally annoys readers.

Background images

Tiled background images can be cool if they're subtle — but too often they make the text utterly illegible. Black text on a solid white background (like the pages of this book) has stood the test of time for hundreds of years.

To set your Web page's background color, follow these instructions:

- **Mozilla Composer:** Choose Format⇨Page Colors and Background from the menu. Click Use Custom Colors to override the normal colors that the user's browser assigns and then click the colored buttons to set the colors of normal text, link text, and other text. If you have a picture that you'd like to display as the background of the page (tiled — repeating to fill the page), enter its name into the Background Image box or use Choose File to choose it from a menu.

- **Word:** Choose Format⇨Background and choose a color. To tile a picture in the background, choose Format⇨Background⇨Fill Effects.

Big images

Many Web pages are burdened with images that, although beautiful, take a long time to load — so long that many users may give up and go away before the pages are completely loaded. Remember that not everyone has a computer or Internet connection as fast as yours.

Take a few steps to make your Web pages load more quickly. The main step, of course, is to limit the size of the images you use by shrinking them with a graphics editor like Paint. A 20K (20,000 bytes big) image takes twice as long to load as a 10K image, which takes twice as long to load as a 5K image. You can estimate that images load at 1K per second on a 56Kbps dialup connection, so a 5K image loads in about five seconds, which is pretty fast; a 120K image takes two minutes to load, so that image had better be worth the wait.

Consider putting a small image on a page and give visitors an option (via a link) to load the full-size picture. We know that you're proud of your dog, and she deserves a place of honor on your home page, but not everyone visiting your site will wait excitedly for your puppy to download. (We hate it when they do that on the rug.)

In GIF files, images with fewer colors load faster than images with more colors. If you use a graphics editor to reduce a GIF from 256 colors to 32 or even 16 colors, often the appearance hardly changes, but the file shrinks dramatically. Set your graphics program to store the GIF file in *interlaced* format, which lets browsers display a blurry approximation of the image as it's downloading, to offer a hint of what's coming.

In JPEG files, you can adjust the "quality" level to a lower quality, which makes the file smaller. You can set the quality of Web images surprisingly low with little effect on what appears on users' screens. Experiment a bit; it could save your visitors some hassle.

You can also take advantage of the *cache* that browsers use. The cache keeps copies of previously viewed pages and images. If any image on a page being downloaded is already in the browser's cache, that image isn't loaded again. When you use the same icon in several places on a page (or on several pages visited in succession), the browser downloads the icon's file only once and reuses the same image on all the pages. When creating your Web pages, try to use the same icons from one page to the next to give your pages a consistent style and speed up downloading.

Live and learn

If you're looking at other people's Web pages and come across one that's particularly neat, you can look at the source HTML for that page to see how the page was constructed. In Mozilla, choose View⇨Page Source or press Ctrl+U; in Internet Explorer, choose View⇨Source.

Putting Your Page on the Web

After you've made some pages you're happy with (or happy *enough* with) and you're ready for other people to see them, you have to release your pages to the world. Although nearly every ISP has a Web server for user accounts, no two ISPs handle the uploading process in quite the same way.

Uploading from your Web editor

To upload your files, you need an FTP program. Luckily, well-designed, convenient, and totally groovy Web-editing programs like Mozilla Composer have an FTP program built right in. They can store the host name, username, and password of your Web server the first time you upload a Web page, so you don't have to enter this information over and over. Here's how to use them in Mozilla Composer to upload your Web pages and the graphics files that contain the pictures displayed on the pages:

1. **Click the Publish button on the toolbar to display the Publish Page dialog box shown in Figure 17-4.**

   First, you need to complete the fields on the Settings tab.

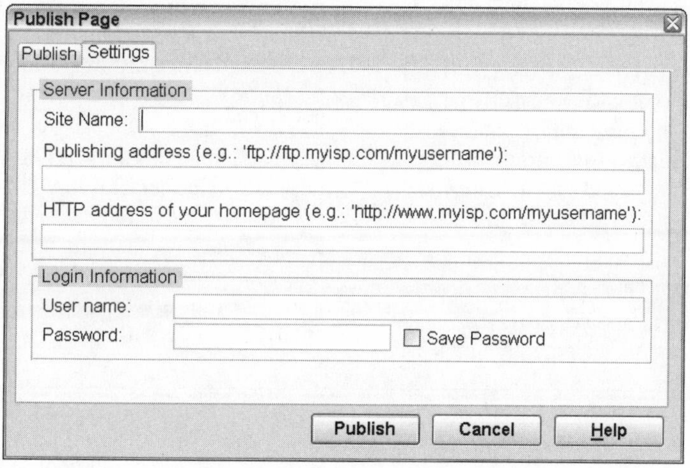

Figure 17-4:
When you click Publish, Mozilla asks for information about how to upload your Web pages to a Web server.

2. **Pick a site name to use when you edit these pages in the future, enter the Publishing Address, the FTP address your ISP gave you to upload your pages, and your username and password.**

   (The HyperText Transport Protocol [HTTP] address is optional.) Most of this information was diligently collected by you in "Web pages on Web servers" section earlier in this chapter. You may not want to select the Save Password check box to maintain the security of your Web site.

3. **Next, click the Publish tab and fill out the Page Title and Filename.**

   The Page Title is the name that you want to appear in the title bar of the browser when your page is displayed. The Filename is the name of the file to use when uploading; usually that's the same as the file that you use on your own computer, to avoid confusion

4. **Click the Publish button to start the upload.**

   Mozilla displays a window with the status of the page file and any image files that appear on the page.

5. **Click Close when it's done.**

A few other Web page editors

If you don't like Mozilla Composer or Word for Web editing, you have lots of other options. Here are a few possibilities:

✔ **Dreamweaver** (www.macromedia.com/ software/dreamweaver): If you get serious about making a Web site, Dreamweaver is the serious Webweavers program. It's not cheap, but it has lots of features, including built-in FTP, error-checking, HTML reference, and code view.

✔ **CoffeeCup HTML Editor** (www.coffeecup. com/software): This Windows Web editor lets you choose page elements from a list,

so you never have to see HTML codes. Your formatting options are limited, but it's a great way to get started. An FTP program is included for uploading your finished pages. This program is no longer free, but it's still a good deal.

✔ **Microsoft FrontPage** (office.microsoft. com): FrontPage comes with Microsoft Office. Watch out, though: FrontPage and FrontPage Express have a nasty habit of inserting Microsoft-proprietary codes that only work if your ISP runs a Microsoft Web server. (So much for standards!)

Some versions of Word include FTP and some don't. (Word 2003 doesn't, so see the next section for how to upload.) If you have an earlier versions of Word, try this:

1. **Choose File⇨Save As.**

2. **Click the Save In box in the upper-left corner of the Save As dialog box and choose FTP Locations.**

3. **To tell Word about the Web server to which you want to upload your Web pages, click Add/Modify FTP Locations. Then type the host name of the Web server, your username (click User), and your password. Click the Add button.**

   When you click OK, you return to the Save As dialog box, and now your Web server's address appears.

4. **Click the server and click Open to connect to the Web server.**

   You see the file and folders you have on the server.

5. **Click Save to upload your page.**

Uploading with an FTP program

Of course, some (crummy) Web-editing programs don't include FTP programs, so you may be on your own when it comes to uploading your Web pages.

Assuming that you have the server details we discuss at the beginning of this chapter, here's what to do:

1. **Run your FTP program.**

   We use WS_FTP (our Web page at net.gurus.com/ftp contains information), although any FTP program will do. If you have Windows XP, you can use its Web Folders feature.

2. **Log on to your provider's upload server, using your own logon and password.**

   You'll have to enter the name of the FTP server, your logon name (usually the same as your account name), and your password (usually the same as the one you use when you connect to your provider).

3. **Change to the directory (folder) where your home page belongs.**

   The name is usually something like /pub/elvis, /www/elvis, or /pub/elvis/www (assuming that your username is *elvis*).

4. **Upload your Web page(s).**

   Use ASCII mode, not binary mode, for the Web pages because Web pages are stored as text files. Use binary mode when you're uploading graphics files.

So, where's my page?

After you finish uploading, if your account name is elvis and your page on the server is called mypage.html, its URL is something like

```
http://www.your-isp-name.net/~elvis/mypage.html
```

Again, URLs vary by provider. Some providers don't follow the convention of putting a tilde (~) in front of your username.

Testing your page

Be sure to check out how your page looks after it's on the Web. Inspect it from someone else's computer to make sure that it doesn't accidentally contain any references to graphics files stored on your own computer that you forgot to upload. If you want to be compulsive, check how it looks from various browsers — Firefox, Mozilla, Internet Explorer, Opera, AOL, MSN TV, and Lynx, to name a few. If you're not compulsive, just check your pages in Internet Explorer and Firefox.

Shortly after you upload your pages, you'll probably notice a glaring mistake. (We always do.) To update a page, edit the copy on your own computer and then upload it to your Web server, replacing the preceding version of the page. If you change some but not all your pages, you don't have to upload pages that haven't changed.

Be Master of Your Domain

Choosing a name is important and that principle is no different when it comes to your Web page. A home page address like

```
www.people.stratford-on-avon-internet.com/~shakespeare/
                PrinceOfDenmark/index.html
```

is just not going to attract as many visitors as

```
www.hamlet.org
```

Getting your own domain name is a lot easier and cheaper than you might think. There are three steps:

1. **Choose a name.**

   You'll want one that's easy to remember and to spell. Pick out a couple of alternate names in case the one you want is taken. Don't use a variation on a popular trademark like Coke or Sony (or Dummies) unless you like dealing with lawyers. Also be sure that it's not already taken; you can check the WHOIS database for .com, .net, and .org at www.whois.net or registrar.verisign-grs.com/whois.

2. **Ask your ISP to "host" your name.**

   That means your ISP breathes some incantations that tell the Internet that when someone types your domain name into their browser, they should see the files stored on your ISP's Web server. Many ISPs charge a fee for this service, but a few do it for free. Your ISP may be able to handle the next step, registration, for you, too.

3. **Register your name if your ISP doesn't.**

   Hundreds of registrars compete for business in the popular .com, .net, and .org categories. The going rate is between $10 to $30 per year.

If your ISP wants to charge you big bucks (that is, more than $10 a month) to register your name and to host your pages, consider using a Web-hosting service. Pair Networks at pair.com and MyHosting at myhosting.com are both reputable, reliable, and cheap.

Blog City

After you've created a few Web pages of your own, you'll probably conclude, with the rest of us, that keeping up a Web site one page at a time is (to put it mildly) a pain in the patootie. If you have better things to do than to fiddle with Web page formatting, you can use automated weblog (pronounced "blog") systems that provide standard formatting while you just provide the brilliant, witty, sparkling content. Chapter 18 tells all.

Wonderful Wacky Wikis

Whereas a blog is basically an exercise in personal vanity publishing, a *wiki* lets a group of people collaborate on a Web site. A wiki (named for the Hawaiian word *wiki-wiki*, meaning "in a hurry" — we are not making this up) can have an unlimited number of authors, all of whom can add and change pages within the wiki's Web site. If this sounds potentially chaotic, it is, but most wikis have ground rules that keep the group moving in more or less the same direction. One of the best wikis is `www.wikipedia.org`, a collaborative encyclopedia which, with over 120,000 entries, is well on its way to including all human knowledge.

It's harder to find places to start your own wiki than your own blog, but it's more fun to find a wiki of interest to you, dive in, and start editing your own little corner of it. If you want to create a wiki for use by your organization, committee, or group of friends, there's a list of *wiki farms* (wiki servers) on the Wiki Science Web site, at

`en.wikibooks.org/wiki/Wiki_Science`

Open a Store Online

Selling stuff on the Internet used to take hundreds of thousands of dollars worth of software and programming talent. A number of sites now let you create a Web store for very modest fees. We like Amazon.com's Marketplace, at `www.amazon.com`, which is particularly easy to set up — as of this writing, you click the Make Money link near the bottom of the page to find out how to set up a seller account, but since Web page designs can change, you may need to look around the Amazon home page. They even process credit card sales for you, eliminating what was once a horrible pain in the neck. Yahoo provides several ways to sell via their site (auctions, a storefront, and classified ads) — see `sell.yahoo.com` for information.

If you're not up for creating Web pages and setting up a whole store, you can still sell individual items either on consignment at sites like www.half. ebay.com or at auction at sites like www.ebay.com. Actually, eBay now owns Half.com, so when you set up an account to buy or sell items on one, you're ready to buy or sell on the other, too.

To sell an item on Half.com (or any other consignment site), first find the item you want to sell (as shown in Figure 17-5). Half specializes in books, movies, and music, and they've got almost everything in print in their database. Once you find your item click the Sell Yours Now link, specify the condition of the item, a description, and your asking price. When you click the List Item link, your listing goes into the Half.com database, and appears on the site within an hour. When you sell your item — which could be minutes, hours, or months later — Half.com keeps a commission.

Figure 17-5:
You've got a videotape to sell on Half.com.

Selling an item on eBay is a little more complicated. You need to write a description for the item and take or scan a digital picture of it. (For some items, like books and CDs, eBay may have your item in its Half.com database, and you can use their description and picture.) Start at www.ebay.com, click the Sell tab or link, and follow the directions. Auctions can be up to seven days long. eBay charges you a listing fee, although if your item doesn't sell, you can usually relist it (try again, perhaps with a lower starting price) for free.

Shout It Out: Getting Your Web Site Found

After you put your pages online, you may want to get people to come and visit. Before you do any online publicity, make sure that your pages have two types of information that search engines and Web directories look for:

✔ **Page description:** You can store a one-sentence description of your page in the hidden codes (*metatags*) at the beginning of each Web page. Yahoo, Google, and other sites display this text when your page appears in their listings, and they use the text to determine how to categorize the page. In Mozilla Composer, you can add a page description by choosing Format➪Page Title and Properties.

✔ **Keywords:** You can provide a list of keywords and phrases that people might search for if they want to find your page. Mozilla Composer doesn't make it easy to add keywords to your page's metatags, but here's how: Choose View➪HTML Source to display the HTML codes that make up your page. Scan down until you find `</head>`. Just above that, add a tag like this:

```
<meta content="chickens, hens, eggs, poultry, domestic poultry"
      name="keywords">
```

Replace the list of chicken-related terms with your own. Then choose View➪Normal Edit Mode to display your page the way it normally looks.

After your page description and keywords are in place, here are a few ways to publicize your site:

✔ Visit your favorite Web directories and search engines, such as Google (`google.com`), Yahoo (`yahoo.com`), and the Open Directory Project (`dmoz.org`), and submit your URL (the name of your page) to add to their database. These sites all have on their home pages an option for adding a new page — it's usually called Suggest URL or Suggest A Site or Add your Site. (Sometimes it's a teeny little link near the bottom of the page.) Automated indexes like Google and AltaVista add pages fairly promptly, but manually maintained directories like Yahoo may not accept them at all.

Don't pay to have your site included: Every respectable search engine and directory has an option for adding your noncommercial site for free, although it may take a while for your site to show up.

✔ Visit `www.submit-it.com`. You can pay Submit It! (a service of Microsoft) an annual fee to submit your URL to a bunch of directories, indexes, and search engines.

✔ Find and visit other similar or related sites and offer to exchange links between your site and theirs.

Getting lots of traffic to your site takes time. If your site offers something different that is of real interest to other folks, it can build a following of its own. Even we *For Dummies* authors have gotten into the action: A few of our home-grown sites that keep growing in popularity are Arnold Reinhold's Math in the Movies page, at `www.mathinthemovies.com`; Margy's Great Tapes for Kids site, at `www.greattapes.com`; Margy's Harry Potter Timeline at `gurus.com/hptimeline`; and John's Airline Information On-Line on the Internet site, at `airinfo.aero`. Just imagine what you can come up with!

Chapter 18

All the World's a Blog

*B*ack at the dawn of the World Wide Web (15 years ago), the plan was that people all over the world would use it to communicate among themselves — a virtual rustic global village. That's not exactly how it turned out, with giant content megamalls like Yahoo making the Net a distinctly non-rustic experience. But now, *weblogs,* or *blogs* for short, are bringing back that early promise along with some truly spectacular opportunities for wasting time.

What's in a Blog?

A blog is just a Web site run by software that makes it easy to add to content. Most blogs are updated frequently by one author and contain lists of fairly short dated entries, like an online journal or diary, with the newest ones at the top. Some blogs are more complex, with multiple topics or pictures as well as (or instead of) words, but they retain the idea of relatively short entries, updated relatively often. Figure 18-1 shows the very popular Boing Boing blog (www.boingboing.net), which offers an eclectic collection of reviews of and links to interesting Web sites ranging from political harangues to art reviews to security locks for ice cream containers.

The best blogs offer cutting-edge journalism and commentary and brilliant, witty, sparkling writing, while the worst disprove the old cliché that a million monkeys at a million typewriters would eventually produce the works of Shakespeare. If you Google for the word *blog* or *weblog* and some topic words of interest to you, you'll invariably find someone blogging away at it. But keep reading to find out better ways to discover and organize the blogs you read.

Slightly too much about RSS and Atom

The key to dealing with lots of blogs is RSS feeds. So what is RSS? It's a highly structured version of a Web page intended not for people to read, but for other computers to read. The idea is that a computer working on your behalf can look at the RSS version of a blog to figure out what's changed and can also reformat the material for a combined display with a bunch of other blogs. The RSS version of a blog is called a *feed* because it's sort of like a system that "feeds" new stories to you as they're available. RSS is nifty because if you find a blog that you like, you can subscribe to its RSS feed and be notified every time a new entry appears in the blog.

Since an RSS feed is a kind of Web page, the RSS feed has its own URL. The RSS feed shown below is www.cauce.org/newsblog/index.rss. An RSS feed is usually located on the same Web server as the material it describes, but there are plenty of RSS feeds located on servers completely separate from the location of the material the feed describes.

RSS isn't totally illegible, but it's a format only a geek could love. Here's the beginning of the RSS version of a blog one of us runs:

```
<rss version="0.91">
<channel>
<title>CAUCE
    Newsletters</title>
<link>http://www.cauce.org/news
    blog</link>
<description>Coalition Against
    Unsolicited Commercial
    E-mail
(CAUCE) newsletters
</description>
<language>en</language>
```

```
<item>
<title>Industry Canada issues
    its spam task force
    report</title>
<link>http://www.cauce.org/news-
    blog/2005/05/30#canada</link>
<description>
<p>Industry Canada, the part of
    the Canadian government
roughly equivalent to the U.S.
    Commerce Department, has
    had a
task force on spam working for
    the past year or so.</p>
```

You can see the codes that mark the title, the link to the blog, the description, a blog item, the link to the item, and so forth. The full RSS file contains a bunch of items, one per story.

It would be much too easy if only one version of RSS were available, so instead, there are about a dozen. The original version 0.90 evolved into 0.91 (that's what the example above is), 0.92, and 0.93. Then a splinter group invented RSS 1.0 (sometimes called RDF), and the 0.9x group leapfrogged them to RSS 2.0. The IETF, the group that maintains Internet standards, has been working on Project Atom, which is intended to be a neutral successor to all the versions of RSS and looks like it may succeed. Fortunately, the different versions of RSS are similar enough that any program that can handle one version can handle them all, and if a blog offers multiple versions, it hardly matters which one you pick. (We'd pick 1.0, which includes slightly more info.)

If you're wondering what RSS means, the most popular meaning is *Really Simple Syndication*, where *Syndication* is the process of making your content available in lots of different places.

Figure 18-1:
Boing Boing
opines.

As blogs have become more popular, many Web sites that weren't originally set up as blogs have become increasingly blogular. Just about every newspaper and magazine with a Web site has made it possible to treat their site as a blog, or as a collection of blogs — one for each section of the paper. My Yahoo (`http://my.yahoo.com`), the customizable Web page you can set up at Yahoo, has added more and more bloggish features so you can now include anyone else's blog as part of your My Yahoo page, and you can use many of My Yahoo's own parts as blogs in collections you make elsewhere.

By using *Really Simple Syndication* (*RSS*), the blogosphere's lingua franca, it's possible to make a blog out of any collection of related material on the Internet. The U.S. Patent Office's Web site has a search engine for patents that doesn't look like a blog, but someone we know used pages from that site to make a blog of patents issued to Microsoft, a blog of patents issued to Google, and so forth — useful to people in the tech business.

How to Read a Blog

Reading a blog is easy; blogs are just Web pages. Point your browser at the home page of the one you're interested in and read it. (Bet you thought it would be more complicated than that.) If you want to see more about a particular story, click the link in the story. (The next section has some suggestions for where to find worthwhile blogs.)

Because blogs change frequently (at least they're supposed to), you might want to bookmark your favorite ones so you can find them again. As you find more blogs, you will soon find your bookmark folder and your brain exploding, trying to keep track of them. Fortunately, you are not the first person to have this problem, so some excellent blog organizing tools are at your disposal.

How to Deal with All the Blogs

Reading one blog is like eating only one potato chip, which never happens. When you find one blog, it usually has links to other blogs. If you search for one blog, you find a dozen blogs, and before you know it, you're mired deep in the swamps of Blogistan, with far too many interesting blogs to keep track of.

The rubber raft to keep you afloat is known as an *aggregator*, a fancy word for something that keeps all your blogs tidily in one place where you can look to see what's new. Aggregators use RSS to track new articles posted to blogs. In your favorite aggregator, you *subscribe* to the blogs of interest, and it shows you all of the interesting stuff in one handy place. Aggregators come in two main varieties. One is Web-based, a Web site that tracks and shows you all your favorite blogs. The other is desktop-based, a program that lets your computer track and show your favorite blogs.

Web aggregators have the advantage of having no software to install, and you can check your blogs anywhere you can find a Web browser. Desktop aggregators have the disadvantage that you may have to download and install software (although two of them are programs you should have installed already) and the advantage that the response is snappier, and they are, debatably, easier to use than Web-based aggregators.

Blogs on the Web

Here are three of our favorite aggregator Web sites. All are available for free.

Bloglines

`www.bloglines.com`

Bloglines is the premier site for people who want to follow a whole lot of blogs. To get started at Bloglines, you set up a free account and then tell it to add the RSS version of the blogs you're interested in. (That's the Add link near the upper-left corner of Figure 18-2.) If you know the RSS feed's URL, you can enter it directly, but it's usually easier to use the built-in search engine. Type in a few words describing blogs you might like and pick the likely looking ones. Many blogs also have a Bloglines button you can click to take you to the Bloglines site and add that blog to your account.

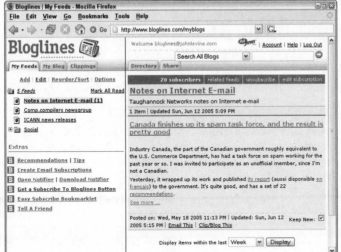

Figure 18-2:
All blogs all
the time at
Bloglines.

For each blog, Bloglines tracks the items in the blog and remembers which ones you've looked at, reporting the number unread in parentheses after the name of each blog. That makes it easy to cruise by and catch up on what's new. You can mark stories of interest to add to your private clipping folder, and you can also publish a blog of clippings, optionally adding notes to each clipping. (Your clipping blog is a real blog with its own RSS feed, so your friends can read it and save entries, and their friends can read their clipping blog, offering blogs within blogs within blogs.)

Newsgator

`www.newsgator.com`

Newsgator offers roughly the same features as Bloglines, but it feels more businesslike. Newsgator makes it easy to subscribe to a lot of news source blogs, newspapers, news services like Reuters, and lots of feeds of industry or topic-specific news. It also offers very cool keyword and URL feeds, in which you give it a few keywords to look for, or a URL to look for, and it synthesizes a feed of all the items in the blogs it tracks with those keywords or that URL. The free service offers one keyword and one URL feed, or you can upgrade to paid services that offer more of them along with other fancier features.

Newsgator also has a clipping folder and lets you publish a clipping blog.

My Yahoo

`my.yahoo.com`

If your goal is just to read blogs, My Yahoo isn't the best place to do it. But if you already use My Yahoo because of all of the built-in content it offers, adding a few RSS feeds (or a lot of RSS feeds) is easy. When you click the Add

Gack, it's a trackback

Bloggers frequently comment on each other. Sometimes the comments are nice, sometimes they're not so nice, but they're certainly, uh, involved. Most blogs let visitors leave comments, but the serious discussions are often between two or more blogs, with each containing comments on the other blog. Anyone reading the blog with comments can see the reference to the original blog, but there's no way for someone reading the original to know where to look for comments. That's where *trackbacks* come in.

Let's say one blogger, call him John (not his real name), posts a provocative entry in his blog.

Then a second blogger, Margy (not her real name, either) posts "For an utterly priceless example of disenchronia, check out this entry in John's blog" with a link to John's blog. If John's blog software is set up to handle trackbacks, Margy's blog system can tell John's blog about the new link, so John's blog adds a trackback note with a link to the comment, thereby making the connection two-way.

The original vision of hypertext, of which the Web is a quick-and-dirty, hacked-up version, made all links two-way. Trackbacks bring the real-life Web closer to what it was originally supposed to be.

Content button, the new content page either lets you enter an RSS feed's URL (there's a tiny link next to the Find button) or it offers a catalog of all the RSS feeds Yahoo knows about. When you add an RSS feed, My Yahoo makes it look just like Yahoo's built-in content.

Conversely, if you use a different aggregator and want to include a few of the My Yahoo sections, visit news.yahoo.com/rss to find RSS feeds for most of Yahoo's news areas that you can add to any aggregator you want. You can even ask Yahoo to make you a custom feed of items that contain keywords you choose, not unlike what Newsgator does, but because it's an RSS feed, you can use it anywhere.

Blogs on your desktop

If you really want to get close to your blogs, you should probably set them up in a program right on your desktop. We have three suggestions about how to do that: a nice but simple program called BlogExpress; our favorite e-mail program, Mozilla Thunderbird, which makes your blogs look like mail folders; and our favorite Web browser, Mozilla Firefox, which makes them look like folders of bookmarks.

Reading blogs in BlogExpress

BlogExpress, shown in Figure 18-3, is an excellent little program you can download from the Net. It's completely free, although the authors wouldn't object if you went back to their Web site and gave them a donation if you use the program and like it. Visit `www.usablelabs.com`, click the BlogExpress link, click the green download arrow to download it, and then run the program you downloaded to install it.

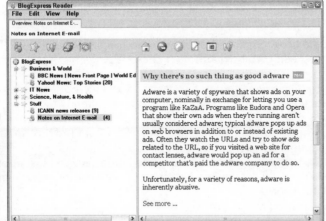

Figure 18-3: BlogExpress makes it easy to keep up with your blogs.

When you start it up, BlogExpress offers some help selecting blogs you're interested in; as always, if you know an RSS feed's URL, you can enter it directly. Then it shows each blog as a page with links you can click. BlogExpress has a built-in Web browser (actually Internet Explorer), so when you click a link, it opens the link as a tab within the Blog Express window, with a Close button at the top to click when you're done with it.

If you minimize the BlogExpress window, it lurks as a little two-blob icon in the Windows system tray, popping up a little window from time to time when it finds new stories, usually saying something like "224 new items." It has a few other features to open and close Web page windows and organize your list of feeds, but it's deliberately a simple, adequate tool that's easy to use, not an all-singing, all-dancing, all-baffling program. For most people, it's all the blog reader you need.

Reading blogs in Thunderbird

In Chapter 13, we encourage you to install Mozilla Thunderbird and use it as your regular e-mail program. If you do that, it's easy to tell Thunderbird to follow a few blogs and show them to you as if they were mail folders. If you follow a whole lot of blogs, T'bird probably isn't the best program to use. But for watching a few as you check your mail, it's quite handy.

First, you have to tell Thunderbird to set up a blog folder:

1. On Thunderbird's main screen, click Create a New Account.

 2. **On the first page of the wizard that appears, select RSS News & Blogs and then click Next a few times until you get to Finish. Then click Finish.**

    Now you have a News & Blogs folder, and you can add RSS feeds to it.

 3. **Right-click the News & Blogs folder and select Manage Subscriptions to open the subscription window.**

 4. **To add a blog, click Add, type or paste the URL of the blog's RSS feed into the Feed URL box, and then click OK.**

Thunderbird offers no automated way to find RSS feed URLs, which is a pain. One approach is to open the blog in your browser, find the XML or RSS link on the blog's page, right-click that link, and select Copy Link Location (in Firefox) or Copy Shortcut (in Internet Explorer) to put the link on the Windows clipboard. Then you can tell Thunderbird to add a new feed, click in the Feed URL box, and select Paste to paste in the URL you just copied. Yes, this process is a pain, which is one of the reasons we don't recommend this for heavy blog users.

When your blogs are set up, each blog appears as a mail folder under News and Blogs. You can see the list of headlines and read the blog entries exactly the way you read mail messages. It remembers the ones you've seen, and you can delete the ones you've read. (They're not deleted from the blog itself, just from Thunderbird's folder.) You can save the ones you like in local folders, just like mail messages, and do everything you can do with mail messages except reply to them — blog entries don't have return addresses.

Reading blogs in Firefox

If you set up Mozilla Firefox as your Web browser, as we suggest in Chapter 13, you're only a few clicks away from having all your favorite blogs as *live bookmarks,* which look like folders in the bookmark menu, containing all of the blog's items as individual bookmarks. The *liveness* is that the folder's contents update automatically as the blog changes. Firefox live bookmarks are much easier to set up than Thunderbird blog folders, but after they're set up, they're not quite as useful.

Whenever you visit a Web page and Firefox can tell that there's an RSS feed related to the page, it shows a little orange feed icon in the status bar at the bottom of the screen. To make a live bookmark for that page, just click the icon. If Firefox found more than one RSS feed for the page, it asks you which one you want. (If they're different flavors of RSS, like 0.91 and 1.0, pick the highest number. If they have different content, Firefox should show you feed names that give you a hint about which is which.) Then it asks you where in your bookmark folders to file the bookmark, and your feed is all set.

To look at a feed, just find its bookmark in the Bookmark menu and click it to see a list of all the current items. Click any one of them to open it or, for a good time, click Open in Tabs at the bottom of the bookmark folder and Firefox opens all of the blog entries at once, with each in a separate tab in the browser.

Firefox doesn't provide any way we can see to remember what items you've already seen, which limits the usefulness of this approach for serious blog-ophiles. We've found it useful to mark a blog that looks promising but we're not sure is worth adding to our Bloglines account so we can look at it a few times before adding it.

Writing Your Own Blog

Now that you've seen all the ways to read other people's blogs, how about starting your own?

To blog or not to blog

If you want to start your own blog, keep in mind our comment at the beginning of the chapter about brilliant, witty, sparkling content. Sparkling is hard, and sparkling on a regular basis is exhausting. So if you do start your own blog, try blogging for a while on your own before telling all your friends about it. Otherwise: "It was okay at the beginning, but now, pee-yew."

Can I make big buck$ with my blog?

Probably not. The alleged path to blog riches is that you start a blog, fill it with brilliant, witty, sparkling content, add some ads down the side, and then millions of people flock to your blog, click the ads, and you use your share of the advertising income to buy a tropical island where you retire.

There are a few famous blogs for which this plan has more or less worked, like Boing Boing (www.boingboing.net, for eclectic techno-gossip) and Wonkette (www.wonkette.com, Washington DC political gossip), but you can probably count them on your fingers, and running each is a full-time job. We've experimented with ads on some of our bloggish Web sites, like John's airinfo.aero, and we've never seen more than a few dollars a day, meaning that our tropical island will be limited to about four square inches.

You can put up a blog with ads for free at Blogger (www.blogger.com), so you have nothing to lose but your time and perhaps your self-esteem. But don't quit your day job quite yet.

Where to put your blog

Running blog software is simple enough that there are probably 10,000 different places that you can host your blog. But three big blog sites let you blog away without having to install anything. Unless you have a friend who's dying to install some blogware on her Web site, use one of these. All three of these sites offer a basic usable blog for free. Some also have extra cost add-ons they hope you'll use. For reasons that will shortly become apparent, we suggest that most of our users try Blogger.

Blogger

www.blogger.com

Formerly known as Blogspot and a couple of other things, Blogger is now part of the Google empire, although Google hasn't Google-ized it, at least not yet. After you create an account, you can add and edit blog entries through the Web site, customize it in any of a zillion ways, and publish your blog. It also supports mobile blogs (moblogs) that let you post text and pictures from your mobile phone.

Blogger is remarkably uninterested in asking for your money. As far as we can figure out, its reason for existence is mostly to be a place for people to display Google ads. But that's fine — it's a nice site and the ads are entirely optional.

Top five reasons not to start your own blog

Blog entries are usually short, so in that spirit we offer you a short list.

5. You work on your blog when you should be working on your day job, annoying co-workers and boss, and you spend hours reading *other* blogs looking for topics to comment on and/or borrow.

4. Every conversation or experience becomes a potential blog entry, rather than part of your life. (Also known as Novelist's Syndrome.)

3. You try to have strange conversations and experiences to have something to blog. (Bad Novelist's Syndrome.)

2. Everything, no matter how trivial, takes on a deep bloggable meaning. ("Did you ever notice all the different ways that rain streaks the dirt on the side of a city bus . . . ?")

1. You realize that you have nothing to say.

We practice what we preach here. None of us has a personal blog, just work-related ones.

LiveJournal

www.livejournal.com

The cliché LiveJournal user is a college student who needs to provide too much information to his or her 100,000 closest friends on topics ranging from taste in music to short-term party plans to personal political philosophy. If this sounds like you, LiveJournal's the place. The basic blog is free, and a paid account can include extra features in your blog, such as polls and surveys.

Xanga

www.xanga.com

Xanga is a lot like LiveJournal except that the average user seems to be about five years younger. Unlike the other two sites, Xanga shows its ads on your blog unless you buy a premium account.

Lights, Action, Weblog!

Text is so 20th century. (Actually, it's more 15th century, but who's counting?) If you find text constraining, just about every blog site, including the three we describe in the preceding section, lets you include pictures as part of your blog, often as a *moblog* (mobile blog) that lets you upload directly from your mobile phone.

If you want to make a blog that consists entirely of pictures, perhaps with some captions, visit Flickr (www.flickr.com), the most popular photoblog site.

And finally, if you want to go the full multimedia route, and you have a camera or phone that records video, www.vidblogs.com hosts video blogs. Since video files are large, only users with snappy broadband connections need apply. But if you think you can make brilliant, sparkling, witty, one-minute movies, here's your chance. Good luck!

Part VI
The Part of Tens

The 5th Wave   By Rich Tennant

"I don't mean to hinder your quest for knowledge, however it's not generally a good idea to try and download the entire Internet."

In this part . . .

We have lots of interesting odds and ends we want to tell you about, so (to provide the illusion of organization) we've grouped them into lists. By the strangest coincidence, each list consists of exactly *ten* facts. (*Note to the literal-minded:* You may have to cut off or glue on some fingers to make your version of ten match up with ours. Perhaps it would be easier just to take our word for it.)

Chapter 19

Ten Problems and Ten Solutions

Gosh, using the Internet is exciting. But sometimes things get so fouled up that you want to push your computer out the window and go back to the communication methods our ancestors used, like newspapers, telephones, and smoke signals.

But don't give up just yet. This chapter offers up some common problems that many Internet users encounter, as well as some solutions to those problems.

My Computer Takes Forever to Boot Up, Popup Ads Have Taken Over My Screen, and It's Really Slow

All these symptoms suggest that your computer is infested with *malware*, sneaky programs that do bad things to your computer, including spyware (which arrive via your Web browser) and viruses (which arrive via e-mail). A full-scale war is going on in cyberspace for control of the world's PCs, and your computer is likely a casualty. Chapter 2 describes both types of malware, Chapter 4 suggests strongly that you install virus-checker and anti-spyware programs, and Chapter 14 describes how to configure your virus-checker. Make sure you have downloaded the latest improvements to your Windows operating system, and check that your virus checker and spyware removers are up to date as well. And if you still use Internet Explorer to browse the Web, consider trying a different browser, such as Firefox.

We like these shareware anti-spyware programs, both of which we use:

- ✔ Spybot Search&Destroy, from `www.safer-networking.org`
- ✔ Ad-Aware, from Lavasoft at `www.lavasoftusa.com`

For both programs, download, install, and run them, being sure to download updates regularly.

The nuclear option

If you have installed and run anti-virus and anti-spyware programs and you still have problems, it may be too late for band-aid remedies. Your computer may be so thoroughly infested that you have no choice but to blow everything away and start over.

Before you reinstall Windows, you *must* get a firewall to protect your computer. The distributed versions of Windows are so insecure that you simply cannot install the program and all its security updates before you are reinfected with viruses and worms. (Installing and updating Windows and your application programs take a couple of hours. Infection takes perhaps 10 seconds.) The routers we mention in Chapter 5 that let you connect several computers to your Internet connection include adequate firewalls that are quite cheap. Even if you have only one computer, the $30 you'll spend for a router is well worth it.

Before you can reinstall Windows, be sure to make a copy of all your files. If you haven't been backing up regularly, make two copies just to be safe. Back up at least one copy to more reliable CD-Rs or DVD-Rs, rather than re-writable media. Make sure you have the install CDs and all the registration codes, license codes, and key codes for all the applications you use.

Before reinstalling Windows, you may want to get a copy of *Windows For Dummies,* by Andy Rathbone, (Wiley Publishing, Inc.) or *Windows XP Home Edition: The Complete Reference* by us, (Osborne/McGraw-Hill) — these books contain more details about how to reinstall Windows that we have room for here. You'll need the original CDs that came with your computer or a new copy of Windows XP or later. Put the Windows XP CD in your CD or DVD drive and reboot. Follow the instructions to where it asks if you want to rewrite or destroy all the information on your hard drive. You may need to select something like "Advanced options" to find this. Take a deep breath and say yes and yes to all the warnings that say all your files will be erased. They will — that's why we had you back them up — but they'll erase the worms, too.

When the reinstallation of Windows is complete, follow the on-screen instruction to re-enter your Internet settings. Then immediately go to `http://windowsupdate.microsoft.com` (which works only with Internet Explorer — sigh) and download all of the suggested updates to Windows, which will take quite a while. Load your anti-virus and anti-spyware software and get their latest updates. Then reinstall all your applications. Yes, this is a real pain.

Next, place your data backup CD in the CD drive and have your anti-virus program scan it. We recommend that you do not reinstall all your data files at first; just the ones you need to use. If you made two copies as we told you to, keep them in two different places, preferably in two different buildings.

Finally, create separate, password-protected accounts for everyone who will be using the computer and make them all "Limited" rather than "Administrator" accounts unless they have a good reason to be installing their own programs. Have a talk with everyone about the risks of free downloads and online game sites. Suggest that, should you have to repeat this process, their use of your computer will be terminated. This is not the kind of problem you want to keep dealing with, as you have no doubt concluded if you just had to rebuild your system.

The switcheroo

Plan B is to consider getting an Apple Macintosh computer, even if only for your e-mail and Web surfing. As of this writing, there aren't any serious online threats to Apple's Mac OS X. This could change, but at least Apple has a headstart over the hackers, instead of the other way around for Microsoft. You should still keep your Mac's operating system up to date and rebuild your PC if you still plan to use it. If you need certain programs for work, look for Mac equivalents or check out Virtual PC, which lets you run your Windows system and programs on your Mac.

This Nice Free Program Won't Run If I Turn Off the Ads

Lots of free programs are supported by advertising. That's the deal. You may be able to find equivalent programs that do not show ads, or you can pay to register the program and make the ads go away. Even if you are willing to trade ad-watching for free software, we do *not* recommend that you use any program that shows Web-based ads — *adware* — while other programs are running. (Ads that display in the program itself rather than in your browser, like Eudora and Opera are fine.) Adware companies swear up and down that it's not spyware and that they don't compile personal dossiers of all the Web sites you've visited to decide what ads to send to your computer, we don't trust them.

I Can't Send Large E-Mail Attachments

Some Internet service providers and some system administrators limit the size of files you can e-mail using their mail servers. In the case of problems at work, it may be as simple as talking to the person in charge of your Internet access and asking for the limit to be changed. Your ISP might not be so accommodating. We have another way to move giant files from point A to point B.

For local file transfer, *sneaker net* (transferring files by walking them from one computer to another) has made a comeback in the form of USB flash drives. Flash drives work with recent versions of all major operating systems. They operate like a removable disk drive but are about the size of your thumb (or smaller, especially if you have big thumbs) and have a shiny rectangular plug at one end. Some geeks carry one on a lanyard around their necks or on their key chains. To use one, just plug it into a USB port on your computer. For very large files (over a gigabyte), you can use an iPod as a portable USB hard drive. After you copy whatever files you want, you need to tell your operating system that you are done with the drive before you unplug it. Windows uses a tiny widget in the system tray that does this. On Macs, drag the disk's icon to the trash.

If your computer has a CD or DVD recorder, you can also burn your files on a CD or DVD to give to your friend. It's not as cute and compact as a USB drive, but it's more durable.

I'm Worried about ID Theft

The U.S. Federal Trade Commission (www.ftc.gov/idtheft) offers this advice to prevent identity theft: First, look out for *phishing*, e-mail that claims to come from a bank or other online account, such as eBay, and claims that there is a problem with your account that you can clean up by clicking a link in the message. These are never real, but they are very dangerous. If your bank thinks there's a security problem, it will not tell you by e-mail. If you are not sure, contact the company by phone or type its home page address (for example, www.*yourbank*.com) into your browser by hand and look for the customer service section. See Chapter 2 for more about phishing.

The Internet isn't the only source of information about you. Keep bills and other documents that bear your account and social security numbers in a safe place and tear up or shred old bank statements and credit card bills. Get a shredder that cross-cuts the paper into short strips rather than the cheaper shredders that make strips the length of the page; patient thieves can paste those together. Those offers for pre-approved credit cards are also a danger if they fall into the wrong hands. Shred them or stop them altogether by calling 1-888-5OPTOUT or visiting www.optoutprescreen.com. If your driver's license still has your social security number on it, get a new license issued.

Get in the habit of scanning your bank and credit card statements when they arrive (or even earlier, online). Don't worry about the bank's arithmetic, but look for charges that you don't remember incurring. If you find any, contact your bank or credit card company immediately. After you have verified fraudulent charges, tell the bank you want new accounts with new credit card numbers. You may need to file a police report, although in our experience, if you have fraudulent charges, the bank will issue new cards without hassle.

I Can't Remember All My Web Site Passwords

The standard advice is to construct passwords out of a mixture of letters, numbers, and special symbols; to have a different password for each account; to never write passwords down; and to change them every few months. Most Internet users who have dozens of accounts ignore this advice because one would have to be a truly unusual person to be able to remember dozens of different random passwords and what account each one goes with.

We suggest a compromise. Make up one good password to use on all your low-risk accounts — accounts in which letting someone else gain access has little consequence, such as online newspaper subscriptions. Use different passwords for the accounts that really matter, such as online banking. If you feel it is necessary, writing those passwords down and keeping them in a safe place is better than picking a password that is easy for someone to guess. Don't list your passwords in your desktop Rolodex or on a sticky note stuck to your computer's monitor.

There are some decent programs for safely storing passwords on personal digital assistants. We like the free, open-source *Keyring* for PalmOS PDAs and cell phones, available at http://gnukeyring.sourceforge.net. Be sure to pick a really strong master password and have a backup plan for when your PDA falls into the bathtub and dies. (Ink on paper has stood the test of time.)

I Get Messages Telling Me E-Mail That I Never Sent Is Undeliverable

There is not much you can do about this after it's happened. Many computer viruses spread by taking over someone's computer and sending copies of themselves to everyone in that computer's address book. The virus uses addresses it finds in the computer's address book as fake return addresses to keep attention away from the infected computer. Most spammers use computers that have been taken over in this way to send spam, again using address book entries or other entries on their list of spammees. Make sure your computer is not the source of such unwanted messages by keeping its operating system and antivirus software up to date, using a router as your firewall (see Chapter 5), and by turning the computer (or at least its connection to the Internet) off when not in use.

People Seem to Know a Lot about Me

The rate at which we are all losing our privacy scares us, too. Here are a few tips:

Get rid of spyware that may be lurking on your machine

Spyware does just what it sounds like — it spies on you and your activities. You think your Internet activities are private, but unless you keep your PC spyware-free, they're not. Browse one mortgage lender site and you'll hear from the universe of mortgage lenders. Buy from one pharmacy and you'll get solicitations for drugs you didn't even know existed from everyone else. Your Inbox is full of names that closely resemble people you actually know — but not quite. If all this sounds familiar, chances are, software is recording your every keystroke. Get rid of it! (The software, not the keyboard.) When we use Internet Explorer (some folks still have Web sites that work only with IE) we often have to clean our machines, since worms and viruses often sneak through security holes in IE. Because IE is so widely used, it's targeted by hackers all over the world, which is why we use Firefox instead (see Chapter 6).

Don't be dumb

Don't put information on your Web page that you don't want everyone in the world to know. In particular, don't include your home address and phone number unless you want calls and visits. We know at least one person who received an unexpected phone call from someone she met on the Net and wasn't too pleased about it. Why would Net users need this information, anyway? They can send you e-mail!

Don't order stuff from a public PC

Normally, ordering stuff over the Web or by e-mail is perfectly safe — at least as safe as handing your credit card to a waiter you've never met! However, some shopping sites store information about you (including a link to your mailing address and payment info) in a file on your computer. This works perfectly when you are ordering from your own computer — you don't have to type all that info when you visit the site the next time you order. But when you order stuff at the library or at a cybercafé, this personal information may be stored on that computer. This means that the next person who uses that computer and goes to that site has all your personal data available and may be able to place an order using it. Better not chance it.

I Can't Get My Kids, Spouse, or Significant Other Off the Computer

Games and instant messaging are highly addictive and seem to be getting more so. Microsoft's Steve Balmer brags about the addictive nature of the games his company sells and smiles as he says he wouldn't let *his* kid play them. That ought to clue you in.

Set clear limits on computer usage and stick to them. Some network routers have features built in that allow you to set time limits that the router enforces. You may have to read the manual. We also suggest you have a talk with your spouse or significant other about what kinds of online chatting are okay and what aren't. Also think about how much time *you* are spending in front of a computer screen. Use some of your Internet time to make a list of outside activities you enjoy and stick it next to your computer screen. Promise yourself you'll do at least one fun off-computer activity every day. Internet addiction is serious — you may need professional help to quit the habit.

On the other hand, if it's your spouse, sometimes it makes more sense to squander $500 on a second computer (see Chapter 5 for hints on connecting them both to the Net) than to squander your marriage.

When I Click a Link, My Browser Says "404 Page Not Found"

Web pages move about or disappear on the Internet. If you type a URL from a printed source, make sure that you type it exactly as it was printed, including capitalization and the funny tilde (~) character; but watch out for the hyphen at the end of a printed line. That hyphen may or may not be part of the URL.

If you clicked a hypertext link or you're sure that you typed the URL correctly and you still get this error message, the data on the site may have been reorganized. Try "walking up" the URL by deleting the portion to the right of the last slash character and trying again; then delete the portion after next-to-last slash character; and so on. If you get a File Not Found message when you try entering this, for example:

```
www.fliberty.com/~smith/recipes/cookies/chocolatechip.htm
```

try these in order:

```
www.fliberty.com/~smith/recipes/cookies
www.fliberty.com/~smith/recipes
www.fliberty.com/~smith
www.fliberty.com/
```

At one of these levels, you may find a hint about where the file you seek can be found. Alternatively, go to your favorite search engine and search for it.

A page long gone may still be found at www.archive.org, a free site that has attempted the daunting task of periodically saving snapshots of the World Wide Web.

I Want to Include My E-Mail Address on My Web Page

Including your e-mail address in a Web page is a sure way to attract spam. Spammers have programs that crawl the Web looking for e-mail addresses to spam. You can thwart them by *describing* your e-mail address rather than just typing it out — "It's `al` at `blahblah.com`" — or use obscure HTML coding on the Web page. At the least, we suggest you set up a separate e-mail address for your Web site at a free site such as `hotmail.com` or `yahoo.com`. If the flood of unwanted mail becomes too great, you can abandon that account and set up a new one.

One useful trick is to ask Web site visitors to include some special word in the subject line of their messages. For example, if your Web page is about belt buckle collecting, you could ask correspondents to include "buckles" in the subject line. You can use an e-mail filter to put just the messages that contain that word into a special folder and send the rest of the messages to the trash.

Chapter 20

Ten Kinds of Files and What to Do with Them

*I*f you've been surfing the Web for a while, you probably have already retrieved zillions of files (or maybe three or four). If not, take a look at Chapter 12 to find out how easy downloading is. When you try to open a downloaded file with your word processor or text editor, however, they may be unintelligible. Different kinds of files need to be opened by different programs. In this chapter, we describe some of the types of files on the Internet and how to tell what they are and what to do with them.

How Many Kinds of Files Are There?

Hundreds of kinds of files exist, maybe thousands. Fortunately, they fall into these general categories:

✔ **Plain text:** Files that contain text, believe it or not, with no formatting codes at all.

✔ **Executable:** Files you can execute, or run; in other words, programs.

✔ **Compressed:** Archives, ZIP files, SIT files, and other compressed files.

> ✔ **Graphics, audio, and video:** Files that contain pictures and sounds encoded in computer-readable form. Graphics files on Web pages are usually in GIF or JPEG format. Audio files can be in WAV (Windows audio), RAM (RealAudio), MP3 (music), WMA (Windows Media Player), or other formats. Video files contain digitized movies, in AVI, WMV, or MPEG format.
>
> ✔ **Data:** Any other type of file. Microsoft Word document files (DOC files) and Portable Document Format (PDF) files are especially popular.

This chapter describes these categories in more detail.

The name of a file — in particular, its *extension* (the end of the name after the last period) — usually gives you a clue about the type of file it is. Although people usually try to be consistent and follow the conventions for filename extensions, file naming isn't a sure thing. In the old days of DOS, filenames usually had a three-letter extension at the end, and the period could be used only to separate the extension from the main filename. Because UNIX, Linux, and current versions of Windows allow the period character to be any part of the filename, hard rules about extensions no longer exist. Nevertheless, old habits cling, and computer people still use conventional extensions to help give files names that convey something about their content. Windows uses the extension to tell what program to use to open a file, so you may sometimes have to rename a file to an extension that will persuade Windows to use the right program. For example, if you double-click a file with the extension DOC, Windows runs Microsoft Word or WordPad (which are both associated with the DOC file extension) to open the file. If you rename a Word document to end with the extension GIF, Windows no longer knows that the file contains a document.

TIP

Stick a fork in it, Mac

Macintosh files, regardless of what's in them, usually come in two or three chunks, one of which is the data file. Although you don't see the chunks on your own Macintosh, you do see them if you try to upload them to a non-Mac server on the Net. In the Macintosh world, the three files are all pieces of one file and are referred to as *forks* — the data fork, the resource fork, and the information fork. When you upload from a Macintosh what you think is one file, it often appears as three separate files with the extensions DATA, RESC, and INFO appended to the filename. Various schemes exist (we describe them in the section "Packing It In" later in this chapter) to glue the forks back together for transportation over the Net.

The Macintosh operating system uses a hidden, four-letter file type to know what program it should run to read a particular file, but you can tell it about Windows extensions by using the File Exchange control panel.

Files attached to e-mail messages don't have to use the right extensions, so a file attached to incoming e-mail could possibly have a GIF or JPG extension that looks like a harmless image, but contains something else, like a virus. If you get an attached file you aren't expecting, treat it with great skepticism — don't open it or run it until you check with the person who sent you the file. (If you don't use Windows, though, you can pretty much ignore this warning, since most viruses run only on Windows machines.)

Just Plain Text

Text files contain readable text without any word-processor-style formatting codes. (What did you expect?) Sometimes, the text is human-readable text, such as the manuscript for the first edition of this book, which we typed into text files. Sometimes, the text is source code for computer programs in languages such as PHP or Visual Basic for Applications (VBA). Occasionally, the text is data for programs. On PCs, text files usually have the file extension .txt (or no extension at all). You can look at these files by using Notepad, WordPad, or any word processor. Mac text files also often have the TXT file type. Read text files on a Macintosh with SimpleText, BBEdit Lite, or any word processor.

Many programs use *Unicode,* a way to store text with non-English characters on a computer. Although standard (ASCII) character codes allow only 94 different characters (which is plenty considering that the English alphabet has only 26 letters), Unicode can represent over 65,000 different characters and tries to cover all the writing systems in use in the world today, including Chinese, Japanese, and Korean ideographs.

Formatted text documents are frequently stored in Microsoft Word (DOC) or Rich Text Format (RTF) format; see the section "None of the Above Files," later in this chapter.

Any Last Requests Before We Execute You?

Executable files are actual programs you can run on a computer. Executable programs are widely available for downloading for PCs and Macs. Executable files are not compatible with all operating systems: A Mac executable file is useless on a Windows machine and vice versa. (Unless, that is, you have purchased and installed Virtual PC on your Mac, which allows the Mac to run Windows executable files; see www.microsoft.com/mac for information).

The most common executable programs are for Windows. These files have the file extension .exe. You run them in the same way as you run any other Windows program: Double-click its filename in My Computer or Windows Explorer.

Some chance always exists that any new PC or Mac program may be infected with a computer virus. (Because of the different ways in which the systems work, UNIX or Linux programs are much less likely to carry viruses.) Programs from well-run software archives are unlikely to be infected; but if you run an unknown program from a sleazy source, you deserve whatever you get.

If you receive an executable file that you weren't expecting by e-mail, even if it appears to be from someone you know, *don't run it.* First, check with the person to make sure that he or she actually sent it. The program is probably a virus that your unsuspecting friend's computer sent to everyone in his or her e-mail address book.

See Chapter 12 for the full scoop on downloading and running programs from the Internet.

Packing It In

Many software packages require a bunch of related files. To make it easier to send such a package around, you can glom the files together into a single file known as an *archive.* After you retrieve an archive, you use an *unarchiving program* to extract the original files.

Some files are also *compressed,* which means that they're encoded in a special way that takes up less space but that can be decoded only by the corresponding *uncompressor.* Many files that you receive or download over the Internet are compressed to take less transfer time (fewer bytes equal fewer seconds to wait). In the PC world, archiving and compression usually happen together by using utilities such as WinZip or Windows XP's compressed folders to create *ZIP files.* In the Mac world, the StuffIt program is popular. In the Linux and UNIX world, however, the two procedures — compression and archiving — are usually done separately: The programs *pax, tar,* and *cpio* do the archiving, and the programs *bzip2* and *gzip* do the compressing.

ZIPping it up

The most widely used compression and archiving program for Windows is the shareware program WinZip. Zipped files (or ZIP files) all end with the extension .zip. Here are programs you can use to create ZIP files that contain one or more files, or get files out of ZIP files:

✔ Windows Me and XP come with built-in zipping and unzipping — they call ZIP files *compressed folders*. Just click the ZIP file's name in My Computer or Windows Explorer.

✔ Windows users with versions other than Me or XP can use the excellent shareware WinZip program, which we mention in Chapter 12. It not only handles ZIP files but also knows how to extract the contents of most of the other types of compressed files you run into on the Net. You can download it from www.winzip.com.

✔ Mac users can download a shareware program called ZipIt from www.maczipit.com.

✔ Compatible UNIX/Linux zipping and unzipping programs called *zip* and *unzip* (the authors are creative programmers but not creative namers) are included with most Linux and BSD packages. The Free Software Foundation, which runs the GNU free software project, offers *gzip*. Files that are gzipped use the filename extension .gz and can also be decompressed by WinZip.

Many ZIP files you encounter on the Net are *self-extracting,* which means that the ZIP file is packaged with an unzipping program; even if you don't already have an unzipper, you just run the archive, and it extracts its own contents. (WinZip is distributed in this way.) Because self-extracting archives are programs, they have the extension .exe rather than .zip. Prudent people will note that just because a program purports to be a self-extracting archive doesn't mean that it really is. Even if we trust the source of the file, we prefer to open it with WinZip and let it tell us what's really inside.

Just StuffIt!

The favorite Macintosh compression and archiving program is a shareware program written by Raymond Lau and known as StuffIt. StuffIt comes in many flavors, including a commercially available version called StuffIt Deluxe. StuffIt files of all varieties generally use the filename extension .sit.

For decompression, you can use the shareware programs StuffIt, or DropStuff, widely available for Macs. Some people also like MindExpander, another unarchiving program. You can download these shareware programs from www.tucows.com.

Other archivers

Dozens of other compressing archivers have come and gone over the years, with names such as Compress, tar, LHARC, ZOO, and ARC. Windows and Mac users can find unarchivers for all of them in shareware repositories such as www.download.com and www.shareware.com. The only other archiver that's widely used is the Japanese LHA because it compresses well and is free.

For the Artistically Inclined

A large fraction of all the bits flying around the Internet is made up of high-quality digitized pictures. About 99.44 percent of the pictures are purely for fun, games, and worse. We're sure that you're in the 0.56 percent of users who need the pictures for work, so here's a roundup of picture formats.

The most commonly used graphics formats on the Net are GIF, JPEG, and PNG. A nice feature of these file formats is that they do a pretty fair job of compression internally, as if they were prezipped.

I could GIF a. . . .

The most widely used format on the Internet is the CompuServe *GIF* (Graphics Interchange Format). Two versions of GIF exist: *GIF87* and *GIF89*. The differences are small enough that almost every program that can read GIF can read either version equally well. Because GIF is well standardized, you never have problems with files written by one program being unreadable by another. GIF files have the extension .gif. GIF does a good job of storing images with limited numbers of colors and blocks of solid color, such as screen icons and cartoon-style pictures.

Dozens of commercial and shareware programs on PCs and Macs can read and write GIF files. Firefox and Internet Explorer can display them as well; just choose File➪Open from the menu. The buttons and little pictures on Web pages are usually stored as GIF files, too.

PNG-a-ding

GIF files use a patented compression method, and until the patent expired, Unisys collected royalties from CompuServe and anyone else it could find who sold software that used its patented technique. As a result, a group of Net graphics users came up with a patent-free replacement for GIF called PNG (with the extension .png, pronounced *ping*). We expected to see GIF fade away eventually and PNG replace it, but it didn't happen, and in the mean-time, the GIF patent expired. PNG handles the same kinds of images that GIF does, and most programs that can handle GIF can read PNG, too.

JPEG's great for photos

A few years back, a bunch of digital photography experts got together and decided that a.) It was time to have an official standard format for digitized photographs and b.) None of the existing formats was good enough. They formed the *Joint Photographic Experts Group (JPEG),* and after extended negotiation, the JPEG format was born. JPEG is designed specifically to store digitized, full-color, or black-and-white photographs, not computer-generated cartoons or anything else. As a result, JPEG does a fantastic job of storing photos and a lousy job of storing other types of graphics.

A JPEG version of a photo is about one-fourth the size of its corresponding GIF file. (JPEG files can be *any* size because the format allows a trade-off between size and quality when the file is created.) The main disadvantage of JPEG is that it's considerably slower to decode than GIF; the files are so much smaller, however, that JPEG is worth the time. Most programs that can display GIF files, including Firefox and Internet Explorer, now also handle JPEG. JPEG files usually have filenames with the extension `.jpeg` or `.jpg`.

Some people occasionally claim that JPEG pictures don't look anywhere near as good as GIF pictures do. What is true is that if you make a 256-color GIF file from a full-color photograph and then translate that GIF file into a JPEG file, it doesn't look good. So don't do that. For the finest in photographic quality, demand full-color JPEGs.

Let a hundred formats blossom

Many other graphics-file formats are in use, although GIF and JPEG are by far the most popular ones on the Internet. Other formats you might run into include

- **PCX:** Many paint programs use this format (with extension `.pcx`). It's also okay for low-resolution photos.
- **TIFF:** This format (with extension `.tiff` or `.tif`) is used by professional photographers and commercial printers. It has hundreds of options — so many that a TIFF file written by one program sometimes can't be read by another.
- **PICT:** This format (with extension `.pict`) is common on Macintoshes because the Mac has built-in support for it.
- **BMP:** This Windows bitmap format (with extension `.bmp`) isn't used much on the Net because BMP files tend to be larger than the equivalent GIF or TIFF.

A few words from the vice squad

We bet that you're wondering whether any free Web sites contain, er, exotic photography, but you're too embarrassed to ask. Well, the answer is yes.

In the early days of the Web, the companies and universities that funded most of the free public sites on the Internet weren't interested in being accused of being pornographers or in filling up their expensive hard drives with pictures that had nothing to do with any legitimate work. (At one university archive, when the *Playboy* pictures went away, they were replaced by a note that said that if you could explain why you needed them for your academic research, they would be put back.) But in the late 1990s, a lot of low-budget entrepreneurs realized that the only thing they needed to turn boring pictures into exotic pictures is fewer clothes. A remarkable number of people seem willing to pay to look at that kind of stuff, and online porn boomed.

Now plenty of sites on the Web *do* show you porn if you give them a credit card number to prove you're of age and to pay for it, and a surprising number show you porn just for the clicking. We're cheap, so we've never looked to see what the pay sites offer. They usually have a few screens of free preview pictures that can be pretty raunchy.

Sound Off!

Audio files — files that contain digitized sound — can be found all over the Web. If you like to listen to National Public Radio news, for example, but can't get around to listening when it's on, you can listen to major news stories from the NPR Web page (at www.npr.org) at any time — totally cool. Many radio stations now let you listen to the station via their Web sites, too. Or, you can download songs from the Web (at modest cost) and play them either on your computer or after downloading the songs to a portable player.

For all kinds of music on the Web, see Chapter 9. The section "What Are You Listening With?" lists the most common audio file types and what programs play each one.

A Trip to the Movies

As networks get faster and hard drives get bigger, people are starting to store entire digitized movies (usually rather short ones, at this point). With faster Internet connections, you can download video clips or watch *streaming video* (video files that start playing on your computer while the rest of the file is still downloading). If you are willing to plan ahead a few hours, you can download entire movies and watch them on your computer.

See Chapter 9 for how to find, download, and play video from the Web. The section "Movies on the Net" lists common video formats and the programs that play them.

Animation in a Flash

Macromedia's Shockwave Flash started out as a way to store little animated cartoons but has evolved into an extremely powerful way to build all sorts of screen-oriented applications. For example, John's bank offers a spiffy little program that creates and manages single-use credit card numbers written entirely in Flash.

The usual way to run a Flash animation is inside a Web browser, and all current Windows and Mac Web browsers come with a Flash player already set up. (If you use UNIX or Linux, you have to set it up yourself.) When you visit a Web page and it shows a little movie, it's probably written in Flash. See, for example, the flying piggy banks at www.voegol.com.br.

You can also download Flash movies and save them to run later. The files end with .swf.

None of the Above Files

Some files don't fit any of the descriptions in this chapter. Here are few other categories of files that you might download:

- **Document files:** You occasionally find formatted word processor files used with programs such as WordPerfect (extension .wpd), Microsoft Word (extension .doc), or OpenOffice Writer (extension .sxw), as well as the older Rich Text Format (extension .rtf). If you encounter one of these files and don't have the matching word processor program, you can usually load the file into a text editor, in which you see the text in the file intermingled with nonprinting junk that represents formatting information. In a pinch, you can edit out the junk to recover the text. But before you resort to that method, try loading the file with whatever word processor you have. Most word processing software can recognize a competitor's format and make a valiant effort to convert the format to something usable so that you aren't tempted to buy the other product.

  For the particular case of Microsoft Word, Windows comes with a program called WordPad that can open many Word documents, and Microsoft offers a free Word Viewer that can display and print Word files. Go to office.microsoft.com/downloads and search for "viewer."

✔ **Portable Document Format (PDF) files:** Another common way to send formatted documents over the Internet is Adobe's Portable Document Format (PDF), with extension `.pdf`. PDF is a proprietary format, and you need a program if you want to *create* PDF files. The program that displays and prints PDF files is free and is included with most new Macs and PCs. It's called Acrobat Reader, and you can download the latest version for PC, Linux, or Mac from `www.adobe.com/products/acrobat`. Several free or cheap PDF creators are now available; we recommend Pdf995, at `www.pdf995.com`.

✔ **Spreadsheet files:** Microsoft Excel saves spreadsheets with the extension `.xls`. OpenOffice Calc spreadsheets have the extension `.sxc`. You can open an Excel spreadsheet with OpenOffice, but not vice versa.

✔ **Database files:** Microsoft Access is the database program that comes with Microsoft Office, and it stores its database in files with the extension `.mdb`. These files can be big and they can contain viruses, since Access databases can contain VBA programs. No other program can open these files (that we know of).

✔ **Presentation files:** PowerPoint is the presentation program that comes with Microsoft office, and its files have the extension `.ppt`. OpenOffice Impress presentation files have the extension `.sxi`. OpenOffice can open PowerPoint files, but not vice versa.

✔ **Web pages:** Web pages have the extension `.html` or `.htm`. If they contain programming, they may have extensions like `.php`, `.asp`, or `.aspx`. You can open HTML and HTM files in your Web browser. PHP, ASP, and ASPX files need to live on a Web server that can run the scripts that these pages contain.

If you run into another file extension, you can look it up at FILExt, at `www.filext.com`.

Chapter 21

Ten Fun Things You Can Do Online

In This Chapter

▶ Taking film-free pictures for family and friends

▶ Checking out short movies and TV advertisements

▶ Playing games and touring the solar system

▶ Taking a look at webcams, blogs, and art museums around the globe

▶ Exploring space, curing cancer, and finding a kid

Y ou can use the Internet in hundreds of ways for work and profit. In this chapter, we focus on fun. When you find new and fun things to do on the Net, let us know. Send e-mail to us at internet10@gurus.com.

Sharing Pictures with Your Friends and Family

E-mail attachments (see Chapter 15) are a great way to ship snapshots anywhere in the world for free. You don't even need a digital camera. Many film developing services will digitize your photos and deliver them to you online or on a CD-ROM (for a fee, of course). Other services, like Kodak's EasyShare Gallery (www.kodakgallery.com) will develop your pictures and let you organize them into albums on its Web site. You can point your friends to your album by giving them the URL, and they can view the pictures online and order prints of the ones they especially like.

Online photography is even simpler if you buy a digital camera. They have become more affordable, especially if you consider how much money you save on film and developing costs, and you can choose to print only the pictures you like. You can find out more about digital cameras and still digital photography at the following sites, all of which review digital cameras and equipment:

✔ **Digital Camera Resource Page:** www.dcresource.com

✔ **Digital Photography Review:** www.dpreview.com

✔ **Megapixel.net:** www.megapixel.net

Editing an Encyclopedia

Wikipedia (wikipedia.org) is not only a free encyclopedia, it lets you edit the articles. If there is a topic you feel knowledgeable about, look it up in Wikipedia. If you find mistakes or have more to say, just click the edit tab. If no article exists, Wikipedia will offer to let you create one. Stop by Wikipedia's Village Pump (at en.wikipedia.org/wiki/Village_pump) for more information on how to get started and work within the wiki culture. See Chapter 17 for more about how groups can edit a Web site communally using a wiki.

Watching Short Movies and TV Ads

The Internet has created a new way for makers of short and experimental movies to find an audience. Many sites feature miniflicks that you can watch for free. IFILM (ifilm.com) has a good selection. You can find a few movie sites at dmoz.org/Arts/Movies/Filmmaking/Online_Venues; click the subtopics listed. The quality of these films varies from dreadful to inspired to occasionally creepy, but you can find some real gems.

If for some reason you don't see as many ads on TV as you'd like, visit www.advertisementave.com, where you can catch up on all the ads you've missed. The excellent AdCritic (www.adcritic.com) also features the best current ads and classics, but now requires a paid subscription. Either way, now you can catch those great Super Bowl ads without the tedious football.

These film sites use a variety of video formats — QuickTime, RealMedia, and Windows Media Player — so you may have to download some plug-ins. A fast Internet connection helps a lot. If you're dialing in, particularly at a slow speed, skip the videos until you can get higher speed access. Check out Chapter 9 for more information about video formats and how to play them.

Listening to Current and Classic Radio Programs

Have you ever turned on your radio, found yourself in the middle of a fascinating story, and wished you could have heard the beginning? National Public Radio in the U.S. keeps many of its past programs available online. If you want to hear the whole program, visit www.npr.org. You can also use the site's search feature to browse for stories that you missed completely.

Many NPR affiliates and other radio stations have live streaming audio of their programs, so you can listen live to stations all over the country — go to Google and search for the station call letters or the program name. (John recommends his local station at wrvo.fm, especially the old shows from the 1930s through 1950s, which they play in the evening.) Many other radio stations now let you listen to their live programs over the Internet, which is particularly handy in large office buildings with poor radio reception. You can listen to stations from around the world and get a taste of world music first hand or hear the news from different perspectives.

Playing Checkers . . .

. . . or chess, poker, hearts, bridge, backgammon, cribbage, go, or any other board game or card game. The classic games hold up well against the ever-bloodier electronic games. Now you don't need to round up live friends to play with — you can find willing partners anytime, day or night, at sites like games.yahoo.com or zone.msn.com (Windows users only).

True bridge aficionados like to think of bridge not as a card game but as a way of life. You can round up a bridge foursome at www.bridgeclublive.com and www.okbridge.com. Each charges $99 per year after a free trial period. There are many free and fee sites listed at www.greatbridgelinks.com. MSN (zone.msn.com) also offers bridge; currently, it's free.

Watching the World Go By

Webcams are live video cameras that you can access over the Internet. They let you see what's happening right now — wherever that camera is pointing. Watch wildlife, events of the day, a city street, a shopping mall, a highway interchange, Slovakia, or even someone's living room. The views are generally updated every few seconds. Go to Online Camera at `www.onlinecamera.com`, WebCam.com at `www.webcam.com`, or `dmoz.org/Computers/Internet/On_the_Web/Webcams` — or just search on "webcams" at `www.google.com` or `www.yahoo.com`.

Shoo any children out of the room before you connect to a webcam site because you never know what you might see.

Journaling Online with Blogs

Posting your diary on the Internet may seem as bizarre as having a webcam in your bedroom, but many people do it and enjoy getting feedback from other diarists. Some people post a series of articles about topics other than their personal lives — for example, about politics, spirituality, or cats. These online journals are called *weblogs* (or just *blogs*), and they are covered in Chapter 18. Here are a few interesting blog sites:

- ✔ **Blogger** (`www.blogger.com`) used to be called BlogSpot and is now owned by Google.
- ✔ **LiveJournal** (`www.livejournal.com`) is one of the most popular blog sites.
- ✔ **DiaryLand** (`www.diaryland.com`), gives you a window into the mind of the young.

Some blog sites require you to register (for free) before you can read the articles.

Visiting Art Museums around the World

Art museums are great places to spend a rainy afternoon. Now you can visit museums and galleries all over the world via your browser. Not all museum Web sites have online art works, but many do. Our favorites include the Louvre in Paris (`www.louvre.fr`), Boston's Museum of Fine Arts (`www.mfa.org`), The Metropolitan Museum of Art in New York (`www.metmuseum.org`), and the State Hermitage Museum in Russia (`www.hermitagemuseum.org`). Check out the spectacular color photographs from Tsarist Russia by Sergei Prokudin-Gorskii, digitally reconstructed by the Library of Congress, at `www.loc.gov/exhibits/empire`. You can find a wide selection of other museums at `dir.yahoo.com/Arts/Museums__Galleries__and_Centers/`.

Building Your Own World

Virtual worlds are electronic places you can visit on the Web — kind of like 3-D chat rooms. Instead of a screen name, you create a personal action figure, called an *avatar*, that walks, talks, and emotes (but doesn't make a mess on your floor). When you are in one of these worlds, your avatar interacts with the avatars of other people who are logged on in surroundings that range from quite realistic to truly fantastic. In some virtual worlds, you can even build your own places: a room, a house, a park, a city — whatever you can imagine. Other worlds let you make money, gain status, and battle complete strangers. People who enjoy role-playing games can disappear into online games for hours, days, or months at a time.

Most virtual worlds require you to download a plug-in or special software. Some are free, most require a monthly or annual subscription.

Here are some places where you can enter or create virtual worlds:

- ✔ **Active Worlds** (www.activeworlds.com) enables you to create your own online world or visit other people's worlds.
- ✔ **Everquest** (eqlive.station.sony.com) is a world of monsters, cities, wilderness, creatures, and deities.
- ✔ **RuneScape** (www.runescape.com), is a medieval-style world.

Web-based online worlds are an outgrowth of *MUDs* (which stands for Multi-User Dimensions, Multi-User Dungeons, or various other names, depending on whom you ask), which were text-based virtual online worlds long before there was a Web.

Touring the Solar System

The last half of the 20th century will go down in history as the time when humans began to explore outer space. Probes visited several comets and asteroids and every planet but Pluto (for a song about planetary exploration, go to www.christinelavin.com/planetx.html). The probes sent back amazing pictures: storms on Jupiter, oceans on Europa, mudslides on Mars, and the Earth at night.

Which generation will actually get to play tourist in the solar system remains to be seen, but here are some great space sites:

✔ You can follow the adventures of the Mars Rovers at `marsrovers.jpl.nasa.gov`, and virtual tours are available now at sites such as `www.seds.org` and `sse.jpl.nasa.gov`.

✔ Be sure to bookmark the astronomy picture of the day at `antwrp.gsfc.nasa.gov/apod/astropix.html`.

✔ Above all, don't miss NASA's incredible montage of human civilization at `antwrp.gsfc.nasa.gov/apod/image/0011/earthlights_dmsp_big.jpg`.

Searching for Extraterrestrial Life or Curing Cancer

SETI@home (`setiweb.ssl.berkeley.edu`) is a scientific experiment that uses Internet-connected home and office computers to search for extraterrestrial intelligence (SETI). The idea is to have thousands of otherwise idle PCs and Macs perform the massive calculations needed to extract the radio signals of other civilizations from intergalactic noise. You can participate by running a free program that downloads and analyzes data collected at the Arecibo radio telescope in Puerto Rico.

If eavesdropping on space aliens seems a bit far out, you may enjoy lending your computer's idle time to solving problems in cryptography and mathematics. Distributed.net (`www.distributed.net`) manages several projects, some of which offer cash prizes to the person who finds the solution. (Feel free to join the Internet Gurus team there.) When you sign up to help a project at Distributed.net, you can run their program on your computer when the computer isn't otherwise occupied, and your donation of computer time helps achieve the goal of the project.

If math and cryptography don't ring your chimes, consider joining the Folding at Home project at `folding.stanford.edu`. This project studies how proteins get their three-dimensional shapes, an important question in medical research. By signing up to run their program, you are helping with basic research that may help find a cure for "Alzheimer's, Mad Cow (BSE), CJD, ALS, Huntington's, Parkinson's disease, and many cancers and cancer-related syndromes" (according to the Web site).

Adopting a Kid

Do you surf the Web for hours each day? Maybe your life needs more meaning. Adopting a kid is more of a commitment than upgrading to the latest Microsoft operating system, but at least kids grow up eventually, and they usually get fewer viruses. Here are two excellent Web sites that list special children in need of homes: www.rainbowkids.com and www.capbook.org. It can't hurt to look.

Glossary

404 Not Found: An error message your Web browser frequently displays when it can't find the page you requested. Caused by mistyping a URL (your fault) or clicking a broken link (not your fault).

address: Internet users encounter two important types of addresses: e-mail addresses (for sending e-mail to someone; e-mail addresses almost always contain an @ symbol) and Web page addresses (more properly called *URLs*).

AIM (AOL Instant Messenger): A free instant messaging program that non-AOL users can use to chat with each other and with AOL users.

America Online (AOL): A value-added, online service that provides many services in addition to Internet access, including access to popular chat groups. Go to www.aol.com for more information.

applet: A small computer program written in the Java programming language. You can download applets by using a Web browser. Applets run in a special way that makes it difficult for them to do damage to your computer.

archive: A single file containing a group of files that have been compressed and glommed together for efficient storage. You have to use a program such as WinZip, PKZIP, tar, or StuffIt to get the original files back out.

attachment: A computer file electronically stapled to an e-mail message and sent along with it.

BCC (blind carbon copy): BCC addressees get a copy of your e-mail without other recipients knowing about it. *See also* CC.

binary file: A file that contains information other than text. A binary file might contain an archive, a picture, sounds, a spreadsheet, or a word processing document that includes formatting codes in addition to text characters.

bit: The smallest unit of measurement for computer data. Bits can be *on* or *off* (symbolized by 1 or 0, respectively) and are used in various combinations to represent different types of information.

bitmap: Little dots put together in a grid to make a picture.

BitTorrent: A method for transmitting large files over the Internet that spreads the load among many cooperating computers.

biz: When these letters appear as the last part of an address (such as `example.biz`), it indicates that the host computer is run by a commercial organization that couldn't get the `.com` address it really wanted.

blog: Short for Web log, which is a personal diary on the Internet. Any fool can publish a blog, and many fools do.

bookmark: The address of a Web page to which you may want to return, stored in your browser. Firefox lets you maintain a list of bookmarks to make it easy to go back to your favorite Web pages. Also called *favorites*.

bounced: Returned as undeliverable, used to describe e-mail. If you e-mail a message to a bad address, it bounces back to your mailbox.

bps (bits per second): A measure of how fast data is transmitted. Often used to describe modem speed.

broadband: A fast, permanent connection to the Internet, such as one provided via DSL or a cable modem. *See also* DSL.

browser: A program that lets you read information on the Web. Some all-singing, all-dancing browsers can do e-mail and other things, too.

byte: A group of eight bits, enough to represent a character. Computer memory and disk space are usually measured in bytes.

cable modem: A box that connects your computer to your cable TV company's wiring. Needed for a cable Internet account.

CC (carbon copy): CC addressees get a copy of your e-mail, and other recipients are informed of it if they bother to read the message header. *See also* BCC.

chat: To talk (or type) live to other network users from any and all parts of the world. To chat on the Internet, you use an instant message program (like AOL Instant Messenger, Yahoo Messenger, or Windows Messenger) or an Internet Relay Chat (IRC) program like mIRC.

client: A computer that uses the services of another computer or a server (such as e-mail, FTP, or the Web). If you dial in to another system, your computer becomes a client of the system you dial in to (unless you're using X Windows — don't ask). *See also* server.

com: When these letters appear as the last part of an address (in `net.gurus.com`, for example), they indicate that the host computer is run by a commercial organization.

cookie: A small text file stored on your computer by a Web site you have visited; used to remind that site about you the next time you visit it.

country code: The last part of a geographic address, which indicates the country where the host computer is located, such as us for the United States. Country codes are always two letters.

default: Information that a program uses unless you specify otherwise.

DES (Data Encryption Standard): A U.S. government standard for encrypting unclassified data. Breakable at some expense, although a newer version, triple-DES, is probably safe. AES is preferred.

DHCP (Dynamic Host Configuration Protocol): A system that assigns IP addresses for a local area network (LAN) or a broadband system that doesn't require individual logins. *See also* PPPoE.

dial-up connection or dial-up networking: The built-in Internet communication program in Windows that connects via an ordinary telephone line.

digest: A compilation of the messages that have been posted to a mailing list recently.

domain: Part of the official name of a computer on the Internet — for example, gurus.com. Microsoft also calls groups of computers on a LAN controlled by a Windows server a *domain*.

domain name server (DNS): A computer on the Internet that translates between Internet domain names, such as xuxa.iecc.com, and numeric IP addresses, such as 208.31.42.42. Sometimes just called a *name server*.

download: To copy a file from a remote computer "down" to your computer.

DRM (Digital Rights Management): Technology that attempts to restrict what you can do with material you find on the Internet.

DSL (Digital Subscriber Line): A technology that lets you transmit data over phone lines at high speed, as much as 7 million bps. Nice if you can get it — ask your phone company.

DSL modem: A box that connects your computer to a DSL line.

dummies: People who don't know everything but are smart enough to seek help. Used ironically.

eBay: The original and most successful Web-based auction site, at www.ebay.com.

edu: When these letters appear as the last part of an address (in www.middle bury.edu, for example), they indicate that the host computer is run by an educational institution, usually a college or university.

e-mail: Electronic messages sent via the Internet.

emoticon: A combination of punctuation or punctuation and letters intended to communicate emotion on the part of the writer, especially in e-mail, chat, or instant messages. Emoticons include smileys (see later in this glossary) and combinations like <g> for "grin."

Ethernet: The most popular kind of LAN. Comes in several varieties, the most common of which run over cables at 10 or 100 million bps.

Eudora: A popular e-mail program that runs on Windows and Macs. You can find it on the Web at www.eudora.com.

FAQ (Frequently Asked Questions): An article that answers questions that come up often. Many mailing lists and Usenet newsgroups have FAQs that are posted regularly. To read the FAQs for all newsgroups, go to www.faqs.org.

favorites: A list of files or Web pages you plan to use frequently. Internet Explorer lets you maintain a list of your favorite items to make it easy to see them again. Same idea as *bookmarks*.

Firefox: A popular, free browser from the Mozilla foundation that competes with Internet Explorer and has fewer safety issues.

firewall: Security software, often running in a router or a user's computer, that connects a local network to the Internet and, for security reasons, lets only certain kinds of messages in and out.

flame: To post angry, inflammatory, or insulting messages. Don't do it! Too much flaming between two or more individuals is called a *flame war*.

Flash: *See* Shockwave Flash.

FTP (File Transfer Protocol): A method of transferring files from one computer to the other over the Net.

GIF (Graphics Interchange Format): A patented type of graphics file originally defined by CompuServe and now found all over the Net. Files in this format end in .gif and are called *GIF files* or just *GIFs*. Pronounced *jif* unless you prefer to say *gif*.

giga-: A prefix meaning one billion (1,000,000,000).

Google: A search engine used for finding things on the Web, with extra smarts to look for the most useful pages. On the Web at `www.google.com`.

gov: When these letters appear as the last part of an address (in `cu.nih.gov`, for example), they indicate that the host computer is run by some government body in the United States, probably the federal government.

header: The beginning of an e-mail message containing To and From addresses, subject, date, and other gobbledygook important to the programs that handle your mail.

home page: The entry page, or main page, of a Web site. If you have a home page, it's the main page about you. A home page usually contains links to other Web pages.

hostname: The name of a computer (or "host") on the Internet (`net.gurus.com`, for example).

HTML (HyperText Markup Language): The language used to write pages for the Web. This language lets the text include codes that define fonts, layout, embedded graphics, and hypertext links. Web pages are stored in files that usually have the extension `.htm` or `.html`. Don't worry — you don't have to know anything about HTML to use the Web.

HTML mail: E-mail messages formatted with HTML codes. Not all e-mail programs can properly display them.

HTTP (HyperText Transfer Protocol): The way in which Web pages are transferred over the Net. URLs for Web pages start with `http://`, although you almost never have to type it.

HTTPS: A variant of HTTP that encrypts data for security.

hypertext: A system of writing and displaying text that enables the text to contain *links* to related documents. Hypermedia extends the concept to images and audio. The Web uses both hypertext and hypermedia.

IM (instant message): A message sent from one person to another that appears immediately on the recipient's computer, allowing a text conversation.

IMAP (Internet Message Access Protocol): One method used for storing and delivering Internet e-mail.

Internet: All the computers that are connected together into an amazingly huge global network so that they can talk to each other. When you connect your puny little computer to your Internet service provider, your computer becomes part of that network.

Internet Connection Sharing (ICS): Windows feature that allows a computer to share its Internet connection with other computers on a LAN.

Internet Explorer: A Web browser vigorously promoted by Microsoft that comes in Windows, and (arguably) UNIX flavors. The Mac version is no longer being upgraded. *See also* Firefox, Opera, *and* Safari.

Internet Relay Chat (IRC): A system that enables Internet folks to talk to each other in real time (rather than after a delay, as with e-mail messages).

intranet: A private version of the Internet that lets people within an organization exchange data by using popular Internet tools, such as browsers.

IP (Internet Protocol): The scheme used to route packets of data through the Net, often used with TCP as TCP/IP. A newer version, IPv6, allows many more addresses. *See also* TCP.

IP address: A four-part number, such as 208.31.42.252, that identifies a host on the Internet.

iPod: Apple's line of personal music players.

ISP (Internet Service Provider): The folks who bring the Internet to you — via dial-up, DSL, or cable modem, including folks like AOL, Comcast, and MSN.

iTunes: Apple's music software and online music store.

Java: A computer language invented by Sun Microsystems. Because Java programs can run on many different kinds of computers, and most Web browsers can run chunks of Java code called *applets,* Java makes it easier to deliver application programs over the Internet. JavaScript is a different language that also is widely used on Web pages.

JPEG: A type of still-image file found all over the Net. Files in this format end in `.jpg` or `.jpeg` and are called *JPEG* (pronounced *jay-peg*) files. Stands for Joint Photographic Experts Group.

K, KB, or Kbyte: 1,024 bytes, kilobyte. Usually used as a measure of a computer's memory or hard drive storage, or as a measure of file size.

Kazaa: Internet-based file-sharing service often used to swap MP3 files.

kilo-: Prefix meaning one thousand (1,000) or often, with computers, 1,024.

LAN (local area network): Computers in one building or campus connected by cables so they can share files, printers, or an Internet connection.

link: A hypertext connection that can take you to another document or another part of the same document. On the Web, links appear as highlighted text or pictures. To follow a link, you click the highlighted material.

Linux: A version of UNIX; an operating system that runs on a wide variety of computers, including PCs. Many Internet servers run UNIX or Linux.

list server: An e-mail mailing list management program; a program that maintains a subscriber list and distributes list postings to those subscribers. Common list servers include ListProc, LISTSERV, and Majordomo. The names of mailing lists maintained by LISTSERV often end with -L.

lurk: To read a mailing list or chat group without posting any messages. Someone who lurks is a *lurker.* Lurking is okay and is much better than flaming.

MacBinary: A file-encoding system that's popular among Macintosh users.

mailbombing: Sending someone vast amounts of unwanted e-mail. *See also* remote mailbombing.

mailbot: A program that automatically sends or answers e-mail.

mailbox: A file on your incoming (POP or IMAP) mail server where your e-mail messages are stored until you download them to your e-mail program. Some e-mail programs also call the files in which you store messages *mailboxes.*

mailing list: A special type of e-mail address that remails all incoming mail to a list of subscribers to the mailing list. Each mailing list has a specific topic, so you subscribe to the ones that interest you. Often managed by using LIST-SERV, Majordomo, Mailman, or another list server program.

mega-: Prefix meaning one million (1,000,000).

mil: When these letters appear as the last part of an Internet address or domain name, they indicate that the host computer is run by some part of the U.S. military.

MIME (Multipurpose Internet Mail Extension): The scheme used to send pictures, word-processing files, and other nontext information through e-mail.

mirror: An FTP or Web server that provides copies of the same files as another server. Mirrors spread out the load for more popular FTP and Web sites.

modem: A gizmo that lets your computer talk on the phone or cable TV. Short for *mo*dulator/*dem*odulator.

moderator: The person who looks at the messages posted to a mailing list, newsgroup, or chat forum. The moderator can nix messages that are stupid, redundant, off the topic, or offensive.

Mozilla: The foundation that supports and enhances Netscape browser software that is now open source. They distribute the Mozilla browser suite, the Firefox browser, and the Thunderbird mail program.

MP3: A music file format available on the Net.

MPAA (Motion Picture Association of America): A group that is attempting to limit Internet file sharing.

MPEG: A type of video file found on the Net. Files in this format end in .mpg or .mpeg. Stands for Moving Picture Experts Group.

MSN: Microsoft Network, Microsoft's Internet provider. It also offers the MSN Explorer, which you can use to browse the Web with your MSN account, and MSN Messenger, Microsoft's instant messaging program.

MSN TV: Formerly WebTV; an online Internet service that includes hardware (an Internet terminal and remote control) you connect to your TV. No computer needed.

Napster: An online music source that charges a flat monthly fee for all you can listen to.

net: A network, or (when capitalized) the Internet itself. When these letters appear as the last part of an address (in www.abuse.net, for example), they indicate that the host computer is run by a networking organization.

.NET: Microsoft's platform for Web services, which allows applications to communicate and share data over the Internet. No relation to .net addresses.

Netscape: A popular Web browser that comes in Windows, Mac, and UNIX flavors (see home.netscape.com). *See also* Mozilla.

network: Computers that are connected together. Those in the same or nearby buildings are called *local area networks;* those that are farther away are called *wide area networks;* and when you interconnect networks all over the world, you get the Internet!

newbie: A newcomer to the Internet (variant: clueless newbie). If you have read this book, of course, you're not a clueless newbie anymore!

newsgroup: A topic area in the Usenet news system. (See the Web page net.gurus.com/usenet for a description of Usenet newsgroups.)

newsreader: A program that lets you read and respond to messages in Usenet newsgroups.

Opera: A small, fast Web browser from Opera Software in Norway, available at www.opera.com.

org: When these letters appear as the last part of an e-mail address or URL (in www.uua.org, for example), they indicate that the host computer is probably run by a noncommercial organization, usually in the United States.

Outlook: An e-mail program (among other things) that is part of Microsoft Office. Powerful, flexible, and notoriously susceptible to worms and viruses.

Outlook Express: The e-mail program that comes with Microsoft Windows. Utterly unrelated to Outlook, not quite as susceptible to worms and viruses.

packet: A chunk of information sent over a network. Each packet contains the address it's going to and the address from which it came.

page: *See* web page.

password: A secret code used to keep things private. Be sure to pick one that's hard to guess, preferably two randomly chosen words separated by a number or special character.

PayPal: A Web-based service through which you can make and receive payments by e-mail or from links on Web sites. Owned by eBay.

PDF file: A method for distributing formatted documents over the Net. Windows and Linux users need a special reader program called Acrobat. Get it at www.adobe.com/products/acrobat.

PGP (Phil's Pretty Good Privacy): A program that lets you encrypt and sign your e-mail, written by Phil Zimmerman. Point your Web browser to net.gurus.com/pgp.

phishing: Using e-mail or IM to trick people into revealing personal information, such as credit card numbers.

ping: Sending a short message to which another computer automatically responds. If you can't ping the other computer, you probably can't talk to it any other way, either.

plug-in: A computer program you add to your browser to help it handle a special type of file.

podcast: To distribute audio files with timely content that are meant to be heard on personal music players, such as the Apple iPod.

POP (Post Office Protocol): A system by which a mail server on the Net lets you pick up your mail and download it to your PC or Mac. A POP server is the computer from which you pick up your mail. The most recent version is called *POP3.*

POP server: A server that stores your incoming e-mail messages until you download them to your e-mail program.

popup: A new window that appears in response to some action you took. Popups are often used for advertising.

port number: An identifying number assigned to each program that is chatting on the Net. You hardly ever have to know these numbers — the Internet programs work this stuff out among themselves.

portal: A Web site designed to be a starting point for people using the Web.

PPP (Point-to-Point Protocol): The most common way a computer communicates with the Internet over a phone line.

PPPoE (PPP over Ethernet): The way you log into a broadband account that require an account and password. *See also* DHCP.

protocol: The agreed-on rules that computers rely on to talk among themselves. A protocol is set of signals that mean "go ahead," "got it," "didn't get it, please resend," "all done," and so on.

proxy server: A program that translates between a LAN and the Internet.

QuickTime: A video and multimedia file format invented by Apple Computer and widely used on the Net. You can download it from `www.apple.com/quicktime`.

RealAudio: A popular streaming audio file format that lets you listen to programs over the Net.

RealPlayer: the program that plays RealAudio streams, available from www.real.com.

remote mailbombing: Subscribing people to lots of mailing lists against their will so that their e-mail mailboxes fill up with unwanted list postings.

RIAA (Recording Industry Association of America): A trade group that is attempting to limit Internet music sharing.

router: A device that connects two or more networks. Can be a separate piece of equipment or software running on a PC.

RSS: A syndication technology that lets you track multiple information sources, with automatic notification of new content.

RTFM (Read The Manual): A suggestion made by people who feel that you have wasted their time by asking a question you could have found the answer to by looking it up in an obvious place.

Safari: The Web browser that comes with Mac OS X.

search engine: A program used to search for things on the Web. Google is the best-known search engine.

secure server: A Web server that uses encryption to prevent others from reading messages to or from your browser. Web-based shopping sites usually use secure servers so that others cannot intercept your ordering information.

serial port: The place on the back of your computer where you plug in your dial-up modem. Also called a *communications port* or *comm port.*

server: A computer that provides a service — such as e-mail, Web data, Usenet, or FTP — to other computers (known as *clients*) on a network.

shareware: Computer programs that are easily available for you to try with the understanding that, if you decide to keep the program, you will send the requested payment to the shareware provider specified in the program. This is an honor system. A great deal of good stuff is available, and people's voluntary compliance makes it viable.

Shockwave Flash: A program for viewing interactive multimedia on the Web. For more information about Flash and for a copy of the program's plug-in for your browser, go to www.shockwave.com.

skin: The arrangement of buttons, menus, and other items displayed by a program. Some programs (such as Opera and Firefox) let you choose among several skins.

Skype: A software product for making free or low-cost long-distance and international telephone calls.

smiley: A combination of special characters that portray emotions, such as :-) or :-(. Although hundreds have been invented, only a few are widely used, and all are silly. Smileys are a type of emoticon.

SMS (Short Messaging System): A format used to send concise e-mail and instant messages to and from cellular phones.

SMTP (Simple Mail Transfer Protocol): The optimistically named method by which Internet mail is delivered from one computer to another.

SMTP server: A server that accepts e-mail messages for delivery to local users or the rest of the Internet.

spam: E-mail sent to thousands of uninterested recipients or Usenet messages posted to many uninterested newsgroups or mailing lists. It's antisocial, ineffective, and often illegal. To fight spam, see www.cauce.org.

spyware: Software that sends information about you and how you use your computer to other people without your permission.

SSL (Secure Socket Layer): A Web-based technology that lets one computer verify another's identity and allow secure connections; used by secure Web servers. A newer version is known as TLS.

streaming audio or video: A system for sending sound or video files over the Net that begins playing the file before it finishes downloading, letting you listen or watch with minimal delay. RealAudio (www.real.com) is the most popular streaming format.

StuffIt: A file-compression program that runs on Macs. StuffIt creates a SIT file that contains compressed versions of one or more files. To restore these files to their former size and shape, you use UnStuffIt.

surfing: Wandering around the World Wide Web and looking for interesting stuff.

TCP (Transmission Control Protocol): The system that two computers use to synchronize data. Usually used with IP as TCP/IP to manage connections over the Net. *See also* IP.

telnet: A program that lets you log in to some other computers on the Net. Many prefer the more secure program ssh. See net.gurus.com/telnet.

tera-: A prefix meaning trillion (1,000,000,000,000).

terminal: In the olden days, a computer terminal consisted of just a screen and a keyboard. If you have a personal computer and you want to connect to a big computer somewhere, you can run a program that makes it *pretend* to be a brainless terminal — the program is called a *terminal emulator, terminal program,* or *communications program.*

text file: A file that contains only textual characters, with no special formatting, graphical information, sound clips, video, or what-have-you.

thread: A message posted to a mailing list or newsgroup, together with all the follow-up messages, the follow-ups to follow-ups, and so on.

Thunderbird: A popular e-mail client from the Mozilla Foundation. See Chapter 13.

Top-Level Domain (TLD): The last part of an Internet domain or host name. If the TLD is two letters long, it's the *country code* in which the organization that owns the domain is (usually) located. If the TLD is three letters or longer, it's a code indicating the type of organization that runs the domain.

Unicode: A method for saving and displaying text in almost any know language.

UNIX: A geeky operating system originally developed at Bell Labs. Used on many servers on the Net. *Linux* is now the most popular version.

upload: To copy your stuff to somebody else's computer.

URL (Uniform Resource Locator): A standardized way of naming network resources, used for linking pages on the World Wide Web.

Usenet: A system of thousands of newsgroups. You read the messages by using a newsreader. (See the Web page net.gurus.com/usenet for a description of Usenet newsgroups.) *See also* newsreader.

viewer: A program to show you files that contain stuff other than text.

virus: A self-replicating program that piggybacks on e-mail messages or other programs, frequently with destructive side effects. *See also* worm.

virus checker: A program that intercepts and destroys viruses as they arrive on your computer.

VoIP (Voice over Internet Protocol): A method for sending telephone calls via the Net. Go to net.gurus.com/phone for more information.

watermark: A message hidden in a music or video file designed to detect copyright violations. *See also* DRM.

WAV: A popular Windows format for sound files (.wav files) found on the Net.

Web Folder: A Windows XP feature that enables you to use Windows Explorer to see, download from, and upload to an FTP or Web server.

Web page: A document available on the World Wide Web.

Web site: A collection of Web pages stored on a Web server. The Web pages belong to a particular person or organization.

webcam: A digital video camera that attaches to your computer and transmits video over the Internet. The video may appear on a Web page or as part of a chat or conference.

WiFi: The most popular kind of wireless network. Also known as 802.11, after the number of the standard that defines it.

Wiki: Short for "wikiwiki," which is Hawaiian for "fast." A technology that lets you rapidly create and edit Web pages using your Web browser.

WiMax: A wireless broadband access technology that hopes to provide an alternative to cable and DSL.

Winsock: A standard way for Windows programs to work with TCP/IP. You use it if you directly connect your Windows PC to the Internet, with either a permanent connection or a modem using PPP.

wireless network: A network that uses radio rather than cables.

World Wide Web: A hypermedia system that lets you browse through lots of interesting information. The Web has become the central repository of humanity's information in the 21st century.

worm: A malicious program that spreads directly from computer to computer.

Yahoo: A Web site (at www.yahoo.com) that provides a subject-oriented guide to the World Wide Web and many other kinds of information.

ZIP file: A file with the extension .zip that has been compressed with ZipMagic, WinZip, or a compatible program. To get at the files in a ZIP file, you usually need ZipMagic, WinZip, or a compatible program.

Index

• D •

• F •

• *N* •

• X •

• Y •

• Z •